GLEN BURNIE

The residence until his death in 1759 of Colonel James Wood, founder of Winchester, Virginia, and the birthplace of his son, Governor and General James Wood. On the lawn stood the first Clerk's Office.

WINCHESTER VIRGINIA
AND
ITS BEGINNINGS
1743-1814

Katherine Glass Greene

HERITAGE BOOKS
2007

HERITAGE BOOKS
AN IMPRINT OF HERITAGE BOOKS, INC.

Books, CDs, and more—Worldwide

For our listing of thousands of titles see our website
at
www.HeritageBooks.com

A Facsimile Reprint
Published 2007 by
HERITAGE BOOKS, INC.
Publishing Division
65 East Main Street
Westminster, Maryland 21157-5026

Copyright © 1926 Katherine Glass Greene

— Publisher's Notice —
In reprints such as this, it is often not possible to remove blemishes from the original. We feel the contents of this book warrant its reissue despite these blemishes and hope you will agree and read it with pleasure.

International Standard Book Number: 978-0-7884-2062-7

TO HIS EXCELLENCY

HARRY FLOOD BYRD

55TH GOVERNOR OF VIRGINIA
UNDER THE CONSTITUTION

REPRESENTING THE HIGHEST TYPE OF THE TWENTIETH CENTURY, AS JAMES WOOD, THE TENTH GOVERNOR, REPRESENTED THE HIGHEST TYPE OF THE EIGHTEENTH

ILLUSTRATIONS

	Page
Glen Burnie	Frontispiece
Autograph Signatures	15
Glimpses of the Lawn and Avenue at Glen Burnie	20
The Braddock Memorial at Washington's Headquarters	52
The Braddock Sash	72
Fort Loudoun As It Is Today	90
Chairing Colonel Wood as Proxy for Washington	96
Seal of Frederick County	115
Map of Winchester	117
Autograph Letter	120
Autograph Letter	122
Admiral Edward Boscawen	122
Ruins of Old Lutheran Church	126
The Burn at Glen Burnie	132
Autograph Signatures	168
Autograph Letter	194
Autograph Letter	206
The Westgate	286
The Trusty Servant	422

TABLE OF CONTENTS

	Page
CHAPTER I	11

Colonel James Wood's Commissions of 1742 and 1743—Tradition Concerning His Early Life

CHAPTER II _____ 16
Commissions Before 1742—Founding of William and Mary College

CHAPTER III _____ 20
Winchester Founded March 9, 1744 New Style—Controversy of the Early Settlers with the Lord Proprietor

CHAPTER IV _____ 26
Glimpses of Early Life in Towns and Homesteads

CHAPTER V _____ 30
First Visit of Lord Fairfax to America—Legal Battles—Charter for Winchester in 1752

CHAPTER VI _____ 35
A Deed from Lord Fairfax—The Suit in Chancery of Jost Hite, Robert McKay and Others

CHAPTER VII _____ 47
The Braddock Expedition

CHAPTER VIII _____ 52
Dedication of the Braddock Memorial, May 27, 1915

CHAPTER IX _____ 60
Address of the Late Captain Robert Y. Conrad at the Dedication of the Braddock Memorial in 1915

CHAPTER X _____ 73
The Story of General Braddock's Sash—Tributes to the Memory of Miss Mary Spottiswoode Buchanan and Mrs. William Ruffin Cox

CHAPTER XI _____ 78
Fort Loudoun—Governor Dinwiddie—Lord Loudoun—Personal Items Concerning Washington—Events in Winchester

CHAPTER XII _____ 89
Fort Loudoun (continued)—General Andrew Lewis—Fort Loudoun As It Is Today—The Formation of the Fort Loudoun Chapter of the Daughters of the American Revolution—Tribute to the Late Dr. Kate Waller Barrett

CHAPTER XIII _____ 97
The Election of George Washington to the House of Burgesses—Colonel James Wood as Proxy—Grabiel Jones, Blue Coat Boy, "The Valley Lawyer"

CHAPTER XIV _____ 105
Wood's Addition—Personal Notes of Ye Olden Tyme—"A Pot of Sugar and a Teacup Full of Tea"—Death of Colonel James Wood

CHAPTER XV ____ 133
Sketch of the Life of Hon. James Wood, Jr., Compiled from Various Sources

CHAPTER XVI ____ 143
The Wonderful Month of May, 1926—Commander Richard Evelyn Byrd and the North Pole—The Sesqui-Centennial at Williamsburg—The Shenandoah National Park

CHAPTER XVII ____ 155
Overwharton Parish—"Gaudia Nuncio Magna," Motto of Rev. Alexander Scott—Letters from Jean Moncure

CHAPTER XVIII ____ 160
The Elusive Charms of Florida

CHAPTER XIX ____ 165
First Reproduction of Military Correspondence—James Wood's Note Book, 1780

CHAPTER XX ____ 187
Letters with Famous Autographs

CHAPTER XXI ____ 195
Garrison Orders, Court Martials, Letters, Etc., 1775-1789, Chronologically Arranged

CHAPTER XXII ____ 249
Personal Letters—Records of the Deaths of Ex-Governor James Wood and His Wife, Jean Moncure

CHAPTER XXIII ____ 287
Romance of Laurence Augustine Washington—His Family—Various Personal Letters—Founding of the Laurence Augustine Washington Society, Children of the American Revolution

CHAPTER XXIV ____ 325
The Founders of the Washington Family in America—Item from General Washington's Will—The Washington and Fontaine Families in Texas

CHAPTER XXV ____ 334
Miscellaneous Letters—Wills—Indentures—Commissions

CHAPTER XXVI ____ 362
Genealogical Notes—Sketches of the Welch and Rutherford Families

CHAPTER XXVII ____ 383
List of Frederick County Clerk's Fees for the Years 1744, 1757, 1761 and 1762—Lists of Officers of the Virginia Line at Winchester and Fort Pitt in 1783—List of Men Draughted from Hampshire County—Catalogue of the Wood Papers

CHAPTER XXVIII ____ 410
Winchester, England—The Cathedral City and Ancient Capital of England—Situated Amidst the Beautiful Scenery of the Itchen Valley in the Heart of the Sporting County of Hampshire

INDEX ____ 431

PREFACE

TO THE PAST

Whatever of true life there was in thee
Leaps in our age's veins;
* * * * *
To thee thy dross in clinging,
For us thy martyrs die, thy prophets see,
Thy poets still are singing.

Here, mid the bleak waves of our strife and care,
Float the green Fortunate Isles
Where all thy hero-spirits dwell, and share
Our martyrdoms and toils;
The present moves attended
With all of brave and excellent and fair
That made the old time splendid.
—*James Russell Lowell*

And upon "the old time," indissolubly connected with the new, "let there be light."

It is the object of this book to present in tangible form letters and other manuscripts pertaining to the lives and times of Colonel James Wood, and of his son, General and Governor James Wood. The papers are published for the first time, and furnish with Winchester as a focus an original and incontestable source of information upon the Colonial and Revolutionary Periods of our country.

It will be noticed that records of the present are for the purpose of bringing subjects to a logical conclusion only or are commemorative of the past; e. g., the addresses of the late Captain Robert Y. Conrad, Miss Kate I. Harris, President Coolidge, and Governor Harry Flood Byrd.

The Sesqui-Centennial year, 1926, is distinguished by the flight of Commander Richard Evelyn Byrd and his intrepid pilot, Floyd Bennett, navy machinist, over the North Pole, an event without parallel of its kind in the history of the world.

Patriotic societies are the granaries of history in detail; therefore the founding of the Fort Loudoun Chapter, Daughters of the American Revolution, and of the Laurence Augustine Washington Society, Children of the American Revolution, are given as being commemorative in a marked degree.

It was a joy to visit Winchester, England, and to find her glory deeply intrenched in her Cathedral, her College, her Hospital of St. Cross, her Great Hall of Justice, monuments to noble influences during a period—reckoning from A. D. 169, when there existed a British church—of one thousand seven hundred fifty and eight years.

Her Virginia daughter in the Indian Valley of the Shenandoah, throughout her comparatively brief space of barely one hundred and eighty-four years, has had a goodly share of saintly pastors and layman, noble patriots, gentlewomen, distinguished jurists and strong men of affairs. In these times of shifting standards in religion and morals, may we in Winchester, Va., ask for the "old paths," whose ways are ways of pleasantness and all whose paths are peace.

But for the persevering research of Eleanor Offutt Barton (Mrs. I. D.), Flushing, New York, and of Harriot Wood Glass (Mrs. William Blackstone Davis), Washington, D. C., the latter of whom may be said to have "discovered" the papers in an old iron-bound chest in the garret at "Glen Burnie," the book could not have been written.

Grateful acknowledgment of assistance is made to Miss Mary I. Bell, Miss Kinnie E. Smith, Miss Camilla C. Rutherford, Dr. Luther W. Welsh, Miss Christine M. Washington, Miss Virginia Lucas, Miss Serena K. (Violet) Dandridge, Mrs. Andrew J. Willis, Miss Lallie Craighill, Mrs. Annie Plummer Johnston, Capt. James S. Phillips, Mr. Harry L. Snyder, Miss Lucy F. Kurtz, Mrs. Julia Washington Fontaine, Miss Maude Patrick, Mrs. Frank B. Crawford, Mr. C. Vernon Eddy, Librarian of the Handley Library, and any others who aided in establishing facts or who lent encouragement to the work.

Several Chapters of Part I were printed in *The Winchester Evening Star* in 1920. The rest of the book appears in print for the first time.

THE AUTHOR.

Winchester, Virginia,
November 6, 1926.

PART I

CHAPTER I

Colonel James Wood's Commissions of 1742 and 1743 — Tradition Concerning His Early Life

Now that Winchester sits in state enthroned amid her hundred jeweled hills, let us turn aside from her famous Apple Blossom Festival; from the prospective Shenandoah National Park; from radio, wireless, flying machines and the glare of electricity, and returning to the dawn of her history, study the background of it all. Let us read by tallowdip, torch and lantern, and travel by stage coach and "waggon" through those early scenes as we find them portrayed in the yellowed manuscripts of such patriots as Colonel James Wood and his son, Brigadier-General and Governor James Wood.

"Who can tell a man what shall be after him under the sun?" Manuscripts in museums are difficult to read and are accessible to few. While it is day, let us put into tangible, portable form these relics of a bygone age.

We cannot imagine in this day of "special delivery," "night letters," and mail by airplane, the weary waiting for news from the frontier, from the battlefield, from the mother country when letters were sent by "post" or "favored" or "honored" by any officer or other traveler who might be going in the desired direction.

The rising generation will surely be interested in the absolutely authentic history contained in the commissions, autograph letters, etc., embodied in this book.

Pause, and let the past speak through this history. The earliest of the manuscripts tell us that James Wood, gentleman, was commissioned Colonel of Horse and Foot in 1742. The commission is recorded at Orange Court House. His commission as the first clerk of Frederick county follows:

> "To all to whom these presents shall come, Thomas Nelson, Esq., sendeth greetings. Know ye that I, the said Thomas Nelson, by virtue of the powers and the authorities to me granted by the Honorable William Adair, Esq., Secretary of his Majesty's Colony and dominion of Virginia, do by these presents nominate, constitute and appoint James Wood, gentleman, to be clerk of the County of Frederick, to have and to hold the said place and office of clerk of said county to him, the said James Wood, with all fees, profits and perquisites whatsoever to the said place and office in anywise appertaining, during pleasure, and I do hereby revoke all former commissions———. In witness whereof I have hereunto set my hand and affixed my seal at Williamsburg the 22nd day of October, 1743, in the seventeenth year of the reign of our sovereign Lord King George the Second.
>
> THOMAS NELSON JUNIOR."

It is not the purpose of this book to quote court records nor to go into the details supplied by the histories of Kercheval, Cartmell, Norris, Scott and others, to whose invaluable works references will be made; but an effort will be made to throw additional light upon the life, character and influence of Colonel James Wood, copying as far as practical commissions, deeds and other manuscripts, an embarrassing wealth of which is at hand. Notes used by one of his grandsons in answer to one of many inquirers for information, are, in brief, as follows:

"Colonel James Wood was an Englishman by birth; and by communication made to me in my youth from his widow, Mary Wood, who lived to a great age, and survived her husband thirty-nine years, I understood he had been a lieutenant in the British Navy before his emigration to this country. He embarked with one of the colonial governors for Virginia, and remained in his family until he located himself adjoining Winchester. He personated Washington in his early life as a candidate to represent Frederick county in the Colonial House of Delegates at Williamsburgh." (Reference was then made to commissions which have been, or will be reproduced). "The inscription of a mourning ring still in the possession of my branch of the family establishes the fact that he died on the 6th of November, 1759, aged fifty-two years."

Family history further affirms that he was from Winchester, England, and that he was educated at Oxford. His clear diction, his handwriting of microscopic fineness and print-like clearness, his thorough knowledge of military tactics, his attention to details, his custom of having witnesses to transactions of whatever nature, his skill in surveying, his strict business methods indicate the legal mind, the trained scholar, the keen man of affairs, the intrepid explorer of the Virginia wilderness.

The obituary of Dr. Robert Wood Dailey, who died at Romney, West Virginia, April 12, 1902, says in part:

"Dr. Dailey's mother was Comfort Wood of Winchester, Virginia, and through her he was the great-grandson of Colonel James Wood, founder of the city of Winchester, Virginia, and the first clerk of the court of Frederick county, Virginia, when that county comprised within its boundaries practically all the eastern part of West Virginia. Colonel Wood was a native of Winchester, England; hence the name of Winchester, Virginia."

In support of this a map in the Corporation Clerk's office in the Rouss City Hall bears this legend:

"Winchester was founded by James Wood previous to the year 1752. The preamble of the act establishing the town of Winchester, dated February 1752, the 25th year of George II, states that 'James Wood, gentleman, had laid off 26 lots of one-half acre each, at the Court House in Frederick county with streets, and sold the same:' he is then by the act authorized to add 54 lots more to the same dimensions of these, 24 acres to be laid off on the side of the former lots and the remaining 30 at the north end of the original 26. The whole to contain commodious streets. The town to be called by and retain the name of Winchester."

"Wood's addition is dated 1758. The addition of Lord Fairfax is dated 1750 (32nd year of George II) and is granted the same privileges as the preceding portions."

Kercheval, in Chapter XV, quotes part of the legislative act passed in 1752 for the establishment of the town of Winchester. This act is given in full by Cartmell. Kercheval adds:

"Tradition relates that Fairfax was much more partial to Stephensburg than he was to Winchester, and used all his influence to make Stephensburg the seat of justice, but that Wood out-generaled his lordship, and by treating one of the justices with a bowl of toddy, secured his vote in favor of Winchester, which settled the question, and that Fairfax was so offended at the magistrate who thus sold his vote, that he never after spoke to him." A foot note says further: "The late John S. Woodcock, Esq., communicated this fact to the author, and stated that he had the information from Colonel Martin."

CHAPTER II

Commissions Before 1742 — Founding of William and Mary College

Before proceeding with later events it will be well to consider some of the services of Colonel James Wood prior to 1472, when he was commissioned Colonel of Horse and Foot.

The first minute on the records of Orange county is in these words:

"At a court held for the county of Orange on the twenty-first day of January, 1734. Present: Augustine Smith, John Taliaferro, and the justices to whom they had just administered the oaths.

"A commission to Henry Willis, Gentleman, under the hand and seal of office of the Honorable John Carter, Esq., secretary of Virginia, bearing date the thirtieth day of October, 1734, to be clerk of the court of this county, being read," etc., etc. This Henry Willis was the same gentleman mentioned by Colonel Byrd as the "topman of Fredericksburg."

At this same meeting Benjamin Cave qualified as sheriff, with Thomas Chew and James Barbour as his securities.

"James Wood, Gentleman, produced a commission from the president and masters of William and Mary College, dated November, 1734, to be surveyor for the county."

Thus James Wood became surveyor for Orange county when George Washington was but two years of

James Maky

[signature]

Wm Green

Fairfax

Fran Fauquier

Thos Nelson Junr

Jno Walker

Andw Lewis

[signature]

Jno Sherman
Tho Wood
Jn Hite

age, and the future Father of his Country was only in his seventeenth year when, in 1748 he became surveyor for Lord Fairfax.

There are hundreds of quaint little drawings of surveys made by James Wood between the years 1735 and about 1744. One, dated December 24, 1735, reads: "Surveyed for John VanMetre fifty acres of land in Orange county lying on the north side of Opequon Creek and opposite to another tract of land formerly surveyed for the said John VanMetre, it being within the limits of 100,000 acres granted by order of Council to Alexander Ross and others."

Another, dated 1739, adds: "This is not claimed by Lord Fairfax." Others are similarly marked, but not earlier than 1739. The oldest manuscript found so far among Colonel Wood's papers is dated 1726, and is still legible, in spite of the fact that it is almost in shreds. It reads:

"Andrew Zimerman.

"At a court for Spotsylvania County on Tuesday, April 5, 1726.

"On petition of Christopher Zimerman in order to prove his son Andrew Zimerman's right to take up land according to the Royal Charter, made oath that he came into this country along with him in the year of our Lord one thousand seven hundred and seventeen and that this is the first time of his proveing his said importation, who upon certificate is ordered to be granted him of right to take up fifty acres of land. Copia Test, John Wallor, Clk. Crt.

"April 11, 1726. This is the first certificate that I have issued.

"Test John Wallor, Clk. Crt."

Quoting again from Scott's History of Orange County, page 30: "The following minutes seem worthy of notice: In 1738 a petition for division of the county by inhabitants of Shenando. This was effective the same year, when Augusta and Frederick counties were formed, embracing all of Virginia lying beyond the Blue Ridge. But Augusta, though formed in 1738, did not really organize as a separate county until about 1745."

In 1739 James Wood was appointed collector of duties for the support of William and Mary College. The full text of the commission is given both because of the honor and responsibility it conferred, and because the conditions under which it was issued, even that relating to liquors, have passed away, a miracle which took place in the year of grace, 1920.

"William Gooch, Esq., His Majesty's Lieutenant-Governor and Commander-in-Chief of the colony and Dominion of Virginia. To James Wood, Gentleman, Greeting:

"By virtue of the power and authority to me given as commander-in-chief of this Colony, I do hereby constitute and appoint you, the said James Wood, collector of all the Rates, Duties, and Impositions arising and growing due to His Majesty by virtue of an Act of Assembly made in the IVth year of the late Queen Ann, entitled an act for laying a duty upon Skins and Furrs for the better support of the College of William and Mary in Virginia, and of one other act made in the XIIth year of his present Majesty's reign, entitled An Act for the better support and encouragement of the College of William and Mary in Virginia, and of one other act made in the Xth year of his said Majesty's Reign, entitled an Act for laying Duty upon Liquors imported by land and better securing the Duty upon Slaves and for other purposes therein mentioned within the bounds and Precincts now called and reputed the County of Orange and Prince William in this Colony. You are therefore carefully and diligently to perform the said office of Collector of Skins and Furrs exported out of and of Liquors imported into the said Countys by Lands to or from any other of His Majesty's Plantations by duly putting in execution all and singular the clauses, articles, and Powers in the said several acts of Assembly contained according to the true intent and meaning thereof. And I do require all His Majesty's

Officers and other his loving subjects to be aiding and assisting to you, the said James Wood, in the execution of the Powers hereby given. And yourself shall ——— all such orders and executions as you from time to time shall receive from me or the Commander-in-Chief for the time being. And Lastly, I do give and grant unto you to have hold and enjoy the said office of collector with all Fees Salaries and Perquisites thereunto belonging during pleasure.

"Given under my hand and seal at Williamsburg the 8th day of April, 1739, in the XIIth year of His Majesty's reign.

WILLIAM GOOCH."

In the category with slaves and liquors may be placed Lord Berkeley's answer to questions sent from Charles II as to "instructing the people, religion, ministry, etc.," in the Virginia Colony. This peculiar man replied as follows:

"But I thank God there are no free schools nor printing, and I hope we shall not have these hundred years, for learning has brought disobedience and heresy, and sects into the world, and printing has divulged them and libels against the best government. God keep us from both."

In March, 1692-83, an act was passed for "ascertaining the place for erecting the College of William and Mary," the first college on the American continent. Since then, so far as America is concerned, kings and queens have passed away, and they are rapidly disappearing from the rest of the earth; slaves and liquors are gone, but "William and Mary" still holds high the torch that "lighteth every man that cometh into the world," witnessing to the fidelity of many hearts and hands through all these years.

CHAPTER III

Winchester Founded March 9, 1744 New Style—
Controversy of the Early Settlers With the Lord
Proprietor

Will you go back nearly two centuries, yet involving three, and imagine yourself on the site of Winchester before there was a vestige of the town? — and that means of any town south of the Cohongoroota (Potomac) and west of the Sherandoah (Shenandoah)? Picture then this vale in 1734 — no pikes, no railroads, no ferry boats; "a waste, howling wilderness," with only the blazed trails of the Shawnees, Tuscaroras, and other warriors of Opekenough (Opockon, Opeckon, Opecquon) leading like threads through the maze of virgin forest. Into this uncharted realm in his official capacity of surveyor for Orange county, came James Wood in 1735. His grandson, in answering some inquirer, as already noted, says, "James Wood remained with the Colonial Governor with whom he had come from England until he located himself, about the year 1735, as I can see no evidence to the contrary, adjoining Winchester, where I now live."

The conclusion that he came about 1735 is confirmed by the survey made for John VanMetre, December 24, 1735. Another reads, "Surveyed for Thomas Farmer eight hundred eighty and eight acres of land in Orange county on the west side of Opockon Creek and between the heads of the Middle Creek and Tuscarora Creek within the limits of 100,000 acres granted to Alexander

Glimpses of the Avenue and Lawn at Glen Burnie

Ross and others — this 22d December, 1735." Another, answering the same description, and surveyed for Walter Homes, is dated February 1735-36. Frequently this double date is used, and it is thus explained by W. W. Scott in his History of Orange County: "It must be borne in mind that 'old style' was yet in effect in the Mother Country and her colonies when Orange was established: that is, the New Year was reckoned from March 25, and not from January 1; and the new style did not become effective until 1752. Thus, though the first court (of Orange County) was held January, 1734, there were yet two months to elapse before the year 1735 began: that is, that January, February and March came after December of the same year."

It is certain, then, that James Wood, with compass, level and chain, was here in 1735. Imagine him, only twenty-eight years of age, coming west from the Opockon and arriving in early spring at the Hollingsworth (now Rouss) and Shawnee springs, and then following a little stream west, past what is known as the old Spring Gardens, and Selma, and the Shenandoah Valley Academy, and Hawthorne, until he arrived at the source of the stream at the head of glen. And then if "the little birds sang east and the little birds sang west," and the crocuses and johnny-jump-ups and anemones were blooming, and the little stream was sparkling and glancing and gurgling for very joy as it does today, can you wonder that it all appeared as fair to him "as the garden of the Lord," and that he must have exclaimed, "Here shall be my home, and I will secure a grant from King and Council, and my friends and companions shall abide here with me." And he named the spot "Glen Burnie," "Glen of the Burn"; and all that he planned came to pass, because on March 9, 1743 (old style), we find him giving bond for one thousand pounds to protect the titles of Morgan Morgan, Thomas Chester, David Vance, Andrew Campbell, Marquis Calmes, Thomas Rutherford, Lewis Neill, William McMachen, Meredith Helm, George Hoge, John White and Thomas Little, Gentlemen, if the title to his grant from King and Council were not completed, and in case his grant should conflict with the old grants of the Fairfax family. "The condition of the above obligation is such that whereas the above bound James Wood having laid off from the tract of land on which he now dwells at Opequon, in the county aforesaid, twenty-six lots of land containing half an acre each, together with two streets running through said lots of the breadth of thirty-three feet, as will more plainly appear by a plan thereof in the possession of the said Morgan Morgan, Marquis Calmes and William McMachen, and whereas the said James Wood, for divers good causes and consideration of the sum of five shillings current money to him in hand paid, the receipt whereof he doth hereby acknowledge, hath bargained and sold, on the conditions hereinafter mentioned, all his right, title, interest, property and claim, to twenty-two of said lots to the aforesaid Morgan Morgan, etc., His Majesty's Justices of the said county, for the time being and their successors, to be disposed of by them for the use of said county as they shall judge most proper, the said lots being numbered in the before mentioned plan as follows: Nos. 1, 2, 3, etc., etc., on the following conditions, viz: that they, the justices or their assigns, shall, within two years from the date of the sale of the said lots, build or cause to be built on each lot one house, either framed work or squared logs, dovetailed, at least of the dimensions of 20 feet by 16, and in any case any person in possession of a lot or lots fail to build within the time limited, the property of the said lot or lots to return to the said James Wood, his heirs or assigns. Now if the said James Wood, his heirs, executors and administrators, shall from time to time at all times hereafter maintain, protect, and defend the said justices, their successors and assigns in the peaceable quiet possession of the fore mentioned lots of land from all persons whatsoever, Thomas Lord Fairfax, his heirs, or any other person claiming under him only excepted. And further if the said James Wood, his heirs, etc., shall hereafter obtain either from His Majesty by patent or from the said Thomas Lord Fairfax or his heirs, etc., shall within one year, if required, make such other title for the said lots to the said Justices or their successors, as their counsel learned in the law shall devise so far forth as his own title shall extend. Now if the said James Wood, his heirs executors and administrators shall well and truly perform all and singular the above conditions, then this obligation to be void, otherwise to be and remain in full force and virtue.

J. Wood.

Sealed and delivered in the presence of
  Wm. Jolliffe,
  Jno. Newport,
  Thos. Postage."

There is no evidence of any foundation for a town earlier than 1743-44.

Conflict about the title arose in 1749, when Lord Fairfax arrived in America, as has been noted, but as will be seen later on, Fairfax not only recognized the James Wood dedication, but added to it in a substantial way.

The following papers show the struggles of the holders of minor grants against the demands of the Lord Proprietor:

"Be it known to all persons whom it may concern, that we, the inhabitors and purchasers of the lots laid off by Colonel James Wood for a town called and known by the name of Frederick Town in the county of Frederick, having been truly informed of Thomas Lord Fairfax's intention of making us pay a yearly rent of five shillings sterling each for our lots, and we not being willing to come under that yoke, have taken this method to make known the same by subscribing our hands hereunto Dated ——— June, 1749.

"Thomas Wood, Jr., Stephen Minor, John Hopes, W. C. ———, Henry Brinker, Andrew Caldwell, Daniel Wurtring, William Green, Joe Dunbar, Jasse Carkins, John Neill, William ———, Hannah Humphrey, Marquis Calmes, Robert Lemen.

"9th, 14th, 1749, Colonel James Wood offered my Lord Fairfax to comply with the rules of his office, though he did not think himself bound by the decree of the King and Council, and that he would pay him the composition of all his lands as also to quit rents from the year 1745, provided he would let him have all within his old lines including the town and said would take ——— as his lordship would please to give him.

Jno. Sturman,
Thomas Wood,
J. Hite."

Thursday, September 14, 1749.

Was present when Colonel James Wood proposed that if Lord Fairfax would make him a title for land he claimed, to-wit, that he lived on, including the town, he would pay composition money and arrearages of quit rents from the year 1745, being the time the said Lord Fairfax claimed them, though the said Wood said he did not imagine himself bound by the decree to do so.

G. Jones.

Mem. Colonel Wood also told Lord Fairfax he was willing his land should be surveyed according to law, if it was not already, provided the survey took in all his lines.

G. J.

CHAPTER IV

Glimpses of Early Life in Towns and Homesteads

The first court of Frederick county, then, was held November 11, 1743, at Glen Burnie (Cartmell, page 289) and for about two years the clerk's office was located on the lawn. The mansion house was probably completed by that time, among the earliest, if not the earliest, of the contemporary dwellings of its class, and apparently the only one of them built of brick. We may imagine the wagon trains carrying feathers, dried fruits, and other products of the clearings to Alexandria and bringing back brick, and the beautiful blue dishes with their fascinating landscapes, and the stiff brocades and gay bonnets for the fair ladies; bringing such luxuries, too, as oysters in the shell.

Best of all bringing the tall and stately grandfathers' clocks. One at Glen Burnie and another at Greenway Court bear the inscription, "C. Chandlee, Maker, Winchester."

At the house, of course, were moulds for the tallow candles, and looms for weaving the vast linen sheets, dear to the housewives, if shivery to the spine, in spite of the billowy feather beds and the voluminous homespun blankets on the high tester bedsteads. What an adventure it must have been for the children to get into them! What royal dishes the bits of blue china and the oyster shells made for the play housekeeping of little Elizabeth and Mary Wood, and how bewitching must have been the home-made dolls dressed in the scraps of gay silk from across the sea!

The house and lawn, and three springs, and the beautiful old garden were surrounded by the long low picturesque stone walls, the old springhouse was built, the famous cedar hedge and the cliff lilies planted, all in English style, a style which characterized the early homes of Winchester, and which still gives the town an old-world air, in spite of our rapidly increasing modernity. Alas, the day when the odor of boxwood shall be only a fond memory! Fancy the herculean task of founding such homesteads as those at Bartonville and Stephensburg, and at the head of the Opequon! The walls at Glen Burnie, built of brick brought as ballast in the slow sailing vessels from England, stand today without a crack. The plastering in those old houses, palatial residences in their time, and worthy to shelter the distinguished founders of our commonwealth, is as hard as marble. The carved woodwork of the high mantels and wainscoting and cornices testifies to the class of homes from which their owners had come, and their serious purpose to build for future generations, in spite of difficulties which it baffles our most vivid imagination to compass.

Colonel James Wood married Mary Rutherford, daughter of Hugh Rutherford. The five children of James and Mary Wood, born between the years 1739 and 1747, were brought up at Glen Burnie. Elizabeth, the future wife of Honorable Alexander White, member of the first Congress, and Mary, who was to marry Colonel Matthew Harrison, of the Revolutionary Army, became, probably, as they grew up, more proficient in domestic arts than their sisters of today can be expected to be; because, from the sheep's back to the family supply of wearing apparel the product was literally homespun and home-made. Each home was in fact, a plant where were produced, and of finest quality, the supplies of the family. At home, James Wood II, the future Revolutionary hero, could learn the arts of war under his father, and from the latter's horse and foot rangers. John, destined to become a physician, was to study medicine in Philadelphia, the metropolis; and Robert, who served three years in the Virginia Line, became known as the father of a large and devoted family. The family seems to have grown up in peace in the midst of the wilderness, although at this point on the extreme western frontier, danger from the Indians was gowing more and more menacing, until as a protection to the growing community, Fort Loudoun was built in 1756.

Colonel James Wood's order from the Virginia Council to "measure out and settle families on such tracts as he surveyed of lands on a branch of the Opeckon Creek not heretofore settled," warranted his claim to his own estate "including the town."

A memorandum of other holdings of his, among still others in addition to the Glen Burnie tract, reads thus:

Patents in the name of Green where I have part:

	Acres
On Brown's Run	2,000
Muddy Creek	1,700
On South Branch	800
On South Branch	370
On South Branch	350
On South Branch (Query)	1,120
On South Branch	1,470
On South Branch	1,080
On South Branch	660
On South Branch	685
	10,235

In my name in which they have part:

On Muddy Creek	350
On Muddy Creek	400
	750

Lands in the New River Grant patented in my name:

The Indian Fields on Crooked Creek	2,000
On the head branches of Holson's Creek	2,193
On Cripple Creek	1,200
Lorton's old place on Tom's Creek	650
The Little Horse Shoe bottom below Tom's Creek	400
On Cedar Creek below Holson's Creek	2,800
	10,043

That he was punctilious in all business transactions is shown by the following note, an example of many of the same kind:

"I have made a promise to my brother-in-law, John Rutherford, on his request, to give him without any expense, three hundred acres of land in some one of my tracts on the branches of the New River or Holson's, on condition he goes to live thereon; but I am not able at this time to determine the place. If he seats on a place that will not suit me to part with, I do agree to pay him for any improvements he shall have made thereon to enable him to make as good on his place which I shall assign him.

J. Wood.

11 October 1752."

CHAPTER V

First Visit of Lord Fairfax to America — Legal Battles — Charter for Winchester in 1752

In 1736, Thomas Lord Fairfax visited America for the first time, spending three years investigating his inheritance, the Northern Neck of Virginia, which included the Colepepper grant, the estate of his mother, Lady Catharine Colepepper. In 1739 he returned to England to lay his grievances about boundaries and minor grants before the King. When he reached America again in 1748, he did not tarry at "Belvoir," the seat of his agent and cousin, William Fairfax, in what is now Fairfax county and near "Hunting Creek," the present Mt. Vernon, but came in 1749 to Frederick county where, at "Greenway Court," about twelve miles southeast of Winchester, he built the famous Lord Proprietor's office, which Washington Irving thus describes: "One story in height, with dormer windows, with two wooden belfries, chimneys studded with swallow and martin coops, and a roof sloping down, in the old Virginia fashion into low, projecting eaves that formed a verandah the whole length of the house. It was probably the house originally occupied by his steward or land agent, but now devoted to hospitable purposes and the reception of guests. As to his lordship, it was one of his many eccentricities that he never slept in the main edifice, but lodged apart in a wooden house not much above twelve feet square" His lordship was at that time forty-nine years of age, and he brought with him George Washington, then but sixteen years old, to be his youthful surveyor. May we duly appreciate his service in introducing thus early to this locality this English-Virginian, the ideal American. All this was the result of his lordship's having found that the Blue Ridge was not the western boundary of his estate, but the eastern rampart of a glorious valley, an El Dorado, and his own! Here would he live, and all these settlers should be his retainers, and pay rent, not only from the date of his arrival in 1749, but from the year 1745, at least.

Not so the settlers! Headed by the wonderful old German, Yost Heite, they flew to legal arms. They were protected by the terms of the minor grants, and they would fight for their rights; and so began the legal battles which lasted until after the death of the Lord Proprietor in 1782, at the age of ninety-two. He had worn out all his contestants and many of the cases were not yet settled. In the interests of the town, now large enough to be established by law, Colonel James Wood chose a different course. He was an Englishman and conservative. He reckoned that it was better to bend than to break. Progress must not be paralyzed by a contest uncertain both as to duration and outcome. Already under the more liberal policy of Lord Beverly, the Upper Valley was filling up more rapidly than the lower. Roads must be surveyed to pass through the gaps in the Blue Ridge; to Cedar Creek; to the Great Cacapon; to Patterson's Creek; to the mouth of the South Branch; from the Court House to Morgan Morgan's; from the Opecquon to the Court House. Winchester should be the hub of a wheel with many spokes. Besides, the Indians were becoming more restless and more aggressive, and relations between the

English and French more strained. It looked as if there would be war in the northwest before long. It was a time to be recruiting troops, not to be fighting about titles. Therefore, he and the brave sharers of his fortunes would pay rent, even for four years in arrears, and secure titles and have peace. But he would protest that in accordance with the King and Council he did not believe they were bound to come under the yoke; and he would stipulate that all his lines including the town should be surveyed. Moreover, he would have Gabriel Jones, the King's attorney, witness his interview with Lord Fairfax and make a note of his terms. James Wood and Stephen Minor, and William Green and John Neill and Marquis Calmes and Hannah Humphrey, and your companions, your protest was the voice of the people!

The cloud of discontent which arose over quitrents, composition money, and the whole subject of taxation extended over the thirteen colonies, and increased, until twenty-five years later it burst in the storm of the American Revolution. Out of the tempest came a voice, the Declaration of Independence, and after the raging elements had died away, behold, the Constitution of the United States!

After yielding to the exigencies of the situation, Colonel James Wood and Lord Fairfax worked together for the advancement of the town, and in February, 1752, a charter was secured. Since it may be read in a detached form by many who would not find it buried within the pages of history, and since each generation should know the story of our origin as a town, the text follows:

"An Act for Establishing the Town of Winchester and Appointing Fairs therein.

I. *Whereas*, it hath been represented to this General Assembly, that James Wood, gentleman, did survey and lay out a parcel of land, at the court house in Frederick county, in twenty-six lots of half an acre each, with streets for a town, by the name of Winchester, and made sale of the said lots to divers persons, who have since settled and built, and continue building and settling thereon; but because the same was not laid off and erected into a town, by act of Assembly, the freeholders and inhabitants thereof will not be entitled to the like privileges, enjoyed by the freeholders and inhabitants of other towns in this colony;

II. *Be it enacted by the Lieutenant Governor, Council and Burgesses, of this present General Assembly, and it is hereby enacted, by the authority of the same*, that the said parcel of land, lately claimed by the said James Wood, lying and being in the county of Frederick aforesaid, together with fifty-four other lots of half an acre each, twenty-four thereof to be laid off in one or two streets, on the east side for the former lots, the street or streets to run parallel with the streets already laid off, and the remaining thirty lots to be laid off at the north end of the aforesaid twenty-six lots with a commodious street or streets, in such manner as the proprietor thereof, the right honourable Thomas Lord Fairfax, shall think fit, be and is hereby constituted, appointed, erected and established, a town in the manner already laid out, and described to be laid out, to be called by and retain the name of Winchester, and that the freeholders of the said town, shall forever hereafter enjoy the same privileges with the freeholders of other towns, erected by act of Assembly, enjoy.

III. And whereas allowing fairs to be kept in the said town of Winchester, will be of great benefit to the inhabitants of the said parts, and greatly increase the trade of that town, *Be it therefore enacted by the authority aforesaid*, that for the future, two fairs shall and may be annually kept, and held, in said town of Winchester on the third Wednesday in June and the third Wednesday in October, in every year, and continue for the space of two days, for the sale and vending all manner of cattle, victuals, provisions, goods, wares and merchandizes, whatsoever; on which fair days, and two days next before, and two days next after the said fairs, all persons coming to, being at, or going from, the same, together with their cattle, goods, wares and merchandise, shall be exempted and privileged, from all arrests, attachments, and executions, whatsoever, except for capital offenses, breaches of the peace, or for any controversies, suits, or quarrels, that may arise and happen during the said time in which case process may immediately be issued, and proceedings thereupon had, in the same manner as if this act had never been made, anything herein before contained, or any law, custom, or usage, to the contrary thereof, in anywise, notwithstanding.

IV. *Provided always.* That nothing herein contained, shall be construed, deemed, or taken, to derogate from, alter, or infringe, the royal power and prerogative of his majesty, his heirs and successors, of granting to any person or persons, body politic and corporate, the privileges of holding fairs, or markets, in any such manner as he or they, by his or their royal letter patent, or by his or their instructions to the governor, or commander-in-chief of this dominion, for the time being, shall think fit."

CHAPTER VI

A Deed From Lord Fairfax — The Suit in Chancery of Jost Hite, Robert McKay and Others

Winchester was thus incorporated in February, 1752, and the minds of her people were left free to grapple with the great events which were brewing and which took form in the first expedition of Major Washington in 1753 to the junction of the Monongahela and the Allegheny; in his second expedition in 1754, when the battle of Great Meadows was fought, and the stockade "Fort Necessity" erected; in the ill-fated Braddock Expedition in 1755, and in the building of Fort Loudoun in 1756. From Winchester, the outpost, the extreme town on the western frontier, these famous expeditions set out over the perilous trail northwest five hundred and fifty miles, past Will's Creek, where Cumberland now sits a queen at the gateway of marvels then unknown and unimagined. But more of these stupendous undertakings at another time. They are mentioned here chronologically to show the importance of Winchester at that early date.

Returning to the subject of titles: Colonel James Wood's wisdom in yielding to the demands of Lord Fairfax was rewarded by his receiving a deed to his own domain in 1753. This precious parchment in the beautiful handwriting of the time, is probably a rare example of similar documents to be found now chiefly in libraries and museums; and it is the more interesting because lineal descendants of Colonel Wood still hold a substantial part of this grant of "waste and ungranted land," surveyed and claimed by him under the provisions of King and Council, probably as early as 1735. The deed, with the omission of technical terms, reads thus:

> "The Right Honourable Thomas Lord Fairfax, Baron of Cameron in that part of Great Britain called Scotland, Proprietor of the Northern Neck of Virginia: To all to whom this present writing shall come sends greeting. Know ye that for good causes for and in consideration of the composition to me paid, and for the annual rent hereafter received, I have given, granted, and confirmed, and by these presents for me, my heirs and assigns do give and confirm unto Colonel James Wood of Frederick County, a certain tract of waste and ungranted land in the said county whereon he lives, joyning Mr. Isaac Perkins on the Branches of Opeckon River and bounded by a survey thereof made by Mr. John Baylis as followeth: Beginning at a Locust stake by sundry markt saplins on the west side of the Great Waggon Road, thence Nor. 61 degrees 30' net three hundred and seventy four poles to a Hickory and two red Oaks at the foot of a Hill, thence - - to a Walnut, red Oaks and white Oak corner to Isaac Perkins, thence leaving Perkins' line and running - - - - to a red Oak and Hickory on a Ledge of Rocks, thence - - - - to Hickorys and red Oak on the side of a Hill, thence leaving Perkins' line and running - - - - to two red Oaks, thence - - - - to a Locust on a Level, thence - - - - by the foot of a Hill, thence - - - - to a stake on a Hill, a Corner to Winchester Town, Lot No. 36, then with the Town Lines - - - - to a stake corner to Lot No. 1, thence - - - - to a stake corner to Lot No. 12, thence with the said lot - - - - to a stake at the corner of William Dobbin's Stone House by the Great Waggon Road, corner to the said Lot No. 12, thence leaving the Town - - - - to the Beginning, containing one thousand two hundred and forty-one acres of Land, Together with all Rights, Members, and appurtenances thereon belonging, Royal Mines excepted, and a full Third of all Lead, Copper, Tinn, Coals, Iron Mines and Iron Ore that shall be found thereon: To have and to hold the said 1241 acres of land, Together with all Profit Rights, and Benefits to the same belonging or in anywise appertaining except before excepted to Him the said James Wood, his heirs and assigns forever. He the said James Wood, his heirs or assigns therefore yielding and Paying to me, my Heirs or Assigns, or the certain Attorney or Attorneys, Agent or Agents, or the certain Attorney or Attorneys of my Heirs and Assigns, Proprietor of the said Northern Neck yearly and every year on the Feast Day of St. Michael the Archangel the Fee Rent of One Shilling sterling money for every fifty acres of Land hereby granted and so proportionally for a greater or

less quantity. Provided, that if the said James Wood, his Heirs or Assigns shall not pay the said annual reserved Rent so that the same or any Part thereof shall be behind or unpaid by the space of Two whole years after the same shall become Due if lawfully demanded, provided also that if the said James Wood, his Heirs or Assigns shall alter or stop or suffer to be altered or stop the water course from his Spring to Pass through the Town of Winchester in the aforesaid county and shall not permit the Inhabitants of the said Town at any time to sink and lay Pipes to convey the Water from the said Spring to the Town for the future and mutual Benefit and advantage of its Inhabitants; That then it shall and may be lawful for me, my Heirs and Assigns, Proprietors as aforesaid Pryor, their certain Attorney or Attorneys, Agent or Agents into the above granted Premises to Re-enter and Hold the same so as if the Grant had never passed.

Given at my Office in the County of Fairfax within my said Proprietary dated this twenty-first day of May in the twenty-sixth year of the Reign of our Sovereign Lord George the second King of Great Britain, etc., A. D. 1753.

FAIRFAX.

Registered in the Proprietor's Office in Book II, Folio 307."

Those who went to law have a different story to tell. Have we no romancer ready to depict the heartaches, the hopes and fears, the bitterness of spirit caused by those weary law suits? Ejected from home! Mere squatters, those heroes who had braved the perils of the deep in a cockle-shell; who in perils in the wilderness, in perils by the savages; in weariness and painfulness, in watching often, in hunger and thirst had ———! But no! The story would be too heart rending. Enough that the incomparable Dickens has painted the picture in caustic!

From the standpoint of history no more convincing proof of the far-reaching consequences of such litigation can be given than that presented by the suit in chancery of Jost Hite, Robert McKay, and others versus The Right Honorable Thomas Lord Fairfax. Here is the hitherto unpublished document with its genuine signatures and seals:

Whereas; a Suit in Chancery hath been commenced (and is now depending in the General Court of Virginia) by Jost Hite, Robert McKay and others, Complainants, against The Right Honorable Thomas Lord Fairfax, Proprietor of the Northern Neck Defendant, for certain lands claimed by the Complainants within the Bounds of the Northern Neck aforesaid which lands were granted by order of Council to the aforesaid Jost Hite and Robert McKay, William Duff, Robert Green, decd., and the said William Duff and Robert Green since the said Order of Council and before the commencement of the said suit did depart this Life, and the said Robert McKay since the commencement of the said suit hath also departed this Life—And the aforesaid William Duff, deceased, did by will Bequeath all his share of the land, aforesaid to John Green, James Green, and Moses Green, and did appoint the aforesaid Robert Green Executor of his will. The aforesaid Robert Green, deceased, did by will Bequeath his share of the said lands to His Sons Robert Green, John Green, Nicholas Green, James Green and Moses Green, and to his wife Eleanor, and did appoint his said wife Eleanor and Sons William and Robert Executors of his said will. The aforesaid Robert McKay did appoint his Sons Robert McKay, James McKay, and Moses McKay Executors of his last will, etc. And the said Jost Hite is now the only surviving Partner. Now it is agreed by the said Jost Hite that the Respective Heirs claiming under the wills of the said Robert McKay, William Duff and Robert Green, deceased, shall severally inherit the shares that the said Robert McKay, William Duff, and Robert Green might have done in case they had lived until a lawful share in the said lands had been obtained and a Division thereof made according to the true intent and meaning of the agreement between the said Partners. And the said Robert McKay and Moses McKay Executors of Robert McKay, deceased, as also the said Eleanor Green and Robert Green Executors of Robert Green deceased, not being present. The aforesaid James McKay for and in behalf of himself and all those claiming under the will of the said Robert McKay deceased, and the said William Green for and in behalf of himself and all those claiming under the wills of the said William Duff, deceased, and the said Robert Green, deceased, and the said Jost Hite do Covenant and agree as followeth, (viz.):

That each party concerned in the said suit against the said Lord Fairfax shall and will pay to the said Jost Hite a proportional part of the money which the said Hite hath expended on account of the said suit according to the Quantity claimed by each party concerned, and Lastly it is agreed and the aforesaid William Green is hereby appointed Agent and Attorney in Fact for managing and acting for the parties in the said suit, and is to pay the Attorneys at Law already employed in the said Suit any sums of money that he shall judge reasonable for carrying on the said suit with vigor, and the parties do hereby obligate themselves and their Heirs to reimburse the said William Green all sums of money or Tobacco that he shall pay out on account of the said Law Suit and to pay him a reasonable reward for his Labour and trouble, each to pay in proportion to the Quantity of Land claimed.

In Witness whereof the said Jost Hite, James McKay, and William Green have hereunto set their hands and Seals this 6th Day of Sept. 1758.

JAMES MCKAY
JOST HITE
WM. GREEN

Test:
    Jost Hite and William Green signed in the presence of us

JOSEPH CARROLL   HARIKENSON READ."

We have here the autograph of the owner of this name of many spellings. It looks rather as if a fly had stepped in ink and performed a small jig on paper. The result is the German text which cannot be reproduced, but throughout the document the spelling is unmistakably "Jost Hite."

Put yourself in the place of an heir to a suit in chancery! No wonder intrepid old Jost Hite died, about 1760, a comparatively poor man!

Charles Dickens, writing in August, 1853, says in his preface to "Bleak House":

"There is a suit before the Court which was commenced nearly twenty years ago; in which from thirty to forty counsel have been known to appear at one time; in which costs have been incurred to the amount of seventy thousand pounds; which is (I am assured) no nearer to its termination now than when it was begun. There is another well known suit in chancery, not yet decided, which was commenced before the close of the last century, in which more than double the amount of seventy thousand pounds has been swallowed up in costs." "In the case of Jarndyce and Jarndyce," he continues, "fair wards of court have faded into mothers and grandmothers; a long procession of chancellors has come in and gone out; the legions of bills in the suit have been transformed into mere bills of mortality; there are not three Jarndyces left upon the earth, perhaps, since old Tom Jarndyce in despair blew his brains out at a coffee-house in Chancery Lane; but Jarndyce and Jarndyce still drags its weary length before the Court, perennially hopeless."

One hundred years earlier, our own people were caught in the toils of this same net. Happily, unlike the annihilated Jarndyces, the descendants of Robert and James McKay and their companions in this misfortune are still leaders in the world's work, while General Duff Green's services are a monument to the name of Duff.

T. K. Cartmell in his wonderful "History of Frederick County," says:

"The celebrated suit makes its first appearance 10th October, 1749, when Hite and his associates filed a bill in chancery in the general court against Lord Fairfax and those claiming under him, setting forth the circumstances——praying that Lord Fairfax might be decreed to make the deeds to the plaintiff for the surveyed lands." (See Calendar Va. State Papers, vol. 4). Lord Fairfax in his answer, ignored all rights of Hite and his associates, and erroneously claimed that the right to convey lands to settlers in the Northern Neck existed in him alone; and thus denied the rights granted through what has been termed Minor Grants. Some conflict of opinion existed in the courts; and considerable delay occasioned by reason of the general caveat entered by Lord Fairfax against all orders of council and patents from the crown office, for lands in his proprietary. The courts finally, in 1786, five years after the death of Fairfax, confirmed the grants to Hite and his associates where it had been shown that settlers had complied with orders of council by retaining surveys of their individual tracts.

"The General Court had on the 15th October, 1771, made a decree that virtually settled the right of Hite and those to whom he had sold land and executed conveyances within the boundaries of the Van Meter grants, and also of the Hite and McKay grants; Hite having seated fifty-four families, pursuant to orders of Council 1730-31.

"Had Fairfax been sustained, every lot owner in Winchester who derived his right under James Wood, would have suffered a loss of his holdings. Fairfax seemed determined to stand upon his rights as the Lord Proprietor of the Northern Neck; and although he had an agreement with Wood, Hite, Rogers and others that he would make them quitrent deeds without payment of the usual fee, yet he declined to withdraw from the contest; and allowed the suit to drag along until all the original litigants were dead. This left Denny Martin Fairfax, his nephew, to contend as an alien for his title to Lord Fairfax's estate, with quitrents and other holdings sequestered by Acts of Assembly passed in 1782 (II Hen. Stat. 128). The court held that Fairfax had no claim against settlers who held Minor Grants for the land West of the Blue Ridge prior to 1738. This virtually determined that Colonel Wood had good cause, and need not have submitted to any demand made by Fairfax for the site of Winchester. Much more could be written concerning these titles; but we must refer the student of such history to Hening's Statutes, vols. 2, 3, 4.

"More than five hundred settlers were affected by these ejectment suits instituted by Fairfax." (Cartmell, page 518; Hening's Statutes, vols. 2, 3, 4).

David Holmes Conrad, Esq., elder brother of Robert Y. Conrad, Esq., father of the late Major Holmes Conrad, in his early History of Winchester, says in describing the settlement of the Wappatomaka (South Branch): "This settlement commenced about the year 1743 or 1745. It does not appear that the first immigrants to this fine section of country had the precaution to secure titles to their lands, until Lord Fairfax migrated to Virginia, and opened his office for granting warrants in the Northern Neck. The earliest grant which the author could find in this settlement bears date in 1747. The most of the grants are dated in 1749. This was a most unfortunate omission on the part of these people. It left Fairfax at the discretion of exercising his insatiable disposition for the monopoly of wealth; and instead of granting these lands upon the usual terms allowed to other settlers, he availed himself of the opportunity of laying off in manors fifty-five thousand acres, in what he called his South Branch manor, and nine thousand acres on Patterson's creek.

"This was considered by the settlers an odious and oppressive act on the part of his lordship, and many of them left the country. These two great surveys were made in the year 1747. To such tenants as remained, his lordship, granted leases for ninety-nine years, reserving an annual rent of 20 shillings sterling per hundred acres; whereas to all other immigrants only two shillings sterling rent per hundred was reserved, with a fee simple title to the tenant."

What bustling days must have succeeded the laying off, on March 9, 1743-44, of the twenty-six original lots by Colonel James Wood, and the dedication of twenty-two of them to the justices! Ground had to be cleared for the Court House, which was built of logs, as was also the jail. At the April term of the Court of 1744, the Clerk of the Court was ordered to write to his Honor the Governor, for "a power to Choose a Vestry for the Parish of Frederick in this County." The first Episcopal Church was built of logs and stood with its burying ground north of the corner of east Loudoun and Water (Boscawen) streets.

The nucleus of the town as at first designed had as its boundaries Loudoun or Main street, "the great road," on the west; Boscawen or Water on the south; Cameron or Market on the east, and Court House avenue on the north. Here stood the public buildings, the Court House, two jails, Clerk's offices, public warehouse, and the Episcopal Church and burying ground.

The sound of hammer and saw and anvil could never have been silent by day, scarcely by night; because according to the wording of the deed, homes must be erected within two years from the purchase of lots. Besides, James Wood had been ordered not only to survey, but to settle families on tracts of unsettled land. With what interest must he have watched the progress of the infant settlement, not yet christened, but called variously Frederick Town and Opeckon! When, however, in 1752, a charter for the permanent establishment of the town was secured, the name given and to be retained was Winchester, after Mother Winchester in England. How could progress and prosperity fail to follow deeds prompted by the spirit of the cavaliers handed down from days of old, when "knighthood was in flower!"

The settlement was attracting residents whose names adorn the pages of history and whose characters helped to make Winchester the thoroughbred representative of Americanism that she is today.

In 1749 arrived Thomas Lord Fairfax, and the question of titles and rents arose. The subject is very big and very interesting. Turn to your histories and study the royal grants as represented by those of Lord Fairfax for the Northern Neck of Virginia; of Lord Baltimore, for what is now Maryland and Delaware; of the Duke of York, for all the territory lying between the Connecticut and Delaware Rivers; and contrast with them the minor grants as represented by those of the VanMeter brothers, Carter, Hite and others. The Northern Neck of Virginia! Surely the most plastic one on record! Uneasy must have rested the head to which belonged such a neck! But, first, think of the name Virginia, a name to conjure with, and try to realize that all of North America between Florida and Nova Scotia was known as Virginia for a number of years, and that it was not until 1607, in the reign of James I, that a settlement was made in Virginia proper. The "Virginia Company of London" granted the right to found a colony one hundred miles square anywhere between the mouths of the Cape Fear River in North Carolina and the Hudson River in New York. The "Virginia Company of Plymouth" granted a similar right between the Potomac River and Nova Scotia. The boundaries of the Jamestown Colony were extended along the coast two hundred miles, north and south, from Point Comfort, and "up into the land throughout from sea to sea, west and northwest, and also all the islands along the coast of both seas." Fancy a grant extending from the Atlantic Ocean to the Pacific! You remember that Captain John Smith sailed patiently up the Chesapeake Bay expecting to emerge into the Pacific Ocean, and that the Shenandoah Valley with its shining river was first beheld in 1716 by Governor Spottswood and his Knights of the Golden Horseshoe, the first to reach the summit of the Blue Ridge.

Remember, too, that the Yosemite Valley was not discovered until 1851, and the maps made by the royal geographers thousands of miles away across an almost trackless ocean, will not seem so fantastic.

As understood in 1736 and 1737, Lord Fairfax's southern limit was the Rappahannock River as it is known today. There was much and long continued contention and litigation about this line, however, between Fairfax and the colonial authorities, but it was finally settled that the Fairfax grant embraced all the land lying between the Potomac and Rappahannock Rivers up to the head springs of each river! Therein consisted the elasticity of this remarkable grant, because the Crown thought that the Potow-mack rose east of the "Blue Mountains," and not far up in the Alleganies as it does in reality. Moreover, the royal donors reserved the right for the purpose of colonization, to make grants within the great grants, requiring the settlers in each case to give proof to the government that such person had settled on his minor grant with so many families, that the tract had been subdivided, and surveys of the subdivisions actually made, and conveyance made to an actual settler on his part. Such grants were to be perpetual, and not to be interfered with by (in this case) Lord Fairfax or his heirs. Hence, the entering wedge of contention between honest Lord Proprietor and honest seekers after liberty, who, with the charter of king and council in their hands, had redeemed from the wilderness and were causing to blossom as the rose great tracts of this fair land; pioneers who "through peril, toil and pain" had brought cosmos out of chaos by building churches, founding schools and doing the most difficult share towards laying firm the foundations of a great and free people.

The Opockon surveys had been made in 1735 and 1736. Who knew then that the Potow-mack included within its sweep the Valley of the Shenandoah? Thomas, the father of the Lord Proprietor, was only beginning to discover the extent of his empire in 1736-7. East of the Blue Ridge the Potomac was called Potowmak, Quiriough, Pot-O-Make, etc.; west of it, the Cohongueroota. Neither Governor nor Council knew the extent of the Fairfax grant. Only the VanMeters, Hites and others who began to come into the Valley from the north about 1730 knew that the two rivers were one. Robert Harper settled at the confluence of the Sherando and built a ferry boat about 1736.

CHAPTER VII

The Braddock Expedition

The young people who daily fare through Braddock street on their way to and from the various schools should be thoroughly familiar with the history of the Braddock Memorial at Washington's Headquarters, because it identifies Winchester with the most important campaign in the history of Colonial Virginia. If we consider the three expeditions of Major and Colonel Washington against the French and Indians as one campaign, we may study their outstanding features and weigh the better their wonderful effect upon the history of the whole country.

Governor Dinwiddie had arrived in Virginia in 1752 and had heard the complaints of the "Ohio Company"—English fur traders with the Indians—against the encroachments of French and Indians from Canada and elsewhere. The General Assembly of Virginia authorized the governor to despatch a messenger to the commandant of the French fort on French Creek, about fifteen miles south of Lake Erie. George Washington, a major of militia, and but twenty-one years of age, was appointed by the governor to this undertaking. Major Washington left Williamsburg October 31, 1753, and came by way of Alexandria to Winchester, now in her eighth year and holding forth like a beacon light in primeval darkness her torch of civilization. Not another ray for many a mile and day was to light Washington and Jacob VanBraam, his Dutch fencing-master, who came with him from Fredericksburg, and John Davidson, Indian interpreter; Christopher Gist, guide; a French interpreter—eight persons in all. They reached Fort Venango on December 12, 1753, accompanied by Tanacharicon, the Half-King, whom they had met at Logstown, and two days later received from Legaudeur de la St. Pierre, the French commander, a courteous reply to the effect that the French refused to vacate the territory along the Ohio. Homeward then, with the reply, walking to save emaciated horses which at last were abandoned; and thrown themselves into the icy waters of the Allegheny River when the raft made with "one poor hatchet" was jammed in the ice. They spent a night of suffering on an island from which they escaped in the morning over the frozen river. Washington arrived at Williamsburg at the end of sixteen weeks.

Governor Dinwiddie and the House of Burgesses, enraged by the reply of the French, appropriated $50,000 to be used in raising troops to drive them out of the Ohio Valley. In 1754 Washington, now Lieutenant-Colonel, again set out from Winchester over the trail through the gaps in the North Mountain by way of the forks of Capon and Will's Creek, reaching Great Meadows in April. His little army of three hundred men was under Colonel Joshua Fry and Major-General Adam Stephen, who had been appointed eldest captain in Colonel Fry's Corps. The skirmish at Great Meadows was disastrous to the French and M. Jumonville, one of their principal officers, was killed. Colonel Washington, expecting to be overwhelmed by advancing numbers, threw up the stockade, "Fort Necessity." Soon a force of nine hundred French and Indians appeared, and in a few hours Fort Necessity was surrendered.

But the garrison was permitted to leave with the honors of war, upon the surrender of the prisoners taken at Great Meadows. Weary and dilapidated, the troops in a pitiable condition reached Will's Creek. From thence Colonel Washington returned to Winchester. According to a footnote in Ford's Writings, vol. 1, page 79, Colonel Fry died at Will's Creek May 31, 1754. Colonel James Wood in his diary says, "Colonel Fry died today." In the catalogue of the Wood papers, Colonel Wood's diary is thus listed. "Wood, J., Father of Colonel James Wood. Manuscript diary kept during the years 1749 to 1754. 12 mo. contains a short but very interesting account of Colonel George Washington's expedition from Fort Necessity, for the purpose of attacking the French fort, his retreat back to Fort Necessity, etc." From this it seems certain that Colonel Wood was with the expedition.

And how was the battered remnant that had escaped from the jaws of death received by Governor Dinwiddie? With anger and despair. He and Governor Hamilton of Pennsylvania appealed to England for assistance. Major-General Edward Braddock was sent with two regiments, the Forty-Fourth Foot under Colonel Sir Peter Halket, and the Forty-Eighth Foot under Colonel Thomas Dunbar. They arrived at Hampton Roads on February 20, 1755.

But the address of the late Capt. Robert Y. Conrad, the orator upon the occasion of the unveiling of the Braddock Memorial, is one of the finest accounts extant of the famous expedition and it is given later.

The details of the bitter defeat of the Braddock Expedition are therefore omitted here.

After caring for the wounded and sending the remnant of General Braddock's troops to Philadelphia under Colonel Dunbar, Colonel Washington returned to Winchester and wrote to Governor Dinwiddie a letter breathing the mature ideas of the patriot, the martyr and the father, yet the author was but twenty-four years of age. Later he went to Williamsburg to try to prevail upon the governor to increase the forces and to build a fort at Winchester. He had written, "I could offer myself a willing sacrifice to the butchering enemy, provided that would contribute to the people's ease." What must it have meant to a man of such a nature to deal with such a one as Governor Dinwiddie, whose indifference to the sufferings of the frontier colonists was so flagrant as to be cowardly and brutal!

Why attempt to review here deeds which are rehearsed by the ablest tongues and pens on each recurring February twenty-second? It is because George Washington is the national hero, our super-man. On such occasions each writes or speaks of him subjectively. It is for us to do likewise and to focalize Winchester as the base of these expeditions to the northwest against the French and Indians; Winchester the extreme limit of civilization before launching into a hostile wilderness and the first hospitable place of firesides to offer shelter, friendship, home, to the returning survivors.

In July, 1758, as commander-in-chief, Washington marched from Winchester, upon still another expedition, his fourth. On November 25, 1758, Fort DuQuesne was in his possession. Other French strongholds fell into the hands of the English and peace was soon declared. In the fall of the same year, he took his seat in the House of Burgesses, representing Frederick county, which comprised the present counties of Frederick, Berkeley, Jefferson, Shenandoah, Clarke, Morgan, Warren and Page. On January 6, 1759, he married the beautiful, wealthy and accomplished Mrs. Martha Custis, resigned his commission, and retired to Mount Vernon to manage his increased estate and to lead the life of ease and culture characteristic of a country gentleman of that age, an age which it has taxed the powers of our most gifted romancers to portray.

Thus from General Washington's sixteenth year, when in 1749 he became surveyor for Lord Fairfax, until the close of his public life, as touching the purely colonial period, Winchester was the center from which he worked, the heart of the school of experience in which he won his laurels. Here were developed the character and the resources which gave to the American Revolution its leader. In short, Winchester must have meant to him friends, refreshment, respite from the horrors of savage warfare. Lord Fairfax at Greenway Court never lost his affectionate regard for him, although he was the leader of the revolution for which his lordship had no sympathy. On the contrary, the surrender of Lord Cornwallis was a deathblow to Lord Fairfax. The gentle, sympathetic letters of the leader of the Revolution never ceased to bring their message of deference and affection to his first patron and revered friend. Washington's whole career exemplifies Emerson's philosophy: "Man is made equal to every event. He can face danger for the right. A poor, tender, painful body, he can run into flame or bullets or pestilence, with duty for his guide." And again, "Go face the fire at sea, or the cholera in your friend's house, or the burglar in your own, or whatever danger lies in the way of duty, knowing you are guarded by the Cherubim of Destiny."

CHAPTER VIII

Dedication of the Braddock Memorial, May 27, 1915

And now for Winchester again, and the Braddock Memorial! In 1915, the Society of Colonial Dames of America in the state of Virginia chose as their objective the marking of the Braddock Trail in Virginia. Two cannon left at Alexandria, Virginia, in 1755, were given by the city of Alexandria to the Mount Vernon Chapter of the Daughters of the American Revolution, who in turn presented them to the Society of Colonial Dames for the laudable purpose of marking the trail at Alexandria and at Winchester. The committee appointed by Mrs. Benjamin Purcell, of Richmond, Virginia, chairman of the Braddock Memorial committee, consisted of Miss Rose MacDonald, chairman of the Alexandria committee; Miss Katherine R. Glass, chairman of the Winchester committee. Mrs. Purcell visited Winchester and was received with enthusiasm. The Town Council offered its choicest locations. Major Holmes Conrad, who was ill at the time, and who died September 4, 1915, suggested the General Daniel Morgan lot in Mount Hebron Cemetery, but the committee on selection, Messrs. Robert L. Gray, Shirley Carter and Alexander T. Jones, appointed by the Common Council, decided that Washington Place, facing Braddock street, would carry out the idea of marking the exact trail, and for that reason the site named was decided upon. The little archaic cannon arrived, and the memorial was constructed by Mr. George W. Haines and his son, Mr.

The Braddock Memorial at Washington's Headquarters

G. Reginald Haines. The pedestal is built of unhewn stones, among them ten from historic localities, and has two white marble tablets. Facing the west the inscription reads: "This monument marks the trail taken by the army of General Braddock which left Alexandria April 9, 1755, to defend the western frontier against the French and Indians. Erected by the Society of Colonial Dames of America in the State of Virginia, May 27, 1915." The tablet facing the east contains the names of the localities from which the ten historic stones are taken. These are described here in order as follows:

1. The Blue Ridge, whose summit was reached in 1716 by Governor Spottswood and his Knights of the Golden Horse Shoe.

2. The Shenandoah River, "the daughter of the stars," the shining natural highway of the splendid Shenandoah Valley.

3. The Shawnee Springs, where once stood the village of the Shawnees, and of whose waters, if one drinks, one must return to drink again.

4. Jost Hite's Fort at Bartonville built in 1750.

5. The Old Opequon Presbyterian Church yard, containing some of the oldest monuments in the Valley. The church was organized in about 1738, in full view of the Valley Pike at Kernstown, and has stood in the pathway of the armies of every war in which Virginia has participated. It has yielded to the ravages of fire and has been twice rebuilt.

6. Glen Burnie, the home of Colonel James Wood, which has been already described, and where stood on the lawn the first clerk's office.

7. Greenway Court, the home of Lord Fairfax. There Lord Fairfax died in 1782, and from there his body was carried in a hearse brought from Alexandria, to be buried in the Episcopal churchyard in Winchester.

8. The grave of General Adam Stephen at Martinsburg. When Major-General Adam Stephen came to meet General Braddock at Winchester on his way to Fort DuQuesne, his daughter, Susan Stephen, accompanied him on horseback. Colonel William Dandridge fell in love with the charming girl in the red riding habit and they were married. Their home, "The Bower," on the banks of the Opequon in Jefferson county, West Virginia, became a renowned center of hospitality. Their son, Adam Stephen Dandridge, married Miss Sarah Pendleton. They were the grandparents of Miss Mary Spottiswoode Buchanan, who contributed so much to the success of the celebration in Winchester, and to whose generosity and patriotism was due the distinctive honor of having at the unveiling the famous sash in which General Braddock was borne from the field of battle.

9. Fort Loudoun, built by General Washington in 1756. The southwestern bastion is still standing. A well, more than a hundred feet deep, and cut through solid limestone, gave the fort an independent supply of water. So effectively did Fort Loudoun preach the gospel of preparedness that its eighteen-pounders, twelve-pounders, swivels and howitzers were never fired to repel a hostile attack.

10. The ruins of the old Lutheran Church in Mount Hebron Cemetery. This church was founded in 1764 and was destroyed by fire from some unknown cause on the night of September 27, 1854.

This is a brief suggestion of the meaning of these stones. They are witnesses of events and actors whose deeds have entered into the warf and woof of the history, not only of the state, but of the nation.

On Thursday, May 27, 1915, the time appointed for the unveiling of the memorial, the sun produced a glorious day, to which the moon added a brilliant night. The wish that the spirit of festivity should be infectious was fulfilled, and Winchester, big and little, young and old, was abroad. Automobiles, and carriages drawn by handsome horses; the Shenandoah Valley Cadets, mounted and afoot; the Boy Scouts, in their sober service uniforms; the Fort Loudoun Seminary and the John Kerr High School students marching gaily with banners flying; the pony carts laden with lovely laughing children, the rarest and fairest of earth's flowers and outshining their brilliant hues, and the sidewalks thronged with smiling, cheering friends and relatives moving with the long procession or standing beneath moving flags and gay bunting produced a scene worthy of the occasion.

The Dames, who had dedicated the Alexandria memorial the day before, arrived in time for luncheon at Fort Loudoun Seminary, after which they were escorted to Washington Place. The parade formed an imposing pageant, skillfully managed by Major W. T. Clement, of the Shenandoah Valley Academy, and his indefatigable aides, Lieutenant Robert T. Barton, of Company I, Second Virginia Volunteers, and Mr. Edmund Lupton. The guests were all comfortably seated through the generosity of the owners of automobiles and carriages, who placed them at the disposal of Miss Mary Spottiswoode Buchanan and Miss Bessie Conrad for the use of the Braddock committee. Among those who thus assisted were Dr. B. M. Roszel, Mr. Thomas Cover, Mr. Loring A. Cover, Mr. W. H. Baker, Dr. W. P. McGuire, Hon. S. L. Lupton, Mrs. John Miller, Mrs. Warren Rice, Mr. H. B. McCormac, Mr. Grover Schlack, Mr. Daniel W. Lupton, Mr. W. W. Tanquary, Mrs. Flora J. Tilford, Mrs. James B. Russell, Mrs. Shirley Carter, Mr. D. W. McIlwee.

Mrs. Thomas W. Harrison, Dr. and Mrs. Robert McC. Glass, Mrs. Robert Y. Conrad, Mrs. Mary B. Campbell, Mrs. Richard E. Griffith, Mrs. Annie R. Hack, Mrs. Robert Arbuckle, Mrs. General John B. Walker, Mrs. Frances Courtney Baylor Barnum, Mrs. Dudley L. Miller, Mrs. Hallie Huck, Mrs. George Jolliffe, The Evening Star and many others contributed to the success of the undertaking, and called for the unqualified praise of the visiting committee and guests. A delightful article by Nemo, the patroness of every good word and work, appeared in The Evening Star of May 29.

The visiting Dames included Mrs. James Lyons, vice-president of the Virginia Society, who represented Mrs. William Ruffin Cox; Mrs. Benjamin Ladd Purcell, Miss Rose M. MacDonald, Mrs. Carter H. Harrison, Mrs. George Eyster, Miss Irene Green Aldridge, Mrs. Mary S. Pechin, Miss Pechin, Mrs. W. R. Beale, Mrs. Morris L. Croxall (Maryland Dame), Mrs. W. B. Davis, Mrs. I. D. Barton, Mrs. Hughes Oliphant, Mrs. Warner Moore, Mrs. Barton Myers, Mrs. Annie Leakin Sioussat, historian general (Maryland Dames); Mrs. Henry H. Castle, Mrs. Alexander Speer. Other guests from a distance included Mrs. William Stone Abert, Miss Caroline Story, Mr. Henry H. Castle, Mrs. Theodore Truesdale Lines, Mrs. Bertha S. P. Jameson. The United States Army was represented by Lieutenant Julian S. Hatcher, the Navy by Captain Louis McCoy Nulton, and the United States Government in foreign lands by Judge Adam Carson, of Manila, P. I. Washington Place was brilliant with bunting. The Virginia banner, faded and worn, the treasured possession of the General Turner Ashby Camp of Confederate Veterans, was withdrawn from the museum in the Washington Headquarters to wave upon this occasion with the British flag and with the national colors. The following program was rendered

Invocation, the Reverend J. Horace Lacy, D. D.

The Story of the Cannon, Miss Rose MacDonald.

The Story of the Stones, and Presentation of the Memorial to Mrs. Benjamin Purcell, Miss Katherine R. Glass.

Remarks upon the work, Mrs. Purcell.

Acceptance of the Memorial for the Society of Colonial Dames and Presentation to the city, Mrs. James Lyons.

The Unveiling, Little Misses Colleen Hughes Glass, Mary Greenway Russell, Virginia Tayloe Boyd, Judith Braxton McGuire, Ellen Fauntleroy Baker, Susan Davis Lougheed Carson. These held the Braddock sash.

Acceptance for Winchester, the Mayor, Dr. Julian F. Ward.

Address, Mr. Robert Young Conrad.

Benediction, the Rev. William D. Smith, D. D.

Not a foot of space was available after the arrival of the procession at Washington Place. A sea of faces was uplifted to the cannon pointing northwest, and to the speakers, and the exercises were given rapt attention. At the close of the program the guests were escorted to the home of Mrs. Daniel B. Conrad, at the corner of Water and Stewart streets where a brilliant reception was held. Mrs. Conrad was assisted in receiving by her daughters, Miss Bessie Conrad and Mrs. Adam C. Carson; by members of the Century Club, the Woman's Civic League, the United Daughters of the Confederacy and the Red Cross. And so the monument devoted to the memory of a great undertaking was dedicated. The marker at Hampton, Virginia, was erected in 1916.

"Address, Mr. Robert Y. Conrad"

How little those who heard that clear, carefully prepared historical account of the Braddock Expedition realized that already we had entered the vortex of a world war, and that many who were that day contributing to the upholding of an ideal, would receive a baptism of fire! Some came through it purified; some were glorified and among the latter the orator upon that occasion. By profession and inheritance, Captain Conrad was a lawyer; but by nature and by inheritance also, he was a soldier. Scarcely could the little boy who loved to play soldier and who was always the leader, have been brought to believe that his services to his country would touch the Rio Grande and the Rhine and that a post of veterans of the greatest war throughout the ages would be called by his name.

Robert Young Conrad, Captain of Company I., One Hundred and Sixteenth Infantry, Twenty-ninth Division, A. E. F., was wounded in action while leading his men.

He died at Malbrouch Hill, near Sanogneux, France, October 8, and he was buried at Glorieux, near Verdun, October 8, 1918. He was born December 30, 1884.

As he poured forth for his country and for the world the exhilarating wine of his young life, he could no doubt exclaim with Robert Louis Stevenson:

> "Under the wide and starry sky
> Dig the grave and let me lie,
> Glad did I live and gladly die,
> And I laid me down with a will."

CHAPTER IX

Address of the Late Captain Robert Y. Conrad at the Dedication of the Braddock Memorial in 1915

In the year 1673, a French subject, Pere Marquette, sailed down the Mississippi River and "took possession" of the entire river valley in the name of France. By the signing of the Treaty of Peace at Aix la Chapelle in 1748, France sought to perfect her title to this vast area, and at once set about the erection of a chain of forts extending from the Saint Lawrence River to the Gulf of Mexico, to defend it.

These strongholds not only checked the growth and expansion of the English colonies, but actually encroached upon territory claimed as part of Virginia. The English claimed this land because it was part of Virginia and also because it had been conveyed to them by the Iroquois.

Both the French and the English claims could be plausibly maintained by force of argument; the real question was, which could be established by force of arms.

The French crossed Lake Erie in 1753 and built fortifications at Presque Isle, now Erie, Pennsylvania, and advanced toward the northern branches of the Ohio River. To protest against this movement, Governor Dinwiddie of Virginia sent Major George Washington, one of the Adjutant Generals of Provincial Militia, to the Commanding Officer of the French expedition, St. Pierre.

St. Pierre's reply was that the Marquis DuQuesne, Governor General of Canada would be notified of the protest and until he was heard from the French forces would remain where they were.

On his way to the French expedition Washington had noted the strategical importance of a point at the juncture of the Allegheny and Monongahela Rivers and had recommended its fortification. A fort was in course of erection when the French captured the place, completed its fortification and named it Fort DuQuesne.

Washington heard of the French action and was also informed that a scouting party under Jumonville was advancing. He captured this force after a fight in which Jumonville was killed. He then retired to Great Meadows where he threw up breastworks to which he gave the name "Fort Necessity." After being attacked here for nine hours by a greatly superior force Washington withdrew, leaving the French in possession of the territory.

The protection of the English colonies in America was the especial concern of the Duke of Cumberland, Captain-General of the British Army, and was a matter of the gravest importance to Parliament. The news of the fall of Fort Necessity spread a fever of excitement and activity throughout all England.

On September 24, 1754, Edward Braddock was commissioned a Major-General, and soon afterward embarked at Cork for America, with the 44th Foot under Colonel Sir Peter Halket and the 48th Foot commanded by Colonel Thomas Dunbar. They arrived at Hampton Roads on February 20, 1755, Braddock proceeding at once to Williamsburg, where he made his headquarters, and the army continuing up the Potomac to Alexandria. This movement was supported by the fleet of Admiral

Boscawen, for whom one of our streets was named. He encountered and defeated a French fleet.

Braddock was intrusted with the command of the entire British campaign, being appointed for the purpose, generalissimo of all the forces in the colonies. He had been a member of the famous Coldstream Guards for more than forty years: was a veteran of Colloden, Fontenoy, Dettingen and was known as a famous disciplinarian and as an expert upon the technical practices of warfare. His whole experience being obtained in campaigns against enemies who followed the rules of war obtaining among civilized nations, Braddock never imagined that any other principles of strategy could be effective. From the first he began his preparations for campaign precisely as he would have done were he then engaged against some European army. He seemed to expect that the roads and towns and even the very forests would be such as he had known in England.

The plan which Braddock was to carry out had four objects:

1. To drive the French from Nova Scotia.

2. To dislodge them from their fort at Crown Point on Lake Champlain.

3. To dispossess them of their fort at Niagara between Lake Ontario and Lake Erie.

4. To drive them from the frontiers of Pennsylvania.

The Deputy Quarter Master General, Lieutenant-Colonel Sir John St. Clair, arrived in America before Braddock, to inspect the field of operations. He made a tour of inspection with Governor Sharpe of Maryland

and was horrified at the wild state of the country. In February, 1755, he wrote from Cumberland to Governor Morris of Pennsylvania to have the road repaired toward the Youghiogeny River and another opened from Philadelphia for the transportation of supplies. When St. Clair had finished his inspection he went down Will's Creek and the Potomac River 200 miles in a canoe to meet Braddock at Alexandria.

Braddock was joined at Williamsburg by Commodore Keppel. There were two regiments of British regulars of 500 men each, which were to be increased to 700 each by men selected by St. Clair from the Virginia forces; artillery and munitions of war conveyed by Keppel. To this force Governor Dinwiddie assured Braddock there would be added about 400 Indians. There were assurances also thought from other sources, that immense quantities of provisions, horses and wagons would be forthcoming at the proper time. Relying upon this Braddock proceeded to Alexandria.

The British troops had disembarked and the Virginia troops had all arrived when Braddock reached Alexandria. Besides these there were two companies of pioneers; six companies of rangers and one troop of Light Horse. The levies were clothed and sent to Winchester to be armed, under command of an ensign of the 44th Foot who was enjoined "to make them as like soldiers as possible."

George Washington was at Mt. Vernon while these preparations were going forward at Alexandria, and Braddock, hearing of his experience and knowledge of the country, invited him to accompany the expedition as a member of his staff. Washington accepted, and upon arriving at the camp, his first impression was one of amazement that the expedition should be trammelled with so huge an amount of baggage and paraphernalia.

On April 20th, Braddock set out from Alexandria. He had been disappointed in the number of horses and wagons provided and in the quantity of provisions delivered to him.

Fortunately when Braddock reached Frederick, Maryland, he there met Benjamin Franklin who was then Postmaster-General for America. Franklin agreed to procure horses and wagons, 150 wagons and 4 horses to each to be at Will's Creek, now Cumberland, by May 20th. Franklin spoke to Braddock of his fear that the slender line nearly four miles long which his army must make would expose him to ambuscade from Indians. Braddock replied, "These savages may indeed be a formidable enemy to raw American militia, but against the king's regular and disciplined troops it is impossible they should make an impression."

After Franklin's departure, Braddock attended by his staff and escort of light horse set out for Will's Creek by way of Winchester, the road along the north side of the Potomac not being yet made. "This gave him," writes Washington, "a good opportunity to see the absurdity of the route and of damning it very heartily." Washington had overtaken Braddock at Frederick and proceeded with him to Winchester, and wrote a letter to William Fairfax from Winchester on May 5 in which he says, "We shall remain here until the arrival of the 2nd division which we hear left Alexandria on Tuesday last."

Washington had three horses knocked up before reaching Winchester and had to buy others, for which he had to borrow money from his old friend, Lord Fairfax of Greenway Court. The fact that Braddock traveled the whole way from Alexandria to Fort Cumberland in great state in a chariot purchased from Governor Sharpe added greatly to his discomfort, but at last realizing that he was not in a region fitted for such display he abandoned his chariot there and took to his horse.

By the 19th of May, the forces were assembled at Fort Cumberland; they consisted of: Two Royal Regiments of Foot 1000 strong increased by Virginia levies to 1400; two Provincial Companies of Pioneers 30 men each; one company of Guides, Captain, two aides and ten men; Troop of Virginia Light Horse under Captain Stewart; detachment of sailors consisting of 30 men; remnants of two New York companies.

The Indians which Dinwiddie had led Braddock to expect, never arrived. The road from Philadelphia was not finished and the necessary forage and supplies had never been provided and there was a woeful lack of wagons and horses. At last, however, the wagons and horses promised by Franklin came, and on June 10th, Braddock set out from Fort Cumberland with his aides, staff and light horse.

Sir Peter Halket had proceeded ahead three days before with his force and for ten days 600 men under Colonel Chapman had been preparing a road supervised by Sir John St. Clair.

On the 16th, Braddock reached Little Meadows, and now seeing that the nature of the country was unlike that of any he had had any experience with, he called upon Washington for advice as to the best course to be pursued. Washington saw the advantage of striking a blow at Fort DuQuesne, if struck swiftly. He advised dividing the forces. One division, of selected men, to push ahead with Braddock, the rest to follow on with the baggage, etc. Braddock for once followed advice, and with 1200 men selected from all the forces and carrying 10 field pieces, prepared to move forward.

At Little Meadows Braddock was joined by the Famous Captain Jack and his rangers, who asked that he and his men be employed as a scouting party. Braddock refused. Washington urged as strongly as the proprieties would permit, that all the friendly Indians be employed as reconnoitering parties; this also Braddock refused, and indeed treated the Indians with such contempt that most of them deserted him.

It was on the 19th, that Braddock set out from Little Meadows. He marched in the way he had been accustomed to march over the plains and roads of Europe and would not listen to any suggestions that his mode of procedure was unfitted for the wilderness.

During the march from Little Meadows, an incident occurred which is of peculiar interest to the people of Winchester. Daniel Morgan was at this time a wagoner, hauling the baggage of one of the Virginia companies. The captain of this company became involved in a difficulty with a great, powerful fellow who accompanied the army and who had the reputation of being an expert pugilist, a bully. The dispute was to be settled by a fight, but Morgan, going to his captain, suggested that he should not fight, because if the bully licked him then the entire company would be disgraced. "Let me fight him," said Morgan. "If he beats me, then no one will think anything of it." The captain remonstrated, but at last saw some sense in the arrangement, and the bully being ready to take on the substitute, Morgan fought him in the captain's place, "and gave him so severe a beating that he was unable to rise from the ground."

Braddock proceeded upon his way with so much pomp and circumstance that he only advanced twelve miles in four days. On June 25th the first ominous event of the enterprise occurred. Three men venturing beyond the line of sentinel were shot and scalped.

On July 4th the forces camped at Thicketty Run.

On July 6th several more men were shot and scalped.

The attack upon Fort DuQuesne was planned for the 9th. Braddock had taken a month to march a little more than 100 miles; his strict and suicidal adherence to the rules of military march as he conceived them, proclaimed his presence all along his route.

The forest was on the same side of the Monongahela River as Braddock's camp, but there was a narrow pass between the river on the left and a high mountain on the right, about two miles wide. Instead of risking being caught in the pass the plan was to cross the river at a ford directly opposite from the camp, proceed along the west bank of the river five miles and then recross the river and push on to the fort.

Washington suggested at this point that the Virginia rangers, who were familiar with Indian fighting and who knew the country, be put forward in advance. Braddock indignantly rejected this suggestion as impertinence on the part of an inexperienced militia officer.

Early on the 9th of July, Colonel Gage crossed the river with the advance; he was followed by Sir John St. Clair with a working force of pioneers of 250 men. A party of Indians attacked Colonel Gage as soon as he crossed, but were put to flight before they accomplished anything. By sunrise the main body turned out in full uniform arrayed more as for a fete than for a battle.

About noon they reached the second ford. Gage with the advance was on the opposite shore. When all had crossed there was a halt at Frazier's Run until Braddock had arranged the order of march.

First, Gage preceded by guides and engineers and six light horsemen. Then Sir John St. Clair and the working party with two six-pounders and four flanking parties thrown out on each side. Then Braddock with the main body; the artillery and baggage being preceded and flanked by light horse and squads of infantry. The Virginia and other provincial troops formed the rear guard.

The space before them was level for about half a mile from the river, where rising ground covered with long grass, low bushes and scattered trees sloped gently up to a range of hills. Generally speaking, the whole country was a forest with no clear opening except the road which was about twelve feet wide and flanked by two ravines, but as has been said, General Braddock "marched through this wilderness as if he had been in a review in St. James Park."

About 9 o'clock firing began. The van of the advance had been taken by surprise. All who were not killed were driven back in confusion upon the advance. Gage ordered fixed bayonets and formed his men in battle array. The attacking party, hidden from sight, kept up a steady and destructive fire, accompanied with unearthly yells. The English soldiers were more terrified by these demoniac sounds than by the withering fire. Most of the officers and many men were killed and wounded in a short while. Gage himself was wounded. The advance fell back upon Sir John St. Clair's force, which was much demoralized itself, and made more so by the precipitate retreat of the advance. The cannon belonging to it were deserted. Colonel Burton had come up with reinforcements and was forming them to face the rising ground upon the right, when both of the advance detachments fell back upon him and put all in disorder.

Braddock was now upon the field. He had the colors advanced in different places to separate the men of the two regiments. He ordered the officers to form their men in small divisions and advance with them, but neither threats nor entreaties could induce the soldiers to advance. The Virginia troops, accustomed to Indian fighting, scattered and concealed themselves behind trees, whence they could pick off the lurking foe, and thus in some degree protect the regular troops. Washington advised Braddock to follow the same plan with the regulars, but he persisted in forming them into platoons and they were shot down as fast as they advanced. Such was the confusion of the regulars that they killed several of the Virginians who were doing their best to protect them.

The officers behaved with great bravery, going in front of their men and encouraging them to charge. The Indians shot at every man on horseback or who seemed to be an officer, and consequently the officers suffered severely. Many were shot by their own men who fired with great rapidity, but with no aim. The soldiers in the front rank were subjected not only to the fire of their hidden enemies in front, but also to the fire of their terrified comrades in the rear. Between friend and foe the slaughter was horrible.

Braddock still remained in the center of the field hoping to stay his falling fortunes. The Virginia Rangers who had been most efficient in covering his position were nearly all killed or wounded. His secretary, Shirley, was killed by his side. Many of his officers had been slain in his sight and most of his light horse had been killed. Five horses were shot under Braddock. At length a bullet passed through his right arm and lodged in his lungs. He fell from his horse, but was caught by Captain Stewart of the Virginia light horse, who with another American and a servant placed him in the folds of a large silken sash, the ends being fixed to the saddles of two horses moving abreast. This very sash has been kept here in Winchester for many years, and will be shown to you today.

The rout was now complete. Baggage, stores, artillery—everything was abandoned. Fortunately for the fleeing soldiers their foe gave up the pursuit to collect the spoils. The shattered army continued its flight after it had crossed the Monongahela. It was shattered indeed; out of 86 officers 26 were killed and 36 wounded. Nearly 700 men of the ranks were killed or wounded. The Virginia troops suffered most. One company was almost wiped out and another, besides great losses in the ranks, lost all its officers, even to its corporals.

About one hundred men were brought to a halt a quarter of a mile from the river ford. Braddock was here, Dr. Craik dressing his wounds and Washington attending him. Braddock had still strength enough to give orders, and seemed to have some hope of holding his ground until reinforced. Most of the men were stationed in a well chosen spot about 200 yards from the road. In less than an hour most of these men had run away. Being thus deserted, Braddock and his officers continued their retreat. He was unable to ride and had to be carried by his soldiers.

On the 13th they reached Great Meadows. The proud spirit of Braddock was broken by his defeat. He was silent the first evening after the battle, only remarking, "Who would have thought it." Next day he seemed to have still remaining in his breast some faint ray of hope, for he said, "We shall better know how to deal with them another time."

He was grateful for the attention paid to him by Washington and Captain Stewart, and expressed his admiration for the bravery displayed by the Virginia troops in the battle. He is also said to have apologized to Washington for the petulance with which he rejected his advice.

He died on the night of July 13th at Great Meadows, the scene of Washington's defeat the previous year. The obsequies were performed before break of day, Washington reading the burial service because the chaplain had been wounded. Braddock was buried in the middle of the road and the troops and wagons passed over his grave that it might not be discovered by the Indians.

His remains were discovered in 1823 when Braddock's road was being repaired and were reburied nearby beneath some pines where they now rest cared for through an appropriation by the Pennsylvania Legislature.

Of Braddock, Washington Irving says:

"His dauntless conduct on the field of battle shows him to have been a man of fearless spirit, and he was universally allowed to be an accomplished disciplinarian. His melancholy end disarms censure of its asperity. Whatever may have been his faults and errors, he in a manner expiated them by the hardest lot that can befall a brave soldier, ambitious of renown—an unhonored grave in a strange land; a memory clouded by misfortune and a name forever coupled with defeat."

THE BRADDOCK SASH

The sash, woven in 1709, was worn by General Edward Braddock's father, who fought under Marlborough. In it General Braddock was borne mortally wounded from the charge upon Fort DuQuesne, July 9, 1755. The sash is a perpetual loan to the Mt. Vernon Association by the heirs of General Zachary Taylor.

CHAPTER X

The Story of General Braddock's Sash — Tributes to the Memory of Miss Mary Spottiswoode Buchanan and Mrs. William Ruffin Cox.

General Braddock's sash, reposing as in the beginning at Mount Vernon, perhaps never again to take part in a public celebration, is one of the most famous relics on the American continent. It is fitting that such relics as the sash, and the key to the Bastile, presented to General Washington by the Marquis de Lafayette, should be preserved at the home of the founder of American liberty. The story of the sash as given by our own Miss Mary Spottiswoode Buchanan is reproduced here in her own words:

"When General Braddock fell mortally wounded at Great Meadows, he said to Colonel Washington, who was one of his aides, 'For God's sake do not let me fall into the hands of the French and Indians. Take off my sash and carry me to a place of safety. In England these sashes were used to carry the wounded officers from the battle fields. This sash was worn by my father, who fought under Marlborough, and I want you, Washington, to have it sent by Bishop, my body servant, to Mt. Vernon.' And there it remained until General Washington, realizing his advanced years and that he must have it preserved, gave it to his nephew, Fielding Lewis, whose daughter married Colonel Butler of Louisiana. When General Zachary Taylor made his brilliant career in the war with Mexico, Colonel Butler said, 'The Braddock sash must be given to General Zachary Taylor, as the hero of the Rio Grande,' but he declined it, saying, 'I am not the hero.' But after he defeated Santa Anna at the famous battle of Buena Vista and entered the city of Mexico, again Colonel Butler urged him to accept it, which he did, valuing it above rubies. When he was dying at the White House as the President of the United States, he left it to his daughter, Betty Taylor, who afterwards married Mr. Philip Pendleton Dandridge. She brought it to Winchester, where it remained in her father's, General Zachary Taylor's mahogany camp-chest until her death, when Mount Vernon begged for it to be allowed to return there, and it was sent there in 1755 and remained there until General Washington's death in 1799. During the life of Mrs. Dandridge, London newspapers became clamorous to know in whose possession in America it was. Dr. Daniel B. Conrad, formerly of the old United States Navy, and later of the Confederate Navy, a most valued friend of Mrs. Dandridge, from his home in Winchester, answered the queries, with the result that the officers from the Coldstream Guards, General Braddock's old regiment, came over from England and offered Mrs. Dandridge $3,000 for the sash, an offer which she declined.

"At Summit, nine miles from Uniontown, Pa., the county of Fayette, and the town have erected a monument to General Braddock, who fell while defending the fort nearby. King George of England sent out a delegation to represent him at the dedication. General Codrington represented the king. He took the sash from me, and with tears filling his eyes, he pressed it to his heart and said, 'General Braddock's father wore this sash when he fought under Marlborough.' Then Colonel Philips, of the Forty-fourth Essex Brigade (General Braddock's brigade), of the Cold Stream Guards, with

General Codrington, lifted me upon the platform. I related how my aunt, Mrs. Philip P. Dandridge, came into possession of the Braddock sash. It was a wonderful experience. Sixteen of King George's officers in their scarlet and blue uniforms, made a picture never to be forgotten. With bared heads and forms erect, they received Uniontown's tribute to General Braddock, amidst thousands who were there. The judge of the Supreme Court of Pennsylvania, their governor and many distinguished professors and men in high places bowed their heads when they saw the bloodstains of General Braddock upon the sash. Time has eaten way the bloodstains. The hollow places mark the ravages of time. The sash was woven in 1709.

"I was the guest of the Historical Society of Pennsylvania and shall ever cherish the privilege of having been present upon so great an occasion."

This is the story of the sash, and these are the reasons why the youth of this generation should understand the meaning of this memorial, the first historical marker erected in Winchester—the little old cannon pointing toward the northwest.

Miss Mary Spottiswoode Buchanan joined the band of the Immortals on September 19, 1925.

Mrs. Robert D. Johnston of White Post, Virginia, the Alabama member of the Board of Regents of Mount Vernon, writes of her:

"To picture dear, adorable 'Miss Spott' as she hangs on the walls of memory is impossible,

> 'Unless to mortals it were given,
> To dip his brush in dyes of heaven.'

"She stood alone in her exquisite personality, so rare, so fine, so charming. There are none of her own kind left.

"One of the greatest honors and rarest pleasures of my life came to me in her friendship. 'I was a stranger and she took me in,' and her loving interest never failed me. I only wish I could put into words what she meant to me, and, oh, how I miss those loving hands, that heaven having now, I need so much, so much."

At the time of the passing of this imcomparable gentlewoman, Mrs. Johnston contributed to her memory the poem than which nothing could be more appropriate:

> "Cherished and choice, at last she goes;
> Like a rose, ancestral rose,
> Which many a summer has alone
> Within an ancient garden grown,
> And when it dieth, leaves behind,
> No more on earth of its own kind.
>
> That lovely presence, fair and fine,
> A gentle sainthood's fitting shrine,
> That delicate and subtile grace;
> An heirloom from an honored race.
> That life, that reads its quiet story,
> In God's own way, to God's own glory,
> And on its very latest page,
> A vivid, beautiful old age."

Mrs. William Ruffin Cox, president of the Virginia Society of the Colonial Dames, under whose direction the Braddock Trail was marked at Alexandria, Hampton and Winchester, was called home on Christmas day, 1925. Mrs. Cox was Miss Kate Cabell, daughter of the late Colonel Henry Walter Cabell of Richmond. Her first husband, Major Herbert A. Claiborne, died in 1902. Some years later she married General William Ruffin Cox, of North Carolina, who died in 1919. Two sons survive her, Herbert A. and Hamilton C. Claiborne.

Mrs. Cox was secretary of the Virginia Society of Colonial Dames from 1894-1897, and president of that society from 1897 until her death; vice-president of the National Society, 1902-1914; and honorary president of of National Society since that date. In addition to these offices she was vice-regent for Virginia of the Mount Vernon Ladies' Association and a member of the Board of Governors of Sulgrave Institute.

Well does the National Society of Colonial Dames of America in Virginia in its memorial of her say:

"Give her the fruit of her hands: and let her works praise her in the gates."

Such noble women as Dr. Kate Waller Barrett, Mrs. William Ruffin Cox and Miss Mary Spottiswoode Buchanan, have raised lasting memorials to themselves in the trails they have marked, the memorials they have preserved, the spirit of patriotism they have fostered, the beautiful examples of Christian womanhood they have been.

CHAPTER XI

Fort Loudoun — Governor Dinwiddie — Lord Loudoun — P e r s o n a l Items Concerning Washington — Events in Winchester

By far the most important relic of colonial days to be found in Winchester is the remnant of the fort built by Washington in 1756. The presence of this fort made Winchester an army post with Washington himself as commandant. On the checkerboard of war Fort DuQuesne, Quebec, Crown Point, Ticonderoga and Louisburg were absorbing the attention of both English and French, and were producing such heroes as Wolfe, Montcalm, Israel Putnam and others whose deeds are part of the alphabet of American history.

The panic caused by the Braddock disaster brought to a climax the tragedy of the Acadians, those guileless peasants from Brittany, simple devoted Catholics, who had been coming to Acadia, the present Nova Scotia, since 1604. In 1713, by the treaty of Utrecht, the territory was transferred to England, but the Acadians could not transfer their allegiance. Absolutely inoffensive, yet a menace because they would not take the oath of allegiance to England, nor would they fight the French, in 1755 their property was declared forfeited to the Crown. On the 10th of September, 1755, their deportation began and by the last of December more than seven thousand of them had been scattered among the colonies from Massachusetts to the Carolinas. Many died on the sea. Families were separated, never to meet again. Their homes were burnt; their farms laid waste.

Ruthless uprooting; exile without palliation, finding a parallel in the carrying away from Judea of the tribes of Israel by the Assyrians, whence the bitter wail, "By the rivers of Babylon, there we sat down; yea, we wept, when we remembered Zion. We hanged our harps upon the willows in the midst thereof."

In Nova Scotia,

"Still stands the forest primeval; but under the shade of its branches, Dwells another race, with other customs and language."

Many an Evangeline and Gabriel lamented each other's loss through weary years, and today "Evangeline's willows" on Grand Pre seem to weep for her sad fate.

While these things were trying men's souls, the future commander-in-chief of the first American army was protecting the frontier with Winchester as a base. No higher thought of reward had he than that of receiving a king's commission. This was never given him because of the jealousy of those who had the power to bestow it. Little did he realize that in a few years, when he would be representing Frederick county in the House of Burgesses, the Stamp Act would be passed, and his fellowburgess, the brilliant patriot, Patrick Henry, would utter the ominous words: "Caesar had his Brutus, Charles I his Cromwell, and George the Third * * * may profit by their examples." Thus from Virginia came the first outburst in opposition to this portentous act of taxation. But this was in 1765. Washington was not, therefore, obliged to resign a king's commission in order to take command of the Revolutionary Army.

In March, 1756, Washington secured an act for the establishment of Fort Loudoun, instead of the system of forts proposed by Governor Dinwiddie, a procedure which, from the nature of the country, the scarcity of troops, and the stealthy, wily methods of the Indians, would have been a waste of time, money, and almost superhuman effort. The act is in these words:

"And, whereas, it is now judged necessary that a fort should be immediately erected in the town of Winchester, in the county of Frederick, for the protection of the adjacent inhabitants from the barbarities daily committed by the French and their Indian allies, Be it enacted by the authority aforesaid, That the governor or commander-in-chief of this colony for the time being, is hereby empowered, and desired to order a fort to be built with all possible dispatch in the aforesaid town of Winchester, and that his honor do give such orders and instructions for the immediate erecting and garrisoning the same, as he shall think necessary for the purposes aforesaid. And the governor, or commander-in-chief of this colony is hereby empowered and desired to issue his warrant to the treasurer for the payment of so much money, as he shall think necessary for the purposes aforesaid, not exceeding the sum of one thousand pounds, who is hereby required to pay the same in treasury notes, to be remitted by virtue of the said act of Assembly, for raising the sum of twenty-five thousand pounds, for the better protection of the inhabitants on the frontier of this colony, and for other purposes therein mentioned."

The fort was a field work or redoubt, having four bastions, whose flanks and faces were each twenty-five feet, with curtains ninety-six feet. The square may be easily constructed by taking the southwestern bastion, still extant, and producing the figure as described above, across Loudoun street, and thence north from this base for the northeastern and northwestern bastions. Washington marked out the site of the fort and superintended its erection. He bought a lot and had a blacksmith shop erected upon it, while his own blacksmith from Mount Vernon made the necessary iron work. Here Washington resided as commandant, his attendants occupying huts or cabins erected within the fort. His own room is said to have been above the gateway of the fort, commanding a view of the principal street. The fort covered an area of half an acre, and in addition to the bastion on the campus of Fort Loudoun Seminary, there are terrace-like mounds on either side of Loudoun street. The work of construction was performed by Washington's regiment. There was a strong garrison, and the fort mounted six eighteen-pounders, six twelve-pounders, six six-pounders, four swivels, and two howitzers. These guns were removed from Winchester at the beginning of the Revolutionary War. The fort was never attacked. A French officer who reconnoitered the location found it impregnable. The wonderful well one hundred and three feet deep, cut through solid limestone, is said to be higher than the sources of the springs in the vicinity, yet the water often rises to the surface. It was near the northwestern bastion.

Winchester was thus rendered so secure that Hessian and British prisoners taken during the Revolution were brought here for safe keeping. The number became so large that barracks were erected four miles north of the town, and in 1784 Winchester was the custodian of sixteen hundred foreign prisoners. But from the time of the erection of the fort, Washington was sadly hampered by the erratic and arbitrary orders of Governor Dinwiddie, demanding that most of the troops be withdrawn from Winchester to strengthen Fort Cumberland, which was now to become headquarters. The most important points were thus weakened, to concentrate a force where it was not needed, and would be out of the way in most cases of alarm. So great was the consternation of the people upon the removal of the troops from Fort Loudoun, thus leaving the inhabitants at the mercy of the Indians that men, women and children appealed to Washington for protection. This appeal, the subject of a painting by Felix O. C. Darley, has been reproduced upon the ceiling of the Empire Theatre.

This irrational removal of troops late in 1756 was caused by the pique from which Governor Dinwiddie had never recovered, caused by the popular elevation of Washington to the command, in preference to his favorite, Colonel Innes. Washington suffered from the governor's ignorance and arrogance until, his administration at an end, he set sail for England in January, 1758, little regretted and leaving a character overshadowed by the imputation of avarice and extortion in the exaction of illegal fees and of delinquency in accounting for large sums transmitted to him by the government—another instance of the incapability of a royal governor through ignorance, and lack of sympathy with loyal colonists, to strengthen the ties between them and the mother country, thus contributing directly to the causes of the Revolution.

Studying these wielders of almost absolute power, we can but see that the Revolution was inevitable. Some times, as in the case of General Braddock, the best of intentions were thwarted through lack of adaptability; but only too often selfishness, greed, a total misconception of the possibilities of a new country, and the aims of a new nation, brought about irreconcilable differences. The royal representatives "never could know why, and never could understand."

Personally, Washington suffered so much at the hands of Governor Dinwiddie that his health was undermined, and he was obliged to retire late in 1757 to Mount Vernon upon the urgent advice of his friend, Doctor Craik, the army surgeon. For months he was ill and so discouraged that he thought seriously of retiring from public life, but gradual recovery and a natural bent for his favorite career induced him to return in April, 1758, to his command in Winchester.

Fortunately, the troops which had been withdrawn by Governor Dinwiddie were returned in 1757 by Lord Loudoun, for whom the fort had been named before his arrival in America, and Washington found himself again in command of seven hundred men with whom to defend a frontier extending more than three hundred and fifty miles. Panic had subsided. Lord Fairfax had decided to remain at Greenway Court, although urged by Colonel Martin to forsake the Valley, but so great was the alarm that a court record of October 5, 1757, says, "James Wood, clerk, is granted the privilege of removing the county records to Fort Loudoun, or anywhere else he may secure them for the imminent danger from the enemy."

In making his returns for the year, this memorandum occurs in Colonel Wood's note book:

"October 8, 1756. To the Honorable Mr. Secretary Nelson:

"I thought it advisable to leave the notes (name illegible) would have returned as delinquents amounting to 1770, in his hands, on his giving the hopes of some returning who were scared off by the Indians. Between this and our next court for———. I will either return the notes or cash for the same. I hope the danger we are in on the frontiers will plead my excuse for not waiting on you. I am, with the greatest respect, Sr, Yr. most obd'nt servant,

J. WOOD."

But why was the fort named Loudoun? Because all hopes were centered upon the coming of John Campbell, Earl of Loudoun, as commander-in-chief. The Earl reached America on July 29, 1756. Washington went to Philadelphia in March, 1757, to meet him, in order to counteract the prejudice which Governor Dinwiddie had caused concerning the state of military affairs in Virginia. His mission was successful in that the troops were returned to Fort Loudoun, as already noted, and Winchester once more became headquarters. On the other vital points Washington was disappointed. The Earl of Loudoun, upon whom the colonists had staked their hopes, was but another Dinwiddie with wider powers. He allowed Field Marshal, the Marquis de Montcalm, quick of mind, enterprising and small of frame, but alert and untiring, to inaugurate and carry through to success a brilliant campaign by which Crown Point and Ticonderoga on Lake Champlain were strengthened, and many forts and an immense amount of military stores were captured. Montcalm ascended the St. Lawrence to Lake Ontario and retired in triumph to Montreal, and Canada, which might have been at the mercy of General John Winslow, was saved to the French for that year. In the meantime, Lord Loudoun, exercising the kind of logic that Governor Dinwiddie had used when he proposed to protect the Shenandoah Valley by fortifying Fort Cumberland, was thinking of establishing a fortified camp on Long Island as a protection against the depredations of the French and Indians about the Great Lakes and on the St. Lawrence River. But the season was too far advanced for such an undertaking.

The great northern campaign upon which so much depended was postponed until the following year, and Lord Loudoun returned to New York, hung up his sword, and went into comfortable winter quarters. In 1757 he sailed for Halifax, where he arrived on June 30, and, joining Admiral Holborne, found himself at the head of a splendid force of more than twelve thousand regulars, besides a fine fleet to support the land forces. But his ardor fled as he landed; the whole summer was frittered away, and nothing done worthy of a Commander. He leveled a parade ground, planted a vegetable garden to prevent scurvy and exercised his troops in absurd manoeuvres and sham battles. Fruitless fuss and parade! Lord Loudoun discovered that Louisburg was more strongly fortified than he expected, and that the French were further reinforcing it. In a moment of zeal he gave orders to go forward, but scarcely was the command given before it was countermanded, because he learned, forsooth, that the French fleet at Louisburg had one more ship than his own—reason enough to his mind, for his return to New York. Not until the administration of William Pitt, for whom Fort DuQuesne, after its capture in ruins by Washington in 1758, was renamed Pittsburgh, was an effort made to retrieve the disgraces of the American campaign. Irving says that as a result of it, "Washington had the mortification to see the noble Valley of the Shenandoah almost deserted by its inhabitants, and fast relapsing into a wilderness."

Lord Loudoun was relieved from a command in which he had attempted so much and done so little. Franklin summed up his character when he pronounced him a man "entirely made up of indecision."

"Like King George on the sign-boards: forever on horseback, but never getting ahead." He never came to Virginia! Yet this is the man for whom Loudoun county, formed in 1757, Fort Loudoun, our Loudoun street, and the names of places derived from them, are named, while many a brave patriot lies "without a grave, unknelled, uncoffined, and unknown." So do we make idols only to find them clay!

In fact, the Earl of Orkney, the Earl of Albemarle, Sir Jeffrey Amherst, and John Campbell, Earl of

Loudoun, Governor General of all the American Colonies, who were governors from 1697 to 1763, never came to Virginia but were represented by deputies.

During these events, Washington was a familiar figure on our streets. Buff and blue, three-cornered hats, knee breeches, silver buckles and buttons were in evidence on all sides. Washington paid much attention to his personal appearance. He was scrupulously neat, but not fastidious, and he had the wisdom to modify the military dress to meet the demands of Indian warfare. Jefferson said that he was "the best horseman of his age and the most graceful figure that could be seen on horseback." Washington often mentions the names of horses and dogs in his letters and diary. Ajax, Blue Skin, Valiant, Magnolia (an Arab), Nelson and others were famous mounts. For his dogs, favorite names were Mopsey, Pilot, Tartar, Jupiter, Trueman, Tipler, Truelove, Juno, Dutchess, Ragman, Countess, Lady, Searcher, Rover, Sweetlips, Vulcan, Singer, Music, Tryal, Forrester. Imagine the tall, well-proportioned figure, the strong, firm face, the brown hair tied back and carefully powdered upon occasion, the far-seeing eyes, calm, eloquent, or flashing. Blue? No. Grey? No. Both!—typical of the ideal union of blue and grey.

Chastellux relates, "He was so attentive as to give me the horse he rode, the day of my arrival, which I had greatly commended. I found him as good as he is handsome; but, above all, perfectly well-broke and well-trained, having a good mouth, easy in hand and stopping short in a gallop without bearing the bit. I mention these minute particles, because it is the general himself who breaks all his own horses; and he is a very excellent and bold horseman, leaping the highest fences, and going extremely quick, without standing upon the stirrups, bearing on the bridle, or letting his horse run wild."

On foot or on horseback, by hedge and highway he must have been known to everyone here, a livable, lovable human being to whom children, horses, dogs, and all growing things were dear. The clerk's office was, of course, a rendezvous then as now, and the young man who began to father his country before he was twenty-one was a welcome guest there and thoroughly in sympathy with Colonel James Wood. As clerk of the court he made this record: "October 4, 1757. On motion of George Washington, Esq., ordered that his tithables be set on the list." Washington was apparently preparing for his election campaign. On a lot he owned on Loudoun street, north of the Shenandoah Valley Bank corner, he had erected a military prison.

Ford gives this item: "Mem. respecting the militia, April and May, 1756: May 11, Colonel Spottswood from Spottswood, with three field officers, five captains, ten subalterns, and one hundred and thirty private men arrived here and encamped in Colonel Wood's meadow." This "meadow" was probably at that time about where the Cumberland Valley Railroad depot now stands. The deed books record that Mary Wood and her son, Robert, in 1797 conveyed thirty-seven acres of their land to Edward Smith, who erected a mill. The deed made the same reservations concerning the water from the town spring that had been embodied in the Wood deed from Lord Fairfax in 1753. In 1826 James Stackhouse acquired four and a half acres of the land deeded to Edward Smith, and to the grist mill with its mill race, distillery, stables and dwelling was added a cabinet-maker's shop and appurtenances. Nothing further is heard of the distillery. Stephen Stackhouse, who had removed to Florida, sold the whole plant to the Cumberland Valley Railroad Company about 1881.

That Colonel Wood was county lieutenant, the following receipts, hitherto unpublished, show:

"June 10, 1755. Received from Alexander Boyd, paymaster, seventy-nine pounds, nineteen shillings and one penny in full payment of my second company of foot rangers for the month of May last, to which I signed Andrew Lewis. 79.19.1

"September 9. Received of the above for the month of June, 77. 7. 6; ditto for July and August. 146. 14.8, for which I signed the receipt, Andrew Lewis.

"8 August, 1755. Received of Colonel Wood the sum of 79. 19. 1, being the sum mentioned on the credit side for the use of Captain Andrew Lewis. Gabriel Jones.

"October 14, 1755. I do acknowledge to have received by the hands of Mr. Gabriel Jones seventy-nine pounds, nineteen shillings and one penny, and from James Wood two hundred twenty-four pounds, two shillings and two pence in full of what the said James Wood received from the paymaster for the months of May, June, July and August, and do allow of his setting my name to the receipt given to the said paymaster.
Andrew Lewis."

CHAPTER XII

Fort Loudoun (continued) — General Andrew Lewis — Fort Loudoun As It Is Today — The Formation of the Fort Loudoun Chapter of the Daughters of the American Revolution — Tribute to the Late Dr. Kate Waller Barrett.

This is the famous Andrew Lewis whose father settled Augusta county. His home was on the Roanoke in Botetourt county. He was the most distinguished of six brothers, among whom was the beloved Colonel Charles Lewis, who was killed at the battle of Point Pleasant, on the Ohio. All the brothers were in one company, of which Samuel was the captain, and distinguished themselves at the capitulation of Fort Necessity, July 4, 1757. They received the first fire in the fatal Braddock engagement. In 1758, during the unfortunate attack of Major Grant upon Fort DuQuesne, both Major Lewis and Major Grant were captured, and as prisoners sent to Canada, where they were, however, soon exchanged. Andrew Lewis, as colonel, attained his greatest fame during the so-called Dunmore War against the famous Indian warriors, Cornstalk, a Shawnee chief, Blue Jacket, Red Hawk, a Delaware, chiefs of the Mingo tribe and Wyandottes, and Logan, of the Cayugas, the famous orator. The six nations had concentrated their forces at the Big Woods, on the Ohio, opposite Point Pleasant. Here occurred, on May 10, 1774, the great Indian battle, as a result of which the Indians were driven west of the Ohio. Cornstalk and six helpless companions were atrociously murdered in a fort at Point Pleasant in the summer of 1777, whither they had come to a conference. The brave Indian chieftain is buried there. The Shawnees had left the Valley in 1754.

General Lewis commanded the Virginia troops when Lord Dunmore, governor of Virginia, was driven from Gwynn's Island in 1776. So hated is the name of Dunmore, who made his little finger thicker than the loins of his predecessors, that it has been erased from every possible record in Virginia. A traitor to friend and foe, among other unpardonable offenses, he collected on board vessels the colony's whole supply of gun-powder, pretending that he feared an uprising of the slaves.

General Lewis resigned his command in 1780, on account of illness. He died of fever on his way home. He was more than six feet tall and possessed a figure of perfect symmetry. In 1768 when with Dr. Thomas Walker he was a commissioner to hold a treaty with the Six Nations in behalf of Virginia, the governor of New York remarked that the earth seemed to tremble under him as he walked alone. In 1774 Daniel Morgan and James Wood, the younger, from Winchester, commanded companies which took part in this famous Indian campaign. Here, on the yellowed page of Colonel James Wood's note book, is the neat signature of this wonderful Andrew Lewis, who, when England declared war against France, May 9, 1756, for the conquest of North America, was associated as major with Colonel Washington and Lieutenant-Colonel Adam Stephen over the new Virginia army of sixteen hundred men.

But what became of the old fort? The guns were removed at the beginning of the Revolution, as already stated. Cartmell says: "Loudoun street was opened as a road from Cork to Piccadilly in 1761, through what

The Southwestern Bastion of the Fort Built By Washington in 1756 from Peyton Street

Fort Loudoun as it is today looking north from Loudoun Street

was termed quagmire. It was not until after 1842 that it was extended from Fairfax lane north and through the stockade on Federal Hill. A roadway had been cut through the timber and hill, but the road or street received its first overseer and work in 1843." Bushels of minie balls, broken swords, shells, and other fragments of the utensils of defense have been seen on the hill within the memory of people still comparatively young. But before the street was graded, the war plant had become the site of educational institutions. About 1830 the Reverend Joseph Baker established on Fort Loudoun a flourishing Baptist academy, which lasted until his death in 1855. He was succeeded by Miss Casey, of New Jersey, who had been a teacher in his school, but who soon became Mrs. Newman. The property was bought by Mrs. Swartzwelder, an eminent musician, in 1868. She and the Reverend James B. Avirett conducted it as an Episcopal Seminary, Dunbar Institute. They were followed by Captain J. C. Van Fossen, who opened a classical school. The late Rev. John P. Hyde, D. D., after conducting the Valley Female College for five years at "Angerona," at that time a well known seat of learning at the head of Piccadilly street, now the residence of the late Mr. Thomas Cover, removed to Fort Loudoun in 1886, where the college continued an influential Methodist center until, at the end of fifteen years, Dr. Hyde, in 1901, retired on account of failing eyesight. It is an interesting coincidence—or was it thus decreed by the fates?—that in 1905 the greater part of the grounds and the main building were acquired by a descendant of Colonel James Wood, and that for the first time the original name, Fort Loudoun, was given to the seminary of today.

James Wood, the younger, was stationed at one time at Fort Loudoun, as colonel of the Virginia line.

The logs from the old stockade were used in various ways. Mr. David Hamilton built a tool house with some of them. Upon the erection of the John Kerr public school building, Mr. Hamilton stored the logs in the cellar of his home. During a bitter winter, when Mr. Hamilton was in Florida in charge of the orange grove of the late Mr. Henry Kinzel, Mrs. Hamilton, unable to obtain fuel, was obliged to use many of the historic logs. The next winter she asked Mr. John Nail whether he would exchange some toys for pieces of Fort Loudoun wood. That versatile genius gladly did so, and the exchange was made again at the next Christmas. He says, "Now I believe I am the only one in town who has any pieces of that wood." Mr. Nail made the gavel presented to Fort Loudoun by Mr. William Spottswood White, and highly prized.

Several of the houses on the east side of Loudoun street have interesting histories. The oldest is the Peyton home, now the residence of Mr. and Mrs. L. E. Rice and their son-in-law, Lieutenant Felix Hatcher, who married Miss Helen Rice. Colonel Henry Peyton, the father of John Peyton, lived in the wing. The front was built by John Peyton when he married, in 1780, Susannah Rutherford, daughter of the Honorable Robert Rutherford. Their ninth child, Louisa Morrow, married William Lawrence Clark, the father of Judge William L. Clark, whom many of us remember. Their daughter, Susan Peyton Clark, married Major Francis B. Jones, who was on Stonewall Jackson's staff, and who lost his life while serving the Confederacy. Louisa Morrow Peyton, the grandmother of Mrs. C. Grattan Crawford; her mother, Susan Peyton Clark, and she herself, Louisa Peyton Jones, were all born there. Later Dr. Robert Baldwin, Jr., son of Dr. Stewart Baldwin, lived there. During the Civil War the house was occupied by northern soldiers, and the oil paintings of Robert Rutherford and of his wife were destroyed.

The house, now owned by the heirs of Mr. George W. Keller, was the residence of members of the Tucker and Magill families, so famous in the history of the state. The house was built by Mr. Isaac Paull, and the wine cellar is still to be seen. The present handsome brick residence is modern, and has the unique distinction of having been mortgaged by Mr. George W. Keller, Senior, who was the father of the late Mrs. Charles L. Crum, to pay a debt upon the Presbyterian Church. The house opposite, just north of the fort on the west side of the street, and bought by Mr. John W. Darlington in 1886, was built in 1853. It was occupied as a parsonage by the late Rev. J. R. Graham, D. D., who married in the same year Miss Fanny Bland Magill. The famous Washington well is in the yard.

Long, long ago, the old fort passed away but still "up and down the people go." O, King Arthur, and your Knights of the Table Round, ye who in your mystical battles slew the dragons of self and sin and struggled towards the ideal until a Galahad was found worthy to behold the Holy Grail, do ye not in spirit today commune with those knights who went out from the old fort and fought to the death, that a countless multitude might, if they would, wear amid the blessings of peace and freedom, "the white flower of a blameless life?"

The Fort Loudoun Chapter of the Daughters of the American Revolution was organized at Washington's Headquarters, December 2, 1921, under the auspices of Dr. Kate Waller Barrett, the late beloved and lamented

State Regent. On that day, Dr. Barrett arrived at Fort Loudoun Seminary in time for luncheon. After the organization of the chapter, she gave one of her inimitable addresses at the Empire Theatre, where she was introduced by Mayor William Wood Glass. The address was followed by a small reception and tea at the residence of Mrs. Robert W. Barton, and Dr. Barrett hurried back to Alexandria to welcome distinguished guests from South America.

She had made her first visit to Winchester, and she had left an indelible impression of the great loving nature which made every age and class reach out to her, and never in vain.

Among her public activities she was known as the State Regent of the daughters of the American Revolution; Member of the Board of Visitors of William and Mary College; Honorary President of the National Council of Women; Honorary President of the Argentine Council of Women; President of the Ivakota School for Homeless and Friendless Girls; State Commander of the American Legion Auxiliary; National President of the American Legion Auxiliary; National President of the Florence Crittenden Mission; Chairman of the International Committee of Immigration, and as such she made several trips abroad for the Federal Government, to the Near East, the Balkans and Asia Minor in 1913-14, to France in 1919-20, to South America in 1920-21. She was Doctor of Medicine and Doctor of Science. She was the mother of five children when she took her degree. Post-graduate work was taken at St. Thomas' Hospital, London, and at the Sorbonne in Paris. She was selected to present the Loving Cup to General Foch in Richmond on Foch Day, November 23.

At the time of her death, February 23, 1925, among other official positions she was Past National President of the American Legion Auxiliary. She has joined the gleaming row with those of ever youthful brows who

> "Come transfigured back,
> Secure from change in their high-hearted ways,
> Beautiful evermore, and with the rays
> Of morn on their white Shields of Expectation."

The Student Loan Fund is the Memorial of the Virginia Daughters of the American Revolution to Dr. Barrett.

The organizing members of the Fort Loudoun Chapter on that memorable occasion were:

Regent, Katherine R. Glass (Mrs. Harry Raynor Green); First Vice-regent, Madge Tabb Cather (Mrs. Howard); Second Vice-regent, Nancy Maynard Rosenberger (Mrs. John W., Jr.); Corresponding Secretary, Edith Jackson O'Neal (Mrs. Samuel D.); Recording Secretary, Grace Enos Rice (Mrs. Warren); Treasurer, Miss Anna Somerville Briggs; Historian, Mary Paxton Baker (Mrs. Louis L.), (resigned on account of ill health); Librarian, Katherine Kurtz Eddy (Mrs. C. Vernon); Registrar, Grace L. Bond (Mrs. Walker McC.); Virginia Athey (Mrs. William B. Sinnott); Retha Blondel Athey (Mrs. Melville Kayser Shirkey); May Baker Baetjer (Mrs. J. George), (deceased); Mary Strickler Collins (Mrs. Michael); Ethel Lovdy Athey (Mrs. Grover Carson Cooper); Susan Baker Faulkner (Mrs. James Gray Beverley); Mrs. Townsend Jolliffe; Mrs. Viola B. Griffith; Louise W. Heist (Mrs. Geo. H.); Miss Lucy Fitzhugh Kurtz; Mollie Tabb Lyon (Mrs. Alexander); Mrs. Virginia B. Maynard (deceased); Mrs. Rosabelle Quantz; Miss Carolyn Quantz; Miss Mary Robinson; Henrietta Sibert (Mrs. J. W.); Susie Glass Strider,

(Mrs. Harry); Florence Light Williams (Mrs. Alex.); Louise Baker Glass (Mrs. William Wood).

At a meeting of the Board of Managers February 20, 1922, these appointments were made to complete the organizing officers: Chaplain, Mrs. Susie Glass Strider; Historian, Mrs. Susan L. Conrad (Mrs. Daniel B.); Genealogist, Louise Waters Miller (Mrs. Godfrey O.); Custodian, Georgia Bryan Conrad (Mrs. Holmes), (deceased).

Other members were Laura Gold Crawford (Mrs. Frank B.); Catherine Baetjer (Mrs. Daniel Crump Buchanan); Miss Sallie W. Boyd; Miss Ellen Boyd; Helen Virginia Bailey (Mrs. Walter); Harriot Wood Glass (Mrs. William Blackstone Davis); Miss Virginia Henkel; Adelaide Victoria Cushing Kern (Mrs. Adam T.); Miss Sallie Miller; Miss Peggie Miller; Miss Mary Miller; Ruth Farley Massey (Mrs. William Pratzman); Rebecca Howland Baird (Mrs. J. Henry Moling, Jr.); Mrs. C. W. Johnston; Gurtha Clute (Mrs. John F. Rodman); Miss Edith N. Wall; Stella Hoffman Whetzel (Mrs. William); Miss Mary Pierce Baker; Miss Julia Tyler; Mrs. Frances Robinson; Rosalie Baker Valk (Mrs. John E.); Rosalie Baker Brown (Mrs. Duncan). These completed the organization for the first year, and are therefore Charter Members.

Chairing Colonel Wood as proxy for Washington in his election to the House of Burgesses July 24, 1758. From Graham's Magazine, 1853

CHAPTER XIII

The Election of George Washington to the House of Burgesses — Colonel James Wood as Proxy — Gabriel Jones, Blue Coat Boy, "the Valley Lawyer"

Founded in 1744, established by law in 1752, the base of the expeditions to Great Meadows and Fort Necessity in 1753 and 1754, of the Braddock Expedition in 1755, and the seat of Fort Loudoun in 1756, young Winchester put a really jaunty feather in her battle-worn cap when she elected to the House of Burgesses in 1758, Washington, the youthful veteran of the famous French and Indian War. And well may she treasure that feather, because Washington, who represented in 1758 and again in 1761 the vast tract known then as Frederick county, is probably today the most colossal figure in secular history. Has the character of any other public man, of any man who has lived through the changes which made of scattered colonies a union of sovereign states, who has held the highest offices within the gift of colonies and of states, whose services covered practically half a century, withstood better the assaults of time? Well may Winchester be glad that this man, whom a Virginian, "Light Horse Harry" Lee, pronounced "First in war, first in peace, and first in the hearts of his country men," received at the hands of her people this measure of appreciation. Well may she be proud that in so doing she secured such lasting honor.

Three times in the County of Frederick, Washington was candidate for election to the House of Burgesses; but his defeat in 1757 exemplified in a way his own favorite quotation from Addison, " 'Tis not in mortals to command success." Certainly he had not then successful political methods at his command. He could not enforce military discipline and be at the same time popular with the soldiers, and he was impolitic enough to attempt an election on prohibition principles. The saloon element rose against him, and he received but forty votes. But in 1758 he was politic enough to place his election in the hands of his friends, and his friends knew the people and knew the music that would please them, as well as did the Pied Piper of Hamlin in another famous instance.

Washington had good reason to deprecate the evil which his friends were obliged to tolerate in order to secure the election upon which they were determined, and by means of which he would be in a position to bring about legislation for the betterment of the community. He had already written to the governor, representing "the great nuisance the number of tippling houses in Winchester are to the soldiers, who by this means, in spite of the utmost care and vigilance, are, so long as their pay holds, incessantly drunk and unfit for service," and he wished that "the new commission for this county may have the intended effect," for "the number of tippling houses kept here is a great grievance." The Virginia regiment was accused in the papers of drunkenness, and under the sting of that accusation Washington declared war on the publicans. He whipped his men when they became drunk, kept them away from the ordinaries, and even closed by force one tavern which was especially culpable. "Were it not too tedious," he wrote the governor, "I could give your Honor such instances of the villainous Behavior of these Tippling House Keepers, as would astonish any person." How little he imagined either the hideous proportions that the curse would assume, or the miracle by which it would be removed! No man ever stood more squarely or fearlessly for law and order than he. Familiar is the story of the inveterate poacher, whom he seized in a skiff, although he was obliged to spur his horse into the Potomac in order to do so. The man leveled his gun at Washington's breast, but after a severe cow-hiding at the irate planter's hands, he concluded to shoot elsewhere in the future than within the Mt. Vernon preserves.

The year 1758 was an eventful one for Washington, as well as for Winchester. During the greater part of 1757 Washington had been ill, but early in 1758 he resumed his duties at Fort Loudoun. In March, attended by Thomas Bishop, who had been commended by the dying General Braddock to Washington, and who was the latter's faithful attendant for nearly forty years, he set off on horseback to lay the needs of the army before the council at Williamsburg. But on the way he met a Mr. Chamberlayne, who with difficulty prevailed upon him to take dinner at his home on the Pamunky, a branch of the York River. Among the guests was Mrs. Martha Dandridge Custis, whose hazel eyes and charming Southern manners must have captivated Washington at first sight. For once Bishop and the horses waited in vain at the door. Not until the next morning did the small cavalcade gallop towards Williamsburg. The White House, the home of Mrs. Custis, was in New Kent County, and there were hurried visits while Washington remained at Williamsburg; but almost immediately he returned to Winchester. On July 2 he was at Fort Cumberland. His friends urged him to return for the election, but his duty to his command forbade his considering his personal interests. When the election took place, therefore, he was represented by Colonel James Wood, who with the genial Gabriel Jones, made July 24 a gala one for the town. Both were lovers of men and natural leaders. Nothing was spared on that day that might contribute to a notable success. Of the votes cast, George Washington received 310; Colonel Thomas Bryan Martin, 240; Hugh West, 199; Thomas Swearengen, 45. We may imagine the enthusiasm with which the people bore aloft the delighted proxy and how lustily he joined in the huzzaing for the Burgess elect. The bill of expense submitted to the successful candidate amounted to £39 6s., about $195.00. Mint was not an item of expense, but that must have been because along the banks of the burn at Glen Burnie, and down through the meadows, Nature had supplied so lavishly that tempting adjunct to the flowing bowl. Well trampled it must have been on that day, and for once at least, its soothing flavor and fragrance were expended in a worthy cause. The great event had been conducted in English style with plenty of good cheer for all who came. The news speedily reached Washington at Fort Cumberland, and that he was pleased with the result is shown by the following letter to Colonel Wood. This letter is recorded in Ford's Writings, vol. II, page 59. A foot note says that the draft is in the Department of State, Washington, D. C.

"July, 1758

"My dear Colonel,

If thanks flowing from a heart replete with joy and gratitude can in any measure compensate for the fatigue, anxiety and pain you had in my election, be assured you have them, 'tis a poor, but I am convinced, welcome tribute to a generous mind such I believe yours to be. How I shall thank Mrs. Wood for her favorable wishes, and how acknowledge my sense of obligations to the people in general for choice of me, I am at a loss to resolve on—but why? Can I do it more effectually than by making their interest (as it really is) my own and doing every thing that lyes in my little power for the honour and welfare of the country? I think not, and my best endeavors they may always command. I promise this now, when promises may be regarded, before they might pass as words, of course.

"I am extreme thankful to you and my other friends for entertaining the freeholders in my name. I hope no exception was taken to any that voted against me, but all were alike treated, and all had enough—it is what I much desired. My only fear is that you spent with too sparing a hand. I don't like to touch upon our public affairs. The prospect is overspread by too many ills to give a favorable account. I will therefore say little, but yet say this, that backwardness appears in all things, but the approach of winter—That joggs on apace."

In spite of his enthusiasm over his election, Washington was so modest that when he went to Williamsburg a few months after his marriage to take his seat in the House of Burgesses, he was quite overcome by the reception which the speaker, Mr. Robinson, was pleased to give him. Attempting to reply to thanks on behalf of the colony for his distinguished military services, he rose to reply, blushed, stammered, trembled and could not utter a word. "Sit down, Mr. Washington," said the Speaker with a smile; "your modesty equals your valor, and that surpasses the power of any language I possess."

Washington was never a speech maker. Thomas Jefferson said that he and Dr. Franklin "laid their shoulders to the great points, knowing that the little ones would follow of themselves," and he and Patrick Henry seemed to come to the same conclusion as if by inspiration. Washington did remember the physical needs of Winchester, and was one of a committee to draft a law to prevent hogs from running at large. The bill was read three times and became a law on April 9, 1761. What a hero anew he must instantly have become! Wild Indians might be driven away and not return, but those squealing, grunting, rooting, wallowing porkers were an ever-present nuisance that even visions of buckwheat cakes and sausage, waffles, beaten biscuits and old ham could not mitigate. Imagine the colonial dames in their voluminous skirts contesting the right of way with a moist, inquisitive snout as they tripped to church or market! Yes, Washington was a public benefactor, and a right gallant gentleman.

And Gabriel Jones, the other principal in the famous Washington election contest—the man with the celestial name and the very uncelestial temper. What of him? Fortunately we are not left in doubt concerning a record too conspicuous to lack detail. Yet it is buried away safe and sound in books, so far as the rising generation is concerned, although his descendants here today are upholding the law and order of which he was such an inflexible exponent. But what a glorious temper he had! What nuts for the wits and wags of that day to lead on the irascible legal luminary that they might enjoy his ebullitions of wrath in a splendid torrent of invective garnished with choice swear words! Once the mischievous Judge Holmes, who was the opposing council in a case in which Gabriel Jones was engaged, dexterously roused his passion to a white heat. To think of punishing Mr. Jones was out of the question, so the presiding judge gave it as the decision of the court that Mr. Holmes should be sent to jail if he did not "quit worrying Mr. Jones and making him swear so."

This most interesting man was born of English parents on May 17, 1724, about three miles from Williamsburg, Virginia. About 1727 his mother, then a widow, returned to England. In 1732 Gabriel was admitted to the Blue Coat School, founded by Edward VI, the Boy King, in 1552.

Here began about 1780 the famous friendship of

Charles Lamb and Samuel Taylor Coleridge, whom the inimitable Charles called "Esteecee".

Gabriel Jones remained at the Blue Coat School until he was fifteen, when he received his discharge and began the study of law. He returned to America and settled in Frederick county, where in 1743, at the age of nineteen, he was made King's attorney. Two years later he qualified to practice law in Augusta county, and as King's Attorney there he began the great career which led him to fame and fortune. In 1749 he married Margaret Strother Morton who had been widowed after a month of married life. Thomas Lewis, surveyor of Augusta, a brother of the famous Charles and Andrew, married one of her sisters. This relationship probably caused "the Valley Lawyer" to sell part of his estate in Frederick county—not Vaucluse, however—and remove in 1753 to Augusta, where he lived on the opposite side of the Shenandoah River from the Lewis family. Here on the former Strayer plantation he died in the year 1806, at the age of eighty-two.

In spite of his hasty temper and speech, Gabriel Jones was a man of intense personal piety. He was elected a vestryman of Frederick parish in 1752, together with Lord Fairfax, the executor of whose estate he became. His family consisted of three daughters and one son, William Strother Jones, of Vaucluse, whose son, William Strother Jones, married Ann Maria Marshall. A daughter, Frances, born at Vaucluse, married David Walker Barton, the father of the late Honorable Robert T. Barton of Winchester; a son, Francis B. Jones, married, as has been already mentioned, Susan Peyton Clark. So the list could be prolonged indefinitely of the descendants of the first lawyer in the Shenandoah Valley.

A portrait of Gabriel Jones shows a small gentleman wearing a high waistcoat and white stock, white ruffles at his wrist, a wig, and a bandage over his right eye. Well could he write to his small grandson, "You must expect many rubs through life, but a firmness of mind will overcome all." His biographers say of him that he had no concealments to make in public or in private; that he was never worse than he appeared to be; that in the relations of domestic life he was punctual, liberal and honorable; that the man never lived who doubted his integrity; that he would never receive more than six per cent for the use of money; that his influence was invariably wielded in behalf of suffering virtue, of sound morals, and of public faith. A few English coins wrapped in a paper on which was written in his own hand, "This is the patrimony I received from my mother; from my father I received nothing," prove that his financial success was due to his own efforts. He represented Augusta county in the House of Burgesses in 1757, 1758 and 1771; he was elected to the Continental Congress from Augusta on June 17, 1779, and in 1788 he and Thomas Lewis were elected members of the Constitutional Convention from Rockingham county. This is the Gabriel Jones who in 1758 neglected his own election in Augusta in order to come to Winchester to help Colonel James Wood to elect George Washington. "The last button on Gabe's coat," if there were any left at the close of that hilarious day—those beautiful silver buttons that made such delightful souvenirs, must have twinkled with delight over the accomplished feat.

Fascinating, the study of the doughty deeds of our forbears and their never ending influence! and in the case of the first election of George Washington to the House of Burgesses, the result leaves us with a smile upon our lips.

CHAPTER XIV

Wood's Addition — Personal Notes of Ye Olden Tyme — "A Pot of Sugar and a Teacup Full of Tea" — Death of Colonel James Wood

The rapidly increasing importance of Winchester induced Colonel Wood in September, 1758, to petition the General Assembly for permission to make an addition to the town. A letter from Dr. Walker, Secretary, has been published in part, but a note concerning the sale, in Colonel Wood's handwriting, has not hitherto appeared in print, and both are given here from the original manuscripts:

"Williamsburgh, September ye 28, 1758

Dear Sir:
The Bill for adding your Lotts to Winchester has been once read and I make no doubt will pass into a Law.
As Mr. Thos. Rutherford informs me that he is very ill I must beg the favour of you if he should not be able to go through the Duty that his present post may require to employ some person to assist, or if he should be unable, to act any part in his stead. If any money should be sent and Mr. Rutherford unable to take care of it, beg you will take possession of it and deliver it in small sums as occasion may require. I shall hope to hear from you if anything extraordinary should happen. 20,000 is voted for ye payment of ye regiment to ye first of December-January.

Dear Sir,
Your most Humble Serv't,
THOS. WALKER."

"16 November, 1758

The subscriber proposeth to set up sundry Lotts in the town of Winchester to be sold at Publick vendue, to the Highest Bidder the Place laid off according to an Act of General Assembly of this Colony may be seen at the House of Mr. Henry Heath: The seller obligeth himself to make a sufficient Title in Fee simple to the Purchaser without reserving a Ground Rent, Title as the Purchaser's Council shall advise. The Purchaser to be restrained from building any House fronting the street with round loggs and from erecting wooden Chimneys.

The seller reserveth to himself the Liberty to bid once at the sale.

Two months credit will be given on the Purchaser's entering into Bond with Security.

J. Wood."

The bill was passed promptly, and was worded as follows:

"Whereas, by an act of assembly, made in the twenty-fifth year of his present majesty's reign, a town was established at Winchester, in the said county of Frederick, which daily increases in inhabitants, and James Wood of said county, gentleman, having laid off one hundred and six acres of his land, contiguous to the said town of Winchester, into lots and streets, hath petitioned," etc., for the same privileges granted the other portions of the town, "it is hereby granted," etc.

The trustees named in the act were Lord Fairfax, James Wood, Thomas Bryan Martin, Lewis Stephens, Gabriel Jones, John Hite, John Dooe, Isaac Perkins, Robert Rutherford and Philip Bush. Stephensburgh was established at this time, and the second town chartered in the Shenandoah Valley had the same trustees as Winchester, the first.

The declaration of Colonel Wood that he would "make a sufficient title in fee simple to the purchaser without reserving a ground rent" seems natural enough to us, but it struck at the root of the rapidly growing discontent of that day over quit rents, ground rents, etc. As late as September 29, 1759, Colonel Wood made this entry in his journal:

"Thomas Lord Fairfax, By quit rents for Lotts to this day, 4. 1. 3."

In fact, Lord Fairfax and Colonel James Wood represent the two great parties of the day; Lord Fairfax staunch royalist to the end; James Wood, loyal colonist, but endued with democratic principles, a type of the last colonial, the first American, who died in faith, not having received the promises of independence.

From March, 1758, dates the seal of Frederick county. The justices in that month ordered a silver seal "about the size of an English half-crown, with the words FREDERICK COUNTY engraven thereon," to be made by William Miller. There were at this time in the Lower Valley, comprising Frederick county, the grand total of 2124 tithables! Winchester and Alexandria were incorporated by a dual act passed by the General Assembly in October, 1779.

Brilliant colonial events of the year 1758 were the reduction on July 21, of Louisburg and the Island of Cape Breton by General Amherst and Admiral Boscawan (for whom Water Street was named), thus retrieving the misfortunes of Lord Loudoun; and, most pertinent to Winchester, was the investment on November 25 of Fort DuQuesne by Washington.

This long task completed, the successful warrior could turn his mind towards the pursuits of peace, and as we know, he was married on January 6, 1759, to Mrs. Martha Custis, and retired to Mount Vernon where he lived in comparative quiet until the call to arms in 1775.

Paradoxical as it may seem, the triumph of English and Colonial arms in Canada was the beginning of the end of English rule in America. Irving in writing of it says; "Thus ended the contest between France and England for dominion in America, in which, as has been said, the first gun was fired in Washington's encounter with De Jumonville. A French statesman and diplomatist, Count de Vergennes, French Ambassador at Constantinople, consoled himself by the persuasion that it would be a fatal triumph to England. It would remove the only check by which her colonies were kept in awe. 'They will not longer need her protection', said he; 'she will call on them to contribute toward supporting the burdens they have helped to bring on her, and they will answer by striking off all dependence.'"

A little later in speaking of the outbreak of Pontiac's War, in 1763, Irving says, "The prediction of the Count de Vergennes was in the process of fulfillment. The recent war of Great Britain for dominion in America, though crowned with success, had engendered a progeny of discontents in her colonies. Washington was among the first to perceive its bitter fruits."

The reference to De Jumonville shows that "the shot heard 'round the world" was fired at Great Meadows, in 1754, during Washington's second expedition from Winchester.

The year 1759 brings us to the close of Colonel Wood's life. He has erected involuntarily a permanent monument to himself in the faithful records so carefully compiled from the time of his appointment to the clerkship in 1743, to his death on November 6 of this year. Into these records he has woven unconsciously the everyday life of the community—a magic web. His mirror reflects world shadows which have grown in importance until we recognize in them some of the foundation fibre of our national existence. Fragments of note books not among the official archives of the city, but preserved among his personal papers, give interesting little hints of manners and customs, quaint or obsolete. For instance:

Sept. 21, 1746. Capt. Thomas Rutherford, Dr.
To cash paid for your wigg 15s.

RUTHERFORD

1745. By my order to Mr. Sam¹ Earle towards his chapel ___ 7.10
By dº to Mr. Calmes towards his chapel _____ 7.10
By dº to Mr. Campbell towards his chapel _____ 7.10
By Mr. Helme for the church _____ 7.10

1745. CAPT. JOHN
15 March. To the duty of 24s Raw Deer skins _____17.

1748.
Mch. cl. To the duty of 500 Deer skins _____1.14.8¾

1744. COL. THOMAS
Aug. 21. To duty of skins and Furrs by Buchannon__1.11.4½

1746. McKENNA
Aug. 12. By schooling 4 scholars three months _____ 1.0.0

1747. Maj. Andrew Campbell.
To clerk's notes delivered you as per receipt.
To Tobacco levied for me by the county.
To Tobacco levied for me by the county.

1747. Aug. 6. Gardener. By a negro woman named Sal, aged 21 years, and two mulatto girls, Jude, aged 2 years in June last, Hannah aged 7 months, £60.

1750. The Honorable Thomas Lee, Esq., President of Virginia, To cash sent down by Mr. Jacob Hite—

1749. April 26, Marriage licenses:
Benj. Grub to Hannah Humphrey.

(*Was this the daughter of Hannah, the protester in June, 1749?*)

April 28. Henry VanMeter to Hannah Bartlett, etc. etc.

1750. Henry Peyton, Deputy Sheriff of Prince William.
To sundry clerk's notes.
The Honorable Robert Dinwiddie, etc.

1755. A list of chairs in Frederick County,
Rt. Honorable Thomas Lord Fairfax _____ 2 wheels
James Wood _____ 2 wheels
John Hite _____ 2 wheels
Marquis Calmes _____ 2 wheels

Ink, a receipt. (A good receipt it must have been, since the ink is faithful to its task at the end of a hundred and seventy years.)

Galls ½ ℔.; copperas ¼ ℔.; gum araback ¼ ℔.; allom ½ ounce; salt ½ ounce.

All the above made fine and mixed together and put into glass or other vessel, and put one pint of good vinegar to it. Let it stand two days, then put three pints of water to it. Let it stand in a warm place for a few days and stir it every day.

1747. Frederick Parish,
To salivating John Higgins, 4.0.0 (*From Dr. Hart's ledger.*)

1752. May 26. Athaliah Minor, Administrator of Stephen Minor, Deceased.

1757. Aug. 27. Robert Rutherford
To a house sold for the use of the Indians, 7.10.

1757. Israel Potts:
To rent of old court house from me 1 day of March 1756 at 4.0.0 per annum.

1750. 1 Jan. By breaking 75 ℔s. Flax at 2½

(*The Winchester Hemp and Flax Factory was established on Picadilly street shortly after the Revolution.*)

By Mr. Jones making a wigg 15s.
By myself three wiggs, £5.
By putting a crown to a wigg, J. Earle, 5s. 9d.
By Capt. Lewis, making a wigg, 15s.

1752. Copy declaration, replication and rejoinder. The King against Campbell, 20 each. Combining the said suit 10.

1757. Aug. 9. Patience Robinson, widow.
To rent of school house from 9th day of February.
To one pistole in cash, 1. 1. 6.
To cash Dble Loon, 4. 7. 1.
Sir Wm. Gooch, Bart. By my bond—

4 Feb. James Caddy brought for Major Washington twenty-four quarts of Dovers' grass seed which he says Mr. Washington bespoke of him and ordered to be left with me.
4 quarts I took myself, sufficient to sow one acre. 1s. 6d. current money per quart.

1749. Jolliffe. By a quarter's schooling 4 children, due Aug. 23, 1.0.0. "Be it remembered that James Wood and John Massey agree as followeth: that the said John is to live on the place formerly seated by Charles Quail until a division be made between the said James and the orphans of Robert Green, deceased. The said John agrees to plant two hundred and fifty peach trees and one hundred apple trees.—"

(*Behold the pioneer orchard of Frederick County!*)

1753. "Honorable William Fairfax, Esq. Dr.
Filing declaration in ejection 10, Docketing, " etc., etc.

1759. April 26. By making a pair of breeches for Jacky ____ 4.6
By making a suit of clothes _____ 1s.
By making a pair of buck skin breeches for James ____ 1.10.0

"The estate of Dr. Daniel Hart paid to sundry persons by James Wood, executor—." And so on and on the broken bits of the mirror reflect other names such as Gordon, Hollingsworth, Love, Capt. Thomas Chester, Glass, Capt. George Robinson, John Griffith, Henry Brincker, William Russell, Benj. Rutherford, Lemen, Joseph Lupton, William Stokes, Lewis Neill, Samuel Earle, Hugh Parker, Edward McGuire, William Reynolds, Jonathan Knight, Heath, William Greenaway, Robert Aldridge, William Hoge, Nicholas Handshaw, Robert Allan, John Bruce, Honorable Lewis Burwell, William Gilpin, Jacob Sower, John Bronaugh, Capt. George Mercer, Peter Burr, Gershom Keys and others, belonging to both the past and the present regime.

A line tucked away in a little old mildewed memorandum book, however, gives a clue to the character of James Wood. It is simply this:

"May 7, 1749. Borrowed of Mr. Hite a sugar pot and Teacup full of Tea." In that token of scrupulous attention to little things is found a key to the success of this man of many duties. Interesting it would be to know the cause of his so charging his conscience. Had Lord Fairfax visited his office, and did he wish to show his lordship the little English courtesy? Had some poor woman come a long way through the wilderness to seek protection from the Indians? Rest assured that it marks "some kindly deed the icy hand hath wrought," and that it points to

"That best part of a good man's life,
His little unremembered acts of kindness and of love."

The inscription in the mourning ring already referred to says that he died November 6, 1759, aged fifty-two. Born at Winchester, and educated at Oxford, England;

according to tradition a lieutenant in the British navy; a pioneer Cavalier in Virginia; the first surveyor of Orange county; the bearer of many other commissions; the last of which it was not for him to fulfill—a commission composed of Colonel James Wood, Captain John Hite and Robert Rutherford, for settling the accounts of troops for their services in the colonial wars and those of persons for damages done by the Indians, and for supplies furnished the Continental Line soldiers—the executor, moreover, of various estates, is it any wonder that he did not live to old age? His will is a very brief and simple instrument. It was written on September 8, 1746, when his children were all minors. Burdened with the care of many people's property, it is not strange that he did not go into detail about his own. He left all he possessed to his beloved wife, Mary Rutherford, appointing her sole executrix, and guardian of their children, "not doubting that she will do a Christian mother's part to them." None of the events of his last days are chronicled. The scribe had laid down his pen, and the first Winchester newspaper, "The Virginia Gazette and Winchester Advertiser," did not appear until July 11, 1787. The first burial ground in the Valley must have been that of the first Episcopal Church which was built of logs and was located at the northeast corner of Loudoun and Water Streets on the original plat of the town. The first known graves at Glen Burnie date from 1801, the family burial grounds becoming necessary, no doubt, because the small spaces about the churches were found to be inadequate. Frederick Parish was created by Act of the House of Burgesses when the county was formed in 1743-4, and by permission of the governor a vestry was chosen soon after.

Christ Church, without a burial ground, was not organized until 1827, and Mount Hebron was not dedicated until June 22, 1844, when Rev. A. H. H. Boyd, D. D., of the Loudoun Street Presbyterian Church, conducted the services. It is reasonable to think, therefore, that James Wood was buried at the old Episcopal Church. But what matter where? He had lived through the storm and stress of the crucial colonial period; he found the colonies weak; he left them almost strong enough to declare their independence; he had seen Winchester become an army post and one of the most important points in the country; he had helped to elect to the legislative body George Washington, even at that time, perhaps, the most famous colonist born in the new world. Twenty-five years of public service in many capacities must have made a lasting impression, not only upon his day, but upon succeeding generations, and results are not far to seek. Of his immediate family, his son James took up his work at once, and as colonel and brigadier-general during the Revolution, and later as governor of Virginia, carried it forward in a way that would have rejoiced the heart of his father.

Of his great-grandsons, William Wood Glass, grandson of Robert Wood and Comfort Welsh, son of Catherine Wood and Thomas Glass, Colonel of the 51st Regiment of Virginia Militia, showed the intense love of home and family that characterized his forefathers. He was always a staunch Democrat, but desired no office. For many years he was an elder in the Presbyterian Church. He died at Glen Burnie, October 28, 1911, in his seventy-seventh year.

Of his great-great grandsons, Robert Wood Dailey, great-grandson of Robert and Comfort Wood and grandson of Comfort Wood and James Dailey, was for thirty-four years Judge of the Circuit Court of Hampshire, Hardy, Pendleton and Grant counties, West Virginia. He died at Romney, W. Va., March 11, 1926, aged seventy-seven. His brother, Benjamin, was also a lawyer, while his brother, Comfort Wood Dailey, was one of the most distinguished lawyers of his day in West Virginia. He represented Mineral county in the State Legislature, was general counsel for the West Virginia Central Railroad, now part of the Western Maryland system, and was a member of the Board of Trustees of Davis and Elkins College. He died at Elkins, W. Va., April 15, 1908, in his fifty-seventh year. Both Judge Dailey and Hon. C. Wood Dailey were elders in the Presbyterian Church, and superintendents of Sunday Schools.

Of his great-great-great grandsons, through Comfort Wood and James Dailey, at least five served in the World War, Robert Wood Baird and his brothers, William and Benjamin Baird, and Griffin and Thomas Dailey.

Robert Browning might have had Colonel James Wood in mind when he described another as:

"One who never turned his back but marched breast forward,
  Never doubted clouds would break,
Never dreamed, tho' right were worsted, wrong would triumph,
  Held we fall to rise, are baffled to fight better,
    Sleep to wake."

SEAL OF FREDERICK COUNTY

(*Coat of Arms of Queen Anne and the I and II George.*)

1. (Upper left corner.) *England.* (3 lions: gules [red] 2 lions passant guardant or [gold] used by Wm. the Conqueror; and when Henry II married Eleanor of Aquitaine he added a 3rd lion).

    Impaling Scotland (or, a lion rampart within a double tressure flory counterflory gules).

2. (Upper right corner.) *France,* azure (blue) 3 fleur de lis, or. (Here rudely given as 3 crosses).

3. (Lower left corner.) *Ireland,* azure, a harp stringed, or.

4. (Lower right corner.) *Brunswick,* Lunenburg, Saxony. On the centre of the fourth quarter, an escutcheon, gules, charged with the crown of Charlemagne.

By an act of the House of Burgesses in November, 1738, old Orange county was divided into three counties; i. e., Orange, Frederick and Augusta. Frederick was named for Frederick Lewis, Prince of Wales (1707), who died before his father, George II. Augusta was named for Prince Frederick's wife.

Frederick county embraced the counties now known as Rockingham, Shenandoah, Jefferson, Berkeley, Morgan, Hampshire, part of Page, part of Hardy, and all of Clarke and Warren. Although named in 1738, the first court for Frederick county was not held until November 11, 1743, because of lack of population, and of men competent to officer the new county. At the November Court, 1743, James Wood was sworn Clerk of the Court, Thomas Rutherford, High Sheriff, and George Home, County Surveyor. Courts were held each month and at the sitting of the justices March 10, 1743-44, Winchester was founded. The first levy was made at the June term, 1744, when 1283 tithables at 59 ℔s. Tobacco per poll were specified.

The first gentlemen justices were Morgan Morgan, David Vaunce, Marquis Calmes, Thomas Rutherford, William McMachen, Meredith Helms, George Hoge, John White.

In 1744, Thomas Little, John Linzy, Jacob Hyte, Thomas Swearingen, Israel Robinson and Solomon Hedges were commissioned justices by Governor Gooch.

The first lawyers were James Porteous, John Steerman, George Johnston and John Newport. At the sitting of the Court, January, 1744, William Russell, John Quinn, William Jolliffe and Michael Ryan took their places at the bar.

March 10, 1744, Gabriel Jones presented his commission as King's attorney.

In March, 1758, the justices ordered a silver seal to be made by William Miller, "about the size of an English half-crown, with the words *Frederick County* engraved thereon."

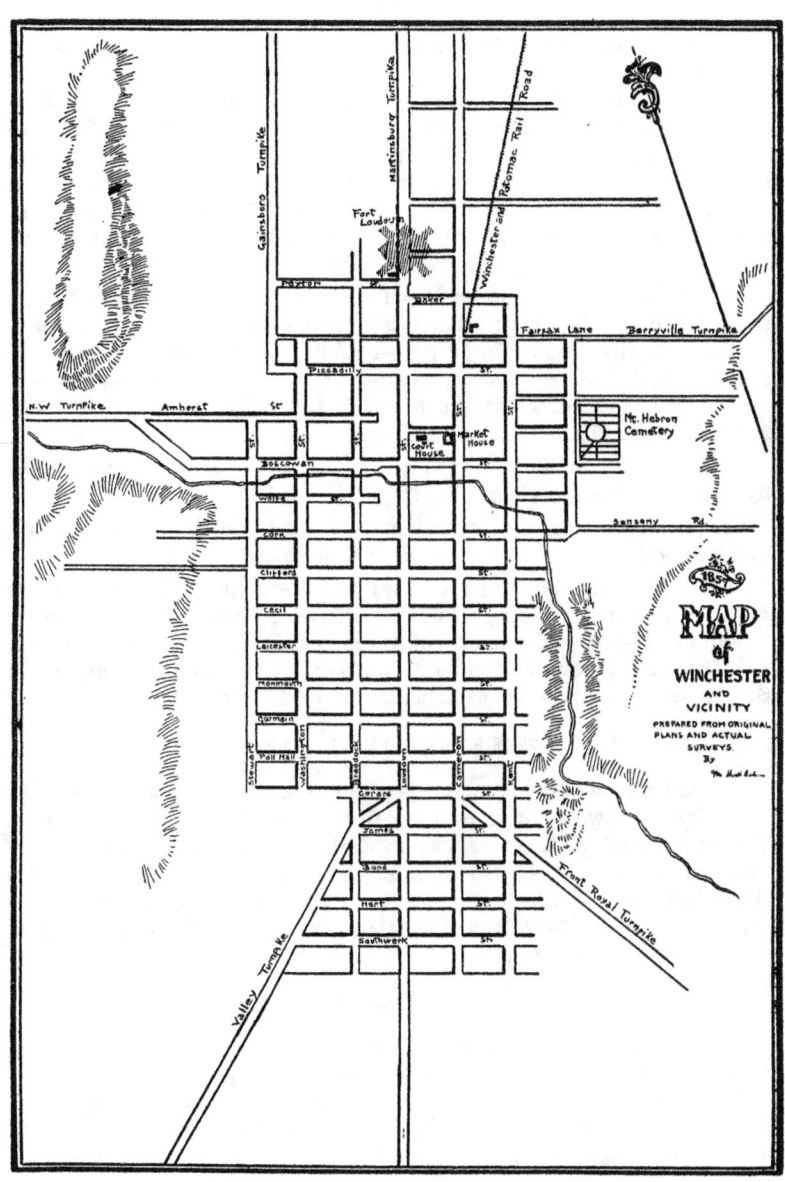

EXPLANATION OF THE OLD MAP IN THE ROUSS CITY HALL

The portion of this Map shaded *Red* represents the "In Lots" in the original plan of the town of Winchester; containing 80 lots numbered from 1 to 80. That portion *surrounded* by red shading represents the "Out Lots" also numbered from 1 to 80, as the purchaser of an "In Lot" was required to take the corresponding "Out Lot." The dimensions of the "In Lots" between Fairfax Lane and Water Street are each 119 feet front by 189 feet, 9 inches deep. Those between Water and Cork Street are each 118 feet front by 189 feet, 9 inches deep.

The Blue shading shows Wood's addition, containing 156 lots of the following dimensions: The lots lying between the Northwest part of the Old Town and Water Street and numbered from 1 to 6 are each 107 feet 4 inches front by 188 feet, 6 inches deep. Those between Water and Cork Street are each 105 feet, 2 inches front by 188 feet, 6 inches deep.

Those between Cork and Gerard Streets are each 117 feet front by 118 feet, 6 inches deep.

The *Yellow* shading represents the addition by Lord Fairfax, containing 173 Lots of the following dimensions:

The Lots between Cork and James Streets are 117 feet front by 189 feet, 9 inches deep. Those on the West side of Kent Street adjoining The Old Town are of the same dimensions as those that join those lying between the Southeast part of the Old Town and Cork Street are each 121 feet, 6 inches front by 189 feet, 9 inches deep.

STREETS, ROADS, LANES

The breadth of Loudoun Street from the corner of lot No. 1 to 12 is 45 feet; elsewhere it is 60 feet, the offset being on the West side. The breadth of Water Street from Stable Alley to Kent Street is 33 feet; the residue of the Street is 60 feet wide. The offset at Stable Alley is 10 feet on the North side and 17 feet on the South side. All other streets are 60 feet wide throughout. All Roads are 40 feet wide; Lanes 20 feet wide.

OUT LOTS

According to the survey by John Bayliss (1752) the Out Lots from No. 1 to No. 40 inclusive, each contains 5 acres; excepting No. 32 containing 7 A. 3 R. 31 P. No. 33, 7 A. 19 P. No. 39, 5 A. 1 R. 27 P. No. 41, 9 A. 3 R. 38 P. No. 42, 5 A. 19 P. No. 42, 4 A. 35 P. From No. 44 to 67 inclusive each 5 acres. No. 43, contains 8 A. 1 R. 22 P. No. 58, 8 A. 2 R. 34 P. No. 59, No. 68, 5 A. 25 P. No. 69, 6 A. 1 R. 29 P. From No. 70 to 80 inclusive each contains 5 A. 20 P., except No. 75, 4 A. 3 R. and No. 76, 5 A.

Dimensions given for the 5 A. lots from No. 1 to 24 is 34.79 Rods in length by 23 Rods Broad.

Courses and Distances Forming the Boundary of the "In Lots of the Town of Winchester," from Lord Fairfax, record of survey, 1759.

Beginning at a Locust post Corner to lot No. 69, and running thence S 19 W 110 poles 10 feet, 5 inches to a post; thence N 71 W 9 poles to a post with the right Honble. Lord Fairfax Lands as follows: S 50 W 74 Poles to a post. S 13 W 153 poles to a post. N 71 W 124 poles to a post, on the east side of the county road, thence with said road N 50 E 46 poles. N 53 E 54 poles to a post, thence crossing said road N 61½ W 2 poles to a Locust Stake Corner to James Wood's land, thence with said Wood land N 61½ W 74 poles to a post, thence through said Wood's land N 19 E 22 1-3 poles 9 feet to a post. Thence S 72 E 26 poles, 9 feet, 11 inches to a post corner to lot number 6 in the town of Winchester. Thence on the town line N 19 E 24 poles, 10 feet, 5 inches to a post, thence with the town line S 71 E 159 poles, 2 feet, inches to the beginning.

Number of Lots in the "Old Town" _____ 80
Number of Lots in Wood's Addition _____ 156
Number of Lots in Fairfax's Addition _____ 173

Total _____ 409

(80 Out Lots).

Latitude, 39 degrees, 11 minutes, 14 seconds, North.
Longitude, 78 degrees, 8 minutes, 46 5-10 seconds, West.
The inscription at the bottom of the map has already been given.

COLONIAL AND REVOLUTIONARY WINCHESTER

Founded March 10, 1744.

The oldest town south of the Potomac and west of the Blue Ridge.

Mr. William Greenway Russell (1800-1891) thus describes the first lots. "Wood laid off at the Court House twenty-six lots; those are the lots on the east and west side of Loudoun street and two on Cameron street.

"At Piccadilly, on the northwest corner, is the first lot, No. 1; at Cork Street, the southwest corner, lot No. 12, making twelve lots on the west and a like number on the east, making twenty-four lots. The market house and jail make twenty-six first laid out. Of the other fifty-four are ten on the west side of Cameron, leaving out the two aforesaid (jail and market house), and twelve on the west side of Kent, making thirty-four lots. Thus Cameron and Kent streets were made.

"Now count the squares from the west side of Kent to Stewart on the north Frederick road and north of Piccadilly, and you will find

Rec'd of mr James Wood by the hands of mr
Lewis Neale thirty three pounds ten shillings
this in Full of all demands this 17th of
April 1759 —

Bennett Price

five squares with four lots each, which make twenty. These with the thirty-four mentioned make fifty-four lots, in addition to the first twenty-six—in all eighty lots.

"By an act passed by the General Assembly in September, 1758, the town was enlarged on the petition of James Wood, and the following trustees appointed: Lord Fairfax, Thomas B. Martin, James Wood, Lewis Stephen, Gabriel Jones, John Hite, John Dooe, Isaac Parkins, Robert Rutherford and Philip Bush.

"Those lots that were laid off in 1758 on the west were thirty-nine lots bounded by Piccadilly and Stewart Streets, Cork Street and the lane called Taylor Lane, by the Lutheran Church, and those on the south to Gerard Street.

"On the east side of Loudoun there are seventy; on the west side are ninety-eight from Cork to Stewart, and half lots beyond Stewart, in all one hundred and seventy-eight lots west and south in Wood's last addition.

"The lots east of Kent were laid off in 1753 by Fairfax as shown by a deed to the Reformed Church.

"Wood's land did not extend quite to Kent Street.

"Those west of Loudoun and south of Kent, were laid off in 1758 and were part of Wood's Addition of that year."

We are indebted to a torch bearer of a later generation than Mr. Russell for a description of the historic names of some of the streets of Winchester. An article by Mr. Housan Kiner Pritchard (1841-1920) is the basis for the brief review of the names here given:

"*Loudoun*, named for the Earl of Loudoun, whose record has already been given. Now the main thoroughfare from north to south, in colonial times Loudoun did not extend above Piccadilly. From its junction with Boscawan southward it was known as the "great road," or the "big road," and it was meant to be a great stage road leading to Staunton, and on to Tennessee, the thoroughfare from Baltimore to Knoxville—our present Valley Turnpike, authorized by law March 24, 1838, although the charter was granted in 1831.

Piccadilly, for the celebrated thoroughfare in London, extending a mile, from the Haymarket to Hyde Park Corner. The name, piccadill or picadilly means "the divisions or pieces fastened together about the brim of the collar of a doublet; a high stiff collar; a hem or band of cut work; a sharp point, from the Spanish "picado," pricked. A tailor made his fortune from this style of collar, and give its name to the street on which he lived.

Boscawan, for Admiral Boscawan (1711-1761), known as "Old Dreadnought." He was at Porto-Bello and Cartagena (1740); Cape Finisterre (May 3, 1747); defeated the French at Newfoundland

16 November 1758

The Subscriber Agreeth to sell sundry Lotts in the Town of Woodstock to be Sold at Public Vendue, to the Highest Bidder, the Plan laid off according to an Act of the General Assembly of this Colony may be Seen at the House of Mr. Henry Hath in the said Town. The Conditions of the Sale are as Followeth.

The Seller Obligeth himself to make a Sufficient Title in Fee Simple to the Purchaser without receiving of said Rent, and no title as the Purchaser shall challenge.

The Purchaser to be restrained from Building any House Seeming the Street, with round Logs and from wasting modern Chimneys.

The Seller covenanth with himself the liberty to Bid Once at the Sale.

Two months Credit will be given on the Purchasers entering into Bond with Security.

J Wood.

ADMIRAL EDWARD BOSCAWEN
From a "Complete History of the Late War"
Dublin, Printed by John Exshaw in Dame Street
MDCCLXXIV

(1755); took Cape Breton Island from the French (1758); defeated the French fleet at Lagos (August 18, 1759).

Admiral Boscawan with his fleet convoyed General Braddock to Alexandria. The name is one of the finest that we have.

Cork, for Cork, in Ireland, because of the Irish who lived on that street.

Clifford, for Sir Thomas Clifford, made Lord of the realm by Charles II. The cabinet was composed of Clifford, Arlington, Buckingham, Ashley and Lauderdale. Their initials form the word "Cabal," famous synonym for political intrigue.

Cecil, in honor of Sir William Cecil (1520-1590), afterwards Lord Burleigh, Secretary of State and Lord Treasurer (1533-1602) under Queen Elizabeth, who produced the bon mot, "Now, Cecil, you are burly both by name and nature." He was a cautious Protestant and a tool of Elizabeth to stamp out the Catholics. Mr. Pritchard remarks that as an evidence of the imperishability of things sacred, there stands here at the corner of Loudoun and the street named for him the Catholic Church of the Sacred Heart.

Leicester, for the weak and profligate Robert Dudley, Earl of Leicester (1532-1588), the favorite of Elizabeth, and a heartless libertine. Who can stand at the ruins of Kenilworth Castle without reconstructing the sad story of Amy Robsart!

Monmouth, for James, Duke of Monmouth (1649-1685), an illegitimate son of Charles II, who asserted his right to the throne as James II, was defeated at the battle of Sedgemoor in July, and beheaded on Tower Hill on July 15, 1685.

Germain, should be German, named for the Germans who lived on it, who furnished some of the members of General Daniel Morgan's Dutch Mess.

Pall Mall, pronounced Pell Mell, from a game resembling croquet, in which the walla, a ball, and mallio, a hammer (Italian), came to mean hand over head fighting—"Pressed close; to come pell-mell to handy blows." (Butler's Hudibras). Pall Mall Street was on the outskirts of the town where presumably the Irish and Germans came to fisticuffs.

Gerard. Origin not positively known. Stephen Girard was probably not born when the street was named: so called perhaps for Charles Gerard of Brandon, eldest son of the Earl of Macclesfield, who was accused of taking part in the Rye House plot (1683), during the reign of Charles II.

Braddock, for General Braddock, marking the trail of the ill-fated Braddock expedition, in 1755.

Wolfe, probably for General James Wolfe (1727-1759), who was killed in the hour of victory at Quebec, when Montcalm, the French commander, was also slain. General Wolfe, with General Amherst and Admiral Boscawan, captured Louisburg.

Amherst, for Baron Jeffrey Amherst (1717-1797), Commander-in-Chief of the British, who captured Crown Point, Ticonderoga and Montreal.

Kent, after Kent County, England. Queen Victoria was the only child of Edward, Duke of Kent, son of George III, and Marie Louise Victoria, of Saxe-Coburg.

Cameron, named by Lord Fairfax for himself. In his deeds Lord Fairfax always used his Scotch title, "Baron of Cameron, in that part of Great Britian, called Scotland."

Washington, for George Washington (Feb. 22, 1732-Dec. 14, 1799). It is to be noted that the name in all the list that has best withstood the acid test of time, and that towers above all the others in the face of results, is that of Washington, whose fame rests upon deeds, and not upon an inherited title often totally at variance with the character of its owner. Washington's military titles were won through self-sacrifice, boundless courage, intrepid daring and marvelous judgment. The honors heaped upon him were the natural result of his prowess. His policies were liberal enough to guide the nation in its widest expansion. His philanthropy embraced the human race. He is the one true benefactor of Winchester among all those whose names are upon the lips of her people daily in calling the names of her streets.

But these old names with all their strength, all their weakness, are a valuable heritage. They connect us indissolubly with the sources from which we sprang; they lend an old-world flavor which even the utilitarian, synthetic terms of trade cannot take away. In spite of the boasted self-development of the day, the most ardent of the so-called self-made must inhale the influence of the past with the very air they breathe.

Mt. Hebron, as befitting God's acre, has a Biblical name.

Although not dedicated until June 22, 1844, there were so many removals of bodies from the old grave-yards together with slabs and monuments, that the cemetery was given the appearance of age.

The dedicatory services were conducted by Rev. Dr. A. H. H. Boyd, pastor of Loudoun Street Presbyterian Church, with an introductory address. Rev. William Rooker, D. D., rector of Christ Church, read the Scriptures, and Rev. William M. Atkinson, D. D., made the dedicatory prayer. A paper was read by Rev. D. H. Bragonier. William L. Clark, Esq., made the principal address, Rev. William B. Edwards, the concluding prayer, and Rev. Joseph

Baker pronounced the benediction. The first interment, in August, 1844, was that of Mrs. Atkinson, wife of Rev. William M. Atkinson, D. D., pastor of the "Old School" Presbyterian Church.

Of Revolutionary heroes we find the following:

Major-General Daniel Morgan. A broken slab, the only memorial here which bears his name, says that he departed this life

> On July the 6th, 1802
> In the 67th year of his age.
> Patriotism and Valor were the
> Prominent Features of his character
> and
> The honorable services he rendered to his country
> During the Revolutionary War
> Crowned him with Glory, and will
> Remain in the hearts of his Countrymen
> A Perpetual monument to his Memory.

General John Smith, to whom Kercheval dedicated his History of the Valley. The panegyric begins thus: "Like Nestor of old you have lived to see 'two generations pass away and now remain the example of the third.' You saw Dunmore's war with the Indians in 1774; you witnessed the war of the Revolution and the war of 1812, with the haughty Briton. In all these great struggles of our country, you have given the most conclusive evidence of unbending virtue and uncompromising patriotism." General John Smith was born "ye 7th of May, 1750 about 5 in the morning." He died May 3, 1836 and he and his wife, Anna Bull, second daughter of General John Bull, were buried in the family burying ground at his home, Hackwood Park, near Winchester; but in 1890 all who had been buried there were removed to Mt. Hebron Cemetery. Of his large and distinguished family but one shining example need be given here—his grandson, Prof. "Archie" Magill Smith, for sixteen years principal of the Shenandoah Valley Academy, and for many years principal of the Episcopal Female Institute, both of Winchester, who is held in particularly tender memory by all who knew him.

"General Daniel Roberdeau, died January 5, 1795, aged 68," runs the brief record on his tombstone. Further details concerning this distinguished Huguenot are thus given by the Biographical Congressional Directory, 1774-1911: "A delegate from Pennsylvania; born on the island of St. Christopher, West Indies, in 1727; moved to Philadelphia, Pa., in boyhood; completed preparatory studies; engaged in lumber business; member of the State Assembly, 1756-1760; manager of the Pennsylvania hospital, 1756-1758, and 1766-1776; member of the council of safety; first brigadier-general of Pennsylvania troops in 1776; elected delegate to the Continental Congress and served from

1777 to 1779; moved to Alexandria, Va., in 1785; died in Winchester, Va., June 5, 1795."

The late Mrs. Mary Rivera Pierce, widow of William Hartman Baker, was fourth in descent from this patriot of many activities.

Obed Waite, February 14, 1766-January 16, 1845. Judge Waite, Mayor of Winchester, married Mary Ann Harrison, daughter of Col. Matthew Harrison, of the Revolutionary Army, and his wife, Mary Wood, who was the second daughter of Col. James Wood and his wife, Mary Rutherford. Mrs. Maria Offutt Barton of Flushing, L. I., is second in descent.

Judge Waite was President of the Bank of the Valley from 1823 to 1845. He was Mayor from 1824 to 1831, and later. His residence was the present home of the Hunters on South Washington Street.

The oldest graves are found in the old Lutheran graveyard, enclosed with Mt. Hebron, which extends eastward from it. Here lies,

Major Peter Helphenstine, of Col. Peter Muhlenberg's company, which was ordered to Charleston, S. C., where they arrived on June 24, 1776, having covered the entire distance on foot and without a tent. Major Helphenstine fell a victim to the climate and died in Winchester in the fall of 1776. The late Mrs. Virginia Beatrice Faulkner, widow of the late Dr. Clinton Maynard, was a direct descendant in the fourth generation.

Captain Daniel Morgan's company which on July 14, 1775, left Winchester on its six hundred mile march on foot and accompanied by one wagon, reached Cambridge, Mass., on August 7. Washington wept as he beheld these old friends and took them by the hand. Their march to Quebec, their hardships, their endurance and marvelous preservation from disaster are household history. Among the privates from Winchester are found the names of George Greenway, William Greenway, Seth Stratton, John Schultz, Jacob Sperry, Peter Lauck, Simon Lauck, Frederick Kurtz, Adam Kurtz, Charles Grim, George Heiskell, Robert Anderson, William Bull and Mark Hays. Among them six Germans, who were intimate during the war and until the end of their long lives formed what is known as the Dutch Mess. The six as given by Mr. William Greenway Russell, who knew some of them and remembered their quaint anniversaries, when memories of their famous campaigns were fondly recalled, gave the six as consisting of Peter Lauck, Simon Lauck, Frederick Kurtz, John Schultz, Charles Grim and Jacob Sperry. A descendant of one of them, who has given the subject serious study, gives Adam Kurtz (1747-1815), Peter Lauck, John W. Grim (perhaps Charles), Adam

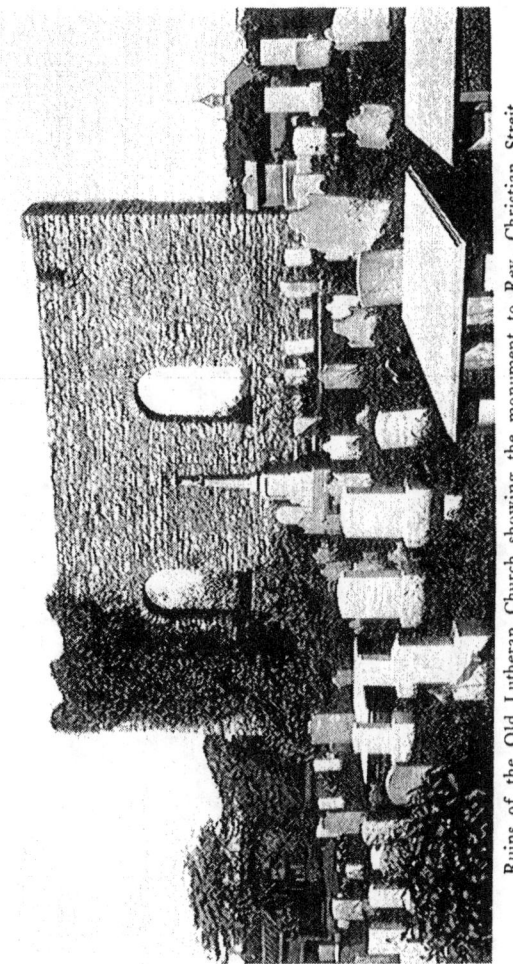

Ruins of the Old Lutheran Church showing the monument to Rev. Christian Streit

Heiskell, Jacob Sperry and John Schultz. Adam Heiskell is buried in Romney, W. Va. The others rest near the ruins of the old Lutheran Church.

An old stone bears the inscription that John Schultz died the 5th day of November, 1840, in the 87th year of his age.

The company of which these heroes were members has the distinction of being the first raised in the Valley in the Revolution. In addition to Captain Daniel Morgan the officers were first lieutenant, John Humphrey; second lieutenant, William Heth; first sergeant, George Porterfield, or Charles Porterfield.

Several worn sandstones in the old Lutheran graveyard bear interesting inscriptions.

Among them are:

"John Tobias Otto, born June 5, 1726, near Mannheim, Germany; died in Winchester, April 11, 1765."

"Hier liegt der Leib Peter Sperry, G. S. 1773, A. 62."

"Hier ruhet der Leib des verstorbenen George Beckers, Sohn der Hannah Beckers, Geboren an 1765 den 7 July, Gestorben on 1790, 11 den May, alt 24 Jahr, 10 Monathe und 4 Tage."

"Philip Bush, born October the 12th, 1733, at Mannheim in Germany; died Decr. the 8th, 1812, after a residence of 50 years in Winchester."

"This stone is erected to the memory of David Holmes, late governor and U. S. Senator of Miss., born March the 10th, 1769; died, August the 20th, 1832. His Death proved by the universal regret of all who knew him that he died without an enemy: His life by his steadfast honor and true Christian charity that he never deserved one."

Close beside the old wall of the Lutheran Church towards the sunrising stands a monument erected to the memory of

"Christian Streit, born in New Jersey, June 7, 1749, died March 10, 1812, the first minister of the Evangelical Lutheran Church born in America. Pastor at Winchester July 19, 1785 to March 10, 1812. 'I have fought a good fight, I have finished my course, I have kept the faith.'"

Beneath Christ Episcopal Church, lie the ashes of Rev. Alexander Balmain, D. D., together with those of Lord Fairfax, removed from the Episcopal burying ground at the northeast corner of Loudoun and Boscawen Streets.

A mural tablet to Dr. Balmain in the rear of Christ Church bears the inscription;

"Sacred to the memory of the Rev. Alexander Balmain, D. D., who died the 10th of June, 1821, in the 80th year of his age, 50th from his ordination and 40th of his ministry in this place.

"Learning, with winning piety combined, adorn'd the Preacher, Scholar, Patriot, Friend.

"His hand with aid, his heart with pity fraught, a living sermon of the truth he taught."

Rev. Alexander Balmain came from Scotland, as did his near kinsmen the Bruce family. He became tutor in the family of Richard Henry Lee, grandfather of Robert E. Lee. He was born in 1740, married on October 31, 1786, Lucy Taylor, a near relative of President Madison, whose marriage ceremony he performed. He died childless. Rev. William Meade, who became Bishop Meade, the author of the famous "Old Churches of Virginia," succeeded him in his pastorate here.

Rev. Alexander Balmain, D. D., Rev. Charles Mynn Thurston, Rev. Peter Muhlenberg, of Woodstock, were called the parson-soldiers or warrior-preachers.

Rev. Mr. Balmain became a Chaplain, while Rev. Charles Mynn Thurston rose to the rank of Colonel, and Rev. Peter Gabriel Muhlenberg to that of General in the Revolutionary Army. These scholars and Christians, thoroughly versed in the Bible, together with such examples as Rev. John Moncure, Rev. William Hill, D. D., Rev. Andrew Hunter Holmes Boyd, D. D., Rev. William M. Atkinson, D. D., Rev. Cornelius Walker, D. D., Rev. Abner C. Hopkins, D. D., Rev. James Randolph Graham, D. D., Rev. Henry Martyn White, D. D., Rev. William Hervey Woods, D. D., with those of other callings who were their peers, represented a type of culture, of piety, of scholarship, of influence in any community, which it is safe to say has never been excelled, and never will be equalled until the Bible and the family altar are reinstated in the home.

The inscriptions quoted from the various markers in Mt. Hebron are among the earliest found there. Since then how many of the gallant, the gifted, the beautiful, the gentle of all callings and all ages have joined them in our sacred City of Rest!

Is it not Goethe who says that "it is natural that the earth should bring forth roses, since so many rose-like forms are gathered to her breast?"

And how have we honored our heroes?

General Morgan has now, as the only memorial which bears his name here, a broken slab pieced out with concrete and flat on the ground, bearing the inscription already given.

Col. James Wood has fortunately a small granite marker on the Court House lawn, a few feet from the place where he was no doubt buried in the old Episcopal graveyard. This and a similar one to Lord Fairfax were erected by a committee consisting of Hon. R. Gray Williams, Hon. Robert M. Ward and other gentlemen who began a work which now appears to be going forward in our tardy marking of historic spots. Fortunately the Robert Y. Conrad Post of the American Legion is taking the matter in hand. But for the records of that day we should not know that Governor James Wood is buried in the Old St. John's Churchyard in Richmond. Only the kindly periwinkle keeps his grave green. There is no marker.

The Daughters of the American Revolution are putting a small marker, costing a few dollars, at the last resting place of as many of the Revolutionary soldiers as they can reach—a noble work.

Gilbert K. Chesterton says, "The size of every man depends upon the height of his ideals, the depth of his convictions, and the breadth of his sympathies and interests."

England is made great by her Westminster Abbey, by her cathedrals, by her innumerable monuments. You review the history of the world as you walk among them. You are with the crusaders at Jerusalem; you are with the martyrs at Oxford; you visualize the Age of Chivalry as you wonder at the armor of the Knights at Windsor Castle.

Comparatively speaking, we are still very young as a nation. Although Jamestown was settled in 1607, it was not until 1716 that the Knights of the Golden Horseshoe first beheld the Shenandoah Valley from the top of the Blue Ridge; more than a hundred years spent before climbing from tidewater to the top of the mountains which are to be distinguished as the first National Park in the east!

Perhaps there may yet be erected for the benefit of all the people a House Beautiful over whose portals and on whose walls may be inscribed the names of heroes who laid the foundations of this great Commonwealth, and of those who reared the superstructure: a temple of art or industry which shall proclaim to all the world, "Look about you: their country is their monument;" while on the flower-laden breath of the evening breeze the silver bells of the Carillon, Virginia's World War Memorial, shall bear to myriads of happy homes their message of, "On earth peace, good will toward men."

PART II

The Burn at Glen Burnie with the stone fence along the Northwestern Grade which leads to Wheeling, W. Va.

CHAPTER XV

Sketch of the Life of Hon. James Wood, Jr., Compiled From Various Sources

The following facts concerning the life of General and Governor James Wood are compiled chiefly from data sent out from the public library at Richmond for Mrs. Eleanor Offutt Barton (Mrs. I. D. Barton, of Flushing, L. I.); and from an address delivered before the James Wood Chapter, Daughters of the American Revolution, at Parkersburg, W. Va., by Miss Kate Innes Harris.

Colonel James Wood, the founder, and Clerk of the Court, died in 1759. On February 5, 1760, Archibald Wager was appointed clerk, and on May 7th of the same year James Wood at the age of nineteen, became deputy.

This by way of connection with the past order.

From the library at Richmond:

"Hon. James Wood, Jr., tenth Governor of Virginia, 1796-99, was born in Frederick County, Virginia, January 28, 1741, and died near Richmond, July 16, 1813. Governor Wood was the son of Col. James and Mary Rutherford Wood, of Frederick County, Va., and he married Jean Moncure, a daughter of Rev. John and Anne Brown Moncure, of Stafford County, Va.

"Mr. Wood became very active in the affairs of the colony of Virginia at an early age. In 1744, when Lord Dunmore, then Governor of Virginia, resolved on the expedition against the Shawanese, which resulted in the battle of Point Pleasant, he commissioned Mr. Wood captain of one of the Frederick County companies in the division commanded by his lordship. Captain Wood presented a petition to the Virginia Convention, December 13, 1777, stating that he had been appointed to command a company in the late expedition against the Shawanese towns, that he had been forced to press a number of guns, for which he gave his receipt, which in many cases had been lost, and had been paid for by him out of his means, and for which he petitioned to have such allowance made as was right. The Convention ordered him to be paid £28.11 for all his losses. He was a member of the House of Burgesses from Frederick County from 1766-1775. He took his seat in the last Virginia Assembly ever convened by a royal governor, Lord Dunmore, June, 1775. With the close of the session ceased forever the authority of the British Crown in the Colony of Virginia. The people had been intensely excited by Dunmore's proclamation, which was regarded as an attempt to incite the slaves to insurrection, and by the removal of the powder from the magazine at Williamsburg, an unwise measure hastened by the action at Lexington, Mass., April 19, the news of which added fuel to the flames of delight in the patriotic hearts of the Virginians. Dunmore's hasty flight to his ships in the James River followed. Amid this excitement the Burgesses met, prepared, adopted resolutions unanimously, with concurrence of the Governor's Council, sent to his lordship for separate addresses, in which they remonstrated against his course, urged his return to his palace, avowed their fealty to the Crown, but also their determination to protect the rights of the people. (See Force's Arch. Vol. II, pp. 1185-1242.)

Captain Wood, Mr. Cary and others were appointed to deliver these addresses to the Governor, which duty they performed. Captain Wood was also appointed at this Assembly one of the commissioners of fifteen "to inquire into the late disturbances and commotions." On June 14, James Wood, Thomas and John Walker, Andrew Lewis and Adam Stephen, Esquires, were appointed commissioners to ratify the Treaty of Peace between the Colony and the Ohio Indians. (Force Vol. II, p. 1240).

Capt. Wood was also appointed in 1775 by the House of Burgesses to visit the several Indian tribes in the western part of Virginia and invite them to the treaty that was to be held at Fort Pitt, September, 1775. This mission he accomplished and his report will be found in Jacob's "Life of Capt. Cresap," and Kercheval's History of Virginia (p. 86 of Jacob's "Life of Capt. Cresap, and also 136). Also see Hon. Brantz Mayer in the "Tah-gah-jute," or "Logan and Cresap" (pp. 143-50 and also Force, Vol. III, 77).

The House of Burgesses appointed on December 28th, 1775, a committee to "inquire into the services of Mr. James Wood, etc." This committee reported as follows:

"James Wood set out on the 25th day of June last in execution of his mission, and in his progress through the several tribes of Indians he was informed that Gov. Carleton's emissaries had exerted their endeavor to persuade them to take up the hatchet against this Colony, and that in consequence thereof many of the said Indians entertained very hostile intentions, etc. (Force Vol. IV, P. 110.)

"In June, 1776, James Wood was appointed on a Committee to sell or rent Lord Dunmore's Berkeley County estates, and also on a Committee to prepare an address to the Shawnee Indians. (Col. Papers I, 272).

"He was a member in 1776 of the Constitutional Convention. He was appointed by that body a colonel in the Virginia line, commanding the 8th Regiment, and rendered gallant service in the defense of Virginia frontiers against the Indians as well as in the cause of freedom. (See Force Vol. III, 761); (See Col. Papers I, 276); (See Jenkins' His. Gywnedd, Pa. 1885); (Col. Papers Vols. I and II; (Lossing's Field Book of the Revolution, Vol. II, 345); (Ford's Writings of Washington, Vol. VIII, P. 480).

"In December, 1781, Colonel Wood was appointed by the Secretary of War superintendent of all prisoners of war in Virginia. (Va. Col. Papers, Vol. II, 673). He was President of the Board of Arrangements of the Virginia line, created by a resolution of Congress, August and November, 1782, to meet at Winchester December 27, 1782. The original report of this Board in the handwriting of Colonel Wood is among the Washington papers. (Rep. 436, p. 32).

"In October, 1783, the Virginia Assembly designated him Brigadier-General. He was a member of the Virginia Society of the Cincinnati, October 9, 1784; elected Vice-President of the Society December 4, 1789, and President of the same January 17, 1802. He resigned as Brigadier-General in 1784."

James Wood was elected to the Executive Council of Virginia in 1784; by seniority he became Lieutenant-Governor. He was in the Executive Council twenty years and died while so serving, June 16, 1813. He was President of the Society of the Cincinnati from October 9, 1784, until his death. (Tyler's Virginia Biography.)

He was elected Governor December 1, 1796, serving until December, 1799, when he was succeeded by James Monroe.

He was an active member of the Protestant Episcopal Church, and was vestryman and clerk of the vestry of Frederick parish until his appointment to the army. The vestry of Frederick parish served as trustees for the churches at Mill Creek (Morgan's), Shepherdstown and Martinsburg.

The County of Wood, now in West Virginia, was named in honor of his patriotic services, which covered a period of over twenty-five years.

Governor Wood was an active member of the Virginia "Society for Promoting the Abolition of Slavery, and Protecting Those Illegally Held in Bondage," and so forth. (See Papers Vol. III, 256 in His. Society of Pa.)

In 1789, he was Presidential Elector from Virginia and voted for Washington for President.

Details from the charming paper of Miss Harris:

"In 1774, Lord Dunmore, the last Royal Governor of Virginia, determined upon an expedition against the Shawanese Indians in Western Virginia. The expedition, which was to result in the battle of Point Pleasant, was organized, and among the captains in Lord Dunmore's own division of forces, was James Wood, Jr., of Winchester. His commission of course was in the name of His Britanic Majesty, George, third of the name, by the Grace of God, King of Great Britain and Ireland. When next Captain Wood was to draw his sword, it was to be as holder of a commission signed by a very different authority. Captain Wood served with marked distinction in this campaign, proving himself an able and efficient officer. Finding that some of his men were without muskets, instead of besieging the commissary for these imperatively needed articles, he promptly supplied them himself, paying for them out of his own means. This expense was afterwards refunded him by the state. With the successful termination of the campaign the colony, freed for the present from the dangers of Indian outbreaks on its western boundary, could now give its undivided attention to the great questions of the day.

"Captain Wood entered the House of Burgesses in 1775 as member for his native Frederick and took a prominent part in the stormy scenes which ensued with Lord Dunmore. The close of this session was to see the downfall of the royal power in Virginia. Lord Dunmore vainly endeavoring to assert the royal authority, was confronted on every side by what he denounced as treason and rebellion. Like the ghost of Banquo, it would not 'down' for all his commands. The people were enraged by his proclamation to the slaves, justly regarding it as an incitement to insurrection and an attempt to kindle a servile war in their midst; and the removal of the powder from the magazine—a precaution taken by Lord Dunmore upon hearing of the fight at Lexington—raised the popular temper to the boiling point. Terrified by the storm he had raised, Lord Dunmore betook himself to his ships in the James River, declaring the colony to be in rebellion and he in peril of his life. The Burgesses appointed Captain Wood, Mr. Cary and others a committee to wait upon his lordship on board his ship, and present to him an address, in which they remonstrated against his action, asserted their loyalty, and in the same breath, their determination to protect the rights of the people. Captain Wood was also appointed one of the commission of fifteen 'to inquire into the late disturbances and commotions.' June 14 the same Assembly, still calmly transacting business in the absence of the Governor—without whose august presence they were not supposed to sit—appointed James Wood, Thomas and John Walker, Andrew Lewis, and Adam Stephen, Esqrs. commissioners to ratify the treaty between the Ohio Indians and the Colony, and at the same time appointed James Wood to visit personally the several Indian tribes in the western part of Virginia and invite them to be present at the signing of the treaty at Fort Pitt, September of the same year, 1775.

"Next year we find Captain Wood a member of the famous convention, which upon the 6th day of May, 1776, was chosen to consider the question of Independence. Events were crowding thick and fast upon one another now, and the air was fairly electric with the coming storm. Lexington and Bunker Hill had been fought the previous year; Ticonderoga had yielded to Ethan Allen's imperative summons to 'surrender in the name of the Great Jehovah and the Continental Congress;' Washington had just compelled Gage to evacuate Boston —thus freeing Massachusetts at last from the incubus of an armed foe in her very citadel. Here at home Norfolk had been shelled and laid in ashes by command of Lord Dunmore as a parting token of his regard for the rebellious colony that coolly cast him forth, and chose as his successor the very man he most hated and feared, Patrick Henry. Everywhere troops were mustering and drilling, munitions of war being collected, delegates from each of the thirteen colonies were assembling in Philadelphia to decide upon the final steps to be taken. What would be the outcome of it all? That it was open war with the mother country few doubted by this time, though a few determined optimists, in spite of the state of actual war which had existed in Massachusetts for over a year, in spite of our own expedition into Canada, still clung to the hope of a peaceful adjustment of difficulties. The convention met in a grimly determined mood. Not for nothing had Patrick Henry and Thomas Jefferson preached and taught, in season and out of season, all these years. The Committees of Correspondence organized by Samuel Adams and Dabney Carr had amply justified their existence. So well had they done their work, that now at this vital moment, the thirteen colonies were practically one. Thoroughly in touch one with another, each resenting the wrongs of the other as his own, no conflicting interests marred the harmony of their concerted action. All along the line they touched elbows, the doubtful and uncertain colonies midway being held firmly in line by the strong colonies of Massachusetts and Virginia on either side of them. The delegates wasted no time in preliminaries, but went at once to their work. They met May 13th and upon the next day adopted a preamble drawn up by Edmund Pendleton, directing the Virginia delegates in Congress to propose to that body to declare the United Colonies free and independent states. We all know the historic scene in Congress some three weeks later when Richard Henry Lee, acting upon these instructions, made the formal motion that the 'United Colonies are, and of right ought to be, free and independent States.' Great were the rejoicings in Williamsburg when it was known that the preamble of Pendleton had been adopted. Bells were rung, the town was illuminated and the state troops concentrated there by order of Governor Henry—Lord Dunmore having long ere this shaken the dust of ungrateful Virginia from his indignant feet—cheered themselves hoarse by way of expressing their cordial endorsement of the action of the convention. Nor did the convention stop here, but upon the 15th of June passed the Declaration of Rights. Since the famous Bill of Rights presented to Charles I by the Long Parliament, no such document had been flaunted in the face of an English king. It was practically a declaration, not merely of rights, but of independence as well. The other colonies might do as they saw fit, but Virginia defined her position, and voiced her claims in no uncertain tones, and she followed the Declaration by deliberately drawing up a State Constitution, not a new colonial, but a state constitution, you will notice, which the convention formally adopted June 29th. Both the declaration and the constitution were prepared by George Mason.

"Massachusetts had already reformed her state government by simply reverting to the terms of her old and much cherished charter. She now promptly followed Virginia's lead by resolving unanimously at a series of town meetings, to support the Declaration of Independence, which it was now expected Congress would pass, so that Virginia and Massachusetts, as beseemed the two most purely English of the thirteen colonies, now stood shoulder to shoulder in the imminent deadly breach. After such a challenge, there was of course but one thing to do—to raise, equip and officer troops as quickly as possible to swell the forces already in arms in New England under Washington, and regiment after regiment, some raw undisciplined farmers, others formed of smart militia companies, were commissioned and sent to the front. James Wood's commission, recorded in the War Department, bears date November 12, 1776, 'to be colonel of the 12th Virginia Regiment in the Army of the United States, raised for the defense of American liberty.' Three years later, he was commissioned colonel of the 8th Virginia Regiment 'to take rank as such from the 12th day of November, A. D., 1776. Given at Philadelphia this 20th day of March, 1779, and in the 3rd year of our independence.' Thus run the original commissions, both of which are in the possession of the descendants of Colonel Wood's younger brother, Robert.

"At one time, from May to September, 1778, the 12th, 8th and 4th Regiments were consolidated under Colonel Wood's command, but his original commission issued in 1776, was to the 12th Regiment of the Virginia line.

"The next year we find Colonel Wood personally mentioned for 'conspicuous gallantry' at Brandywine. Then followed the repulse at Germantown, the cheering news of Burgoyne's overthrow and surrender at Saratoga; Monmouth, the victory lost by the treachery of Charles Lee, calling forth from the self-controlled commander-in-chief one of those rare but tremendous bursts of passion, before which it was said strong men cowered like frightened children; and the terrible winter at Valley Forge where the Prussian, Von Steuben, the veteran of Frederick the Great's campaigns, drilled the awkward squads into efficiency, alternately swearing at and cajoling the men whose awkwardness drove him well nigh to frenzy. 'Je ne puis plus,' (I can curse dem no more), he was wont to sigh tragically, when he had exhausted the resources of three languages.

"Late in the autumn of 1778 the men of Burgoyne's surrendered army were transferred to the vicinity of Charlottesville, Va., to await their regular exchange. Colonel Wood was put in charge of these prisoners of war, and won golden opinions from them by his kindly ways and prudent management. Indeed the good order and temper which notoriously prevailed among these prisoners, was largely attributable to Colonel Wood's efficient handling of the situation.

"Finally, after years of alternate success and failure, triumph and despair, came Yorktown with its decisive victory, when the bands of the surrendered army marched out playing dolefully 'The World Turned Upside Down.'

"Though the treaty of peace was not signed until two years later, the fall of Yorktown October 19, 1781, ended the war, and henceforth Colonel Wood's history is identified with that of his native state. In December, 1781, two months after the fall of Yorktown, he was appointed superintendent of all prisoners of war in Virginia, and when in 1782 Congress created 'A Board of Arrangement of the Officers and Men of the Virginia Line,' Col. Wood sat as President of the Board. In 1783 he was commissioned Brigadier-General of the state troops, and once more served the state against his old enemies, the Indians, who were again harassing the border. This was General Wood's last campaign, for at its close he resigned his commission, and sheathed his sword forever.

"But such a man was not allowed to retire to the seclusion of private life. Other offices and duties now claimed him. He had served his state as soldier, henceforth he was to serve her as statesman. In 1784 he became a member of the Executive Council of Virginia, succeeding John Marshall, and in 1789, when our first presidential election was held, he was elector for Virginia, and in that capacity cast Virginia's first electoral vote. That vote, it is needless to say, was cast for his old chief and friend, Washington.

"The same year General Wood became Vice-President of the Society of the Cincinnati, of which he had been a member since 1784. Seven years later, years spent in almost constant public service, Virginia conferred upon him the highest honor in her gift, electing him Governor of the state. He served from 1796 to 1799, when, upon the expiration of his term of office, he was succeeded by James Monroe, afterwards President of the United States. Governor Wood's administration was marked by no one conspicuous act, but by the general peace and good order which prevailed. Probably the most noteworthy act of his administration was the erection of the state armory in Richmond.

"In 1802 he became President of the Cincinnati, holding this rank for the rest of his life. For more than twelve years he was a member of the Legislature and for more than twenty years a member of the Executive Council, being still a member of that body at the time of his death, which occurred near Richmond June 16, 1813. Truly he might have said with Othello, 'I have done the state some service.'

"Governor Wood was a member of the Episcopal Church, was a vestryman and clerk of Frederick Parish until his appointment in the army. He married Miss Jean Moncure, but left no children to glory in their father's stainless record and proudly wear his honored name.

"With military pomp and honors, amid the tolling of bells and the roll of the muffled drums, as befitted a soldier and a Governor of

Virginia, he was buried in the churchyard of old St. John's, in Richmond, where his ashes rest amid many of his old comrades clustered around the quaint old building wherein were held many of the stormy meetings of that turbulent time. Here Patrick Henry cried, 'I know not what others may choose, but as for me, give me liberty or give me death.' Truly old St. John's should be a hallowed spot to all admirers of the Continental buff and blue."

Governor James Wood died childless, but the James Wood Chapter of the Daughters of the American Revolution, at Parkersburg, W. Va., has proved a noble heir to a noble name. And could a name be more fitly honored than by a living, working, self-perpetuating body of human beings? Not a club, not a clique, but an organization of men or women of liberal minds, descendants of men or women who have performed some patriotic service in a common cause? Those who thus honor the past are always instant in every good word and work in the present and are laying the foundation for a better future.

The history of the James Wood Chapter is very interesting. It was organized in 1903, the second or third chapter in the state. Pioneer work in forming a Chapter had been done since 1894, when Miss Kinnie E. Smith, the first Daughter of the American Revolution in West Virginia, was commissioned to form the Parkersburg Chapter. Years of toil and tireless zeal were rewarded by results in a Chapter in Marietta, Ohio, in the Point Pleasant Chapter and monument, in the Parkersburg Chapter; and the James Wood Chapter, the first officers of which were: Regent, Mrs. B. D. Spilman; vice-regent, Mrs. G. W. Peterkin; recording secretary, Miss Carrie Shrewsberry; corresponding secretary, Mrs. William H. Smith; historian, Miss Kinnie E. Smith; registrar, Mrs. C. A. Hiteshaw; treasurer, Mrs. Nannie Bradenbaugh.

Of these, Mrs. Spilman and Mrs. Smith became officers in the National Society.

Miss Kate Innes Harris, whose sketch of James Wood has been quoted, and who died in 1912, was a graduate of the Episcopal Female Institute, Winchester, Virginia, under the late Rev. J. C. Wheat, D. D. This tribute to her worth and work is here rendered in the name and spirit of her Alma Mater.

The James Wood Chapter now numbers more than eighty members and enjoys a well deserved prestige.

Dear Miss Kinnie Smith, "atavis edite (a) regibus," are you not rewarded for your long years of seed sowing? Is not the world better for the things for which you have labored—the ideals fostered through the chapters formed, the monuments erected, the Sequoias preserved, the earth sent from Point Pleasant for the monument in California, the purchase of Monticello, the names of patriots rescued from oblivion?

CHAPTER XVI

The Wonderful Month of May, 1926 — Commander Richard Evelyn Byrd and the North Pole — The Sesqui-Centennial at Williamsburg — The Shenandoah National Park

> I will make mention of Egypt and Babylon to them that know me: behold Philistia, and Tyre, with Ethiopia: this man was born there.
> And of Zion it shall be said, This and that man was born in her: and the highest himself shall establish her.
> The Lord shall count, when he writeth up the people, that this man was born there.
> Psalm 87:4, 5, 6.

Surely no history of Virginia written in 1926 would be complete which did not mention the great events of her mascot month of May. (Was not Jamestown founded May 13, 1607?) The press of the whole world has sent forth the name of Commander Richard Evelyn Byrd as the first to reach the North Pole by airplane, second only to Admiral Peary in reaching it at all.

Sunday, "Mother's Day," May 9, Commander Byrd, the "Miss Josephine Ford," Fokker airplane, the sun, the sun compass of Albert Bumstead, the North Pole!—ignis fatuus, aurora borealis, which had lured men to death since the first hollowed log manned by a dauntless spirit crept out from shore! The unattainable attained! Science had caught the secret of the feathered airplane, the eiderduck. Science had overcome the variation of the magnetic needle and had perfected the sun compass, and the only two in the United States were in the skillful hands of a navigator than whom there is none better.

The great opportunity had come; "der schoene Monat Mai" produced just the right combination of earth and sky; a son of Winchester, Virginia, was ready; not by chance, but by a long preparation whose foundations were laid generations ago. The vision of Milton was no longer a vision but a reality. The representative of a great and free nation, of a universal and free press, on that momentous day became the realization of his ideal, and in a literal sense of which the poet never dreamed: "Methinks I see in my mind a noble and puissant Nation rousing herself like a strong man after sleep, and shaking her invincible locks. Methinks I see her as an Eagle muing her mighty youth, and kindling her undazl'd eyes at the full mid-day beam, purging and unscaling her long abused sight at the fountain itself of heav'nly radiance." Such a triumph of science and skill calls for the language of inspiration. No longer need Bryant devote his divine art to the marvels of the instinct of the waterfowl; with equal, nay with greater truth might he apply it to the spirit of man, who has transcended nature, and exclaim:

"Whither, midst falling dew,
While glow the heavens with the last steps of day,
Far through their rosy depths dost thou pursue
Thy solitary way?

* * * * * *

"There is a Power whose care
Teaches thy way along that pathless coast—
The desert and illimitable air—
Lone wandering, but not lost."

"And from the depths of personal conviction we exclaim with the sweet singer of Israel: "O Lord our Lord, how excellent is thy name in all the earth: who hast set thy glory above the heavens.

* * * * * *

' 'When I consider the heavens, the work of thy fingers, the moon and the stars, which thou hast ordained:

"What is man that thou art mindful of him? And the son of man that thou visitest him? for thou hast made him a little lower than the angels, and hast crowned him with glory and honor. Thou madest him to have dominion over the works of thy hands; thou has put all things under his feet:

"All sheep and oxen, yea, and the beasts of the field: The fowl of the air, and the fish of the sea, and whatsoever passeth through the paths of the seas. O Lord our Lord, how excellent is thy name in all the earth."

The Sesqui-Centennial of the signing of the Virginia Resolutions must also enter into any history of Winchester, as the follow-up of the event properly stressed in the sketch of James Wood by Miss Harris. The delegates from Frederick County to the memorable convention which lasted from May 6 to July 5, 1776, were James Wood and Isaac Zane.

At the Sesqui-Centennial, May 15, 1926, Calvin Coolidge, President of the United States, was introduced by another of Winchester's sons, Hon. Harry Flood Byrd, Governor of Virginia, and older brother of the aerial navigator. President Coolidge struck the keynote to his address in his declaration that the states are the sheet anchors of our institutions—a sentiment in the class with Woodrow Wilson's famous appeal to make the country "safe for democracy." Part of President Coolidge's historical and history-making address was as follows:

"Fellow Americans:

No one who is interested in the early beginnings of America, or who is moved by love of our country, could come into these historic and hallowed surroundings without being conscious of a deep sense of reverence. In a land which is rich in the interesting records of the past, that portion of Virginia lying between Washington and Norfolk stands out unrivaled in important events and great names. Colonial importance, Revolutionary fame, the statesmanship of the early republic, the great struggle for the supremacy of the union—these epoch-making stories can not be told without relating the history of this locality and recounting the eminence of its illustrious sons. Very much of this narrative centers around the venerable town of Williamsburg and the old College of William and Mary.

"Within this locality are Jamestown, where the English settlements began, and Yorktown, where English dominion ended. From Petersburg to Arlington stretches a land marked by many battlefields where the shedding of fraternal blood rededicated the Constitution. Here began the first preparation within our country for the establishment of a college. But the unfortunate interruption of hostile natives deferred the completion of the project so that this institution ranks second in age with all our other universities. Here are the three capitals of this sovereign commonwealth. If the work which is represented by the great names which have been associated with the growth and strength of this region were struck from the annals of our country, the richest heritage of progress and fame that ever glorified the actions of a people would sink to comparative poverty.

"What a wealth of distinguished figures from the time of John Smith down to the present day! I can not relate them all, these statesmen and soldiers, these founders and benefactors, who here lived and wrought with so much of enduring glory. They are represented by such stalwart characters as Patrick Henry, George Mason, Richard Henry Lee, Thomas Jefferson and George Washington. Later came Monroe, Marshall, Madison, Randolph and Harrison, with a long list of associates almost equally eminent in the history of our country. All Americans. It was into this region that Abraham Lincoln made his last journey from Washington.

"This richest of all our historical settings made so great an appeal to me when I was approached by your two distinguished senators, Mr. Swanson and Mr. Glass, whom I cherish as friends, honor for their devotion to their country, and esteem for the support they have often given when we have been mutually striving for sound government, bearing the invitation of your General Assembly to participate in the observance of this day, which was supported by Col. Henry W. Anderson, a lawyer who has contributed so much of his great learning and talents to the service of his country, and emphasized by my former secretary, Mr. Slemp, for many years a prominent leader in Congress, a man whose loyalty and devotion has imposed upon me so much obligation, that it seemed almost a patriotic duty to respond.

"It is difficult to determine where or when the great movements in human progress had their original inception. Our life is complex and interwoven with thousands of varying motives and cross currents. One act leads to another. Yet certain actions stand out with so much prominence against the background of the past that we are justified in saying of them that at least there is an event which is one of the beginnings of a new epoch. In accordance with this standard, we are altogether warranted in asserting that 150 years ago, on the 15th of

May, 1776, formal action was taken in this city by a patriotic band of loyal Virginians, in their public capacity as servants of the common cause of the American colonies, which had a most direct influence in leading to the Declaration of Independence.

It is not necessary at this time to relate again the various events that preceded and caused the American Revolution. The people of this commonwealth had been constantly alert in the assertion and maintenance of their constitutional rights against British encroachment. Under the lead of Samuel Adams, the Boston town meeting in May, 1764, adopted resolutions against the proposed stamp tax, but the first formal defiance of that act after its passage came from Virginia, when in May, 1765, Patrick Henry introduced a series of resolutions in the Assembly declaring that the only power of taxation lay in the people themselves, or in their chosen representatives.

"Again, in May, 1769, the House of Burgesses, numbering among its membership Washington, Henry and Jefferson condemned the laws of Parliament taxing the colonies and requested other colonies to join them in this protest. When the governor took the desciplinary measure of adjourning them, they met at the Raleigh Tavern, where Washington prepared a resolution pledging themselves to continue the policy of non-importation, which was adopted. Also in March, 1773, the Virginia Assembly unanimously voted to establish a system of inter-colonial committees of correspondence. As great an authority as John Fiske calls this 'the most decided step toward revolution that had yet been taken by the Americans.' This original suggestion appears to have come from the eminent divine Jonathan Mayhew, who suggested to James Otis that the communion of churches furnished an excellent example for a communion of colonies.

"Again, late in 1772, a Boston town meeting had taken the lead in adopting a committee for correspondence for the Colony of Massachusetts, and Samuel Adams wrote to Richard Henry Lee, who had already expressed the same idea, urging a like action for Virginia. But in March, 1773, this colony had already anticipated that course and enlarged upon it by making it an inter-colonial committee. The convocation of such a body would result in the setting up of a Congress which would represent the united authority of the colonies.

"Events moved rapidly, and in the closing days of 1775, incensed by his tyranny, a body of patriots, including John Marshall, drove Lord Dunmore, the governor, out of Norfolk, a place of 9,000 inhabitants, and took possession. In retaliation the governor set fire to the town by shells from the harbor on New Year's day, and it was consumed.

"Confirming my statement that it is difficult to date and locate the exact beginning of any event, we find that on the 22nd of April the people of Cumberland county adopted a resolution prepared by Carter Henry Harrison instructing their delegates to the Virginia Convention, which was to meet in this town in May, 'positively to declare for an independency' and to 'promote in our convention an instruction to our delegates now sitting in Continental Congress to do the same.' A like sentiment was being unofficially, though publicly, expressed in other counties. On the 20th of April Lee wrote from the Congress in Philadelphia to Henry to propose in the coming convention a separation of the colonies from Great Britain.

"It was on the 6th of May, 1776, that there assembled at Williamsburg a convention which was to become historic. It was presided over by Edmund Pendleton, who had opposed the stamp act resolutions of Patrick Henry, but 11 years and the wanton cruelty of the royal governor had made a great change in the public opinion of the colony and he had become a loyal supporter of independence. He now joined with Patrick Henry and Meriwether Smith in drafting resolutions to 'America,' and after setting out the grievances that it had endured and 'appealing to the Searcher of Hearts for the sincerity of former declarations' and a discussion in which Mason and Madison, to be known to future fame, took part, on the 15th of May, 1776, it was

" 'Resolved unanimously, That the delegates appointed to represent this colony in General Congress be instructed to propose to that respectable body to declare the united colonies free and independent states, absolved from all allegiance to, or dependence upon, the crown or Parliament of Great Britain; and that they give the assent of this colony to such declaration, and to whatever measures may be thought proper and necessary by the Congress for forming foreign alliances, and a confederation of the Colonies, at such time, and in the manner, as to them shall seem best: Provided, That the power of forming government for, and the regulation of the internal concerns of each colony, be left to respective colonial legislatures.'

" 'Resolved unanimously, That a committee be appointed to prepare a declaration of rights, and such a plan of government as will be most likely to maintain peace and order in this colony and secure substantial and equal liberty to the people.'

"The import of these resolutions was well understood in this locality. The event was marked that evening by a celebration, the ringing of bells, and the firing of guns. The British flag went down at the statehouse never to rise again, and in its place was flown the crosses and stripes, the temporary emblem of a new government.

"These resolutions coming by the action of the duly constituted representatives of the largest of the colonies were of an importance that can not be described as anything less than decisive in the movement for independence. Other localities held the same opinions, but this action of the Old Dominion was needed to make such opinions effective. Richard Henry Lee now had the assurance of the support of his constituents. On the 7th of June he moved the Congress—

" 'That these United States are and of right ought to be free and independent states; that they are absolved from all allegiance to the British crown and that all political connection between them and the state of Great Britain is and ought to be totally dissolved; that it is expedient forthwith to take the most effectual measures for forming foreign alliances; that a plan of confederation be prepared and transmitted to the respective colonies for their consideration and approbation.'

"This motion was at once seconded by John Adams, of Massachusetts. In this great crisis the Pilgrim and Cavalier stood side by side united in the common cause of human liberty under constitutional law.

"The excellence of the official documents of the Revolutionary period has often been remarked. It was such as to draw praise from the foremost British statesmen. In that respect the Virginia resolutions of May 15 left little to be desired. They are characterized by a most admirable restraint, clear and logical in their presentation of facts, and clothed in appropriate language. They have a dignity and strength that are compelling and a courage and reserve that are convincing. They were composed by no ordinary men. Such a document could only be produced by character and culture. The influences which had flowed from the eighty-odd years of existence of William and Mary College can not be separated from the form and substance of these resolutions. Into their making went all that was best of some of her most distinguished sons.

"What purpose had planted these institutions of learning in the American wilderness? What raised up Harvard, that it might become the teacher of Otis and Hancock and the Adamses? What nourished William and Mary, that it might furnish inspiration to Bland, to Wythe, to Nelson, and to Jefferson? These two seminaries had a common benefactor in the famous Robert Boyle. And when the wanton ravages of war reduced this once flourishing institution that had spoken so boldly in the cause of liberty to a state that left little but the vibrant tones of the college bell and the fervent prayers of a devout President, it was a distinguished son of Harvard, Senator Hoar, who plead her just cause with such eloquence in the halls of Congress that a dilatory government at last made restitution for a part of the damage done, that this seat of learning might be restored to take its active place again as a citadel of truth and liberty and righteousness. No one can contemplate these events without a deep realization that those who participated in them were guided by an inspired vision.

"It has been the experience of history that political ideals do not spring into full development all at once. They are the process of continued study. The Virginia resolutions in the fewest possible words map out a course of action and lay down the fundamental principles by which America has since sought to guide and direct its political life. The members of the convention, however, would not have argued that they were embarking upon a new theory of political relationship with so much assurance as they would have contended that they were adapting well-established theories of constitutional law to their own condition.

"They declared for complete independence. They abjured both the crown and the Parliament of Great Britain. Much emphasis has been placed on our political independence. It has become one of our most fundamental traditions of government, and rightly so. In our domestic affairs our sovereignty rises to its most complete state. We tolerate no outside interference. But as the devout Mayhew had seen the communion of colonies in the communion of churches, so these resolutions, even though unconsciously, recognized a communion of nations when they authorized the forming of foreign alliances. They could not escape the conclusion that as the individual derives his liberty from an observance of the law, so nations derive their independence and their sovereignty from an observance of that comity by which they are all bound. As modern developments have brought the nations closer together, this conclusion has become more and more unavoidable. While the rights of the citizens have been in no wise diminished, the rights of humanity have been very greatly increased. Our country holds to political and economic independence, but it holds to cooperation and combination in the administration of justice.

"The resolutions did not fail to recognize the principle of nationality. It was the 'united colonies' that they proposed should be declared independent, and it distinctly authorized 'a confederation of the colonies.' This was an early and authoritative statement of the theory that this is all one country bound up in a common interest, destined to the experience of a common fortune. It was the expression of a desire for a yet unformulated plan for a federal government. How great a part Virginia was to play in the final adoption of such a government was by this action already indicated. When that great test came some years later it was the known wish of the great Washington, aided by the superb reasoning powers of Marshall, notwithstanding the direct opposition of Henry, that caused Virginia to ratify formation of the union. For a second time the action of this great commonwealth was the determining factor in the destiny of America.

"To attempt to proceed upon any other theory can only end in disaster. No policy can ever be a success which does not contemplate this as one country. Not only is this one country, but we must keep all its different parts in harmony by refusing to adopt legislation which is not for the general welfare.

"The resolutions did not stop there. Had they done so, they would have been very far from comprehending and expressing the necessities of the American people. They went on to provide that the regulation of the internal concerns of each colony be left to respective colonial legislatures. This was a plain declaration of the unassailable fact that the states are the sheet anchors of our institutions. If the federal government should go out of existence, the common run of people would not detect the difference in the affairs of their daily life for a considerable length of time. But if the authority of the states were struck down disorder approaching chaos would be upon us within 24 hours. No method of procedure has ever been devised by which liberty could be divorced from local self-government. No plan of centralization has ever been adopted which did not result in bureaucracy, tyranny, inflexibility, reaction and decline."

Governor Byrd's review of history, given from the standpoint of a Virginian, standing where the framers of the famous Resolutions had stood, is particularly pertinent, and is given almost in its entirety:

The Governor said:

"Mr. President, Ladies and Gentlemen:

One hundred and fifty years ago, at the other end of this street where we now are, 112 members of the Colonial Convention highly resolved that Virginia renounce her allegiance to the British flag. Before sunset that memorable May day the familiar flag of the mother country was lowered and furled forever in this old capital of Virginia, and the resolutions penned by Edmund Pendleton were sent on their long journey over narrow trails and rough roads to the Continental Congress, then in session at Philadelphia.

"Thomas Jefferson, who was to draw the Declaration of Independence to be adopted in Philadelphia some six weeks later, says in his memoirs: 'On the 15th day of May, 1776, the convention of Virginia instructed the delegates in Congress to propose to that body that it declare the colonies independent of Great Britain, and a committee was appointed to prepare a declaration of rights and a plan of government. This 'plan of government' was to be Virginia's first constitution as a state independent of Britain, if not the first written constitution in the new world. Some other colonies had, indeed, empowered their delegates to vote for independence, but Virginia's convention that met here went further and actually directed Virginia's delegates to propose that the united colonies be declared 'free and independent states absolved from all allegiance to or dependence on the crown or Parliament of Great Britain.'

"British troops had burned Norfolk five months before, and George Washington was straining the strength of his steadfast spirit to make effective the army of independence. The royal government had proclaimed these men rebels, and they had debated these bold, brave resolutions in the very shadow of treason if the colonies failed. But these Virginia delegates were not then to take counsel of their fears.

"Not only the fiery orator, Patrick Henry, but also the conservative, cautious Edmund Pendleton, was ready to break the bonds that so long had bound Virginia to the British crown. George Mason, the successor of Washington as the representative from Fairfax, and James Madison, only twenty-three and fresh from Princeton College, were equally ready to make the great decision. And it was a great decision, for Virginia then stood first in population and wealth of all the colonies, and her influence in the Congress, then in session at Philadelphia, was powerful.

"Massachusetts with her 350,000 inhabitants compared with Virginia's half million, must have submitted had not Virginia come forward. It was by no means easy to sever the ties with the mother land. John Adams estimated that one-third of colonial Americans remained loyal in sentiment to the crown, even after their fellow Americans were fighting.

"While Pendleton is thought to have actually penned the resolutions, they appear to have been the product of the convictions and counsels of Patrick Henry and Meriwether Smith, as well. One may imagine the fire with which Henry championed them.

"Indeed, Henry's hand was quite probably the one which later qualified the assent of the colony to the formation of the confederation with the clause that no constitution adopted should interfere with the internal concerns of any state—a state right's reservation, foreshadowing the opposition of Henry to be displayed years later in Richmond, when Washington and Marshall urged Virginia to ratify the constitution of the United States.

"Inspired by the Williamsburg resolutions, one of Virginia's representatives in the Philadelphia Congress, Richard Henry Lee, on June 7 proposed a resolution for American independence, and for forming foreign alliances of confederation. In the meantime, however, the Virginia convention itself dealt with the second resolution proposing that a committee adopt the declaration of rights and a plan of government for Virginia.

"George Mason's Bill of Rights was adopted June 17 following—an adoption that will be celebrated on the 12th of next month. In recognition of the influence of the Williamsburg resolutions in hastening American independence, the Virginia Assembly provided for this celebration and appointed a committee, consisting of Mr. Ashton Dovel, Mr. I. N. Coleman and Mr. H. E. Hanes from the House of Delegates, and Senators H. B. White and Julian Gunn from the Senate, who deserve our appreciation for this fitting celebration of a significant event.

"It is with something of a thrill that I now approach the introduction of the President of the United States at this historic meeting. He comes here the chief executive of the most peaceful, powerful and prosperous nation in the world, only a short century and a half after powerful leaders of feeble colonies proclaimed their will to be free.

He is here at the heart of the movement for American Independence. Just six miles from here the first permanent English settlement in America was made at Jamestown on May 13, 1607, and twelve years later the first legislative assembly to be held on American soil assembled in the church at Jamestown. In 1689 the capital was moved from Jamestown to Williamsburg, and while the capitol was being built the wing of this very college was the accustomed assembly hall of the House of Burgesses.

"It was in the old capitol that Patrick Henry spoke in favor of his resolutions denying the right of Parliament to levy taxes upon Virginia. In this speech Henry had the courage to proclaim that 'Cæsar had his Brutus, Charles I his Cromwell, and George III ———.'

"When the speaker was interrupted by cries of 'Treason! Treason!' Henry dauntlessly continued, '—and George III may profit by their example. If this be treason, make the most of it!'

"A young law student stood there in this town at the door of the House that day and heard Henry. His name was Thomas Jefferson, and that speech confirmed his determination to devote his life to Virginia and the liberty of America.

"As we revive patriotic memories we are startled sometimes to think how very young we are as a nation. From Jamestown to the Declaration of Independence we worked under the British flag longer than we have labored under the Stars and Stripes since July 4, 1776.

"And may I not pause here in this day when the common sacrifices of British and American boys as comrades in the World War have wiped away all stains of bitterness between the English speaking people, to utter Virginia's word of sympathy to all Englishmen in this time of their internal difficulties, and to pray that peace and harmony may be restored quickly, and that they will bring happiness and prosperity to their king and country?

"Our independent life as a nation has been short, but it has been strong, progressive and prosperous, in part because the same patriotic devotion to duty shown by the fathers has been manifested by their successors in high places.

"The power of the President of the United States today might have astonished Thomas Jefferson and Patrick Henry. And yet the trend of public sentiment is to centre yet greater authority in the President in order to promote efficient and economical government. The popularity of the presidential office, the respect and loyalty its occupants command, is a notable tribute to the high average of ability and fine public spirit exhibited by the heads of our governments.

"The Presidents of the United States have reverenced God, lived good lives and dedicated their talents and their strength unreservedly to the service of their country."

At William and Mary College only two weeks earlier were dedicated the beautiful memorial gates in honor of Dr. Kate Waller Barrett by the Commonwealth Chapter, Daughters of the American Revolution, Richmond, Virginia, of which Mrs. Benjamin Ladd Purcell is regent. It is interesting to remember that the beauty of Pocahontas, another charming woman, who visited England in 1616, inspired the English to found a college for the education of the Indians. Funds were collected by the bishops of King James, and finally in the reign of William and Mary, who pledged 2,000 pounds, to which was added money raised by taxes on tobacco and liquor, quitrents, and that obtained from three pirates by Dr. James Blair, the college was founded in 1693, according to plans drawn by Sir Christopher Wren. Thus Williamsburg and William and Mary College stand as a link between the old world and the new, representing mutual sacrifice and service.

The third event of the Month of May, 1926, of untold importance, not only to Virginians but to all who love the beautiful out-of-doors, was the signing by President Coolidge on the 22nd of the bill creating the Shenandoah National Park, the first National Park in the east. Countless travelers, when they reach the crest of the Blue Ridge and look down upon the shining waters of the Shenandoah, "daughter of the stars," will in imagination hear again the clink of the golden horseshoes of Governor Spottswood and his mystic knights, rejoicing in the romance that envelops a land so fair.

CHAPTER XVII

Overwharton Parish — "Gaudia Nuncio Magna," Motto of Rev. Alexander Scott — Letter from Jean Moncure

The scene changes from Williamsburg and the bonny month of May, 1926, to Overwharton Parish, Stafford County, and the thread of the narrative is resumed. Both parish and county were formed about 1666. Rev. Alexander Scott, born July 20, 1636, died April 1, 1738, was minister for twenty-eight years. He never married. His curate for a short time before his death, and his successor, was Rev. John Moncure, a Scotchman, but descendant of a Huguenot refugee who fled from France at the revocation of the Edict of Nantes. His name, together with those of the vestry, is painted on one of the panels of the gallery in Old Aquia Church under date of 1757. He died in March, 1764, and is buried at Old Aquia Church. He married a daughter of Dr. Gustavus Brown, of Port Tobacco, Md. Their daughter, Jean, married James Wood. In 1820 she wrote a letter to a cousin, the granddaughter of the Rev. James Scott, whose wife was her aunt, another daughter of Dr. Gustavus Brown, through whom they were related to George Mason. Bishop Meade records this letter as the best account extant of the circumstances of her parents' early life. It may be found in his "Churches of Old Virginia," Vol. II, page 200, and is here reproduced:

"I was only ten years old when I lost my dear father. He was a Scotchman descended from a French ancestor who fled among the first Protestants who left France in consequence of the persecution that took place soon after the Reformation. He had an excellent education, and had made considerable progress in the study of medicine, when an invitation to seek an establishment in Virginia induced him to cross the Atlantic, and his first engagement was in Northumberland County, where he lived two years in a gentleman's family as private tutor. During that time, although teaching others, he was closely engaged in the study of divinity, and at the commencement of the third year from his first arrival, returned to Great Britain and was ordained a minister of the then Established Church; came back to Virginia and engaged as curate to your gr. uncle Alexander Scott, who at that time was Minister of Overwharton Parish in Stafford County and resided at his seat of Dipple. Your uncle died a short time after, and my dear father succeeded him in his parish and resided at the Glebehouse. Your grandfather, the Rev. James Scott, who inherited Dipple, continued there until he settled at Westwood, in Prince William. He was my father's dearest, kindest friend, and one of the best of men. Their intimancy brought my father and mother acquainted, who was a sister of your grandmother Scott. Old Dr. Gustavus Brown, of Maryland, my maternal grandfather, objected to the marriage of my father and mother. Although he thought highly of my father, he did not think him an eligible match for his daughter. He was poor and very delicate in his health. Dr. Brown did not, however, forbid their union, and it accordingly took place. The old gentleman received them as visitors, and visited them again, but would not pay down my Mother's intended dowry, until he saw how they could get along, and to let them see that they could not live on love without other sauce.

"I have often heard my dear mother relate the circumstances of her first housekeeping with tears of tender and delightful recollection. They went home from your grandpapa's, where they were married, with a slenderly supplied purse and to an empty house—except a few absolute necessaries from their kind friends. When they arrived they found some of my good father's parishioners there; one had brought some wood, another some fowls, and the third some meal, and so on. One good neighbor would insist on washing for them, another would milk, and another would tend the garden; and they all delighted to serve their good minister and his wife. Notwithstanding these aids my mother found much to initiate her into the habits of an industrious housewife, and my father into those of an active, practical farmer and gardener, which they never gave up.

"When the business of preparing their meal was over, a small writing stand was their table, and the stair-steps furnished one a seat and a trunk the other. Often, when provisions were scarce, my father took his gun or his fishing rod, and with his dog, sallied forth to provide their dinner, which, when he returned, his happy wife dressed; and often would she accompany him afishing or afowling, for she said they were too poor to have full employment in domestic business. Though destitute of every luxury they had a small, well-chosen library which my father had collected while a student and tutor. This was their evening's regale. While my mother worked with her needle, he read to her. This mode of enjoyment pleasantly brought around the close of the first year. When the minister's salary was paid, they were now comparatively rich. My dearest father exchanged his shabby black coat for a new one, and the next year was affluent. By this time the neighboring gentry found out the value of their minister and his wife, and contended for their society by soliciting visits and making them presents of many comforts.

"Frequently these grandees would come in their splendid equipages to spend a day at the glebe and bring everything requisite to prevent trouble or expense to the owners—merely for the enjoyment of the humble inhabitants of this humble dwelling.

"In the lapse of a few years, by frugality and industry in the management of a good salary these dear parents became quite easy in their circumstances. My father purchased a large tract of land on the river Potomac. He settled this principally by tenants; but on the most beautiful eminence that I ever beheld, he built a good house and soon improved it into a very sweet establishment. Here I was born; my brother and two sisters, considerably my seniors, were born at the glebe. My brother, who was intended for the Church, had a private tutor in the house. This man attended also to my two sisters, who previously to his residence in the family were under the care of an Englishman, who lived in the house, but also kept a public school under my father's direction about a mile from the house. Unhappily for me, I was the youngest and very sickly. My father and mother would not allow me to be compelled to attend to my books or my needle, and to both I had a decided aversion, unless voluntarily resorted to as an amusement. In this I was indulged. I would sometimes read a lesson to my sister or the housekeeper, or if their authority was resisted, I was called to my mother's side. All this amounted to my being an ignorant child at my father's death, which was a death-stroke to my mother. The incurable grief which it plunged her into could scarcely be a matter of surprise, when the uncommonly tender affection which united them is considered.

"They were rather more than middle-aged, when I was old enough to remember them: yet I well recollect their inseparable and undeviating association. They were rarely seen asunder. My mother was an active walker and a good rider. Whenever she could do so, she accompanied him in his pastoral visits—a faithful white servant attending in her absence from home. They walked hand in hand and often rode hand in hand—were both uncommonly fond of the cultivation of flowers, fruits and rare plants. They watched the opening buds together, together admired the beauty of the full-blown blossoms, and gathered the ripening fruit or seed. While he wrote or read, she worked near his table—which always occupied the pleasantest place in their chamber, where he chose to study, often laying down his pen to read or comment on an impressive passage. Frequently, when our evening repast was over (if the family were together) some book, amusing and instructive, was read aloud by my dear father, and those of the children or their young associates who could not be silent were sent to bed after evening worship—which always took place immediately after supper. Under the void which the sad separation occasioned, my poor mother's spirits sank and never rallied. The first six or eight months were spent in a dark, secluded chamber, distant from that formerly occupied. The management of the family devolved upon my brother and second sister. My eldest married two or three years previous to this period. I was left pretty much to my own management. The education of my brother and sister was so far finished that they not only held what they had acquired, but continued to improve; but alas, poor me! I, as usual, refused everything like study, but became, unfortunately, immoderately fond of books. The key of the library was now within my power, and the few romances it contained were devoured. Poetry and a botanical work with plates came next. This gave me a useless, superficial knowledge of what might have been useful, but what in this indigested way was far otherwise. The Tattler, Guardian, and Spectator were the only works I read which contained beneficial instruction; and of these I only read the amusing papers; and taking the beautiful and sublime allegories which abound with moral instruction, in a literal sense, I read them as amusing tales. This kind of reading made up a pernicious mass of chaotic matter that darkened while it seemed to enlighten my mind, and I soon became romantic and exceedingly ridiculous—turned the branches of trees together and called them a bower, and fancied I could write poetry and many other silly things. My dear mother suffered greatly towards the close of her life with a cancer; for this she visited the Medicinal Springs, and I was chosen to attend her. It was a crowded and gay scene for me, who had lived almost entirely in seclusion. I did not mix with its gayest circle; yet it was of service to me, as it gave me the first view of real life that ever I had. My beloved parent was not desirous of confining me, but I rejoice at the recollection that I very seldom could be prevailed on to leave her.

"There I first became the favourite and devoted friend of your most excellent mother. Forgive the vanity of this boast, my dear cousin, but I cannot help observing that she afterwards told me that it was the manner in which I discharged my duty that won her esteem and love. At this place, I first met with General Wood, who visited me soon after my return home, and became my husband four years after."

Jean Moncure need not have had so humble an opinion of her powers. Her verses, "Flowers and Weeds of the Old Dominion" were published in 1859. She is mentioned in Appleton's Cyclopedia of American Biography and in the National Cyclopedia of American Biography.

Colonel William Byrd II, of Westover (born March 18, 1674, died August 26, 1744), was describing such delightful people when he wrote:

> "My minde to me a kingdom is:
> Such perfect joy therein I finde
> As far exceeds all earthly blisse
> That God or nature hath assignede."

Here at old Aquia Church, in Stafford County, is buried Dr. Kate Waller Barrett (January 22, 1858-February 23, 1925), in her native soil, near the place of her birth, among generations of her own kin, beneath the shadow of the old church where her young husband, Reverend Robert South Barrett, was rector. Could any one wish more for the last resting place of one who lives in so many hearts, and whose works are destined to follow her in so many helpful ways?

CHAPTER XVIII

The Elusive Charms of Florida

By the Proclamation of 1763, three new Colonies were established in America; namely, Quebec or Canada, East Florida and West Florida. Lands were also granted to the officers and soldiers, who had served in the late war, and who resided in America, on their personal application for the same, in the following quantities and proportions: To any Field Officer 5000 acres; to any Captain 3000; to every subaltern or Staff Officer 2000; to every non-commissioned officer 200, and to every private, 50; and all to be free of quitrents for ten years. The land could be chosen, however, only in one of the above three new Colonies. (Sparks, Vol. II, page 369.)

This move to colonize in Florida was made by an association styling itself the "Military Company of Adventure," composed of those who had served in the Provincial Army in the late war. This company expected to obtain the grant from the British government of a large tract of territory in West Florida (now Mississippi) on the Mississippi and Yazoo Rivers—territory that had been thrown open to settlement by the creation of a new state, Florida, after the peace of 1763. This company appointed General Phineas Lyman of Connecticut, to press its claims on the ministry, but he found so much opposition to it that he was unable to effect his purpose without waiting for a formal grant. The company in January, 1773, sent a party from New York to take possession. "After a long voyage they arrived in Pensacola, and then to their great disappointment and chagrin, found that the governor had no authority to grant them lands as had been represented. Considerable time was spent in negotiation on the subject and exploring the rivers and adjacent country; but no settlement was made." (Ford's Writings of Washington, page 373.)

James Wood is said to have been the first Englishman to stand on the present site of Memphis, Tenn. His mission to that new land is explained by the following letters from George Washington:

13 March, 1773

Dear Sir:

Herewith you will receive Lord Dunmore's certificates of my claims as well in my own right as by purchase from Captain Posey and Mr. Thruston, in the location of which in the government of Florida, I shall rely on your friendship and care. Unnecessary it is to add that I shall choose good lands or none. But as many things occur to make land valuable, it is impossible for me at this distance and under my present knowledge of the country, to be explicit in any direction. Suffice it then to observe generally, that I would greatly prefer the land upon the river, to land back of it; that I should not like to be in a low morassy country nor yet in that which is hilly and braken; and that, from the idea I entertain of that country at this time, I should like to be as high up the Mississippi as the navigation is good; having been informed that the land is better and the climate more temperate in the Northern part of the government than below.

If I could get the lands equally good in one survey, I should prefer it. If not, then in one or more as circumstances require. Perhaps some locations already made upon the river might for a small consideration be bought, if so, I would rather advance a little money than put up with less valuable land. You will please to have the grant surveyed and effectually secured with such indulgences as those claiming under the Proclamation of 1763 are entitled to; and do all and everything in my behalf which shall to you seem right and proper; the cost of doing which I will pay for, and moreover for your faithful discharge of this trust, allow you the sum of one hundred pounds Virginia currency on the due execution of it.

Wishing you a pleasant tour and safe return to your friends, etc.

Virginia,
25th March, 1773

To William Edwards,
   Governor of West Florida.

Sir:

  Mr. Wood, the bearer of this, is a gentleman of Virginia, going upon a tour of Florida. He proposes, before his return, to explore some of the ungranted lands in your government, and, as I have never been able to designate the lands to which I am entitled under his Majesty's Proclamation of October, 1763, he has promised, if he meets with any lands as he thinks will meet with my purpose, to have ten thousand acres surveyed for me. To four thousand acres I am entitled in my right, by virtue of that Proclamation; to the residue, by purchase, certificates of which will be presented to your Excellency by Mr. Wood, under the seal of Lord Dunmore, our present Governor. My entire ignorance of the climate and soil and the advantages and disadvantages of the country of West Florida is the reason why his Lordship's certificates are couched in such general terms; and of my giving Mr. Wood a discretionary power to select the lands or not as he may be influenced by these appearances. Should he meet with a spot favorable to my wishes, I have no doubt of your Excellency's granting the land with such indulgence as have been practiced in sundry cases, agreeable to his Majesty's gracious intention, with the terms of which I shall endeavor strictly to comply.

  Could I, Sir, a stranger, take it upon me with propriety to recommend Mr. Wood, I should briefly add, that he is a gentleman well esteemed in Virginia, and I am persuaded will duly appreciate any little civilities you may be pleased to bestow on him.

  I have the honor to be, Sir, with very great respect, etc.

GEO. WASHINGTON.

(Sparks' Writing of Washington, Vol. II.)

Mt. Vernon,
30th March, 1773

Dear Sir:

  I intended to have a little further conversation with you on the subject of the Florida lands, but my haste to leave Williamsburg and your dining out the day I did do so, prevented it. I addressed a short letter to you by way of memorandum and left it with Mr. Southal. I hope you received it; that I may be satisfied you did so, please advise me, as the Governor's certificates of my claim were inclosed therein. These certificates will be sufficient authority for the Governor of West Florida to warrant the surveys, and if any scruple is intertained of my purchases from Mr. Thruston and Captain Posey, I shall remove it by transmitting their bonds, which should have accompanied this letter, could I have been assured of its reaching your hands before your departure. You will readily perceive by the tenor of my last that it is good land or none I am in pursuit of; and that I could wish to have it procured in such a part of the country as from your observation aided by information, you shall judge most valuable, although in accomplishing of it, I pay a little more—For these reasons it is I avoid particular directions. I shall place a generous confidence in your integrity, having no doubt either of your ability or your inclination to serve me. By meeting with Mr. Gist, and others of your old acquaintances, you will have it in your power of forming from their accounts a pretty general, and perhaps, just idea of the nature of the country, and of determining by your own observations then whether the lands on the Mississippi, the Mobile or elsewhere, promise in future to become most valuable—Not till after which I would recommend it to you to fix on your locations. Dr. Connolly is curious in his observations and sensible in his remarks. To him, therefore, I have wrote (as he has been pleased to solicit my correspondence) requesting his assistance to you. I have also taken the liberty of writing to the Governor of West Florida, expressing my hopes of obtaining this land (and more) in case you think proper to locate in that Government, agreeable to the tenor of his Majesty's Proclamation; mentioning at the same time your intended tour, and the descretionary power I have vested in you; and as Lord Dunmore promised me that he would give you an introduction to him, I hope you received it. It would appear to me from the words of his Majesty's Proclamation of October, 1763, that those who obtain land under it are not only entitled to an exemption of quitrents for ten years, but exempt also from cultivation and improvement for the same term. Of this latter, however, please to be informed from the best authority—as in the event of it, I should be strongly inclined to extend my views beyond the quantity I here claim, especially as the time allowed for doing it is not short, and difficult to be complied with. This therefore, is a matter I would beg leave to refer to your consideration, requesting, in case you find the country from a comparative view of it, desirable; good lands easy to be obtained and not difficult to keep under the established rules of government, that you would increase my quantity to fifteen, twenty or twenty-five thousand acres. In short, I could wish to have as much good land located in a body or country more together (for the convenience of superintendence) as I could secure without much difficulty or expense. Even if the first one thousand should be subject to the same laws of cultivation with the last. Various are the reports concerning the quit rents and purchase money of these lands, but it appears evident to me from the strict sense and letter of the Proclamation, that the Governor has no right to exact more than is demanded of any other of his Majesty's colonies; in none of which I believe more than two shillings sterling rent and ten shillings right money are required.

Mount Vernon,
Feby. 20, 1774

Dear Sir:

I have to thank you for your obliging acct. of your trip down the Mississippi, contained in a Letter of the 18th of October, from Winchester. The other Letter therein referred to, I have never yet received, nor did this come to hand till sometime in November as I was returning from Williamsburg.

The contradictory accts. given of the lands upon the Mississippi are really astonishing—some speak of the country as a terrestrial Paradise, whilst others represent it as scarce fit for anything but slaves and brutes. I am not satisfied however from your description of it that I have no cause to regret my dissapointment. The acct. of Lord Hilsborough's sentiments of the Proclamation of 1763, I can view in no other light than as one among many proofs of his Lordship's malignant disposition towards us poor Americans; founded equally in malice, absurdity and error; as it would have puzzled this noble Peer, I am persuaded, to have assigned any plausible reason in support of this opinion.

As I do not know but I may shortly see you in Frederick and assuredly shall at the Assembly, I shall add no more, than that it will always give me pleasure to see you at this place whenever it is convenient to you, and that with complimts. to your good Mother, I remain, Dr. Sir.,

Yr. most Obed. & Hble. Servt.,

GEO. WASHINGTON.

To James Wood, Esq'r
    in Winchester

By favor of Capt. Crawford.

(*Autograph letter hitherto unpublished.*)

CHAPTER XIX

First Reproduction of Military Correspondence — James Wood's Note Book, 1780

The memorandum book of James Wood's official letters from Albemarle Barracks during the year 1780 is given first, although there are earlier letters, because it is a unit, a little mildewed book 3½x5¾, entirely in the handwriting of James Wood, the addresses and subscriptions not complete because the letters are copies of those issued. The exactitude of such memoranda is the more remarkable because of the great scarcity of stationery. Any scrap of paper available is pressed into service. There is no evidence of haste. On the contrary the utmost neatness is shown, exemplifying the value of little things.

At a session held in November, 1762, the General Assembly by royal authority increased the electorate. The freeholder clause was more literally construed. The General Assembly was to be held once in three years at least. On July 17, 1775, the Colonial Convention elected delegates to represent the Colony of Virginia in General Congress then assembling in Philadelphia. In the autumn of 1775 the Convention took charge of necessary legislation, supplanting the House of Burgesses. Six regiments were ordered to be raised in the counties of Augusta, Dunmore, Frederick, Berkeley, Hampshire, Culpeper and Fincastle. One of the regiments raised in the Valley was to be called the German regiment. The General Congress was to appoint general officers; the Convention to appoint field officers, and the several County Courts to appoint Captains, etc., upon recommendation of the General Committee. (Cartmell). Hence the term "Convention troops" found throughout the letters.

The extreme use of capitals used at the time is not observed because of the greater difficulty in reading the text.

MAJOR FORSYTH D. COMY. GEN'L.

Sir:

I am extremely sorry to inform you that this post is now in the most alarming situation for want of provisions: the whole magazine consists of no more than 40876 weight of salt beef, and not a single ounce of flour or Indian meal: the Convention troops have at least fifteen days allowance of flour due them. Without the most unwearied exertions to remove those difficulties, I foresee the most terrible consequences. For God's sake don't delay a moment in proceeding here in order to take the most vigorous measure for alleviating the distress of such a number of people who look to you for supplies.

6th March, 1780

GENERAL SPECHT

Sir:

I have the pleasure of your letter of the 8th instant. The polite terms in which it is couched is extremely flattering to me. The command at this post has devolved upon me at an unlucky period, a time when appearances are very alarming from the apparent scarcity of provisions, but I am happy to inform you that from the fullest investigation the scarcity does not proceed from a real, but from causes altogether artificial, and I have hopes with proper exertions the troops will in future be much better supplied.

This Sir, you may rely on, that nothing shall be wanting on my part to render the situation of the convention army as agreeable as possible.

I should not do justice to the troops if I did not inform you that their conduct since I have had the command has been perfectly consistent with good order and propriety.

I have enclosed a renewal of sergeant Snowar's permission to remain with you and will give Mr. D'Burgsdorff passports for the two noncommissioned officers agreeable to your request.

11 March, 1780.

JOHN HARVIE, ESQ.

Sir:
I have very carefully examined all the papers respecting your wood account, and cannot devise any mode of settlement, but what must make you a very considerable loser; the one prescribed by General Hamilton will be making you an allowance perhaps for a tenth part of the quantity used but I really can't see any other way of doing it, so as to render his accounts passable upon his settlement with the British Auditors.

12th Mar., 1780.

GENERAL WASHINGTON

Sir:
The enclosed are letters from Brigadier General Hamilton who commands the Convention troops, to Major General Phillips at New York. The Brigadier desires me to enclose them to your Excellency with a request that they may be forwarded by the first Flag.

The letters were examined by me before they were sealed. They contain besides several matters respecting the internal police of the Convention troops, a representation of the scarcity of provisions which has prevailed at the post for some time past; he mentions the difficulty the troops labour under in being obliged to give the most exorbitant prices for the necessaries of life and particularly enumerated the prices of some articles. I mention these particulars that your Excellency may judge of the propriety or impropriety of suffering information of this kind to be communicated to the enemy. When I took the Command of this place, I found it in the most alarming situation for want of provision and forage, owing, I believe in a great measure to the extreme severity of the winter and the purchasing commissary not being supplied with an adequate sum of money in the fall of the year when a sufficient quantity of beef and pork might have been readily procured. On this subject I have wrote very fully to the Board of War. A number of the officers of Convention who are and have been for some time Valetudinary, are exceedingly desirous of taking the benefit of the ensuing season at the warm springs in Augusta and Berkeley if they can obtain permission. This indulgence I am not at liberty to grant, by the resolution of Congress of the 21st of August last, unless the indulgence is approved by your Excellency or the Board of War. I should do great injustice to the Troops of Convention if I did not inform you that their conduct since I have had the Command has been perfectly consistent with good order and propriety.

I have the honor of inclosing your Excellency the present state of the Troops of Convention.

16 March, 1780.

Arnold

Nath. Greene

James Wood
Alex. White
Lau. Washington

Horatio Gates

John Hancock

John Jay
Th. Jefferson
Lafayette

BOARD OF WAR

Gentlemen:

I have the honor of inclosing you a return of the present state of the Convention Troops; and a monthly return of the guards doing duty at this Post. When I took the Command, there were one Captain, three Lieutenants, one Ensign, seven Sergeants and thirty-six militia, rank and file, out of which upwards of one half were rendered unfit for duty for want of clothing. The proportion of rank and file compared with the number of officers being so small, I thought it best to discharge the whole.

I am sorry to inform you that we have been for some time past extremely scarce of provisions, but am happy to find from a thorough investigation that the scarcity does not proceed from a real, but from causes altogether artificial and principally from the purchasing Commissary not being supplied with an adequate sum of money in the fall of the year, when any quantity of beef and pork might have been laid in with great ease and convenience. The Commissary of Forage informs me that he has engaged a sufficiency of forage to answer the purpose of his department; upon the whole I have the greatest reason to believe that with proper exertions in the Commissary a sufficient quantity of Indian meal may be procured, but I have great reason to apprehend a very considerable difficulty in procuring a sufficiency of animal food between this and the time grass beef will be fit for use; and would beg leave to suggest that the most probable means of the Post being better supplied in the future would be to make this a separate and distinct department.

On my taking the Command, I found that the line of picquets round the barracks which had been nearly completed, were mostly pulled down, burnt and destroyed by the Convention Troops in the course of the winter, which from the weakness of the guards was impossible to prevent, as they took the advantage of doing it privately in the night. In the present weak state of the guards, I think it would be a necessary precaution to erect a separate magazine detached about six or seven miles from the barracks, for the purpose of storing all the spare arms, ammunition and accoutrements; and to call in a sufficient number of militia as a guard for that particular purpose; if your Honorable Board should approve the measure, I will immediately have it carried into execution.

Several officers of the Convention who are Valetudinary, are extremely anxious to obtain permission to go to the warm springs in Augusta and Berkeley the ensuing season. This indulgence I don't think myself at liberty to grant, unless it is approved by the Board of War, or the Commander-in-Chief. Before I had seen the resolution of Congress of the 21st August last, I had with the concurrence of the Governor of Virginia permitted three or four officers to go to the adjacent counties for a short time, on visits to their acquaintances, who were known to be friends to the Liberties of their country, and at the particular request of a member of Congress, consented to a British officer's going to the warm springs in Augusta.

I should do great injustice to the Troops of Convention if I did not inform you that their conduct since I have had the command, has been perfectly consistent with good order and propriety.

The letter directed to Congress is from Brigadier Hamilton, which contains a representation of the past. May I beg the favor of you to forward the letter directed to His Excellency General Washington and Col. W. A. Henry by the first express.

I have the honor to be, etc.

16th March, 1780.

Colonel Grayson

Dear Sir:

Since I had the pleasure of seeing you in Philadelphia, I have been appointed to the Command at this Post. On my arrival I found everything in the utmost confusion, every department in the staff in the most wretched situation; that of the Commissary without an ounce of flour, and not above eight days allowance of salt beef. We are now in rather a better way, and I hope with industry to have the troops tolerably well supplied in future, if the Commissary can be furnished with money, without which we must inevitably starve. The present state of the guards doing duty here is extremely weak, as you will see by the returns sent to the Board of War. Would it not be a good scheme to pardon all deserters (I mean from the Virginia line) who should repair to this post, and deliver themselves up within a limited time? I am well assured it would have a good effect. By it we should recover a great many men, who will otherwise seek an asylum in the new country and become entirely useless the remainder of the war.

It will always afford me real pleasure to hear from you. If anything worthy your notice should happen in this quarter, you may depend upon having it.

16th March, 1780.

Colonel Archibald Carey

I am favored with your letter of the 17th instant, and am exceedingly obliged by your polite invitation; if I can by any means make it accord with my duty, I shall do myself the honor of waiting on you. It really gives me pain that I am precluded by the resolution of Congress of 21st August last (a copy of which I enclose) from gratifying gentlemen you mention, without the approbation of the Board of War or the Commander-in-Chief being first obtained. You may be assured that I should take great pleasure in obliging gentlemen who have in every respect, so far as I have been able to judge, conducted themselves with the strictest propriety. Before the resolution of Cangress came to my hands, I had given a Captain Blackwood of the 21st regiment and two or three other officers permission to visit the adjacent counties, of which I have since acquainted the Board of War, and as the indulgence was granted before I had any knowledge of the resolve of Congress, I expect to escape censure.

I shall immediately write to the Board of War and hope to obtain permission for Mr. Mumell and the other gentlemen to make the excursion they desire.

I am, etc.

22nd March, 1780.

General Washington

Sir:

I have the honor of enclosing your Excellency the proceedings of a general Court Martial held at this Post yesterday. I would beg leave to add that the prisoner, LaBrun, was enlisted but a few days before he deserted, appears extremely ignorant, and is in my opinion an object worthy of mercy.

I am, etc.

26 March, 1780.

Governor Jefferson

Sir:

I am to acknowledge the receipt of your letter of the 20th instant, with the letters and packets for General Specht, Hamilton and Gall, all of which I immediately forwarded.

I have the honor of enclosing your Excellency a return of the horses belonging to the officers of the Convention Army, and would beg leave to observe that by the reports of the Commissaries of forage and provisions, they have engaged a sufficient quantity of meal and forage to answer the purposes of their departments.

The garrison regiment is at this time in the most wretched situation for want of clothing, particularly shirts, overalls and shoes. There are nearly one half of them unfit for duty for want of those articles, and really make so despicable a figure that I am ashamed to see them on the parade. I must therefore beg your Excellency's interposition that you will be pleased to give the necessary direction to the proper board for furnishing them and will forward the [*illegible*] returns by the first opportunity.

I have also enclosed a copy of the parole taken of Messrs. Geddis, Clark and Hochesly, which I hope will meet with your approbation.

As a number of the Convention officers wish to write by the return of the Flag, I shall be glad to know whether their letters are to be examined by me, or sent altogether to Your Excellency. I see a considerable difficulty in examining those of the Germans, as I have but a very imperfect knowledge of the language.

I am, etc.

27th March, 1780.

EDWARD McGUIRE, ESQ.

Sir:

I received your letter last night. The horse, saddle and bridle you mention certainly belong to Major Irving of the 47th British Regiment. The same night his horse was stolen, a coat belonging to an officer of the 21st regiment was taken.

I am extremely sorry the villain will escape the punishment he so justly merits, by the peculiar situation of Major Irving. I mean his being an enemy and a prisoner of war and therefore not a competent witness by the laws of the land against a citizen; so that I think the only probable means of bringing him to condign punishment would be to send him to Maryland, where his former sentence might with propriety be executed.

I have enclosed one of Major Irving's advertisements and would recommend it to Captain Gilkeson (as it is impossible for the gentleman to come to Winchester, it being out of his parole) to bring the horse saddle and bridle immediately to the post, where he will undoubtedly receive the reward.

I have lately understood that you have received instructions to send the prisoners of war in your neighborhood to this place. If so, I am to inform you that I have no place proper for confining them, and that a great scarcity of provisions has prevailed at this place for sometime past.

I am, etc.

29th March, 1780.

COLONEL SOUTHALL

Sir:

Mr. Hochesly, the British commissary of stores, will be with you in a few days to receive the stores lately arrived in the Flag of Truce from New York and will want a considerable number of waggons. If you can furnish him with waggons you will be pleased to do it, or allow him to hire them, provided he does not exceed the hire given by your department.

If any letters should come by post or otherwise to Richmond, directed to me, may I beg the favor of you to forward them by the earliest conveyance.

I am, etc.

29th March, 1780.

Brigade Major Cleve

Sir:

On the subject of examining letters intended to be sent by the Flag. I have wrote to Governor Jefferson and am in daily expectation of receiving his determination whether the letters are to be examined by me, or sent altogether to him; if I am to do this piece of duty, I shall be at a very great loss, as I am unacquainted with the German language.

I am with great personal respect, Sir, etc.

31st March, 1780.

Brigade Major Cleve

Sir:

I am honoured with your letter of this day. The proposition you make of sending an officer with the letters of the German Corps to Governor Jefferson at Richmond is perfectly agreeable to me, and will give the necessary passport to the officer who may be appointed for that purpose, upon his giving the usual parole.

I hope, Sir, you will believe me sincere when I assure you that I never had an idea that any officer in the convention army would give improper intelligence or do anything inconsistent with their parole of honor; at the same time your own good sense will suggest to you that I am under an indispensable obligation of complying with my instructions in every instance.

I am, etc.

4th April, 1780.

Governor Jefferson

Sir:

I received a letter last night from Colonel Southall informing me that the Flag of Truce had got to her moorings.

My not hearing from you gives me reason to believe that something had turned up to detain you longer at Williamsburg than you expected. I have therefore thought it best to send the guard immediately to Richmond for the purpose of escorting the British paymaster.

I have directed the sergeant to wait on Your Excellency for any orders you may think proper to give him.

The officers of Convention seem exceedingly anxious about sending their letters, and not having received your determination with respect to examining them, at the earnest request of the German Officers, I have permitted one of them, whose parole I have taken, to wait on you with the box of letters belonging to the German Corps. Those of the British, I shall keep until I know your pleasure.

I have the honor to be, etc.

9th April, 1780.

B. GENERAL HAMILTON

Sir:

The subject you mention of soap being made a part of the ration is entirely new to me. I shall inquire into the matter, and nothing final shall be done until I have the pleasure of seeing you.

The order of the 10th instant was in consequence of an information that some of the officers' servants made a practice of associating with the slaves by going to their dances in the night. The order is not meant to prevent their going in the day time to purchase anything for their masters' use which the slaves may have for sale, provided it is with the knowledge and consent of their owners.

I am happy to find it the inclination of the officers in your army to give me as little trouble in my command as possible. Their conduct in every instance since I have been at the post has been perfectly consistent with propriety.

I had an opportunity by Colonel Harvie, who set off yesterday, of sending your letters to Messrs. Clark and Hochesly. The guard of Light Dragoons set off the day before. I am amazed that I have not heard from Governor Jefferson; I wrote him the 27th ultimo on the subject of your letters intended to be sent to New York by the return of the Flag of Truce, and to know whether it was his wish to examine the letters at Richmond, or whether it was his idea that I ought to do it here, and to be ingenuous with you I had hopes of being exempt from the trouble. Whenever I obtain Governor Jefferson's determination, I will immediately inform you.

I am exceedingly obliged to you for the writing paper. I was entirely without and had been obliged to make use of wrapping paper for several days before it came to hand.

I am with great personal esteem, etc.

11th April, 1780.

GOVERNOR JEFFERSON

Sir:

Since I had the honor of writing you the 9th instant, I have received a letter from the President of the Continental Board of War in which he says, "The Guards are in our opinion weak and therefore we think there should be an augmentation by militia. The necessity of removing the arms would be superseded if you have the proper addition to your strength, on which subject we beg you will write to the Executive of the state.

"We think it reasonable to indulge the officers who are sick in their request to reside at the springs, but we do not choose to direct it without the concurrence of the Governor and Council to whom you may always write on the subject of such applications, and as they are best acquainted with the propriety of the places of residence requested by the officers, we shall consent to any in which they concur."

I expect this post will soon be infested with speculators, money changers and villains of every denomination, upon hearing of the arrival of the Flag of Truce. I have thoughts of publishing the inclosed, in hopes of restricting them in some measure. If your Excellency shou'd approve the idea, you will be pleased to give the paper to Captain Rice, who will get it published. If not, be so good as to destroy it.

A Captain Sheldon of the British has requested me to mention his desire of making a visit to Governor Hamilton at Williamsburg.

I received a letter some time ago from Colonel Arch. Carey requesting me to permit four or five of the British officers to make him a visit. I shou'd be very happy in gratifying the Colonel as well as the gentlemen, if you approve it.

I am, etc.

13th April, 1780.

Officer Commanding at Barracks

Sir:

The bearer Edward Tarr (who is a free man) has lately been robbed of a considerable sum of money in paper and specie by a woman who lived with him. He suspects one Richardson of the Royal Artillery to be an accomplice. He has obtained a warrant from a Civil Magistrate to search for his money and other effects which were taken at the same time, and to apprehend the culprits. You will be pleased to direct that no insult be offered to the constable while in the execution of his office and that Richardson be delivered to him to be examined by the magistrate.

I am, etc.

17th April, 1780.

Field Officer of the Day

Sir:

As it is improper that the orders given to the Light Dragoons should be made public, you will be pleased to direct the noncommissioned officer to patrol the different roads, at the times you may think proper to appoint, as well by night as by day, giving him positive orders to apprehend and bring to the main guard, either noncommissioned or privates who shall be found out of the bounds, belonging to the Garrison or Convention troops, who have not papers.

On the vigilance of the Light Dragoons a great deal depends, and any neglect of duty or remissness in them will meet with the severest punishment.

When you are relieved be pleased to communicate those orders to the field officer on duty. I wou'd wish that the times of making the patrols both night and day shou'd constantly vary, as it will increase the difficulty of evading them.

I am, etc.

18th April, 1780.

GOVERNOR JEFFERSON

Sir:

Since I had the honor of writing your Excellency, I find a Captain Cherry of the western battalion, who was a supernumerary Captain in the Virginia line, conceives himself injured in his rank. He says that he was appointed a Captain by the Governor and Council in June or July, that he neither received money or recruiting instructions; that he has received his commission dated in November last, and subsequent to those of Captain Kinley, who was a Supernumerary Lieutenant and Captain Miller who was never before in any service. Captain Cherry has requested me to mention the matter to your Excellency. I wou'd beg leave to observe that he served in the 4th Virginia Regiment with reputation until he became supernumerary in the year 1778.

I am requested by General Hamilton to desire your permission for Lieut. W. O. Neill of the British to go to the Warm Springs. The surgeons have given it as their opinion that there is great probability of his losing the use of a limb, and have recommended the use of the bath.

I am, etc.

23rd April, 1780.

GOVERNOR JEFFERSON

Sir:

I had the honor sometime ago of writing your Excellency on the subject of Captain Cherry's rank, and respecting the applications of some of the British officers, but have not received your determination on those points.

Since my last we have been reinforced by detachments of Colonel Crocket's Corps, about sixty rank and file with their officers, which I think will supersede the necessity of calling in the militia. I am under great apprehension the troops will suffer for want of salt provisions before grass beef will be fit for use. Our supplies have been very partial of late, and extremely bad in quality. The troops have twenty days meal due them this day.

I have understood that Congress have called upon the state for the necessary supplies of the Post in future; if this matter shou'd come before the Assembly, I wou'd very willingly attend them in order to give them any information in my power, being well assured that the Post cannot be properly supported without some very material alterations.

We have under close confinement upwards of sixty prisoners of war who have heretofore deserted and been retaken; I must think this a very improper place to confine them, as we have no place of security, and are obliged to keep a number of sentries, notwithstanding which they very frequently escape.

I have enclosed your Excellency the proceedings of a General Court Martial: the unhappy culprit is an Indian and had made a practice of taking the Bounty in different counties; but as desertion has not been very prevalent at the post, I hope he may be pardoned.

I am, etc.

15th May, 1780.

General Hamilton

Sir:

I have received your letter of yesterday, and sincerely lament the situation of the Troops; no exertion in my power has been wanting to remove the difficulty in procuring supplies. I shall direct the quarter master to have an Express in readiness whenever you may think proper to dispatch him. At the same time I wou'd recommend the sending your letters by post, as the expense of an express will be enormous. There is now at Mr. Hochesly's a Mr. Pringle March of Baltimore, who I dare say cou'd be prevailed upon to wait for Dispatches, and who cou'd readily forward them from thence by post to Philadelphia. I should be glad to have the state of the Convention Army, if possible, before the Express sets off.

I am, etc.

22d May, 1780.

Board of War

Sir:

General Hamilton who commands the Convention troops has made application to me for an opportunity of representing to your Honorable Board the present situation of the Troops. When I last had the honor of writing you I expressed my apprehension that it would be extremely difficult to supply the Post with meat before grass beef wou'd be fit for use. I am now very sorry to inform you that our supplies of late have been very partial and insufficient, insomuch that there is at this time twenty-five days meat due the troops, and I am under the disagreeable necessity of observing that there is no probability of procuring meat without the Purchasing Company cou'd be supplied immediately with a very large sum of money. He has been entirely without for a considerable time past; this you may rely on, that no exertion on my part has been wanting.

I was happy enough to have anticipated your wishes in allowing the Troops to procure provisions when we cou'd not supply them by taking off the former restriction, and am happy to find the effect very different from what was expected. In two weeks after it every kind of provision and vegetable fell very considerably in the price, owing to the quantity brought in being much larger than the Troops cou'd find money to purchase.

I have never seen the resolves of Congress referred to in your letter. By some mistake they were not inclosed. I immediately wrote Governor Jefferson on the receipt of your letter, respecting the augmentation of the guards by dragoons from the militia, but have not as yet received his answer. Since the last return we have been reinforced by about forty recruits raised for the purpose of defending the Frontier against the Indians and who have been ordered by the Governor and Council to do duty at this Post till further orders.

I have the honor of inclosing you the present state of the Troops of Convention and am, etc.

24th May, 1780.

GENERAL WILKINSON

Sir:

The Commissary of Hides Department at this Post is in the most wretched situation, owing entirely to the want of an adequate sum of money to carry it on to advantage. Mr. Marche who superintends the Business is exteremely active and industrious and if he was properly supplied with money wou'd, I am well assured, make it an object of great consequence to the states.

I am, etc.

24th May, 1780.

GOVERNOR JEFFERSON

Sir:

The situation of this Post at present is really shocking. The Troops are deficient since the 10th April about 28 days allowance of meat, the different Staff Departments unable to make purchases for want of money, and a great part of the salt provision sent from Richmond so exceeding bad that after being brought here at an enormous expense is entirely unfit for use; an inspection of the Provision sent from thence would be a great saving to the public. Several of the Convention officers have made application to remove from their present quarters to Louisa and the adjacent counties, which I did not think myself at liberty to grant, but at their request promised to make your Excellency acquainted with their desire.

General Hamilton has desired permission of me for a Quarter Master Serg. Fleming to go to New York in the Flag; he alleges that the sergeant was exchanged but returned for the purpose of settling his accounts. I have inclosed the only papers he has produced in support of his application, and beg leave to refer the matter to your Excellency.

I am, etc.

31st May, 1780.

B. GENERAL HAMILTON

Sir:

It has always given me real pain that the Convention troops could not be better supplied. No exertion on my part has been wanting. I have made frequent and repeated representations of the state of the post to Congress, the Board of War and Executive of Virginia. In my last to the Board of War I inclosed your letters, which I sent by a Mr. Thompson then on his way to Philadelphia who engaged to deliver them.

I have directed the Commissary not to issue more than two rations of fish weekly. Our late deficiency of meat has been owing principally to the want of a sufficient number of waggons. I have had two or three hands out for ten days past endeavoring to procure an additional number of waggons.

I am, etc.

5th June, 1780.

GOVERNOR JEFFERSON

Sir:

I am extremely sorry that I am under the disagreeable necessity of being so troublesome to you in repeating the distressed situation of this Post.

As our whole supplies of meat are brought from Richmond by land, we find notwithstanding every exertion having been used to procure a sufficient number of waggons, that it is really impossible to procure more than one half the quantity absolutely necessary. This must be owing to the Quartermaster's Department being for some time past entirely without money and his being restricted to a certain price, in my opinion quite inadequate to the service. Captain Rice, the principal of the department, will have the honor of waiting on your Excellency. To him I must beg leave to refer for particulars.

I wrote to your Excellency some time ago respecting the Prisoners of war who are closely confined. I shall be exceedingly obliged to you for your direction concerning them. Their close confinement and bad provisions has brought on them violent symptoms of the scurvy. The surgeons are of opinion that many of them must perish unless they are enlarged or removed to a better air.

I am, etc.

8th June, 1780.

JOHN WALKER, ESQUIRE

Sir:

I have had upwards of Forty of the Convention Troops who deserted and were retaken, closely confined at this Post for many months past, and who are considered as Prisoners of War. I represented the disagreeable situation they were in to the Governor who has recommended it to me to send them to Frederick Town in Maryland, and that I wou'd apply to one of the delegates from this state to procure an order from Congress or the Board of War to the proper person for receiving and providing for them. I shall accordingly send them off with a guard on the 14th. I must therefore request that you will procure the necessary instructions to the Commissary of Prisoners, Quartermaster and Commissary of provisions at Frederick Town.

The bearer, Mr. St. Lawrence, will deliver them with all possible Expedition; and although he does not go to Philadelphia for the express purpose of delivering this letter, yet I think he ought to be made some Compensation, as I have prevailed upon him to set off sooner than he intended, and he has engaged to use the greatest Expedition.

I am, etc.

11th June, 1780.

GOVERNOR JEFFERSON

Sir:

I am honored with your letter of the 9th instant with the several inclosures, and shall think myself happy if I am able to carry your ideas into Execution. I have issued peremptory orders for all the officers without distinction to repair within five days to the Barracks, and shall certainly enforce them with strictness; at the same time I must beg leave to suggest it as my opinion that in case it shou'd be necessary to remove the troops, it wou'd have greatly facilitated their march for the officers to have remained at their Quarters; they will certainly when confined to the limit of the Barracks conceive themselves discharged from their paroles, will encourage desertion among the soldiery, and in case of being obliged to remove, throw every obstruction in the way. It will be altogether impossible to secure the Troops and prevent desertion with the Guards I have, and the state of Provisions and the prospects of procuring supplies will not admit of my calling in any of the militia at present.

From the state of the post which I have frequently made to your Excellency, you will please to observe that the waggons which are employed are not more than half sufficient to transport Provisions and Forage, and that unless my hands are strengthened by Government, it will be morally impossible for me to remove such a body of men without a day's provision beforehand, without money to purchase, or without authority to impress Carriages, Horses, Provision or Forage.

I am well assured had the Assembly extended their resolution no farther than to have restricted the officers' limits to the County, and called in all their supernumerary servants, it wou'd have answered a much better purpose. I hope I shall be excused for giving my opinion thus freely, as your Excellency may be assured it proceeds from my zeal for the service.

I shall immediately order two hundred of the militia from each of the Counties of Albemarle and Augusta to be appointed and held in the most perfect readiness to march at the shortest notice. At the present I am inclinable to think in case of the rapid approach of the Enemy, it wou'd be better to march the Troops through Orange and Culpeper and cross over at Chester's Gap. My reason for this is that if the Convention troops shou'd be the object of the Enemy, they will most certainly keep the upper road as far as possible above the Blue Ridge, and there will be a much better prospect of my being supplied that route than the other.

I shall be extremely glad to be informed by the return of the Light Dragoon whether the officers are to be closely confined to their Barracks. Whether some of them who have built huts within the distance of four miles are to be removed? and whether I am to demand other Paroles of them and what the Tenor of the new ones are to be?

General Hamilton requests to know whether the General Officers, their aides, Brigade Majors and servants are to be included. He desires me to inform you that they will willingly give any Parole that may be thought necessary.

I must again repeat that without the most ample supplies of money to the different Staff Departments, the Troops when they are collected cannot be supplied at the Barracks.

I have been closely confined for five days past with a violent fever. It is with the greatest difficulty I sit up to write, therefore hope your Excellency will excuse all imperfection in this letter.

I have the honor to be, etc.

13th June, 1780.

LIEUT. TAYLOR

Sir:

I have thought proper to reduce the number of your Command to a Sergeant, Corporal and Twelve Privates of the Regiment of Guards and a Corporal and four Light Dragoons, and as there will be no possibility of drawing provisions between this Post and Winchester, you will be pleased to draw six days' Provision, or seven if you should think it necessary, for which you have an order inclosed to the Commissary. You will parade your guard on Tuesday as early as possible, and receive the prisoners of war from the main Guard, taking a list of their names, the Corps to which they belong, and a particular description of each, and proceed with them the nearest route to Winchester, quartering them on your march in barns or out houses the most likely to prevent Escapes, posting a sufficient number of sentries to secure them effectually.

I shall rely on your utmost attention to the discipline of your detachment and that you prevent them from doing the least injury to the Inhabitants through which you pass. You will receive letters to the County Lieutenant of Frederick, the Commissary of Prisoners and Quarter master at Winchester. I have requested that the Prisoners may be received. If the requisition is agreed to, you will please to deliver them to Mr. Edward McGuire, taking his Receipt for them. On the contrary shou'd it be refused, you will draw a sufficient quantity of provisions at Winchester to serve your detachment and proceed to Frederick Town in Maryland and deliver your charge to the Person appointed to receive them.

I am, etc.

13th June, 1780.

COUNTY LIEUTENANTS ALBEMARLE AND AUGUSTA

Sir:

The rapid Progress of the Enemy from South to North Carolina has induced his Excellency the Governor with the advice of the Council to impower me to call upon any number of the Militia of your County whenever I may think the Public Security requires it. You will be pleased, therefore, to hold two hundred men with their proper officers in the most perfect readiness, properly armed and accoutred to march at the shortest notice. I hope the men will attend in a very particular manner to this order. At the same time they may be assured that I will not call upon them without an absolute necessity.

I am, etc.

13th June, 1780.

CAPTAIN READ

Sir:

It has been thought expedient in the present situation of the Enemy to the southward to form a line of communication from thence to this post for the purpose of facilitating the necessary intelligence. You will be pleased to select twelve Light Dragoons, the most to be depended on for their fidelity and industry and take command of them yourself, observing in a very particular manner from time to time the following instruction, viz. to have your party ready to march tomorrow morning when you will take the most direct route towards Cross Creek in North Carolina. At the distance of every forty miles you will leave a Light Dragoon at a proper station and proceed yourself (constantly keeping one of the Dragoons with you) as near the Enemy as you can consistent with safety, where you will remain, always changing your Position with that of the Enemy and observing to send proper instruction to the Dragoons in your rear to make the necessary changes in their Stations, in order to straighten the line of Communication.

Through those Dragoons you will please to communicate to me from time to time every important movement of the enemy. The Dragoons must go their distance from Post to Post by night and by day without regard to weather, taking receipts of the Hour and Minute at which they deliver to each other their Dispatches.

I must recommend the utmost caution as you will be in a Country generally disaffected, and always liable to be surprized and taken to the Enemy. You will take the two thousand pounds received from the Governor with you for the purpose of defraying contingent Expenses, taking particular care to procure proper Vouchers for your expenditures. I have the utmost confidence in your judgment, vigilance and Zeal for the service, and very sincerely wish you an agreeable tour and safe return.

I am, etc.

13 June, 1780.

GOVERNOR JEFFERSON

Sir:

I am extremely sorry to inform you that Desertion has prevailed among the Troops in a very great degree since the late orders. I have retaken near one hundred and fifty within a few days. How many have escaped I cannot at present ascertain.

I sent off Captain Read on Thursday last week with a party of Horse to the southward and have fixed a Light Dragoon at Rutherford's Ordinary. I sent off a Guard with the prisoners of war a week ago with directions to the Commissary of Prisoners at Winchester to receive them if they can be supplied with provisions. If not, I directed the officer to proceed with them to Frederick Town. On this subject I wrote to the Board of War a few days before I sent them off.

I am, etc.

17th June, 1780.

GOVERNOR JEFFERSON

Sir:

Since my return I have received a letter from the Board of War, with a resolution of Congress, copies of which I have the honor of inclosing your Excellency; as also a copy of the proceedings of the General Court Martial, which I mentioned to you at the Council Board. The unhappy Culprit I think an object worthy of mercy. He is a Frenchman, appears extremely ignorant and has undergone a long and painful confinement in irons ever since the 20th of March last.

The Commissioners in this county are busy and it is hoped will be able to collect some salt Provisions, which with what shall be collected in the adjacent Counties I hope you will think expedient to order for the use of this Post.

The Quarter-master has not been able to increase the number of waggons and he is under great apprehension that those now in the service will leave it, unless they are immediately paid the arrears due them. I shall hope for your instructions by the return of the Light Dragoons.

I am, etc.

13th July, 1780.

GENERAL HAMILTON

Sir:

I shall be much obliged to you to direct the Officers of the Convention Army to make out a list of their servants to be delivered to you, and transmitted to me as soon as possible; I mean to call in all the old papers and to issue new ones, allowing each officer one servant to pass to and from the Barracks and seven miles round his master's Quarters, and the other servants as usual.

If the Gentlemen will take the trouble individually to write the Papers agreeable to the usual form it will be easing me of a good deal of trouble.

I am, etc.

17th July, 1780.

GOVERNOR JEFFERSON

Sir:

I am induced at the earnest request of the Captains and Subalterns of the Regiment of Guards to send a Light Dragoon with their letter to your Excellency. They appear to be so much disgusted by the Officers in the other regiment getting a supply of clothing that they seem determined to quit the service unless they are supplied in a short time.

Colonel Crockett has made application to me for an order on the Commissary of Hides for as much leather as will make each of his men a shot Pouch and a Hoppess strap. As the Tan yard is carried on at Continental expense, I don't think myself at liberty to do it without your Excellency's direction, Colonel Crockett's being a State Battalion.

Mr. Money, a Chaplain belonging to the British, who is in a bad state of Health is very desirous of going to the warm springs. He has lost an eye and still has a violent inflammation in the other. A Lieutenant McNeill who obtained your permission to go there sometime ago, lately sent an Express requesting that a surgeon might be sent to him, being in a dangerous situation. As his case wou'd not admit of delay, I permitted Dr. Bowen to proceed to the springs for that Purpose.

The Commissioners in this County have not been able as yet to collect above a thousand weight of salt Provisions. If your orders respecting live stock have not already been sent to this and the circumjacent counties, and you will be pleased to send them by the return of the Dragoon, I will immediately forward them.

The Convention troops are now fifty-four days in arrear of their allowance of meat, since the first of May last. I am exceedingly sorry to be under the necessity of troubling your Excellency so often.

I have the honor to be, etc.

21st July, 1780.

Governor Jefferson

Sir:

I am honored with your letter of the 28th ultimo. In answer to it I am to inform your Excellency that my Regiment was marched in the Spring 1777 to the Northward without arms, and that I drew arms and accoutrements for them out of the Continental Magazine in Philadelphia. When I took command of the regiment four of the companies were stationed at different posts on the Ohio, armed with rifles belonging to the state, which I was directed by the Board of War to put into the hands of the militia who relieved those Companies, which I accordingly did.

We have received but few cattle from the Commissioners. The difficulty in collecting them is very great and will be attended with considerable expense. I have thought it best to appoint a Bullock master and five Drovers, who find their own Horses, to be constantly employed in this Business, which I hope will be approved by your Excellency and the Council. I have not made any agreement with them respecting their wages, which I must beg leave to refer to your consideration. In the mean time I have directed that they shou'd draw the usual allowance of Provision and Forage.

I have the honor to be, etc.

12th August, 1780.

CHAPTER XX

Letters With Famous Autographs

I have heard nothing from Lord Latham and expected him here before this time as I am accused of obstructing His Majesty's Service and am to answer that accusation on the last day of the General Court before the Governor & Council. I request you will be pleased to attend there that day with your orders received of me from time to time whilst you was in the service and to answer such questions as that Honorable Board are pleased to ask relative to that affair. I am with esteem,
>   My Dear Captain,
>   Your Most Obedt. humble Serv't.
>   ADAM STEPHEN.

Octo. 28th, 1764.
Captain Wood.

(*Endorsement on back*)

To Capt. James Wood, of the Frederick Militia.

Sir:
   I have herewith troubled you with a warrant for the purpose of reinlisting the Virginia Troops in your Brigade and when you send it to the Pay-Master General, if you will direct the Officer who may carry it to call at Head-quarters I will transmit you the necessary instructions or if an earlier opportunity offers, I will do it then,
>   I am Sir,
>   Yr. Mo. Obet. Serv.
>   GO. WASHINGTON.

West Point, 19 September, 1778.

P. S.
   Do not delay a moment in sending for the money, and let me beseech you to use every exertion possible to facilitate the recruiting the men in General Scott's Brigade. Endorse the warr't. to the Off'r. who goes for yr. money.
>   G. W————N.

Colo. Wood, Commandant of General Scott's Brigade.

   NOTE: The body of the above letter was written by Alexander Hamilton, who was Geo. Washington's Secretary, and was signed by Geo. Washington, also the P. S. was written and signed by Geo. Washington.

Staunton, March 8, 1780.

Sir:

With a great Deal of Pleasure I have heard that the Command of the Troops of Convention which was in Colo. Bland's Hands and vacant since several months is devolved upon You.

The Troops have wished for your arrival long ago, convinced that in all just Demands You will give them all Relief that lies in Your Power; I therefore recommend them to Your best Protection and assure you, that Brigadier General Hamilton as well as I will take a particular care, that all Orders, which you may think proper to give them, shall be punctually executed, and that it will be a real pleasure for us to give you Proofs of our personal Esteem.

Not being able yet to come nearer to the Barracks, but obliged to stay at Staunton about 4 weeks longer, I beseech you, to procure to my Aid-de-Camp Lt. de Burgsdorff (who will have the honor to deliver you this letter) two Passes for orderly Non-Commissioned Officers, that when it is necessary they may be sent hither. Lt. de Burgsdorff will deliver You a Pass for Serg't. Snower of the 47th Regiment Brittish, signed by Colonel Bland, which you will please to renew.

I will be answerable that these Passes shall be employed to no other use, than what they are asked for.

I am with particular Esteem,

Sir,
Your Most obed't.
and most humble Serv't.
J. W. SPECHT, *Brig.-Gen'l.*

(*Autographed and signed*)

Richmond, May 13, 1780.

Sir:

Permission having been granted by Sir Henry Clinton to two American Officers to come out on parole on condition that the same indulgence should be granted to Lord Torgohicken and Lt. Hadden of the Convention prisoners and these gentlemen desirous of going to New York in the Flag Patsy now lying at this place you will be pleased to furnish them with passports and take proper paroles. Mr. Hochesley and Mr. Collier of the Convention being also exchanged you will be pleased to furnish them with passports to New York, taking such paroles and prescribing such routes as you shall deem proper unless either of them should choose to go by the Flag in which case the same measures will be taken by you as in the case of the gentlemen first above mentioned. Gen'l. Washington has informed me of these exchanges. I am Sir,

Your very Humble Servant,
TH. JEFFERSON.

The Governor's compliments to Colo. Wood. He is sorry he was preengaged. Gene. Gates dines with the governor and wishes to have conversation with Colo. Wood. perhaps for this reason he might excuse himself from his enjoyment.
July 7, 1780.

Mrs. Schuyler's Compliments to the dear Col. Wood Should esteem it a particular favor wou'd he honor her with a visit to morrow morn. Will My dear sir ever view me in the light of an effectionate friend—I gratefully acknowledge such you have ever been to
       your sincere Shinah Schuyler.
Thursday Night.

          In Council, Annapolis,
          21st. December, 1780.
Sir:
 We received yours of the 15th. & 17th. inst. Mr. Murdock by this opportunity will receive £1000 which, we hope, will obviate the difficulties you have been involved in by the Sheriffs not paying our orders. From your representation of Mr. Geddes's conduct we should be inclined to comply with Brig. General Hamilton's request, but as he may transact his business without going to Baltimore himself, the indulgence desired is unnecessary. We are sir.
    Your Mo. Obed't. Servts.
         Tho. S. Lee.
Colo. James Wood.

         Richmond, Jan. 12, 1781.
Sir:
 The enemy having retired from this place & fallen down James River, and the German Prisoners being represented by you to be in a distressing situation for want of covering & food, you will be pleased to march them back again to the Barracks in Albemarle.
    I am Sir,
    Your very humble servt.,
        Th. Jefferson.

        Richmond, Feb. 13th, 1781.
Sir:
 I have laid before the Council the several certificates of enlistment you were pleased to inclose to me. They are very clear that an enlistment to serve until the prisoners should be removed from Albemarle can by no fair construction be deemed at an end by any occasional crossing of the line with an intention to return. A man is not said to be removed from his residence by taking a journey from it. You will find endorsed on two certificates an opinion of the Board in

favour of the parties. We cannot enlist men for twelve months, but shall be very glad to re-enlist these for the War, as I have no doubt but the Germans will be removed. Mr. Brown about a fortnight ago received money to purchase three months' animal food for the Germans; meal he is authorized to procure under the provision law.

      I am with great esteem Sir,
      Your most obedt. Servt.
         TH. JEFFERSON.

        Richmond, Feb'y. 15th, 1781.
Sir:

I have just received information from General Green that Lord Cornwallis maddened by his losses at the Cowpens and Georgetown has burnt his own wagons to enable himself to move with facility, and has pressed forward as far as the Moravian towns. General Green being obliged to retire before him with an inferior force. We are endeavoring to gather a force around him from which I hope he will not escape, nevertheless as the event is hastening on, till it be in some measure known, I think it will not only be prudent for you not to leave your present post, but to hold the Convention troops and guards in readiness to march at a moment's warning. I would also advise that you recall Capt. Reed's troops, as it may be more useful with you, if it be necessary to remove the Germans, and will be wanting here, should their removal be not necessary. I am with much esteem sir

    Your Most obed't. humble ser't.
        TH. JEFFERSON.

        Richmond, Feb. 18, 1781.
Sir:

Lord Cornwallis's approaches are so rapid that we know not where they will terminate. He was at Boyd's Ferry on the 14th inst. Without Arms as our Countrymen are, there is no safety for the Convention troops, but in their removal. You will therefore be pleased to remove them in the instant of receiving this, only allowing them time to package their Baggage, that it may follow them in waggons. As the Prisoners taken at the Cow-Pens will be at Staunton by the time this reaches you, & will proceed on along that Valley, I think it most advisable that you should keep below the Blue-ridge. But of this you will judge yourself. Time does not allow me to send you formal Warrants for taking Provisions: I can therefore only give you this general authority to issue such Warrants yourself. I have given notice to Congress of this measure, who will no doubt send you orders at what place these people are to end their Journey.

    I am with much respect & esteem,
      Sir,
    Your most obedt. humbl. Servt.
        TH. JEFFERSON.

Brooklyn, March 19th, 1781.
Sir:

The universall Satisfaction Your generous Conduct has given all the gentlemen of the Brunswick Troops of Convention, as evry one gratefully acknowledges who have been exchanged, and Brigadier General Specht in particular, induces me to return you my warmest thanks for that kindness and attention you, Sir, have so politely shown the Troops of His Serene Highness, my Master; and to assure you that the continuance of such behavior, which is the undoubted emanation of a noble mind, will ever be remembered personally by myself and generally by the whole of the Troops of Brunswick, who have been under your care, with the utmost gratitude. I am convinced the same Honorable Sentiments that has hitherto influenced your actions towards them will ever prevail on You, Sir, to follow their dictates and alleviate the unavoidable attendant misfortunes of Captivity which every Heart impressed with your sensations must feel. Repeating to you, Sir, the sincerity of my thanks and flattering ideas of your favor towards the said Troops, I have only to assure you, Sir, of the obligations I feel myself under, and to add with what perfect truth I have the honor of being.
    Sir,
     Your very Obedient,
      Humble Servant.
       RIEDESEL.

Colonel Wood.
Lea Lea Lea.
General (Baron) Riedesel.

Leonard's Farm, 13th April, 1781.
Sir:

I have received a letter from Mr. Loring Commisary of Prisoners, dated New York, the first of April, mentioning that Lt. Gen'l. Sir Henry Clinton had given his consent that Lt. Col. Hill of the Troops of Convention may be immediately exchanged on account of his bad state of health; and should it not be agreed to, that Col. Hill might have your permission to go on parole to New York, which I hope you will have no difficulty in granting, should the exchange fail as proposed in Mr. Commissary General Loring's letter to Mr. Shrinnor, a copy of which I here enclose. I am
    Sir,
     Your Most Obed't. servant.
      JAS. HAMILTON.

Col. Wood.

Wilderness, 4 June, 1781.
Dr. Sir:

I wrote you yesterday enclosing the resolve of Congress and the Board of War's letter, respecting the removal of the Convention

Troops from Winchester to the Eastern States, requesting you to march them from that place immediately. The enemy's having pushed a considerable body of horse to Louisa Court House last evening, intended as they give out against Charlottesville, and the insurrection in Hamshire being more considerable than I at first apprehended renders the removal of the Convention Troops a matter of the highest importance, more especially if the information I received this day is to be relied on that 15 sail of vessels appeared in Powtomack——— I have the honor to be
    Your Most Obed't. Servant.
      (Signed) LAFAYETTE.
Coln. Wood.

  Colo. Taylor will please expedite the march of the Troops with all the expedition possible.
      (Signed) J WOOD.

      Camp before '96, June 15, 1781.
Sir:
  I have received your favor of the 2nd. Ultimo.
  That part which respects Dr. Oliphant has been copied and forwarded to Lt.-Colonel Balfour the Commandant at Charles Town. I have not heard from him upon the subject, but hope the determination of Congress will produce the desired effect.
    I am Sir,
     with esteem.
    your very hum'l. Serv't.
      (Signed) NATH. GREENE.
Colo. Jas. Wood.

      York Town, Aug. 15th, 1781.
Sir:
  Knowing the enclosed to be from General Gist on public Service, I took the liberty to open it. Colonel Miller carrys letters from me to countermand the March of the Troops from the several Cantonements, but should any arrive at Lancaster and not have received them, I request you will be so good as to inform the officers it is my desire that they return.
    I am sir,
    Your Most Obedint Servant.
      WM. IRVINE.
Col. Wood.
    (Endorsement on back)
PUBLIC SERVICE.
Col. James Wood.
Lancaster.
(Favour of Col. Miller).

Philadelphia, Jan. 6, 1783.

Having unluckily got the blade broke of the sword you were so kind as to lend me. I brought it with me to this place & have got a new blade made to the same handle & scabbord. Being just on my departure for Europe, I leave it with Mr. Madison, one of our delegates, who will delivery it to your order. Accept my sincere thanks for the friendly loan of it & assurances of the esteem & respect with which I am, Dr. Sir,
    Your Most obedt. humble Servt.
          TH. JEFFERSON.
Colo. James Wood, Winchester.

Office of Finance, 10th January, 1783.

Sir:

I have received your favor of the 7th. of last month and would write an answer particularly directed to the several objects of its contents, but I find it is unnecessary to trouble you on the subject. The Minister of War having determined to remove the prisoners from Winchester and the Legion of Armand being already removed. I am sir with perfect respect
    Your Most Obedient & Humble Servant,
      (Signed) ROBT. MORRIS.
Colo. Wood, at Winchester in Virginia.

3rd April, 1783.

Dear Colonel:

Mrs. Gates received the letter you was so obliging to forward to her from Mrs. R. Rutherford's. I got home Sunday night and found her alarmingly low and ill. Dr. Mechey who is now with her thinks her in no immediate danger and all that remains to do is to restore her wonted strength. This will take time and necessarily detain me here longer than I intended, but peace is proclaimed in Europe and will be so in America, perhaps is so this day, therefore the presence of particular officers may be dispensed with. Monday Surnight Congress, that is Nine States passed the Commutation Act, Viz; for allowing five years full pay instead of half pay to such officers as choose to accept it. There now only wants funds to be established for the regular payment of the Interest and that business is finished. The Pay-Master Gen'l. is gone by order of Congress to the Army to settle the amounts and ascertain the balance due. America is surely too honorable to be unjust to a brave body of men who after eight years' toil and hazard have established her freedom and independence. My very respectful compliments to Mrs. Wood and your fireside concludes me
    Dr. Col., Yr. Affectinate Humble Serv't,
          HORATIO GATES.
Addressed to Col. James Wood, Winchester.
(*Autograph letter signed*).

West Point 29th Sept. 1770.

Dr Sr

Do not delay a moment in sending for the Money — and let no boaschyer [boat?] for the money exertion hop [be] able to face. he no every exertion possible to face. [cite?] the Recruiting of the Men in Gen.l [Gen.ls?] Scotts Brigade. endorse the[?] or hear[n] to the off.r [officer] who goes on s Jersey Money.

Gs Washington

Cl. Jno. Dick, Ass.t D. Q. M. G. [or similar]

D.10.1 Ass.t D. Commandant

CHAPTER XXI

Garrison Orders, Court Martials, Letters, Etc., 1775-1789, Chronologically Arranged

Romney, Feb. 9, 1876.

Cousin Julia:

The Historical Society of our honored Mother State, Virginia, has conferred upon me the distinguished office of examining and preparing for publication such material parts of the Journals and Correspondence of our Kinsman, Gov. James Wood, as may be important to elucidate an important era in our nation's history.

I should hesitate to ask the privilege of examining such of his papers as exist at "Glen Burnie" if I did not stand in the place of direct relationship to both him and you.

My honored mother bore her middle name of "Jean" after Jean Moncure, General Wood's wife, and my grandmother in her orphanage was reared at her house at Richmond.

Will you kindly grant the permission I ask, and either allow the papers to be sent here to me, or that I come to Winchester and spend a few days in the examination, and believe me with the kindest wishes for your health and welfare,

With respect and affection,
Yours,
AND. W. KERCHEVAL.

The privilege of examining the papers was not granted, and they appear in this volume for the first time.

Charles Town, South Carolina, 3d June, 1775.

Hond. Sir:

I am informed by several gentlemen from your parts, and by Colo. Hight particularly, that there is two hundred thousand acres of land laid out on the Ohio River for those men, that were in the engagement in the year 1754 with Colo. Washington and your honour at the Meadows.

I have therefore taken this opportunity to acquaint your honour that I am in the Land of the living, and to beg you will write me a Letter by Colo. Hight or by the post and directed to the Post Office in Charles Town, in which letter be pleased to inform me whether it is worth my while to come and claim my property in that Survey on the Ohio or whether there is any objections against my receiving it as my dividend in the Land. Your answer to this by Colo. Hight or the post will much oblige.

      Hond. Sir,

        your most obedt. humb. servt.,

            PHILEMON WATERS.

To Colo. Adam Stephen in Virginia.

(Copy)

Mr. Philemon Waters.

Sir:

 I receivd. your favor by Jacob Hite, and had no opportunity of answering before this.

 You are intituled to 600 acres of Land by your being at the battle of the Meadows, and had it depended on me you should have had a double share for firing the first gun at the Enemy that day July 3d. 1754.

 That Country is settled 100 miles below Fort Pitt, that is 150 miles below Gist's Plantation, and there is a great run to it, as ever was to Carolina. They could raise about 6000 fighting men over the Mountain.

 They whip the Indians whenever saucy.

 It will be an excellent Country in a short time, and some spots of Land sell at a pound per acre already; I will be glad to hear of your welfare, and am,

      Dr. Phil,
      Your most Humble Servt.,

           ADAM STEPHEN.

Berkeley County, Virginia.
July 17th, 1773.
To Mr. Philemon Waters,
in Charles Town, Carolina.
(Copy)

 I do hereby certifie that the Bearer Mr. Philemon Waters was a Soldier at the battle of the Great Meadows in the year 1754, and that he this day applied to me to receive his claim to Land under Mr. Dinwiddie's proclamation of 1754. But as the 200,000 acres granted by that proclamation hath been long since surveyed, distributed and patents issued in the names of those who put in their claim before Novr. 1773, it is not in my power to give him any relief now.

 Given under my hand this 20th day of April, 1775.

(Copy)   GO. WASHINGTON.

Virginia, Prince William County, Sct. 23rd. May, 1775.

This day came before me the subscriber one of his Majesty's Justices of the Peace for the said County, Philemon Waters Junior of Orrangeburg District in the Colony of South Carolina and made oath on the holy Evangelists of Almighty God that he being a Soldier at the battle of the Great Meadows in the year one thousand seven hundred and fifty-four became intitled to a part of two hundred thousand acres of Land on the Ohio granted by the honourable Govr. Dinwiddie's Proclamation and the said Deponent upon his oath hath declared that being a resident of South Carolina he never heard in any manner whatever until about the middle of April last that any time was limited for the several Claimants under the aforesaid proclamation to come in and make good their several claims to the above Lands or he the said Deponent should have used his best endeavours to have entered his Claim in due time.

HENRY PEYTON.

Baltimore County, Novem. 11th, 1773.

Dr. Sir:

This will be handed you by Mr. Chas. Wells who comes out to look at some of Bryan Bruin's Lands Mortgaged to our Company. If it lies in your power to render him any Service I shall be much obliged to you.

From Yours, &c.
CHARLES RIDGELY.

I should be glad to see you; am very sorry you past me when last in Town. I understand Mr. Watson is dead; he bought some Lands near the Springs. I past his bond for them to Watson the Bath Keeper. Watson past the sd. bonds to Mr. Couller and Mr. Couller had good of me for them. I should be mutch obliged to you for your advise who I shall ask to gett my money or the Land. Pray let me know and send from you by Mr. Wells.

C. RIDGELY.

Capt. James Wood,
in or near Winchester.

Sir:

As Capt. James Wood had not an opportunity of Bounding any lands on the Ohio River, and the situation of the Tract in the Fork of Kentucky with Ohio that I have offered you 3500 acres, is a situation he will be glad to have a part in, have proposed and promised him the other 3500 acres, joyntly with you. I did not go out to that Country on a monopolising scheam. Mr. Wood as well as yourself is a Friend. If you can secure it between you I shall have pleasure in it. It is I am to survey Smaller Tracts. Lands might be culled, but that would not be a just principle. However, as you have the plot sent out by the Commission, let Mr. Wood joyn you in it as my half, and let him have the plot or see the situation of the Land. If he should miss you, I have subjoyned the coarses.

Beginning Trees are Two Beaches and a poplar on the South Bank of Ohio River, 224 poles above the mouth of the Kentucky River, and upper corner to a survey made for Coll. Peachy; thence up the River Ohio North 45 degrees. East 740 po. to a Mulbery and Black Walnut on the River Bank. Coarse contd. North 45 degrees. East 140 po. North 55. East 105 po. to Two Wild Cherry Trees & Walnut on the River Bank; thence S. 36 degrees. E. 1240 po., to a shugar and Red Oke Trees thence S. 60 degrees W. 1002 poles to a shugar Beach and Black Oke Trees; thence N. 35. W. 1020 Poles with Coll. Peachy's line to the beginning. The above land as I told Mr. Calmes may have bin resurveyed or in part last year. If you do not chuse to run the risque of my first survey, let me know.

Sir I have sent you by Mr. Bennit an open letter to Mr. Calmes as Mr. Bennit will act for me. I have left the matter open to him to take measures for securing the lands if you do not.

Yours with esteem,

THOS. BULLITT.

Dumfries, March 21st, 1775.

To Messrs. Marquis Calmes & Capt. James Wood.

Sir:

As I cannot be up or have an opportunity of seeing you before Capt. James Wood passes you on his way to the Indian Treaty, shall be obliged to you to let him have a Copy of the Plot of the seven thousand acres of Land above the mouth of the Kentucky, as he is to have the Half. If it does not suit you to keep the other half, you can let him have the plots and he can have it copyed and leave me the copy or original.

I am yours with esteem,

THOS. BULLITT.

To Mr. Marquis Calmes, Sept. 3d, 1775.

Head Quarters, Jany. 24th, 1779.

BRIGADIER SMALLWOOD
MAJOR ADAMS
B. MAJOR KIRKPATRICK

The Regimental Paymasters are immediately to make returns of shoes actually wanting in their respective Regiments, which the Brigade Majors will digest into Brigade returns, have them signed by the Officers Commanding Brigades, and deliver them into the orderly office next Thursday Afternoon.

(J. W.)

Headquarters, January 28th, 1779.

BRIGADIER GENERAL WAYNE
MAJOR STEPHENSON
B. MAJOR MINNIS

John Mechelm Esqr. being appointed Commissary General of Hides for the State of New Jersey, with full power and authority to collect and receive all Hides, Tallow, Horns, and all other usefull offal of Cattle slaughtered in the said State for the use of the Continental Army, or the use of any persons appertaining to it; all persons belonging to the same are to respect him accordingly, and deliver the articles before mentioned without order.

The Discharge of three Pieces of Cannon at Lt. Sterling's Quarters will be the signal for an alarm in which case the Troops are instantly to be put into the Position lately ordered.

(J. W.)

Head Quarters, Jany. 31st, 1779.

BRIGADIER MUHLENBERG
LT. COLO. WILLIAMS
B. MAJOR MCCORMACK

The Morris Town Guard to be increased to a Captain's Command, and relieved Monthly 'till further orders. The Officers will see that all the Ammunition in the Men's hands be returned to the Regimental Quarter Masters, and in future when their men return from Guard or detachment, they are in like manner to see it returned.

D. O. February 1st, 1779.

The General Directs that the Virginians now in His Excellency's Guards be furnished with their Proportion of Clothing from the several Regiments to which they formerly belonged.

B. O. The Brigade to be mustered next Thursday 10 o'clock beginning on the right of the 4th Regiment; the Rolls to be completed and delivered to the Adjutants of the respective Regiments by Saturday Evening.

If the Paymaster General of the Continental Army will advance to Major Jonathan Clarke for my use the sum of Three Hundred and twenty pounds, it shall be duly accounted for by

O. TOWLES, *Major*,
6th Virga. Regiment.

Long Island, September the 12th, 1779.

1778. Dr. Mr. Samuel Mills of Colo. Seldon's Regiment

1778. Dr. Mr. Samuel Mills of Colo. Seldon's Regiment L. D. May 31. To Cash advanced to you & for sundries furnished for your use when a Prisoner at Philadelphia as per settlement between us __ } Sensa. Curry. Solid Coin £ 10.17.0

There is no error or omission to except.

Sepr. 17, 1779.
O. TOWLES.

1779

Head Quarters, Middle Brook, Jany. 4th, 1779.

BRIGADIER GENL. WAYNE
COLO. WILLIAMS
B. MAJOR KIRKPATRICK

The Commanding Officers of Brigades are to make report of their Hutts and how far completed, as soon as possible.

B. O. The Commandant directs that an Officer from each Regiment attend at the Clothier General's store tomorrow with proper lists of deficiencies of Cloathing agreeable to general orders at West Point to receive the Cloathing due to their respective Regiments.

(J. W.)

G. O. January 7th, 1779.

The Clothier General is immediately to deliver out to the respective Regiments any deficiency of the cloathing allowed at Fredericksburg. When that is completed, the Commanding officers of Brigades, are to make returns into the Orderly Office of what will be then deficient.

At a Court Martial, whereof Colo. Newill was President, Colo. Thomas Price Commanding the 2nd Maryland Regiment, tried on the following charges: 1st. Cowardice on York Island in the face of the Enemy. 2d. With disgraceful behaviour in refusing to take command at Hackinsack of the Regiment, Colo. Smallwood's, when ordered to Fort Lee. 3d. Scandalously leaving Hackinsack at 12 o'clock at night, when raining, on the report of the Enemy's approach. 4th. Disgracefully leaving Kingston on the approach of the Enemy. 5th. Cowardice at Brandywine. 6th. Cowardice at Germantown. 7th. Ungentlemanly behaviour in not complying with his promise to leave the service made at the Court of Enquiry at White Marsh, by which he induced many of the witnesses through compassion to suppress their evidence. After maturely considering the charges, evidence and defence, the Court do acquit Colo. Thomas Price of the 4th and 6th charges. They also acquit him with honour of the 1st, 2nd and 3rd and 7th charges. Major General Lord Sterling, Commander in Chief at Middle Brook, confirms the sentence of the Court, and orders Colo. Price to be released from his arrest.

Lieutenant Robert Porterfield of the 7th Virginia Regiment is to do the duty of Brigade Major in General Woodford's Brigade 'till further orders, Brigade Major Porterfield being absent.

(J. W.)

Head Quarters, January 10th, 1779.

BRIGADIER GENERAL WAYNE
COLO. HUMPTON
BRIGADE MAJOR HITCHCOCK

A Sub Sergeant and 20 Privates to mount guard at Morris Town over the Quarter master and Commissary's stores. The men for guard tomorrow are to be furnished with three days' provision and Forty rounds, except those for Morris Town Guard, who are only to have their Cartridge Boxes full; the Fatigue to parade tomorrow with axes; Provost guard with three days' provision.

D. O. ———————— 11th Jany. 1779.

One man from each of the Virginia Regiments, and a Sergeant from Woodford's Brigade to be sent to Mr. Dyers, who will give them Directions for the Building of a Hutt for the Virginia Cloathing, now here and shortly expected.

(J. W.)

Head Quarters, Jany. 12th, 1779.

BRIGADIER MUHLENBERG
LT. COLO. GASKINS
B. MAJOR MCCORMACK

The Deputy Clothier is immediately to make a return of all the Blankets and every species of Cloathing, and of any other articles he has on hand, into the orderly office.

Captain Thomas March, Foreman, is appointed Aide de Camp to Major General Lord Sterling, in the room of Major Monroe resigned the 20th of December last, and is to be regarded and obeyed accordingly.

For a month's command one Field Officer, Five Captains, 10 subs, 10 Sergeants, 10 Corporals, 6 Drums and Fifes, and 240 Privates from the line to Parade next Thursday morning at Guard Mounting; such men to be taken from this service who are well Cloathed and have

Blankets; their arms are to be in perfect good Order, to be furnished with forty rounds each, and four days' provisions cooked. The Commanding Officer of the parade is to have the men examined, to take none but such as are above described, and to report to the Adjutant-General. The Field Officer of this Party is to call at the Orderly Office Wednesday afternoon for Instructions.

The Commissary General of Issues or his Deputy is to call at Lord Sterling's Quarters for instructions where to provide provisions for the party—Two Captains, 4 subs, 4 Sergeants, 4 Corporals, and 100 men for Fatigue to be on the Grand Parade tomorrow morning at ten o'clock with three days' provisions. Mr. Shute, D. Q. M. Gen'l., will attend the party.

(J. W.)

BRIGADIER GEN'L. WAYNE
COLO. N. GIST
B. MAJOR MINNIS

A Subaltern from the Pennsylvania Line and one from Muhlenberg's Brigade to be sent immediately to Brunswick, to superintendend the sick at the Hospital at that place. They will receive orders from Colo. Buford, at Brunswick.

B. O. January 14th, 1779.

A Court of Enquiry to sit tomorrow at the President's Quarters to enquire into the conduct of Lieut. Brown, relative to the battle of German Town. Major Clark will preside. Returns to be immediately made of the state of the Huts, agreeable to General orders.

(J. W.)

Head Quarters, Middle Brook, Jany. 14th, 1779.

BRIGADIER MUHLENBERG
COLO. NICHOLLS
B. MAJOR. KIRKPATRICK

A Fatigue Party of one Captain, 2 subs, 3 Sergeants, 3 Corporals and 60 privates to parade with Axes tomorrow on the Grand Parade.

Head Quarters, Middle Brook, Jany. 17th, 1779.

BRIGADIER MUHLENBERG
LT. COLO. HAWES
B. MAJOR PORTERFIELD

At a Brigade Court Martial whereof Major Grier was President, Lieut. Patrick Fullerton, of the 2nd. Pennsylvania Regiment, was tried for ungentlemanlike Behavior; unanimously found guilty of the charge, and sentenced to pay Capt. Talbot a reasonable price for two shirts, two stocks, and one Blanket, and to be dismissed the service agreeable to the 21st article of the 14th section of the Articles of War. Major General Lord Sterling, Commander-in-Chief in the Jerseys, approves the sentence, and orders it to take place immediately.

The Brigade Majors are reminded of a general Order to bring in their general returns punctually every Saturday at orderly time. Fatigue the same as yesterday.

B. O. The Commanding Officers of Regiments are requested to have ditches dug in the rear of their Huts, agreeable to a General Order for that purpose.

(J. W.)

Head Quarters Feb. 6th, 1779.

BRIGADIER MUHLENBERG
COLO. GIST
B. MAJOR PORTERFIELD
(*Orders lacking. Paper torn.*)

Head Quarters, Jany. 21st. 1779.

BRIGADIER GENERAL SMALLWOOD
MAJOR MASSEY
B. MAJOR MCCORMACK

The Deputy Clothier General is to issue one woolen cap to each effective man in the Brigade in this camp, on returns made by the Commanding Officers of Brigades Countersigned by the Adjutant General; men on detachment at Monmouth to be omitted in the returns, as they will be drawn for separately; the Brigade Commissaries to regularly return all the Cattle's Horns and feet with the Hides to the Commissary General of Hides, at least once a week. They will see that the butchers carefully take off all the Hides from the feet as much waste has been occasioned by a contrary practice. The Officers commanding those Brigades which have not yet complied with the Orders of the 26th. December relative to Ammunition are desired to see that the returns are made out and it drawn, agreeable thereto immediately. Fatigue the same as Yesterday.

B. O. Jany. 21st, 1779.

At the request of Lieut. Brown of the Delaware Regiment a Court of Enquiry was held the 15th. instant, whereof Major Clark was President, to Enquire into the Conduct of Lieut. Brown at the Battle of German Town; the Court at his Further request did also enquire into his conduct at Brandywine. It appears from the testimony of the Evidences that there were supernumerary Officers in the

Delaware Regiment in both actions, and that it did not appear that Lieut. Brown was not one of them, and that it does not appear that **Lieut. Brown was at Brandywine** or that he left the field at German Town and that the reports prevailing against Lieut. Brown were without foundation.

(J. W.)

Head Quarters, January 22d, 1779.

Brigadier Wayne
Major Murray
B. Major Porterfield

The Fatigue the same as yesterday. A Corporal and Six Privates to mount guard at Bound Brook.

Head Quarters, February 2d, 1779.

Brigadier Muhlenberg
Major Clark
B. Major Minnis

All the Non-Commissioned Officers and soldiers quartered upon the Inhabitants are immediately to join their respective Regiments in Camp and none in future to lodge out of it. A Court Martial of the line to sit next Friday at ten o'clock at the new Office Room for the Trial of all Prisoners brought before them; Colo. C. Hall is appointed President. Lt. Colo. Gashmis, Major Mentzes, and two Captains from Woodford's, two from Muhlenberg's, two from the 1st. Pennsylvania, and one from each of the other Brigades on the ground to attend as members.

The Brigade Majors of the Virginia and Maryland line are furnished with the names of the men of their Brigades who are sick at Albany, and are unable to return for want of Cloathing, the Commanding Officers of their respective Regiments will send Cloathing to the new office room on Thursday Morning 10 o'clock, where a waggon will be ready to take them with an Officer from the Virginia line to superintendend the conveyance of the Cloathing and Deliver them to the men at Albany, and Conduct them to Camp. He is to call at the Orderly Office for Instructions. Fatigue the same as yesterday.

D. O. A General Court Martial will sit at the President's Quarters the day after tomorrow at 10 o'clock A. M. for the Trial of Lieut. Jenkins. Major Massey will preside, and each Brigade will give two Captains and two Subs as members.

(J. W.)

Head Quarters, Feb. 4th, 1779.
BRIGADIER MUHLENBERG
MAJOR MOORE
B. MAJOR HITCHCOCK

The Brigade—(*Page torn*).

Head Quarters, Feb. 7th, 1779.
BRIGADIER SMALLWOOD
MAJOR GRIER
B. MAJOR MINNIS

The Honble. the Congress have been pleased by their resolution of 23d. January last to direct that the Commander-in-Chief be authorized and directed to take the most effectual measures to reinlist for the continuance of the War, all such of the Continental Troops as are not expressly raised for that period, to complete the Battalions to their proper complement, and for those purposes besides the Bounty of Cloathing and Land heretofore granted by Congress for Encouraging the recruiting service, to grant to each able bodied soldier now in the service and who shall voluntarily enlist for during the war, a bounty according to the circumstance of present engagement but not to exceed in any case two hundred Dollars. The Commander-in-Chief therefore engages to every able bodied soldier whose time of service will expire between this and the last day of June next, who shall enlist during the War, a Bounty of 200 Dollars besides the usual Bounty of Cloathing, &c., and to every able bodied soldier who shall enlist to serve during the war whose time of service extends beyond the last day of June next, a Bounty of 100 Dollars besides the usual Bounty of Lands, &c.—As an encouragement to the Officers to exert themselves in the reinlistment of the men, the Honble. the Congress have been pleased to allow ten Dollars per man, for every man so inlisted, and who shall pass muster. The Officers of One State are not on any acct. to endeavour to reinlist the men of Another, neither are the Officers of one Regiment for the present to reinlist the men of Another. The Commanding Officers of Regiments are to call at Head Quarters for Warrants for enlisting money. Officers are to make use of every precaution to avoid being imposed upon by those who have been already reinlisted for the War. Regimental returns of the names of men reinlisted to be made monthly to the Officers Commanding Brigades, who are to make a Brigade returns to the Adjutant General to be by him transmitted to the Commander in Chief. The arrangement and rank of the officials in the Virginia line as settled by the Committee of Arrangement at the White Plains is immediately to take place and the Officers are to repair and take rank in their respective Regiments to which they were appointed.

(J. W.)

Head Quarters Middle Brook Feb. 12, 1779.

Brigadier Muhlenberg
Lieut. Col. Hawes
B. Major McCormack.

General Muhlenberg and the Field Officers of the Virginia Line are requested to meet tomorrow morning 10 OClock at the Orderly Office Room, when the Commanders in Chief will lay some Business before them respecting their Line. — Complaints having been made that the Soldiers have abused the Indulgences of Congress entered on their Resolutions, by buying money of the two Licias in Confusions of Arrears not belonging to the Army. The Paymaster General is directed to receive no more of these Confusions after the 12th of Instant, and notice is further given that any One possessed of the Certificates above mentioned will be permitted with the utmost severity ... to facilitate the Collection of Bills at present in the Possession of the Soldiers, they are to deliver them to the Regimental Paymasters who will have them Exchanged with the Paymaster General.

Head Quarters Middle B. Feb 11, 1779.

Brigadier Smallwood
Lt. Col. Brent
B. Major Porterfield

Head Quarters, Middle Brook, Feb. 12, 1779.

BRIGADIER MUHLENBERG
LIEUT. COLO. HAWES
B. MAJOR MCCORMACK

General Muhlenberg and the Field Officers of the Virginia Line are requested to meet tomorrow morning 10 o'clock, at the orderly Office Room, when the Commander-in-Chief will lay some business before them respecting their line. Complaints having been made that the Soldiers have abused the Indulgence of Congress contained in their resolution; by Buying money of the two called in Emmissions, of persons not belonging to the Army, the Paymaster General is directed to receive no more of these Emmissions after the 12th. Instant; and notice is further given that anyone convicted of the practice above mentioned will be punished with the utmost severity. To facilitate the Collection of Bills at present in the possession of the Soldiers, they are to deliver them to the Regimental Paymasters who will have them exchanged with the Paymaster General.

(J. W.)

Head Quarters, Middle B., Feb. 11, 1779.

BRIGADIER SMALLWOOD
LT. COLO. BRENT
B. MAJOR PORTERFIELD

A Formal Complaint having been lodged with the Commander-in-Chief against Colo. Craig for beating and otherwise illtreating Caleb Brecaw, an Inhabitant of this State, a Court of Enquiry to examine into the circumstances of the affair to sit next Saturday 10 o'clock A. M., at the Court Martial Room. The Court will consist of Colo. Russell as president, Colonels Williams and Butler, Lieut., Colo. Williams and Major Posey as members. They will report a State of facts with their opinion to the Commander-in-Chief. Accurate returns of Arms, Accoutrements, Ammunition, &c., according to the printed forms which will be delivered out are to be forthwith made by the Commanding Officers of Regiments to the Officers Commanding Brigades who are to have them digested into Brigade returns and transmitted to the Adjutant General.

(J. W.)

1780

Albemarle Co.

This is to certify that Meshai Hitchcock came before John Henderson, Jn., a Justice of the Peace for the County of Albemarle and made oath that he was present when Zacariah Fortune agreed to serve as a Soldier in the State Troops at Albemarle Barracks in the place of James Step a Soldier in Capt. Mattison's Company and that the said Fortune applyd to Colo. Taylor and acquainted him that he was willing to serve in the place of the above Step as a Soldier till Jan. 7, 1780 and no longer.

JNO. HENDERSON.

6th April, /80

Sir:

No accounts of the Truce Vessel's having come to her moorings, I must confess I am both uneasy on that account, & the uncertainty we are in with respect to the Box of Letters for the Troops come by it, which if you have any information of, I should be glad to learn, by a line sent on Sunday Morning to the Barracks.

At the same time I wish to know if you are to examine the letters here before they are put up in the Box for New York. Those of the Germans will be sent to Mr. Burgsdorf. The British may all be sent to Major Forster's Quarters at the Barracks or where it will be most convenient for you. This you will please to signify.

I am
Sir
Your most obedient Servt.

JAS. HAMILTON.

Colo. Wood.
Genl. Hamilton, 6th April, 1780.

Albemarle Barracks, March 25, 1780.

At a Garrison Court of Enquiry held by order of Colo. Wood respecting the loss of a considerable quantity of Bacon by W. Master Hugh Hayse's Brigade.

LT. COLO. CROCKETT, *President.*

Members—Capt. White, Capt. Young, Lt. Taylor, En. Meriwether, Capt. Burton, Lt. Brent, Ensn. Paulett, En. McGathick.

The Court being sitting, Andrew Boyle a waggoner in the above mentioned Brigade, being sworn deposeth that he knew nothing of any of the Bacon being disposed in any shape except about ten pounds which the waggoners made use of on the road; and further observes that W. Master Hays was constantly with the Brigade from the time that they left James River till it was delivered at the Barracks, and cannot form any conception of the manner in which it was lost.

Nicholas Smith a waggoner in above mentioned Brigade deposeth and saith that he knows nothing concerning the loss of the Bacon. Jacob Stretchbury waggoner as above confirms the testimony of the above mentioned Smith.

Joseph Boyle waggoner confirms the above witnesses. Mr. Hugh Hayes waggoner Master, in Vindication of himself declares that he delivered to the following men, waggoners in his Brigade, the Quantity of Bacon anext their names:

	Pieces Received	Pieces Lost
Rich'd. Shirs and Patrick Gray	310	7
Andrew Boyle and Joseph, a Negro	316	4
Nicholas Smith and Peter, a Negro	356	9
Jacob Stretchbury	167	39
James and Kurry	331	23

The Quantity lost amounts to 1456 Pounds.

JOSEPH CROCKETT, *President.*

Proceedings of Court of Enquiry on Waggon Master Hayes.

Albermarle Barracks, March 27th, 1780.

At a Garrison Court Martial held by order of Colo. Wood for the trial of Hugh Hayes Waggon Master, and Andrew Boyle, Joseph Boyle, Patrick Gray, Richard Shirs, Nicholas Smith, Jacob Stretchbury, Peter and Sam, Negroes belonging to Edward Sniggars of Frederick, Kurry a negro belonging to William Brady of the said County waggoners under the said Hayes charged with loosing Bacon out of their waggons to the amount of one thousand four hundred and fifty six pounds:

COLO. CROCKETT, *President.*

Members—Capt. White, Lieut. Brent, Lt. Pettus, Ensign Paulett.

The prisoners being brought and the court being sworn proceeded to the trial of the above mentioned prisoners. The Prisoners unanimously plead not guilty. Hugh Hayes being sworn deposeth that he delivered 13800 ℔s. of Bacon to the above mentioned Waggoners and that they were deficient in the weight on its being delivered to the receiving Commissary at the Barracks 1456 ℔s., the Court are of opinion that the owners of the different wagons shall make good the loss of the Bacon by stoppage of their wages to the amount of what the Bacon lost was purchased at and if it cannot be discovered by the Commissary's books what each waggon lost it shall be brought to a avairrige by judging the weight of the pieces each man lost.

Nicholas Smith and Peter, a Negro belonging to Edward Sniggars of Frederick County since the above mentioned loss of Bacon have each of them lost three peaces which the court are of opinion they shall pay for as above directed.

The Waggoners in Pollock's Brigade were brought before the court charg'd with loosing twenty four peaces of Bacon. Mathew

Pollock being sworn deposeth that Richd. Tyler was two pieces deficient in what was delivered to him. Ruben Finney being sworn deposeth that he saw Richard Tyler with something which he took to be Bacon at the distance about two hundred yards which the sd. Tyler was going off with but cannot tell whether it was Bacon or not. Roger Cooper, Waggoner, Mr. Pollock observes was deficient eleven peaces in what was delivered to him and that Bristor belonging to Bartlet Turner was deficient eighteen peaces in what was delivered to him, and that in searching the waggons after unloading found four pieces in the waggons drove by Louis a Negro belonging to Drury Williams and three pieces in the Waggon drove by John Dyhan belonging to David Mims. The Court are of opinion that Richd. Tylor receive thirty nine lashes on his Bare back and that the loss of the whole of the Bacon be made good as before directed.

JOSEPH CROCKETT, *President.*

Proceedings of Court Concerning Bacon.
Colo. Wood.

At a General Court Martial held at Albemarle Barracks April 21st, 1780, for the tryal of James Cragy, who is charg'd with Disertion from the 5th Virginia Regiment:

COLO. CROCKETT, *President.*

Members—Majr. Roberts, Capt. Burnley, Capt. Cherry, Capt. Young, Lt. Brent, Lt. Pettis, Lieut. Taylor, Lieut. Pollett, Lieut. Magill, Ensn. Slaughter, Ensn. Moore, Ensn. McGavock.

The Court being duly sworn, and the prisoner brought before them, pleads quilty of Disartion.

The Court are of Oppinion the prisoner is quilty of a Breach of Article the 1st., of section the 6th., of the Articles of War, and sentince him to run the Gauntlet twice through the Brigade.

JOSEPH CROCKETT, *Presdt.*

Proceedings of Court Martial on James Cragy.
Colo. Wood.

13th May, 1780.

Sir:

Hearing that you was returned by Mr. Hochesly, & having it confirmed by Colo. Hill, I shall first congratulate you on your safe arrival, and am sorry so soon to have occasion of troubling you.

The enclosed Complaints I meant to have laid before you this Day, having been at Charlottesville for that purpose, & not finding you returned, wrote Colo. Taylor, who either has or will show you my Letter and shall wait on you on Monday morning. In the meantime have enclosed the Complaints with the proceedings of a Garrison Court Martial, which will be order'd to sit again on Monday to try all Prisoners brought before them and if the evidence makes their appearance that Day they have orders to proceed on the trial of the two men of the 20th., and make no doubt of your taking the proper steps of checking insults and threats unprovoked to the officers mentioned in the enclosed.

I am
Sir
Your most obedt.,
Humble Servt.
JAS. HAMILTON.

Colo. Wood.

Charlottesville, 13th May, 1780.

Sir:

I enclose the Field Officer on Duty's Letter to me of yesterday, with the copie of Captn. McLean of the 9th Regt's Letter to him and that of Captn. Marlay's of the 10th.

The very extraordinary matter contained in those Letters (copies of which I have order'd to be made out and deliver'd to you) has occasion'd my coming here in expectation of seeing Colo. Wood & entering my complaint to him on the above subject. His not being arrived occasions my application to you, which cannot be made clearer than by the manner I have taken to lay it before you and expect that Justice such very unprecedented & outragious Insults merit.

The abuse and threats contained in the Letters require redress as speedy as exempliary.

I am
Sir
Your most humbl. Servt.,
JAS. HAMILTON.

Colonel Taylor.

Albermarle Barracks, August 25th, 1780.

A Board of Officers set to enquire into the enlistment of such Soldiers in the Regt. Guards may claim a discharge:

COLO. CROCKETT, *President.*

Members—Capt. Porter, Capt. Cherry, Lieut. Karney, Lieut. Glenn, Ensign. Paulett, Ensign. Kennedy.

Capt. Burton being sworn respecting the enlistment of Tacha. Fortune deposeth and sayeth, James Steep came to Colo. Taylor with sd. Fortune, and told him he had got sd. Fortune to take his place. Colo. Taylor asked Fortune if he was willing to take Stapp's place. He answer'd yes. Fortune was asked for how long. He making no answer Colo. Taylor replied, I suppose as long as the Troops (or as long as the rest of the Soldiers or something to that effect)? The sd. Fortune answered yes. The Court after hearing Capt. Burton's evidence and examining the inclosed depositions are of oppinion that the sd. Fortune is properly a Soldier during the stay of the Convention Troops.

The Board after perusing the depositions inclosed of Geo. Wright and Wm. Edmunds respecting the enlistment of Wm. Lavender are of oppinion he is intitled to a discharge.

Elijah Linch produced the within certificate which the Board are of oppinion is forged and the sd. Linch a Soldier during the stay of the Troops at the Barracks.

JOSEPH CROCKETT, *President.*

Colo. Wood.

Albemarle Barracks, September 5, 1780.

At a Board of Officers set to enquire into the enlistment of Jassee Toney, James Williams, Wm. Lowrey, Soldiers belonging to the Regt. of Guards:

COLO. CROCKETT, *Presdt.*

Members—Capt. Cherry, Capt. Young, Lt. Karney, Lt. Taylor, Ensn. Paulett, Ensn. Kennedy.

Joseph Headon being sworn sayeth respecting Toney's enlistment that Capt. Herndon informed him that the sd. Toney was enlisted by Capt. Holman Rice for but six months after the sd. Holman Rice was broke and Herndon took command of his compy. He told Toney that if he would agree to be return'd for one year he should then receive his cloathing and have a discharge from the said Regt. He further sayeth that it was proved before him by Sundrey witnesses that Toney enlisted with Capt. Rice for but six months and no longer.

Joseph Headon further sayeth concerning the enlistment of James Williams that Lt. Herndon who enlisted sd. Wms. inform'd him that he had enlisted him for twelve months or during his stay at the Barracks as an officer. He also sayeth that Jno. Lisle, Charles Aiken, and Jean Williams all of them made oath before him to the above enlistment of James Williams.

Joseph Headon deposeth concerning Wm. Lowrey's enlistmt. that he saw the deposition of four or five deferent persons sworn to before Capt. Thurman certifying that the sd. Wm. Lowrey enlisted with Capt. Holman Rice for but six months. He further sayeth that Capt. Herndon after taking the commd. of Rice's company directed him to tell the said Lowry who was at that time sick at his father's that if he would return to the Barracks he would make the same agreement with him that he had done with Toney; that was he should be discharged at the expiration of twelve months.

The Board are of oppinion that the above Soldiers, Toney, Williams and Lowrey are entitled to a discharge.

JOSEPH CROCKETT, *Presdt.*

Proceedings of Board of Officers 6th September 1780.
To Colo. Wood.

War Office, Sept. 20th, 1780

Sir:
We have been honoured with your Letters of the 11th and 15th instants. We can say nothing agreeable on the subject of Forage which cannot to provided 'till the Q. Mr. gets Money, & at present there seems little prospect of a supply. The embarrassments you meet with in finishing the Picketts are very distressing, & the more so as the Diminution of the Guard would more than pay the expense of the Picketts. If you can get the Business done on Credit & will send us the Bill we will do all in our power to obtain payment. There is a strong Probability of the enemy's moving towards Philadelphia, & therefore we cou'd wish every possible means of securing the prisoners should be taken. There are Tools at Lebanon if they could be transported. As to the difficulty of the Delivery of the Rations we think it easily remedied by your directing the Contractors to have their Provisions delivered at the Barracks, and if the contract will not comprehend it, on their refusal we must have a contract made for the purpose. But we cannot conceive the Gentlemen will make farther Difficulties on this Head as the Prisoners were the principal objects of the Contract & they should remove their Store to the principal place of delivery which is at the Hutts.

However contrary to our private Feelings we must as public Officers disagree to your issuing Provisions to the Families of Officers as there is no resolution of Congress to warrant it, nor will the Contractors be paid for such issus.

We have the Honour to be
very respectfully,
Your obedt. Servt.

RICHARD PETER.
By Order.

Colo. Wood.
At Lancaster

We have put an extract of your letter to the Dr. (?) for the state. I directed him to give you every assistance in his power.

Genl. Orders, 10th Oct., 1780.

Brigadier Hamilton has received a copy of the proceedings of the Court Martial on Mr. Lewis, one of the American Commissaries, for assaulting Sergt. Fleming, of the 47th Regt., in which he observes the evidences produced by Sergt. Fleming were neither examined or admitted of. This the Brigadier has complained of as diametrically opposite to every principle of justice.

Considering the sentence of the Court, Colo. Wood has in his orders made all the reparation in his power, provided always that former orders prohibit the hearing of or admitting evidences adduced by any complainant in the Convention Army.

War Office, October 19th, 1781.

Sir:

The Board cheerfully consent to your leaving the Superintendance of the Convention Troops to proceed on your private affairs to Virginia of which you will please to inform the officers at the respective Posts. Should you be employed by the Commander-in-Chief in the Army, we shall endeavor to manage the Officers of the Prisoners without you, tho' we with much Pleasure inform you that we have the greatest Reason to be satisfied with your Conduct during your Superintendance. You will be pleased to leave in Writing a full account of all the Business of these Prisoners, & give your opinion as to anything you deem necessary to be done which will promote the public serivce so far as concerns them.

We have the honor to be
very respectfully
Your very obed. Servant,
RICHARD PETER.
By Order.

Colo. James Wood.

Albemarle Barracks, Oct. 30th, 1780.

A Board of officers set to enquire into the Enlistments of such Soldiers in the Regt. of Guards as may claim a discharge.

COLO. CROCKETT, *Presdt.*

Members—Capt. Chapman, Ensn. Paulett, Ensn. McGavock, Ensn. Kennedy.

Charles Lavender claim'd a discharge and produced a certificate return'd him for during the stay of the Convention Troops but sayeth from John H. Woodroof that he enlisted the sd. Lavender and his Reason for returning the sd. Lavender for during that time was that he had returned Lavender's brother so.

Huddleston Carter produced the deposition of Jno. Carter and Stephen Davis that he was only enlisted for eighteen months but being returned by Capt. Thomas for during the stay of the Barracks. The Board are of Oppinion he is to serve. The Board are also of oppinion that Charles Lavender is to serve during the stay of the Convention Troops in the State.

JOSEPH CROCKETT, *Presdt.*

Proceedings of Colo. Crockett's Board, November, 1780.

Colo. Wood.

At a General Court Martial held at Albemarle Barracks on Friday the 3rd. day of November 1780 for the trial of L. Anderson of the Western Battalion, who is under an arrest for overstaying the limits of his Furlough Six weeks, & not taking care of Deserters under his charge.

COLO. CROCKETT, *President.*

Members—Capt. Burnley, Capt. Purvis, Capt. Porter, Capt. Chapman, Capt. Young, Capt. Tipton, Lt. Brent, Lt. Paulett, Lt. Kerney, Ens. Meriwether, Ens. Kennedy, Ens. Green.

The Court being sworn and the charge read, the prisoner pleaded not guilty except to the part of the charge of overstaying the limits of his Furlough, & gives for reasons that he was after Deserters.

Major Walls being sworn deposeth that on Monday the 2d ulto., he saw Lt. Anderson at Martinsburg and two deserters belonging to said Battalion, were also present; that he gave Lt. Anderson orders to take immediately in possession said deserters & carry them to Winchester & join with the deserters there; proceeding from there to Woodstock for the same purpose and from there on to the Barracks with all such deserters; and to the best of his knowledge Lt. Anderson did not apply for said deserters till the Friday following. Thomas Berryman one of said Deserters mentioned to be at Martinsburg being sworn deposeth that Lt. Anderson did not apply for him till the Friday above mentioned, & being asked if Lt. Anderson received hand cuffs for the purpose of confining them, Answered he did. Q. Did he put them on? Ans. No. Q. At what time did Lt. Anderson receive said handcuffs? Ans. At the time the Deserters were taken out of Custody.

Lt. Anderson in his defence produced a piece of writing which was read and is hereto annexed. Uppon considering of the matter, the Court are of Opinion he is not guilty of the Charges for which he was arrested.

JOSEPH CROCKETT, *Presd.*

Gentlemen:

When the Governor and Council of this State agreed that the British Troops of Convention shou'd be quartered at Frederick Town, they informed me that in consequence of a petition, the Trustees wou'd be empowered to rent the Poor House, and to provide by other means for the support of the poor. If such a law shou'd pass, which

I have no doubt of, I shou'd wish to rent the whole house for the purpose of quartering the Guards, provided that the terms shou'd not be unreasonable. Now, what I have to request of you, Gentlemen, is that you wou'd meet and agree upon the terms of renting the house in case you shou'd be authorized to do it, and that you will in the meantime give me permission to occupy the vacant rooms for the Guards, untill I can procure other quarters for them, in case we shou'd not agree for the house. In case this is complied with, I give you my word that every possible care shall be taken that no kind of damage is done the building, and that I will remove the troops as soon as I can procure other quarters. Your readiness in complying with other requests of this kind, induces me to hope that you will give me every assistance in your power.

       I am &c.
                (J. W.)

Ltt. to Trustees,
Fk. Town
13 Dec. 1780.

1781

          Frederick Town, New Year, 1781.

Dear Sir:

  The inclosed is all the letters I have received of yours since you left Town, with a general return of the Convention troops in Maryland now under your Command.

  It is with singular satisfaction I can inform you I have had less trouble than could be expected since your absence. The troops have been well supply'd as yet, but have only a small stock of provision on hand.

  A greater number of the married men than you had an apprehension of got leave to settle in town. No complaint respecting their conduct as yet. The Officers have sign'd their paroles and a great number of them are now living in the country. When it is convenient for you to moove here it will give me great satisfaction. Colo. Zohson has given me every assistance in his power. Major Read and myself are very happy in our Quarters.

      I am Dear Sir,
        Your Hble. Servt.,
          JOSEPH CROCKETT.

GENERAL LIST OF THE DETACHM'T OF THE ROYAL ARTILLERY, 6th April, 1781

Serjeants	Richd. Church	John Greenlaw
John Syple	Davd. Davies	Andrew Dunlap
William Haytor	Joseph Groves	Alexr. Fraser
John Bush	Jams. Short	Jams. Boggs
William Hobson	John Simm	Robt. Ireland
James Somerville	Jams. Smith	John Shiecleft
Alexr. Rothney	Alexr. McDonald	Thoms. Monelly
Arthron Leslie	Malcom Cameron	Davd. Moore
Alexr. Patrick	Deserted Apl. 7	John Law
Willm. Roxbrough	Arch. Peacock	Richd. Warren
Robt. Jameson	Jacob Hain	John Bridgland
James Jack	Jams. Chambers	Famies Holdon
Jams. Kidd	Deserted Apl. 7	Andw. Davidson
John Vickers	Thos. Harington	Niel Betton
Willm. Carter	John Christy	Thoms. Byres
Chars. Hinds	Thos. Langford	Geo. Patton
Davd. Witt	Thos. Richardson	Robt. Watkinson
Syprus Stagg	Willm. Westmoorland	Geo. Sutton
John Robeson	Robt. Sewell	Edwd. Green
Alexr. Yeats	Jams. Watson	Willm. McHeitchcon
Alexr. Hickie	John Hutchison	Josia Gaven
Jams. Richardson	Jams. Edwards	
George Kidd	Thoms. Miles	
Willm. Law	Deserted Apl. 7	
Jas. Carr	Thoms. Grigg	

Winchester, 1st, May, '81.

Sir:

The Officer who was left in Albemarle Barracks with the baggage, reporting to me, that he was obliged to hire 4 Waggons, 30 silver Dollars each, for bringing on the remainder of the Brunswick baggage; I submit it to your consideration, if we are not entitled to have this money repaid on the following reasons:

When February last we were removed from the Barracks there was no doubt of furnishing us with the necessary carriage; the British Troops were allowed that, and had more Waggons than we ever pretended to; it was only for want of the necessary Waggons, we always have been under the necessity of leaving most of our baggage behind. From the midst of Febr., to the 5th April when the Resolution of Congress was published to us, there was more than twice the time for the baggage joining as here at Winchester, the same Waggons returning always, though often a sufficient number of Waggons existed at Albemarle Barracks. Should we suffer by that delay? and it is not but just the resolution of Congress should be put in execution from the very place it has been published to us, viz. Winchester.

I have likewise to represent to you, Sir, that the men left with the Baggage had for many days no provision of any kind issued to them, nor in the Barracks nor on the road.

I have the honor to be and with great esteem,
Sir, Your
Most obdt. humble Servant,
DUMENGEN, *Lt. Col.*

I must not omit mentioning that almost a whole Waggon Load Picaxes, axes, etc., etc., was brought from the Barracks belonging to this contingent and delivered to Colo. Taylor.

Sir:

It has been represented to me by the Senior Officer of the Convention troops that about the 11th instant, a Mr. Daniel Hopkins, who I am informed is in your employ, came to Winchester and purchased from the German troops, bills of exchange to the amount of £163 Sterling, with Continental Currency, after it was known in your State that Continental money had ceased to circulate. As these people are under my direction, and the above transaction appears to me to be fraudulent; I think it but just to inform you of my sentiments; expecting from the good Character I have had of you, that you will direct the Bills to be returned, or any circulating currency paid in lieu of the Continental. If this is not complied with, I shall think it my duty to take proper steps for stopping the payment of the bills, and collecting the same money which was paid by Mr. Hopkins. I hope that you will be persuaded that nothing but the love of justice, would have induced me to trouble you on this occasion.

(J. W.)

Mr. D. Bowly,
Baltimore
21st. May, 1781.

Fort Frederick, 24th May, 81.

Dear Sir:

Your favour by Capt. Baily came safe to hand. Am sorry to inform you that the command you take over the prisoners in this State prevents me altogether from acting in my office as Commisary of Prisoners for the State. All prisoners that has been in Maryland for this year or two past, has been entirely under my direction, particularly at this Post. I believe the Governor and Council of this State wrote to you to that purpose, and begd. that if you could consistently with your instructions from Congress relative to the prisoners, to give up the direction of them wholey to me. If you cannot do that, be pleased to make such necessary appointments as you know will be wanting here. Please to answer this as soon as possible untill which I will do everything in my power for the security of the prisoners.

As the matter at present is circomstanc'd I am totally at a loss how to act; whether to make any returns of prisoners in this State or not. Militia and everything at this place has been under my command. I have acted at this post from a particular request from the Board of War, and unless the authority by which I have always acted is taken from me I cannot think of giving up the command.

I hope my dear Coll. you will not think that any part of this letter is ment to give offence. I can assure upon my word tis not. I have only made a true state of the matter. No gentleman in the army I would sooner be commanded by than yourself in any other Instance than this. I am sorry to say that almost every necessary of life (bread excepted) at this place in wanting. At this time I have not 300 weight of Meat, and Don't know where to get another ℔. Tools or workmen to carry on building, is out of the question. I have not one farthing of money, and what is worse, no kind of paper money passes in this part of the state. What will become with the guard & prisoners, God only knows.

      I am Dr. Sir, with perfect esteem
       Your obt. servt.
           Mo. Rawlings.

(Public Service)
Colo. James Wood.

              26th May, 1781.

Sir:

As I have no doubt but that a considerable Number of the Convention Troops are still in the Neighborhood of this Place and concealed by the Inhabitants, and there being the Invalids and other Prisoners confined in the Gaol of Frederick, I think it absolutely necessary that an active Officer should be continued here, to fall upon every possible method of collecting and confining all the Prisoners who can be apprehended; to direct a Guard over the Invalids when he shall think it necessary and to sign the necessary Provision returns. From these considerations I must beg that you will continue to act at this Post; and as you know I am instructed to send an officer to George Town to superintend the landing of the necessaries for the Troops, I must likewise request that you will undertake this Business. Your Expences must be paid out of the Order on Mr. Edelin if he shou'd be able to answer it to enable you to comply with this. I think you had better keep the Continental Horse and draw Forage for him.

Before I conclude, I think it a Duty incumbent upon me to express my entire Approbation of your Conduct in every Instance, since you have commanded the Guards over the Convention Troops. Be pleased therefore to accept my warmest Acknowledgments, and be assured that nothing on my Part shall be wanting in Certifying your Services, and make no Doubt that they will be amply rewarded by your Country.

(J. W.)

Captain Baily,
26th May, 1781.

Reading, June 18th, 1781.

Sir:

I received your favor of the 17th instant requesting me to let you know the circumstance we are in at this place with the prisoners and provisions.

The Prisoners are lying near the River of Schuylkill about half a mile from Reading and a Guard of fifty men placed over them.

As for provision there is no Beef, and upon the whole everything is scarce.

I shall do my endeavors to secure them to the best of my judgment. I should be very glad to have them removed soon upon that account.

As for Capt. Van-Hair's Horse, I shall have none, for the Commanding Officer has ordered them in the Country.

No more at present, but remain
        Sir, your Hm. Servt.,
           VAL. ECKERT, L. C. B.
           (Colo. Eckert.)

Colo. Wm. Bayley.

PRESIDENT READ

30 June, 1781.

Sir:

I have lately received instructions from the Board of War to Hut the Convention prisoners, the British in the neighborhood of York Town, and the Germans near Reading; but have not as yet received your determination with respect to the identical places, or the manner of executing the work. The Guards for the British while the Huts are building and stockading, ought not to be less, in my opinion, than 150 men with their officers, as I am confident they will improve every oppy. to effect escapes. I think a Guard of Fifty will be very sft. for the Germans, and it will be unnecessary to inclose them with Picquets, as none of them have attempted to escape for a considerable time past. I shall keep the British at this place 'till I hear from your Excellency. I have the honour to be, etc.

(J. W.)

PRESIDENT REED

13th July, 1781.

Sir:

I have just now the Honour of your Excellency's letter of the 9th instant, and have communicated the contents to Colo. Hubley, who will take the necessary steps to prevent any further preparations being made in the neighborhood of York Town. With respect to accommodating the whole of the prisoners including those of the Convention Troops within the Picquets, I think your information erroneous. There is at present upwards of 200 men with 427 women and children without the Picquets, sheltered with blankets and planks procured by themselves, and yet the Barracks are exceedingly crowded. Add to this, a malignant Fever prevails among them, of which many have died, and upwards of 100 are down with it. Upon the whole, if your Honble. Board determines to keep them here, I think it will be absolutely necessary to enlarge the Picquets, and to direct a quantity of Oak Plank to be provided, with which they cou'd make shelter for themselves, and which might answer as a temporary expedient. Besides, I think it wou'd be an exceeding proper measure to have a House detached from the Barracks, appropriated for an Hospital, and to remove the sick as they are taken down; for the security of which a small detached Guard wou'd be sufficient. The present Guards consists of 300 non-commissioned and privates with their proper officers, part of which were intended to guard the British to York, and likewise a Guard to remove the seamen confined here to Philadelphia. I am clearly of opinion that 150 men properly officered, will be a sufficient standing Guard for this post.

I am happy to inform your Excellency that I have found a real disposition in the Commissary of prisoners, and the commanding officer of the Militia, to do everything in their power for the good of the service. I shall set off tomorrow for Reading, and will return in a few days to this place, where I shall be ready to receive any further commands which you may honor me with.

I am with the greatest respect and esteem,
Sir
Yr.
Excellency's
Very obt. Servt.
(J. W.)

PRESIDENT REED

16th July, 1781.

Sir:

I am exceedingly embarrassed how to act with respect to Hutting the German Troops in the vicinity of this place. The lands alluded to in your letter to Colo. Echert and which you supposed to be invested in the Proprietaries, is claimed by the inhabitants, under former agreements, has been surveyed and the taxes paid by the persons in possession, so that I conclude, altho they have no legal titles yet they are entitled in equity; and being altogether unacquainted with the laws of the State, I have thought it prudent to refer the matter to your Excellency, and to postpone any proceedings 'till I received yr. further instructions. The place adjudged the most proper for buildings the Huts is claimed by a Mr. Heister, as you will perceive by the inclosed letter from his son. Another place was thought of by Colo. Echert, claimed in the same manner, by a man who has obsconded, which is distant about three and a half miles from Town, and which I have viewed, but am of the opinion it will be very inconvenient from the Badness of the road to it, and the stream of water being small and uncertain. Colo. Echert and myself are of the opinion that the Continental stables and a large store house might be converted into Barracks, by raising them about two feet, and underpinning them with stones, by which it wou'd make them two stories, and wch. with some small additions wou'd shelter the whole of the troops. However, this wou'd be attended by inconvenience and expense as their firewood must be waggoned, but I am told not any considerable distance. My Intention is if the troops are to be Hutted, and the Quarter Master can procure tools and a person acquainted with building to superintend the work, to have them built by the troops, and in such a manner as to be of use upon any other or future occasion. I mentioned the matter to the Quarter Master, who tells me that the situation of his department is such, as to render it very difficult to procure the necessary tools, and that it won't be in his power to get a superintendent for want of money. I am just setting off to Lancaster in expectation of receiving our orders respecting the British troops, and shall return to this place as soon as I have adjusted matters there. In the meantime any orders addressed to Colo. Echert or Major Bailey will be strictly complied with.

    I have the honor to be, etc.

                    (J. W.)

COLO. SCOTT

21st July, 1781.

Sir:

  His Excellency the President, and the Supreme Executive Council of the State, having directed that the British Convention prisoners shou'd be Hutted in the neighborhood of this place, and have desired me to apply to you, as Lieut. of the County, for your advice and assistance in carrying their ideas into execution; in consequence of which I take the liberty of requesting you to furnish a Guard from your Militia consisting of One Hundred and Fifty men and their proper officers; and that you will be pleased to engage a person acquainted with carpenter's work to superintend the building the Huts and to have charge of the tools, and also eight or ten rough carpenters for the purpose of building Huts for the Guards, store houses, and Picqueting in the prisoners' Barracks; and that you will endeavour to procure the following tools, viz. one Cross cut saw, sixty narrow axes, 6 Broad axes, six frows, six pair of iron wedges, six pick axes, six spades, and six shovels. A few draft horses for the purpose of hauling timber will likewise be wanting.

(J. W.)

PRESIDENT READ

Lancaster, 2nd August, 1781.

Sir:

On receipt of your Excellency's letter of the 19th ultimo, immediately fixed on a situation for Huting the German Troops, on the lines between Daniel Heister and the heirs of one Bowers, in order to make it as little injurious as possible to either. With the assistance of Colo. Echert I procured as many tools as will answer the purpose, and set the troops to work on their Huts. My meaning in having a Superintendent appointed was, that he shou'd be a workman well acquainted with building, to direct that the Huts shou'd be regularly built, in such a manner as to be useful on any future occasion, and to have charge of the tools. I mentioned this matter to the Quarter Master before I wrote on the subject, supposing that someone in his Department might be spared for a short time to do this duty, but he having declined complying with my requisition, occasioned my troubling you with it. I have since prevailed on one of the Militia Officers on duty, to overlook and direct the work. I have fixed the B—— troops on good ground (the property of a non Juror) between York and the Susquehanna, so as to be very convenient to throw them across the river on any emergency.

(J. W.)

Sir:

The approach of the enemy will make it necessary for the security of the prisoners to augment the Guard under Major Bailey to 250 men with their Officers, which I bg. you will order with all possible expedition. I think it wou'd be a very proper measure to place a Horseman at Jeffers's on Susquehanna, for the purpose of expediting intelligence between this post and Lancaster. I have directed that letters directed to Colo. Miller shou'd be directed to you in my absence and beg that you will where necessary, immediately communicate the contents to Major Bailey, and by express to me at Lancaster. I am, etc.

(J. W.)

Colo. Scott,
8th Augt. 1781.

York, 8th Augt., 1781.

Sir:

In case of my absence, and you shou'd receive certain information of the landing of the Enemy, at any place likely to affect the safety of the prisoners, and their landing shou'd be on this side of the river, you will please to throw the prisoners across the Susquehanna at Wright's and Anderson's Ferrys; if, on the other hand, they shou'd land on both sides, or approach in any manner so as to make that improper, you will then move them by way of Lebanon towards Easton, leaving the women and children at their present encampment. I have requested Colo. Scott to augment the Guards, and make no doubt but you make every precaution to prevent their escapes, and that you will always be in the most perfect readiness to move at a moment's warning. I thought to have called on you, but have determined to return to Lancaster tonight. I think it essentially necessary to detach a Corporal's Guard to each of the Ferry's, for the security of the boats.

(J. W.)

Major Bailey.

Permission to Colo. Hill, etc., to remain at his Present Quarters.

8th August.

Colonel Hill, Captains Swethanham, Bailie, and McLean of the Convention Troops, who have resided for some time past in the County of Fluvanna, have hereby my Permission to remain at their Present Quarters until any future Order to the contrary. And, as they are Officers on Parole, and considered by me as immediately under my Protection, any insult or improper treatment offered them by Citizens of the State, will be Prosecuted by the utmost rigour of the Law. On the other hand, wherever it shall be made appear that their conduct is inconsistent with the Tenor of the Parole, they will be removed and restrained to Narrower Limits.

(J. W.)

Sir:

I take the liberty of requesting that you will be so good as to take into consideration the several matters laid before you in my last letter. The time is elapsed in which I engaged Payment to the People. I am extremely uneasy at having public debts hanging over me, which is increased by an apprehension that you as well as Mr. Morris may be induced to quit the service of an ungenerous Public, and my anxiety to make a speady settlement of all my Public Transactions.

Since the general Rendezvous at Winchester the Post has been supplied with Forage by contract made by G. M. He is very much pushed by the People for Payment and wishes to be informed in what manner that is to be done, and how the Post is to be supplied in future. I think the number of teams at present more than necessary and am of Opinion that it wou'd be a proper measure to sell the most indifferent of them.

(*Neither date nor address*)   (J. W.)

Sir:

At the Posts of Frederick Town and Winchester thirty-two German Prisoners have been liberated. Out of the money arriving, I paid £270 to Captain Stricher, the recruiting Officer; and the Ballance to sundry persons for Corn and Hay supplied Colo. Armand's Legion. A Ballance still remains due to the people for Forage, wch. was procured on my own credit, and for which orders were drawn by Colo. Armand's Quarter Master, and accepted by me to the amount of £269 Virginia currency. There is also due sundry persons for Waggonage for the Legion, hauling Corn, etc. £239. 8. 0. V. currency, for which I am likewise answerable. Colo. Armand is in Town, and can assure you that he cou'd not be supplied by any other means, than that of my becoming liable to the people. I expect a number of the German Prisoners will liberate themselves, as they have lately received some pay from the British, and a supply of Cloathing.

I was enabled to inclose the Winchester Barracks with Pickets agreeable to your orders by borrowing One hundred Pounds, Virginia Currency, and prevailing upon the Inhabitants, who expected to be benefited by the removal of the Prisoners from Frederick Town, to subscribe £50 in addition to it. For this Business, I am liable for the sum borrowed and Waggonage of the Timbers, and about a £140 Virginia Currency in addition to it. The people who subscribed the additional £50 think they ought to be repaid that sum, as the order for removing the Prisoners to that Post was countermanded, and they did not receive the benefits expected.

(*Mem. letter nither date nor name.*)   (J. W.)

Note: Debts incurred in Public Service at Winchester for supplies for prisoners.

                                             COLO. BUCHANON.
                                             GENL. IRVINE
                                             COLO. MILLER
8th Augt., 1781.   GENL. GIST.

GENL. IRVINE

                                                        8th Augt., 1781.

Sir:

I received letters last night by Express from the Board of War, informing me that a Considerable part of the British Army were proceeding up the Bay, and that Baltimore was their apparent object. Copies of the letters which came by Express will be inclosed you by Major Moore. As there are upwards of two thousand Prisoners of war at this Place, Lancaster and Reading which wou'd certainly be an object with the Enemy, Considering the dispersed and unprepared state of the Militia, I wou'd beg leave to refer it to your Consideration, whether it wou'd not be a proper measure to call the recruits from Carlisle and Hanover to this place, and those at Reading to Lancaster and to put arms into their hands. These recruits and the Militia which cou'd be suddenly assembled, wou'd in all probability be sufficient to check any body of Horse they wou'd be able to detach from the Head of the Bay. I shall be at Lancaster and will forward any orders to Reading you may think proper to send.

I have the honour to be with great respect and esteem,
    Sir,
        Yrs.

(J. W.)

Colo. Miller

8th Augt. 1781.

Dr. Sir:

It gives me real Pleasure that you have been so obliging as to undertake to place a Detachment of Volunteer Horsemen at proper Stages between this and the Head of the Bay for the purpose of facilitating Intelligence of any movement of the Enemy to this Post. I must request that you proceed with all possible expedition to Bush Town leaving a Horseman at equal stages and equal distances on the route between this and that place, with positive orders to be in constant readiness to move to the next stage whenever any Dispatches shall be sent to him. You will be pleased to keep one of these Horsemen constantly with you, in order to carry your letters to the first Stage, from which they are to be conveyed from stage to stage, Day and Night, without loss of time.

Upon delivering the letters, each Horseman returns to his Post and waits for further Orders.

By this channel you will be so obliging as to inform me as to the situation of the Enemy, and of every material movement which you think likely to affect the safety of this Post or Lancaster. In case of my absence, your letters had better be directed to me or Colo. Scott, as I am authorized by the Board of War to call into service whatever Horsemen I think proper. They will be paid by the Public, and found their Provision and Forage. Where there is no Public Provision or Forage, you will please to pass certificates to the People, keeping an exact list of such Certificates, which are to be returned to me; you will likewise keep an account of your own Expences which will undoubtedly be repaid. If one of the Continental Officers wou'd be so obliging to go with you, and to fix himself between you and the

Mo. of the Susquehanna, so as to Correspond with each other, I think it would be of the utmost Consequence.

I am, etc.,

(J. W.)

Dr. Sir:

I have just received letters by Express from the Board of War, informing me that the Enemy were proceeding up the Bay in considerable force; and as there is at this place, Lancaster and Reading, upwards of 200 Prisoners of war, which may be an Object considering the dispersed and unprepared state of the Militia, and I am much afraid the disaffection of the people pretty considerable. I have for the purpose of facilitating Intelligence, fixed a Chain of Horsemen, at proper stages from hence to Bush Town, and shall be exceedingly obliged to you to forward by express to me, through Colo. Henry Miller, who will remain at Bush Town, any material movement of the Enemy you may think likely to affect the security of this Post or Lancaster. I have the Honor to be with great respect etc.

(J. W.)

CIRCULAR TO GENL. GIST & COLO. BUCHANAN, LT. OF BALTIMORE

8th Augt., 1781.

Dr. Sir:

You will perceive by the ltt. from the Minister of War, his motive of sending the Guard which you command with the Prisoners. In addition to his Orders, I shall only add, that you will please to give your Direction to the Q. M. as to the place of encampment, and that you will Prevent every waste of fire wood, or Destruction of Property either in the Prisoners or Guards. I think it very probable the commanding officer at L. will relieve your Guards; if not, you must proceed to Elizabeth Town. I wish you an agreeable March.

I am,
Dr. Sir,
Yrs.

(J. W.)

Ltt. Officer Command.
Guards.

Dr. Sir:

I expected it wou'd have been within my Power to come with the Prisoners to York, but Dispatches which I have recd. from Philadelphia, render my presence at Reading indispensably necessary. You will discover a considerable part of the Prisoners have families; those, I think there is little reason to apprehend will attempt to escape; but the others, who have no families, will require to be well guarded, as I am certain they will avail themselves of every Oppy. of escaping.

The Sergeant Majors have always behaved well, and have been indulged with the limits of a mile round the Barracks, as well as a number of other Sergeants who have been recommended by the Sergeant Majors. You will please to deliver to the orderly Sergeant of the British, a copy of the Inclosed Order to be communicated to the Prisoners.

(J. W.)

PRESIDENT REED

August 16th, 1781.

Sir:

I have the honour of inclosing your Excellency a list of the articles of provision taken by my order in this State, under the resolve of Congress of the 4th of June. Give me leave to assure you that the powers have not been exercised but in cases of the most absolute necessity. I find very great inconvenience in the constant changes in the Militia officers, intrusted with the command of the Guards over the Prisoners. If it can be done with propriety I cou'd wish to have power to continue an officer on this duty, when I find him properly qualified for it, and where he is willing to remain.

(J. W.)

BOARD OF WAR

23rd Aug., 1781.

Sir:

I have the honour of inclosing you a letter which I have just now received from Doctor Weir who has been confined to the limits of one mile, since I received the direction of the Board of War in April last. I have the pleasure to acquaint you that I have got everything in a very good train at the three Posts. The officers appd. to do the duty of Town Majors are, Colo. Gibson, at York, Colo. Hubley at Lancaster, and Captain Bowen at Reading; the Posts are well supplied by the contractors with the specified articles, good in quality. For many months before the Convention Troops were removed from Virginia, they were supplied with Provisions altogether by the Executive of the State, empowering me to empress and, as in almost every instance, the people parted with their provisions at my request willingly, I think myself bound in Honor to see their accounts settled, and that justice is done them. I must beg that the Board will permit me to go to Virginia some time next month for a short time on this business and as the distance from York is not more than two Days ride, if the Enemy shou'd make any movement up the Bay, the Board may rely upon it, that I will instantly return to my charge. During my absence, I will leave such instructions, as to prevent any bad consequences attending it, which will not be long. I shall be glad of a line by the return of Mr. Slough. As I was anxious to have the

Huts built in such a manner as to answer a future purpose, I directed that the prisoners should draw the full ration for 14 days, while employed in their Buildings; which I hope will not be disapproved by yr. Honble. Board. The Convention Officers have been delivered to the Executive of Connecticut, as you will perceive by the inclosed receipt. *(J. W.)*

Sir:

Not having received an answer to my letter of the 23rd ultimo, I beg leave again to repeat my request for permission to go to Virginia for a short time to settle the accounts of the people who furnished provisions and forage for the Convention Troops while in Virginia. They are so exceedingly uneasy about the settlement of their accounts, that two expresses have been sent to me on that account; my stay will be very short. I mentioned in the same letter the situation of Dr. Weir, Director General of the Convention Troops, and inclosed his letter to me on the subject. I shall be much obliged to you for a line in answer to this and my letter of (Aug. 23rd) by the bearer, Major Wirtz, who will forward it to me.

(J. W.)

16th Sept., 1781.
B. War.

Oct. 25, 1781.

I, the subscriber, John Wier, Surgeon General of the Convention Army under Lieut. General John Burgoyne in the service of the King of Great Britain, being a prisoner to the United States of America and having permission to go from Lancaster to Elizabeth town in the State of New Jersey, on my way to New York do hereby pledge my word and sacred honor that I will proceed and keep the direct public road from Lancaster aforesaid by way of Reading and Easton to Elizabeth Town aforesaid, avoiding and as much as possible keeping at a distance from the main body and other posts of the Army of the aforesaid United States; and at Elizabeth Town, on my arrival there, will surrender myself to the Commissary of Prisoners or other person there having charge and direction of prisoners of war to the said States, and abide and observe his orders and directions as to my further proceedure and during my journey and stay at Elizabeth Town on parole I will not do or say or cause to be said or be done, any matter or thing whatsoever injurious to the interests or welfare of the said United States or any of them or the Armies or inhabitants thereof, or give intelligence in any manner either directly or indirectly to the enemies of the said States, but in all things conduct myself as an officer prisoner of war ought to and should do. I do further engage that Archibald McDonald and William Law, also two of the Convention Prisoners who wait on me and who are permitted to attend me shall remain with me within the limits aforesaid and observe and comply with the same restrictions I am subjected to by this parole.

Witness my hand at Lancaster the Twenty-Fifth day of October, in the year of our Lord, One Thousand, Seven-Hundred and Eighty-One.

JOHN WIER,
Surgn. G. C. Army.

1782

January, 1782.

Sir:

I was honoured a few days ago by your letter of the 12th ultimo by Lt. Colo. North and I shall think myself peculiarly happy if I can contribute towards carrying your ideas into execution wth. respect to the removal of the Prisoners of war. As soon as Colo. North communicated his instructions to me, I made an immediate requisition for the necessary Guards, and had the greatest reason from the assurances which were given me, that the Guards would be in readiness to move the first Division today; but to my great surprise, I am now informed by the County Lieutenant that he cannot order the Militia on this service without the direction of the Executive of the State. In consequence of wch. Colo. N. is under the disagreeable necessity of waiting here till the return of an Express from Richmond.

As the State has repealed all the laws for empressing, I found it entirely out of my power to procure waggons, either on the credit of the State, by empressing, or upon any other terms, but that of giving my own private Bonds to the people for the waggon Hire, payable in one month, at the rate of twelve shillings Pennsylvania Currency per day. By this means I have secured a sufficiency of teams to answer the purpose. In all probability, the bearer, Mr. B. will return from Philadelphia, as soon as the Express from Richmond, and the Militia Guards are got in readiness to move the Prisoners. I beg you will be pleased to inform me whether the No. of waggons for transporting the baggage of the prisoners is to be limited, or whether I am to furnish them agreeable to the requisitions of their Officers. As there has been no regular mode adopted of furnishing the Guards and Prisoners with Provisions, they have been frequently without Bread for many days together; this I represented some time ago to the Executive of the State, but have not as yet received any answer from them. I have purchased one hundred Barrels of Flour on my Credit, which I hope will serve them until other measures can be adopted, I hope, Sir, that you will be persuaded that I have, and will, exert my utmost Influence in assisting Colo. North in complying with your Instructions. I am endeavoring to collect the Prisoners who are much dispersed, and which cannot be effected in a short time, as I am informed by good authority they are scattered through the different Counties from York to this place. Until this can be done, I think it wou'd be necessary to have some Person appointed to this Post to procure provisions for a small Guard to receive the Prisoners as they are brought in, and to supply them until they can be forwarded to Frederick and Lancaster. I am now engaged in settling the public Accounts for Provisions Forage and waggon Hire furnished the Convention Troops while under my superintendence, and endeavoring to do the People who advanced their Property at my instance, that Justice in the settlement of their Accounts which they have a right to expect and which I conceive myself bound in Honor to afford them. This Business in all probability will employ me two months. During that time, I shall give every assistance in my power to have the Prisoners collected. I am afraid there will be a bad acct. of the Eutaw Spring Prisoners. They have, I understand, been long on the road and much dispersed. Mr. Bush, I believe, can give you some information respecting them.

(J. W.)

Genl. Washington and Genl. Lincoln.
January, 1782.

I have the honor to inform your Excellency that the Secy. at War has been pleased to direct the immediate removal of Prisoners from this State to Maryland and Pennsylvania, under the direction Lt. Colo. North; General Lincoln at the same time directed me to make requisitions for the necessary Guards of Militia as well as for waggons for Transportation of their Baggage; which I accordingly did; but find the County Lt. does not consider himself at Liberty to comply with Genl. Lincoln's request, without instructions from your Honble. Board; which obliges Colo. N. to delay the removal of the Prisoners, until your direction to the County Lt. to furnish the necessary Escort. I am afraid a very considerable proportion of the Prisoners are straggling in different parts of the Country, owing to the inattention of the Militia Guards on their march to this Place, and in want of proper supplies since their arrival. Indeed they have had every oppy. to escape as there has been no mode adopted for supplying them with Fuel, but by sending them under Guards to cut their own fire wood, which gave them the most favorable oppy. of escaping from their Guards.

(J. W.)

Sir:

I have the honour of reporting to you that it has not been in my power to comply with the Resolution of Congress for closely confining the British prisoners of war at Winchester and Frederick Town, owing to the insufficiency of the Guards, and there being no plans of security for the purpose of confinement at either of the Posts. At Winchester the prisoners consist of about 500 of which 80 are Germans, guarded by a Company of Militia. The situation about four miles from Town with great convenience of wood and water and in a country abounding with all kinds of Provisions, there is Huts erected sufficient to contain 1800 or 2000 prisoners, which might be inclosed by Pickets at a very inconsiderable Expence.

The Barracks at Frederick Town, with the Huts erected for the prisoners are sufficient for 1200 Prisoners and wou'd be a very proper place of confinement if it cou'd be Picketed in, and one or two wells dug within the Pickets and a proper Guard established. At this place timber is inconvenient and must be purchased. There is now at Frederick Town upwards of 1200 Prisoners of which 180 are British. The Guards at Frederick Town are furnished by drafts from the Militia by order of the Executive of the State, but in such an irregular manner that the prisoners have been frequently left with less than a Sergeant's Guard.

(J. W.)

To Majors Debenst & Scheer

Gentlemen:

I have the honour of your letter of yesterday's date and am extremely sorry that I am engaged in business of a public nature, which will prevent my being in Frederick as soon as I cou'd wish and where I think my presence is indispensably necessary. The disagreeable circumstance you mention respecting Lieutenant Bohlin gives me pain. At the same time I give it to you as my opinion that his conduct, whatever the provocation might be, when his peculiar situation is considd. was highly improper. I have invariably considered every officer admitted upon parole as a Gentleman, and have endeavoured to treat him as such until any part of his conduct gave me reason to alter my opinion, and have never failed where they have been treated improperly by any person amenable to a Military Tribunal, to have them tried by a Court Martial; and where any prisoner has been abused by a citizen, had the offender prosecuted by the Civil Magistrate.

I have wrote Major Bailey and have directed him upon Lt. Bohlin signing a parole, which I have sent, to enlarge him.

I expect to be at Frederick within ten days and will have the matter in dispute fully enquired into. I am, etc.

(J. W.)

Dr. Sir:

I have just now received your letter of yesterday's date with several inclosures. I am very sensible of the difficulties you have met with by my own. I have long been using every endeavour to collect the prisoners who are dispersed over this State, but find I have almost every man in the upper Counties to contend with. Your Application to the Genl. Assembly was extremely proper, and has rendered service to your Country. I have made the same application to our Assembly, and expect a similar law has been adopted before this time. You will

please to enlarge Lt. Bohlin upon signing the inclosed parole. I am in daily expectation of hearing from the Governor of Virginia, and I shall as soon as I do, come to Frederick, where I will have the dispute between Capt. Read and the Hessian officer fully inquired into.
I am, etc.

(J. W.)

Major Bailey.

Sir:

You will be pleased to move on with the first Division, and after consulting the officer commanding the Guard as to the distance the Division will be able to reach, pitch on a convenient place for encamping each night. I think you had better agree for a sufficient quantity of wood standing, to answer the purpose of each Division, as I shall direct the 2d. Division to encamp on the ground left by the first. You will contract for ferriage on the best terms you can; and provide other Waggons and Teams at Lancaster, if you can't engage the Waggons now employed to go the whole route, on reasonable terms.

(J. W.)

Capt. Summers.

Frederick Town, 15th March, 1782.

Dr. Colonel:

I am very happy to hear by Mr. Jackson that Robert Morris, Esqr., approved of my extending my contract to the Post of Winchester. Mr. Jackson informs me that he is very short of meat, which gives me much concern, oweing he says to the want of cash which is not at present in my power to furnish him with, but expect I can next week as I have sent an express to Philadelphia for that purpose. I have advanced him all the money I had by me, which I am sencible is very inaddiquate to the present consumption of provisions.

I shall send him an reinforcement the moment the cash arrives which I am certain will be next week—in the meentime I shall esteem it the greatest obligation if you will be so kind as to make the people satisfied for a few weeks that may incline to credit Mr. Jackson. I am sencible of your wish to serve me. I hope to have the pleasure of your Company to Phila., about the first of April.

I have the honour to be Dr. Colonel
Yr. mst. obedt. hble. servt,

MOSES RAWLINGS.

Dr. Sir:

I find that I cannot with any Degree of Convenience come to Frederick Town as soon as I expected; I must therefore beg that you will act for me in the best manner that you can, observing in a very particular manner, that none of the prisoners are permitted to indent themselves for any term above three years. If those Prisoners who belong to the Convention Army have been married, and been allowed the rights of Citizenship in any of the states shou'd come in, and you find them unable to liberate themselves by paying the Eighty Dollars, you will please to give passports to return under an obligation of appearing once a month. I forgot to mention to you, that the Secretary of War has permitted the Officers, Prisoners at Frederick Town, to amuse themselves by Fishing within the limits of their Parole. You will please have an Extract from the last Orders issued at Frederick as far as relates to the Prisoners, translated into the German Language, Printed and Dispersed among such of the Sergeants as you have reason to think are Desirous of remaining in the country.

I shall endeavour to be with you in a few days.

(J. W.)

(No address. Mem. on a fragment of a letter.)

GENERAL LINCOLN

4th April, 1782.

Sir:

I am honored by your letter of the 20th ult. I intended long before this to have forwarded the Prisoners I have been able to collect to Frederick Town, but upon visiting that Post, I discovered there was not room in the Barracks to contain them, nor was there any Place of security to confine them. Those already at Frederick are kept within a Chain of sentinels, which is no security, when it is considered that the Guards are Militia and take every opportunity of letting the Prisoners out in order to get their Labour. I was very disirous to have the Barracks picketed in, if I cou'd have had any Assistance from the State; but upon inquiry, I found that I cou'd not get a waggon and Team, nor timber for the purpose, as the State were without money and the Assembly had repealed all their empress Laws. This Business I think might be done with an inconsiderable Expense, as the work might be done by Fatigue parties from the Guard, so that there wou'd be nothing to pay for but the Timber, and Teams to haul it in, by which a great expence in the Guard wou'd be saved. I have found it a very difficult matter to collect the Prisoners, as I have the country in general to contend with, who are anxious to conceal them, as Labourers are exceedingly hard to be got and the Guards which I have are all composed of People who are interested in keeping them; however, I have been able to collect upwards of Four Hundred; but am really afraid to trust the present Guard with them to the Place of their Destination. I have considered the matter and think it best to apply to the Executive of this State to empower me to select a Guard, which I will, if granted take under my own Direction and escort them to such place as you may direct; in the meantime I shall mount a few Persons who may be depended upon and endeavor to collect all the Prisoners who are scattered in different parts of the Country. I intend to go myself immediately to all the Posts in Virginia where Prisoners have been and forward all the sick and others to this place, by which time I shall hope for your further Orders. From every information I have been able to collect, but very few of the Prisoners have attempted to escape with the Enemy; they seem to have aimed very generally to conceal themselves in the Country, and a great number of them, particularly the Germans and Irish are exceedingly desirous of taking the Oaths to the States, if they can be permitted to become Citizens.

When I first visited the post at Frederick Town I found that Major Bailey had been appointed by Colo. North, pro tempore, to do the duty of Town Major. From the situation of the Post and considering their regular manner which has been practised in issuing Provisions, and my knowledge of Major Bailey's integrity and fitness for the office, I continued him till your pleasure shou'd be known. I still think it a necessary Appointment, and am well assured the country will be greatly benefited by it. I have the honour of inclosing you an extract from my Orders at Frederick, and hope the regulations I have adopted will meet your Approbation. I thought it a necessary Precaution to oblige the senior officer among the Prisoners to sign every Provision return, in order to obviate every Dispute on the general settlement of the two Nations. The women taken with them have been hitherto allowed Rations, being included in their returns. If this shou'd be thought wrong, please inform me, and it shall be discontd. I have taken the liberty of drawing on you for two Hundred Dollars in favor of Mr. Samuel May. You may rely upon it that a shilling shall not be laid out unnecessarily, and that I will take proper vouchers for my expenditures.

I shall use my best endeavours to make a general collection of the Prisoners, and to be in readiness to remove them to any place you may direct, with all the expedition possible. May I beg to be informed if I am to collect the Convention Prisoners at the same time. I shou'd have had no doubt of the propriety of it, but from a letter which the Governor of Virginia wrote to some of the inhabitants, explanatory of a Proclamation which he had issued for calling in the Prisoners, and which he says in his letter was not meant to extend to the prisoners taken at Saratoga. Many of those prisoners have married, and been admitted by some Magistrates to take the oaths of the United States.

Mr. May will return immediately, and will, if you shou'd have any further commands, wait on you for them. I have the Honour to be, etc.

(J. W.)

(*No address*)

COLO. RAWLINGS

9 Apl., 1782.

Dr. Sir:

I intended the pleasure of seeing you at F. Town on the day appointed, but some things have intervened which disappoint me. Major Bailey will send by you transcripts of the issues at the Post, from whose exactness and knowledge of the business, I think you have no reason to apprehend the least difficulty in settling your accounts. My principal reason for wishing to be in Frederick Town before you went to Philadelphia was to see whether there was a possibility of procuring shelter for the prisoners who have been collected here; but recollecting that Major Bailey had reported to me when last at Frederick Town, that the Barracks were incapable of holding any additional numbers, I wrote immediately to G. Lincoln for his further directions. As you purpose being at Annapolis soon, I beg the favor of you to apply to the Executive of Maryland, to adopt some effectual mode for calling in the Prisoners who are much dispersed in that State, and concealed by the Inhabitants and that you will in the meantime use every possible endeavour to have them collected and confined at the Barracks.

(J. W.)

A SYSTEM ON WHICH PROVISIONS ARE TO BE ISSUED

1st. When a regiment, independent corps or detachment is to draw provisions, their Quarter Master or some commission'd officer appointed in order to do his duty shall make out and sign a provission return, seting forth in columns the number of persons with their ranks or stations; the number of days to be drawn for; the commencing and ending of the time, both days included and the number of rations—this return to be countersign'd by the commanding officer of such regiment, corps or detachment. When the contractors shall issue the provisions and have taken a receipt sign'd by the proper Quarter Master or officer doing his duty, by the commanding officer of a detachment, Quarter Master, Sergeant or some person in his absence not under the rank of a Serjeant, this return and receipt so executed shall be admitted at the Treasury as a sufficient voucher for the Contractor.

2nd. All orders for provissions for General Officers and the Quarter Master General and their families shall be sign'd by themselves or one of their aids or assistants and a receipt sign'd by the servant who shall receive it shall be a sufficient voucher for the Contractor.

3d. No person whatever in the departments of Quarter Master General and of Military Stores shall sign any order or return for provisions except the heads of those departments or such persons as shall be respectively appointed by them to perform this Business. Of such appointments, the Contractors are to have notice in writing. No return is to be made for any except those who are necessarily employed in the service of said Departments and who do not draw provisions in any other Character. The rations allowed to each individual must be fix'd and the returns might specify the number, stations, or occupations of the persons; the number of days to be drawn for; the commencing and ending of the time, both days included and the number of rations in the whole. This return with proper receipts will be a sufficient Voucher for the Contractors. No fatigue rations to be issued in either of the departments of Quarter Master General or of Military Stores but by the particular authority of the superior officer, a copy of whose order must be transmitted monthly with the Contractors accounts.

4th. Hospital. No officer or other person whatever belonging to the General Hospital shall sign or countersign any orders or returns for provisions or Hospital stores excepting the superior officer of that department at the post or place where such provisions or stores are necessary to be drawn. Such superior officer shall make out and sign two distinct returns as follows, viz:

One return for all the sick and convalescents under his care, setting forth the number of persons, the number of days to be drawn for with the commencing and ending of the time, both days included; the number of rations, and at what allowance per day for each class of sick or convalescents, also pointing out by different lines what regiment or corps the persons belong to. This return with the proper receipt sign'd by the Steward of the Hospital will be a voucher. He shall make and sign another return for himself and all the officers and others under his command or direction setting forth the number of persons with their rank or station in distinct columns—the number of days to be drawn for, with the commencing and ending of the time, both days included, and the number of rations. This return with a proper receipt or receipts will be a voucher. When such superior officer draws an order for hospital stores, he shall express the quantity of each article in words at full length, and the Steward of the Hospital shall sign a proper receipt for them in like words also. No fatigue rations to be allowed any person in the Department except by order of the Physician or Surgeon Genl., a copy of which order to be transmitted with the Contractor's accounts.

5th. All orders or returns for provissions for prisoners of war at settled ports must be sign'd by the Commissary of prisoners or Town Major; if none, to be counter sign'd by our commanding officer, if any. These returns must show in proper column the number of each, rank and station, as also the women and children allowed to draw, with the number of rations to be drawn—the number of days with the commencing and ending of the time. No prisoner is to draw more than two thirds of a ration and that without liquor saving such who are allowed otherwise by Capitulation. When whole rations are allowed, vegetables and other necessary articles are to be substituted for the Liquor. In no return is liquor to be drawn for the women with the prisoners or any compensation made for it. No provision is to be drawn for any prisoners who are out at work.

6th. The commanding officer of any corps passing a port shall sign the order for provisions for such corps to be countersign'd by the commanding officer of the port, if Senior; but for detachments not commanded by a commission'd officer, the order must be sign'd by the officer then commanding at the port.

7th. All soldiers acting as servants with arms shall draw with their corps, and all such soldiers who are annex'd to officers and are without arms shall be drawn for by the officers respectively with whom they serve.

8th. As all victualling returns are to be examin'd and check'd at the war office in all the returns of regiment and independant corps the absentees will be accounted for on the back of the returns.

9th. The commissary of prisoners, or where is none, the town Major shall call the roll of the prissoners daily, sign their returns for provisions and inspect the barracks and see that they are preserved from injury and properly supplied.

B. LINCOLN, *Secy. at War.*

War Office, April 26, 1782.

[*Long ss generally used.*]

(*A system for issuing provisions*)

COLO. WOOD

1782—Dr. The United States to Bargis Ball Lieut. Colo. Comd. To my allowance of 6 rations per day from the 1st. day of January 'till the 30th. April, 1782 inclusive.

1782—To my allowance in lieu of Rations from 1st May 'till 31st August Recd. Aug. 5th, 1782 of Wm. Constable a Certificate in the name of Colo. Wm. Heth for two months' subsistence signed by J. Pierce, Paymr. Genl. Paybl. the 1st. Inst.

150 dollars.   WM. WISTER.
Rect. Colo. Wm. Heth's Certificate.

I have been directed by the Minister of War to contract for Forage for your Legion. But from the shortness of Crops and the difficulty of procuring hay, I find it altogether impossible to get any person to undertake this Business, of which I shall inform General Lincoln immediately. I wou'd therefore recommend it to you to remain where you are till further orders, as there is no stable or public building of any kind. I believe I cou'd on my own credit procure two thousand bushells of corn, but hay or fodder can't be got at any price. If the situation shou'd be such, at any rate if you can't stay where you are, you must give me immediate notice that I may have some corn provided, which cannot be had sooner than the 20th instant, and not then without I have at least four days' notice of your determination of coming.

To Colo. Armand,
11th Sept., 1782.   (*Mem. Col. J. Wood.*)

I have received your Letter of yesterday's date, and have been prevented from answering it sooner by being engaged in a multiplicity of Business. As you have determined it improper for the Officers of the Legion to sit as a Court Martial on the private soldier confined, I shou'd suppose that the proper mode of proceeding wou'd be to have a report made to Genl. Morgan, who will appoint a Court; as to myself, any proceeding of mine wou'd be improper, as I am the prosecutor. With respect to the affair between your Officer and the Civil Magistrates, I know nothing of it, as that matter had subsided before I came to the place; the officer had gone to his quarters, and the people had dispersed. The crime of Brown was altogether distinct from the other matter. Having observed him behaving very disorderly in the streets, I determined to confine him. In order to send him to the Guard, I went to him and ordered him to go with me, informing him who I was, and that I shou'd confine him; he immediately resisted, flew at me and struck me, and was aided by a number of Others, who declared that they would rescue him and that they would pay no respect to any officer but those of their own Corps. Before Brown struck me, he had not received a stroke from me or any other Person. After it, he was knocked down and severely beat, previous to his commitment; but after his confinement not the least violence was offered him.

I mean to send an Express to General Lincoln on Sunday, in order to inform him what I have done respecting Forage for your

Legion, what engagements I have entered into, and the prices of the Corn, Waggonage, etc.

If you have any commands to Philadelphia, they will be agreeable.

(J. W.)

Colonel Armand
October 10, '82.

Dr. Sir:

Lieut. Howell of the 1st. Reg. Dragoons has died since the return was made out. I must beg you to mark his death among the Casualties.

I am very respectifully & Most hastily yours,

Oct. 10, 1782.   J. BARNETT.
Genl. Muhlenberg.
Commanding in Virginia.

BY THE UNITED STATES IN CONGRESS ASSEMBLED

November 19, 1782.

On the report of the Committee to whom was referred a report of a Committee on a letter of the 30 October from the Secretary at War.

Resolved. That the Senior Officers of each grade sufficient to form Corps agreeable to the Act of the 7. August last (the regiments to have their complement of Officers as established by the Acts of the 3 and 21 of October 1780 except as to the therein proposed supernumerary Subaltern for receiving the Recruits who shall be omitted) shall be retained in service for the Command of the said Corps and the redundant Junior Officers of the several grades shall retire from immediate Service agreeable to the said first recited Act, but the said Junior Officers so retiring shall retain their Rank in the Army and be liable and entitled to be called into actual Service only when regiments or Corps shall be raised for them by their respective States. But any senior officer entitled to remain in service shall have the liberty of retiring with the emoluments of Officers retiring under the Acts last recited for reasons satisfactory to the Commander-in-Chief or the Commanding Officer of the Southern Army on such retiring Officer's relinquishing his Command and future right of promotion in the Army and signifying the same on or before the first day of January next, to the Commander-in-Chief or the commanding Officer of the Southern Army, who shall duly transmit lists of such retiring Officers to the Secretary at War, any act or Resolution of Congress to the contrary hereof notwithstanding.

November 20, 1782.

Resolved, That Commissions issue on promotions properly Certified for all regimental Officers entitled to fill vacancies happening before the first day of January next, excepting vacancies occasioned by senior Officers retiring agreeably to the resolve of the 19th instant, any resolution of Congress to the contrary hereof notwithstanding.

Extract from the records in the War Office.

W. JACKSON, *Assistt. Secy. At War.*

Arrangement of the 1st. Virginia Regiment.

Note. Officers marked in the Column for remarks Desire to retire with the emoluments of Officers retiring under the Acts of Congress of the 3d and 21st October, 1780. relinquishing Command, and future right of Promotion in the Army.

Arrangement of the Virginia line, as it ought to stand in case the officers who have signified their wishes, are permitted to retire, agreeable to the resolutions of Congress of the 19th. November, 1782. 5th. Regimt.

James Wood, Colonel
Samuel Hawes, Lt. Colonel
Samuel Finley, Major.

Captains		Lieuts.	
1	William Johnston	1	Thomas Miller
2	Clough Shelton	2	Joseph Conway
3	Nathaniel Pendleton	3	Wm. Eskridge
4	John Stith	4	Jacob Brown
5	Thomas Edmunds	5	James DeLaplaine
6	Abraham Kirkpatrick	6	Javan Miller
7	John Anderson	7	Geo. A. Washington
8	James Williams	8	John Heath
9	Robert Woodson	9	Edmund Clark
Lieut. 1	Thomas Martin	10	Surgeon Cornelius Baldwin
2	Charles Stockley		
3	Nathaniel Darby		
4	David Walker		
5	Robert Brackenridge		
6	Thomas Coverley		
7	Samuel Basherville		
8	John Hackley		
9	John Harrison		
10	Albert Russell		

Junior Lieutenants who have made their election to supply the places of vacant Ensigneys retaining their rank and pay agreeable to the resolve of Congress of 11th. July, 1782.

The Board have also added an accurate arrangement of the Line, as it ought to stand, if the officers who have signified their wishes, are permitted to retire, agreeable to the resolutions of Congress of the 19th November, 1782.

Major Smith Sneed

Captains 1. Alexander Parker
2. Samuel Booker

Lieuts. 1. John Scarborough
2. Richard Worsham

Lieuts. 1. John Wm. Sudderian—To do ensigns duty.

Arrangement of Officers for 101 Non-Commissioned and Matrosses belonging to the 1st. Regiment of Artillery.

Captain Wm. Pierce
Capt. Lieut. Ambrose Bohannan

Lieuts. 1. Richard Claiborne
2. John Drew
3. Elias Langham
4. Wm. Whitaker

Mem. to Search if Colo. Washington's entries are made agreeable to his letter to Mr. T. Rutherford.

Enquire of Colo. Lewis concerning five entries and surveys made for Sam. Echerling in the year 1752, one at the Mo. of Dunker's Creek. Do. On the opposite side of the River. Do. 2 Miles lower down on the West side of the River. Do. on the East side on Crabb Apple Creek Partly Opposite to the last mentioned. Do. 2 miles above the Mo. of Dunker's Creek on the East side.

To make entries for Mr. R. R. of 100 in the forks below the Mo. of G. Kanawha.

Do. in the names of R. & T. Rutherford 4,000 acres between Sandy Creek and Scioto River being the Lands surveyed June 1773 by John Wood, Robert Wood, Thomas Lewis, and Simon Butler on which they built Cabbins.

To write Colo. Preston in the name of T. R. See Colo. Washington's letter to him on the same subject.

(J. W.)

Frederick County, Decemb. 22d, '82.

Mr. President and Gentlemen:

I have presumed to state my case and with what propriety I claim rank before you, hoping it will meet with your assent, trusting to your equity in similiar cases.

When Virginia Line marched Southerly under the Comd. of Genl. Woodford, Doctr. Roberts as full Surgeon and myself as mate to the 2d. Battalion, the Surgeon resigned at Richmond. I immediately made application to the Commanding Officer, but was answered that the Surgeon General of the Army was the Gentleman authorized to appoint. The Troops then being on their way to South Carolina I could not make the proper application, after which we fell Victims to Brittish Tyranny, and then it could not be determined. After thirteen months Captivity, I was exchanged, and joined the Southern Army. On my arrival, I informed Doctr. Brown, Surgeon General, the circumstances relative to my rank and on what account I claimed it. He gave it in my favour and told me to consider myself as full Surgeon, but could not appoint me to particular regiment as he did not know the mode of the late arrangement. On my return from the Southward, I repaired to the Genl. Rendezvous and considered myself a full Surgeon from the authority of Doctr. Brown, and requested Genl. Muhlenberg to appoint me to a particular Regiment. It met with his approbation, but not with the Governor's. The answer of the Governor was that my Claim was just, but was sorry he had never a Regiment for me, and must wait till I could be appointed with more Propriety. Now Gentlemen, there was a number of Officers in the Line who had no Command, yet still took rise upon Resignations as a matter of right. Why I am denied that privilege is a doubt with me, tho' with the same propriety claim it. You Gentlemen will determine whether it is just or no.

Since my being in the State Doctrs. Monro and Davis have been appointed in the Line as Officers. Every Nidwall? Gentleman is certainly intitled to the same emoluments, if a General one which I shall always consider it, unless they had some peculiar recommendation. I submit these matters, Gentlemen, to your Candour, probity, to give it its final issue.

    I am Gentlemen with respect,
     Your Humble Servent,
          JOS. SAVAGE.

Colo. Wood Presd.,
Winchester.

         Fredericksburg, Decer., 24th.
Dear Genl.

Not until this morning was I informed that there was orders for the arrangement of the Virginia line, and as I immagine you will have the management of it, and as my indisposition will prevent my attending, beg leave to acquaint you if I can be included in the arrangement, it is my desire to be continued. Beg to be remembered to your family and the officers of my acquaintance.

    With much esteem,
     I am Your Obdt. Svt.,
         GEO. WASHINGTON.

Genl. Muhlenberg, Winchester
Hond. By Colo. Walker.

(L. Washington's letter J. Wood.)

1783

Gentlemen:

In the general squabble for Rank I crave the Attention of your Board to my Pretentions. Prior to your determination in favour of Major Willis I was perfectly contented, but I find my seniority is grounded on the same principles with his.

I was a first Lieutenant in a Company Commanded by Capt. Andrew Waggoner in the State Service and Junr. to Capt. Casey in my State Commission, but on receiving orders to enlist our men into Continental Service, Capt. Waggoner's Company were reinlisted to Capt. Asby's in whose Company Capt. Casey was a first Lieut. On these principles, Gentlemen, I trust I shall have the Rank Capt. Casey had, which was from the Resignation of Capt. Jos. Mitchell.

I am ready with my witnesses to wait on the Board to prove my pretension.

               I have the honr. to be
                    Gentlemen,
           Yr. most Ob. hum. Svt.,
                         GRES. G. NEVILL.

Colo. James Wood,
President of the Board of Arrangement, Winchester.

                                Winchester, Jan. 6th, 1783.

Note in Colo. Wood's writing:

"The Board are of Opinion that Capt. Nevill ought to take rank from the Resignation of Capt. Mitchell the 1st September, 1779."

As this will be delivered you with the Arrangement of the Virginia line and as I was President of the Board who made the Arrangement, I take the liberty of mentioning that the Board were of the opinion that by the Resolution of Congress of the 12th November, they were obliged to arrange the senior Officers of each grade for the command of the men now in service, which they have done, and noted such as wished to retire. I am desired by most of those Gentlemen to mention their inability to serve, particularly Capt. Bowyer, who is really aged, and so infirm as to be wholly unfit for service. The Board considered themselves at liberty to arrange Junior Lieutenants to do the duty of Ensigns, by the Resolve of Congress of the —— April, 1782, as there was vacant Ensigneys in the line. All the Majors in the line who were not Prisoners, wish to retire, except Major Finley and Major Sneed. As Major Finley is with the Southern Army, and Major Sneed on the Eastern Shore, I dare say you will think it best to arrange Major Finley to the first Reg. as he is with the detachment serving with the Southern Army. Jany. 13th, 1783.

                                                    (J. W.)

Genl. Lincoln.

Frederick, 25th March, 1783.

GARRISON ORDERS

The Intendant of prisoners is to call in immediately all Prisoners of war, except such of the British who have been taken out on bail, agreeable to the resolves of Congress. The officer commanding the Guard is to keep all Prisoners within the limits of the Barracks, and not to suffer any to go out with out a Passport from the Intendant of Prisoners, who is the only Person authorized by the Minister of War to give such Passports. Whenever the Contractor serves the Post with good Bacon, ten ounces is to be issued to each Ration, which is deemed equivalent to three-quarters of a pound of salt Pork.

JAMES WOOD, *Colo. Com.*

From that part of Colo. Nevill's testimony, that the G. of V. approved of the app. of L. L. The above proceedings are referred to the Governor for his consideration; at the same time on considering the facts as stated, I am of the opinion that Lieutenant Lane from the time of his appointment and the nature of it, is the senior Lieutenant in the 12th Regiment, and that he have the Command and Rank as such; and upon his junction with Captain Langdon's Company, he is to serve in that Company as First Lieutenant.

(J. W.)

To the T. Sy.

MEMORANDUMS

Genl. Muhlenberg's Subsistence.
Forage in the future.
Settlement of Forage and Waggonage accts.
Genl. Morgan's Waggon certificate.
Genl. Morgan's Saddle, Pistols, etc.
The times of payment of Rations to be stipulated—the forms of Contract, etc.

(J. W.)

I do certify that John McGuire Esq., entered the Service in June, 1775, was afterwards promoted to the rank of Captain in the Continental Army, which Commission he resigned in the year 1778—his time of service supposed to be three years.

Given under my hand this 6th May, 1783.

JAMES WOOD, *Colo. I. V. L.*

This certificate is too vague to ascertain Capt. McGuire's claim.

THOS. MERIWETHER

I do authorize and employ Brigadier-General Morgan to settle and receive the within mentioned certificate.

JOHN McGUIRE.

May 6th, 1783.

Sir:

Please issue four Days' Provision for Ten Light Dragoons. Commencing the 27th. & ending the 30th. June, 1783.

J. WOOD, Colo. Com.

Mr. Jackson.

N. B. Issue in future on the return of the Sergeant Major at Winchester Barracks the 27th. June, 1783, Recd. from the Contractor for Winchester Barracks the Number of forty Rations within mentioned. JONATHAN WHITE.

Provision Return for Four Pennsylvania Soldiers of the 4th Regiment of Artillery for Four Days Commencing the 3d and ending the 6th June 1783. JAMES WOOD, Colo. Com.

---

4 Men,
16 Rations.

At Winchester Barracks the 3d. day of June 1783, Recd. from the Contractor for Winchester Barracks, sixteen Rations above mentioned.

Pennsylvania Artillery
June 3d & 6th, 1783. WM. FORD BOMBR.

1784

Alexandria, May 19th, 1784.

Dr. Sir:

I wrote you the 8th instant by Thomas West, Esqr., and at the same time inclosed you the Commercial Agent's Certificate to George Harmar, Esqr., for sixteen thousand three hundred and eighty nine pounds crop Tobacco. If you have been so fortunate as to receive it or any part thereof or if it will answer the pay into the Treasury be pleased to let Charles Lee, Esquire, have it, as he is to pay money into the Treasury and discount is esteemed good pay. I shall be happy to render you any service that you may command from
Your most Obedt. Servt.,

DENNIS RAMSAY.

General James Wood.

Honored by Charles Lee, Esqr.

Richmond.

Winchester, June 7th, /84.
Dear General:

As you were kind enough to undertake to settle my business in Richmond, I shall be much obliged to you to get for me the pension Warrents if to be obtained before the Money's due. I am in doubt whether they will issue them before. Indeed Major Magill informs me they cannot, but I suppose it cou'd make no difference having it specified in them that they were not to be paid before the time they became due. They would be of service to me at this period. I believe I could exchange them for money which I want much as a necessary ingrediance at Bath this Season. Major Magill will do me the favor to take charge of them.

I am Dear Sir with the Highest
Respect and Esteem,
Yours,
WM. McGUIRE.

General James Wood, Richmond.
Honoured by Mr. Stribling.

Sir:

My son waits on you with a certificate I received a twelve month ago and you were so kind as to promise payment on the receipt of the cash. I did not make application as I did not know when the cash was collected. If you will be so good as to let me have it at this time I stand in great need to pay my harvest people. If you do not think proper to pay it, please to let me know when I must apply for it, and you will much oblige, Sir,

Your Obedient Servt.,
ANNA McDONALD.

July 12, 1784.

1789

THE ELECTION OF THE FIRST PRESIDENT

Dr. Sir:

I have just now recd. your favor by Paddy Kirch, who tells me he shall set off immediately—Not having a sheet of paper in the house, I am obliged to write on a dirty wrapper. We have not a word of news—party seems to subside in a great measure. Mr. Henry was an elector, attended in perfect good humour and was extremely anxious than Genl. Washington shou'd not lose a single vote in this or any other State. Ten electors attended, three of whom were antifederalists and voted for Clinton—five for Adams—myself and L. Johnston against him, both for the same reason; viz., that we knew him to be an enemy of Genl. Washington and not a Republican, One of us voted for Hancock, the other for Jay.

I shall be happy to hear from you, and shall in return give you every occurrence worthy of your notice which may happen here. The letter to Sherman shall be delivered. I am told he is in Wmsburg., but will return next stage.

Below you have a list of the representatives returned. My wife joins with affectionate compliments to the ladies.

I am, Dr. Sir,

Yr. very obt. servt.,

JAMES WOOD.

(No address)

17th Feb. 1789.

Sam Griffin	F
Theod. Bland	A
Isaac Coles	A
Jno. Page	F
Josiah Parker	A
Andrew Moore	F
Richd. B. Lee	F
James Madison	F

Note. Previous to 1804, each elector voted for two candidates for President. The one who received the largest number of votes was declared President, and the one who received the next largest number of votes was declared Vice-President. The electoral votes for the first President of the United States were: George Washington, 69; John Adams, of Massachusetts, 34; John Jay, of New York, 9; R. H. Harrison, of Maryland, 6; John Rutledge of South Carolina, 6; John Hancock, of Massachusetts, 4; George Clinton, of New York, 3; Samuel Huntington, of Connecticut, 2; John Milton, of Georgia, 2; James Armstrong, of Georgia, Benjamin Lincoln, of Massachusetts, and Edward Telfair, of Georgia, 1 vote each. Vacancies (votes not cast), 4. George Washington was chosen President and John Adams Vice-President. *(New Century Book of Facts.)*

CHAPTER XXII

Personal Letters — Records of the Deaths of Ex-Governor James Wood and His Wife, Jean Moncure

> I, for my part, value letters as the most vital part of biography ——We should all be ready to say that if the secrets of our daily lives and inner souls may instruct other surviving souls, let them be open to men hereafter, even as they are to God now. Dust to dust, and soul-secrets to humanity—there are natural heirs to all these things.
> *(From the Letters of Robert Browning and Elizabeth Barrett Barrett. Copyright 1899, by Harper & Bros.)*

> "The human touch,
> Life's tokens dear,
> These need I most,
> And now, and here."
>
> The bravest are the tenderest,—
> The loving are the daring.
> —*Bayard Taylor.*

Winchester, 17th July, 1775.

Madam:

I received your favour of the 7th instant this morning, and am happy in having so early an opportunity of conveying you agreeable intelligence from Mr. Wood. Your intrusting me with the care of your letter requires no apology. This confidence, tho' in a small matter, I consider as an earnest of future Friendship, and the pleasure I shall hereafter enjoy in your Company. Your apprehensions of Mr. Wood's danger are natural, tho' I can venture to assure you of the friendly disposition of those Tribes towards a Person on his business; and their Expectations of a Treaty undoubtedly afford a sufficient security for his personal safety. I thank you for your kind Enquiries after my Wife's health. She has been somewhat better than when I wrote Mr. Wood. Yesterday she had a relapse and is since confined to bed in great pain. She desires her compliments to you, Colo. Blackburn, his Lady and Family, to which please add those of

Madam,
Your very humble Servt.,
ALXR. WHITE.

Mrs. Jenny Wood at Colo. Blackburn's near Dumfries.
To be put into the Post Office at Fredericksburg.

My dear Jenny:

I am sincerely sorry to hear of your long Suspense but I make no doubt but you have heard before this that Capt. Wood is safe at Fort Pitt. Harry Lee received a letter from old Harry a few days ago, wherein he informs him that Mr. Wood is very well. The Indians are not yet met or at least not all that were expected, old Cornstalk and several others of the Indian Chiefs were met. The others are daily expected. Sister Becky expects Mr. Blackburn towards the end of this month when I suppose you may expect Capt. Wood.

Miss Aggy has promised that if you have no objection she will come with you up to Westwood some time next week. Pray Jenny do. Perhaps Miss Aggy and I together may raise your Spirits. Let me know how Mrs. Conway is.

N. B. Pray excuse this Scrawl and burn it the instant you read it. I would copy it but I scarcely have a moment to write.

I am ever yours,
A. Scott.

My Dearest Love:

I am exceedingly unhappy that I did not know of the Opportunity which now offers time enough to write fully to My Dearest Love; the Tents are now struck and the men paraded to march off without anyone knowing whether to the North or the South. We are now on the Borders of New York Government about 40 miles No. of Morris Town. As I shall send back an Officer in a few days, I shall only at this Hurrying time inform my Jenny that I am extremely well and that from the Constant hurry of the Camp, time passes faster than I cou'd have Expected, but to think of a moment's happiness 'till I see my Heart's Delight and My Sweet Little One, is altogether vain and impossible. Let me beg that you take care of your health. The Drum beats ——— Must conclude.

My Dearest Love,
Yours ever,
J. Wood.

Camp head Qrs. 20 July, 1777.
Don't fail writing Colo. Heth.
To Mrs. Jean Wood of Winchester.

My Dear and Only Love:

I intended the inclosed letters shou'd have gone yesterday by one Mr. Lewis (a brother of Mrs. McFarland's) who intended through Winchester but before I had closed my Letter he had set off. Major Hunter by whom you will receive this, returns in a few days. Let me beg my Love that you will let me hear from you on his return. I am unhappy beyond description until I know how you are, and shall be happy to hear the little Occurrences at Bath, what Company you have and how your time passes. I understand Mr. Hartley and Mrs. Smith are there. Colo. Hartley is a Brother Officer, and I am told his Lady is a fine woman. In all probability the army will lie here a considerable time. I am extremely anxious to have you nearer to me whenever your Health will permit, and it is agreeable to you. I shall be exceedingly glad to fix you either at York Town or about 20 miles from Philadelphia, where Mrs. Brown boards; I saw the Doctor as we passed through Philada. He tells me that she is in a most agreeable Place and that the people can accommodate you in the same House. The distance from the Army is not more than a day and a half's ride to either that or York Town, so that you will have an Opportunity of choosing either. I am sure I can get leave to come for you, but if I shou'd not I can send Billy Baylis (who is appd. paymaster and has leisure time) with a stage waggon for you. I hope my love will have no Objection to coming to me whenever her Health permits. Till that blessed time arrives I cannot expect or desire it. The expence will be very Trifling, and what I can well afford, considering how saving I live—not that I want for anything. Our Provisions are good, plenty of Soap and Candles found us, so that I am at little Expense. We draw but one ration each Officer, and receive money for the remaining five, with which we are enabled to purchase Milk and pay every other Expense without breaking on our Pay. This among the extravagant wou'd be thought penurious so that I wish to keep it to myself.

Don't, my Love, be the least uneasy on my account. The Danger is trifling compared to what People at a Distance generally imagine. The Enemy keep close, and I dare say they will be kept in such narrow Bounds that they will soon look out for better Quarters on some other shore. We have had near thirty Prisoners brought in since last night which makes upwards of eighty within this three Days past. The Army is remarkably Healthy and in high Spirits. I have not had an Hour's sickness since I left you, though I am not near so fat as I was, which does not a little please me when I know that you like it better so than otherwise. Do my Love send me a small Plat of your hair to wear around my neck besides the Article mentioned in my other letter. Oh my dearest life, how I long to press you to my fond bosom and how slow the time passes which is to bring about that greatest of Felicities—Adieu, my Sweet, my Amiable Jenny. Don't forget to give me a full account of my Dear Maria in your next. I have recd. only three Letters from you, the latest date of which was the 22nd of last Month. I know my Love has wrote oftener but they have not come to hand. Ten thousand fond adieus to my soul's Delight. I am with every sentiment of the warmest affection,

My Dearest Life,
Yr. sincere and very Affectionate Husband,
J. WOOD.

Near Wilmington, 31st Aug., 1777.
For Mrs. Jean Wood, Winchester, Virginia, by Major Hunter.

My Dear My Lovely Jenny:

I just now received your letter of the 26th August the contents of which gives me Heartfelt Pain. I always flattered myself that the Springs wou'd have restored both you, and our Poor Little Girl's health. We must, My Love, submit ourselves with patience, to the will of the Infinite Wise Disposer of every event. If it shou'd please Him to take from us our sweet Innocent, I can bear it with a Christian Fortitude, in full assurance that the Decrees of the Supreme Being are right and best, and that it is gone to a place of eternal Happiness. While you, My Love, My Amiable Jenny, are spared, I can be happy under any misfortune or in any Circumstance of life. If it has pleased God to take our Child, let me beg that you endeavor to bear the loss with Patience and Discretion and that you will inform me with all possible Expedition; I shall immediately return and remove you to some agreeable Place near me, or if your Health shou'd not permit, I will immediately quit the service. I am more and more convinced that I can't live without you, my sweet, my amiable wife. I dare say we are fixed at this Place for the campaign; the Enemy in my Opinion have nothing in view but to secure the Eastern Shore, which they are attempting to do, by extending their lines, from the Head of Chesapeake to the Delaware Bay, which is but Ten Miles. I reconnoitered their lines yesterday with two other Officers. We went so near as to see their Centinels. They have extended about 4 miles towards Delaware. Major Dark attacked one of their Picquets yesterday and drove them until they were reinforced, killed several, without any loss on our side except one man of my Regiment badly wounded, and two missing. Mr. Gamball led the attack and behaved well. I have been exceedingly uneasy for fear of your wanting money, and wrote to Mr. White, to supply you with any sum you wanted, but lest he shou'd be out of the way I have now inclosed you a small sum, and have desired Major Hunter to send it by Express.

For God's sake, my love, keep up your spirits, and take care of your Health; on it depends all my hopes of Happiness. I can bear any other loss or misfortune that can befall me; that alone can only make me wretched. I have never recd. the Letter you mention nor any others but the first three. I am in Expectation that I shall receive them all, as I hear of many people from Virginia being on the road. Don't, my love, be the least uneasy on my account, be assured that I am in no kind of Danger and in perfect Health. The army are remarkably Healthy and in High Spirits. I hear the Inhabitants of Winchester have been greatly frightened and that a party of brave Volunteers had set out in pursuit of their imaginary Enemy. I am greatly surprised at the timidity of the people. It is full as possible that the Indians shou'd penetrate to Philada. as Winchester.

I have not missed a single Oppy. of writing since I left you. Indeed I have some times wrote twice a Day. You may rely upon hearing from me whenever an Oppy. happens. I have never heard where Mrs. K. stays. I shall be glad you would give directions that particular attention be paid the Mare. I shall want her if I shou'd remove you to (*illegible*) in fine order. I am with every sentiment of the most ardent affection,

My Dearest Jenny,
Yrs. Eternally,
J. WOOD.

Camp near Wilmington, 2nd Septm., 1777.

My Dearest Jenny:

I am exceedingly unhappy at being disappointed in sending my Letter of the 5th as I find it has been generally circulated that I was killed in the attack of the 4th. Shou'd the report have reached you, I dread the consequences, as I am truly sensible of your great affection and extreme tenderness for a Husband who loves, who doats on you, with the most uncommon Passion. I have just received your two affect. letters of the 23rd, and 28th, of Sept. Believe me, my best beloved, that they came very opportunely. They came at a time when I was truly malancholy and distressed. Your dear idea had been constantly present to my disturbed imagination, and something hung over me which affected me beyond conception. I now feel myself relieved on hearing that my all on this side of eternity was tolerably well, and still had the same sentiments for a Husband who adores her even to idolatry.

I am Heartily sorry to find that some Expressions in my letter of the 5th, of Sept., shou'd give my beloved Jenny the Pain I find they did. At the same time the pleasure I feel in finding your Sentiments agree so exactly with mine, make me happy beyond Conception. At the time I wrote the letter, it came into my head that I had said a great deal at different times to you on the subject, perhaps too much, and although I still had it as much at heart or more than ever, I concluded it to be the surest method to leave you totally absolved and at your own free will to act as you thought proper, well knowing your extreme Generosity and Tenderness for a beloved Husband would operate more powerfully on a generous mind than anything else. Since I know your sentiments, I can now give mine with Freedom. You know them perfectly, I am more fully confirmed in them and am well assured that if I cou'd bring myself to believe that you would ever call another yours, I shou'd never enjoy a single moment's happiness in this world. Nay, I must go farther, I am convinced that I cou'd not be happy after I leave it were it possible that I cou'd know it. Mr. Kinkead is well except his being unfit for duty by a number of Boils. He is at a Country house near the Camp and may not have an Opportunity of writing. If you think you can come as far as York Town, pray let me know. I long with an impatience greater than I ever experienced to press you to a Heart overflowing

with love and Tenderness. I find it won't be possible for me to come to Winchester until the 1st of December and to be without my only Comfort 'till that time will be intolerable. I am, thank God, in perfect Health and Spirits, which proceeds from a consciousness of having deserved well of my Country. General Stephen has mentioned me with great Respect to the commander in chief as the last Regiment who left the Field. Now pray, My Love, remember me affly. to my Mother, Mr. White and Bobby and their families and Mrs. Kinkead. I am obliged to conclude with bidding my only Treasure ten thousand fond Adieus, and that I have no doubt of being more happy (if Possible) than ever in the fond arms of my Dear and Only love.
I am, with the most ardent affection,
My Dearest Love,
Yr. fond and afft. Husband,
J. WOOD.

Camp 28 miles from Philada., 10th Oct., 1777.

P. S. The complaint of our little girl is quite new to me and is to the surgeon of our Brigade. I hope it will go off without any prejudice to her. I am greatly obliged to my love for the Ribbands. If you can get a pair of your gloves with fingers I shall pay you in Kisses. I want a pair of Leather Breeches made by the man who made the last, of something thicker leather. He knows the size. I want them to come high up and Boot straps sewed behind. I shall be much obliged to my dear wife to send them by the first opportunity. They are for a particular friend in the army.

Whenever my Dearest love wants money, apply to Mr. White. Deliver the inclosed Order to Bobby. I think it would be proper to get Mr. White to write a line to Thomson Mason to jog his memory. I think you had better get the Mare broke to draw in the Chair. Bobby will do it for you.

My Dearest and Only Love:

I have just now heard of an Opportunity to Frederick Town. I sit down with extreme pleasure to write a line to my Dearest Jenny. I am exceedingly uneasy that I never cou'd get an opportunity of writing since the action of the 4th instant till yesterday. I find it has been very generally circulated that I was killed, as I was among the last who came in, and as I have frequent experienced that most People are fond of communicating bad news, I am much afraid the report reached you before my Letters will come to hand. Conscious of your extreme Tenderness, I dread the consequence if that shou'd have been the case. Oh, my beloved Jenny, with what impatience I long to press you to my fond Bosom. Time hangs so heavy upon me that I know not what to do. I am wretched beyond description without you. Believe me I did not know how Dear you were to me 'till this tiresome separation. You are constant in my thoughts, from whence nothing can drive you. Not the most imminent Dangers have ever put you out of my mind a single moment. Everything has been quiet in our Camp since the 4th, and is likely to remain so as we are 26 miles from the Enemy and no talk of moving nearer. I obtained leave to come to this place to see Colo. Blackburn who is in a fair way of doing well. Doctor Brown and Mrs. Brown are here. I have used every endeavour to procure something for a Gown without the least effect. I have had an Opportunity of sending to Trenton, Lancaster and every Town near us for that, and a piece of Cloath for a Cloak for you, but have not been so happy as to get either. Pray my love take the first opportunity of sending to Williamsburg, where I hope they may be had. Mrs. Brown tells us there is a Quantity of Gauze, Lace &c. at Dumfries. Pray send to Mrs. Blackburn to send you a Quantity. She tells me there is Satin, which I am sure you are in great want of for a shade, &c. Mr. White has a large sum in his hands. Believe me, my Dear, I shall be exceedingly happy if you can lay out 50 or 60 pounds in any articles you want. I hope my love you have complied with the directions I sent you in the last letter I sent you by Gilkeson; it is a matter I have much at heart. Pray don't neglect it. Perhaps we will meet sooner than you expect, and I am certain my Love wou'd wish to have things in the best order possible. Send me my Love an exact measure of the thickest part of your arm below the Elbow. By it I can tell if you are any fatter than you were.

We have just had an account that General Gates had found the Enemies' lines to the Northward, killed a great No., took 300 Prisoners, 18 Pieces of Cannon and 600 Tents, and that the Hessians desert in great numbers to us. This comes by an Express and is generally believed.

I can't possibly write to my Mother or any body as the gent. waits for this. Our loss at the last Battle is computed at one thousand, that of the enemy much more. It was a busy day. I think much warmer than the last. My best wishes for my Mother and all friends, and am with every sentiment of the most ardent Affection,
My Dearest Jenny,
Yr. most affectionate and Tender Husband,
JAMES WOOD.
Bethlehem, 14th October, 1777.

P. S. I have sent an order to my Brother which pray deliver to him. It is for money advanced to Capt. Wallace. Let me beg my love that you want for nothing that money will purchase.

18th Oct., 1777.

Unhappily before I cou'd finish my letter, the Gentleman who was to have conveyed it to Frederick Town had set off, since which I have received, my dearest Love, two letters by McDowell and Furgeson.

How is it possible My Jenny to give you the least Idea of my feelings on receiving so many proofs of your inviolable attachment; those proofs must make me happy in any situation of life. I am exceedingly sorry to find you despond so much. I assure you sincerely I think our affairs in a very prosperous way. Our successes against the Northern Army, you may be assured, greatly over-balance our misfortunes here. We have just now received certain Intelligence that Burgoyne and his whole army have surrendered themselves Prisoners of war to General Gates; there is to be great rejoicing on the Occasion in Camp at five o'clock this Evening.

I am greatly surprised at Bobby's carelessness of the letter, considering the Great Charge I gave him. There was an Order inclosed on the Treasury for whatever money was due to me, as I did not know the sum. Desire him to endeavour to get the letter. What makes me more anxious is, that I had more time and wrote more fully than I had ever an Opportunity of doing before or since. You desire, my angel, to be Candid as to the time that I am certain of returning to your arms. Believe me, my Beloved Jenny, I long with as great a desire and as much Impatience for that wished for time, as it is possible for you. I have come to a Determination not to ask leave till the first of December, when I am determined to Quit the service. My wish is that you wou'd come as far as York Town, where I have no doubt I cou'd obtain leave to meet you and conduct you back, but how to ask it I know not. Many things which I am unacquainted with may render it Impossible. I know you are badly off for a Cloak and many other things and what I most dread is that your Health will not admit of your taking such a Journey. I cou'd send Billy Baylis or get Bobby to come down with you; they have both repeatedly offered it. Holliday went off without letting me know of his going. You may be assured my Sweet, my too Amiable Wife that I have never missed a single Oppy. since I parted with you. It is all the Pleasure I have. I feel myself happy and relieved after writing to my Beloved wife. I am much afraid you have not received half of my Letters. I am confident I have wrote upwards of thirty. I have been much Indisposed with a violent cold and sore throat but have got much Better. It is generally believed here that we shall have little more fighting this Campaign. The Bearer waits, I must therefore conclude with my sincere and ardent prayers for your Health, and every happiness.

I am my Dearest and Only Love,
Yr. only tender and fond Husband,
J. WOOD.

Camp, 20th Oct., 1777.

My Dearest Love:

Although I wrote yesterday to My Dearest Jenny, since which nothing material has intervened, I can't let an Opportunity pass without writing. You will receive this by one of the Quakers who was sent down with the Militia. He has promised to carry it to you from a grateful principle as I interested myself in getting their Discharge. From every account we receive from Philadelphia the enemy must have suffered greatly in the action of the 4th instant. General Agnew was certainly killed and two Hundred waggons with their wounded was seen by different People going to the Hospitals in Philadelphia. On the other hand our Army are in High Spirits, and are much stronger by several reinforcements than they were before the two Actions. We have just now heard that General Howe is retreating from Philadelphia. It is not fully confirmed but is generally believed. They have been baffled in many attempts to get up the River and their shipping considerably damaged by our Gallies. Inform Mr. White and all friends of this Intelligence and that I shou'd have wrote but for the want of Paper. Adieu my angel, ten thousand fond adieus. Endeavor to make yourself as easy as possible; the time will soon come I hope that we shall meet and be happy.

      I am,
      My Dearest Love,
      Yr. Affec. and Tender Husband,
          J. WOOD.

Campt, 20th Oct., 1777.
To Mrs. Jean Wood in Winchester by Tho. McClure.

      Winchester, November 10th, 1777.
My dear Sister:

  I have long sought an oppy. of writing to you but in vain. I never cou'd since I saw Mr. Fitzhugh at Bath meet with one; by him I wrote. I hope you received it. This goes by one Glascock who has promised to leave it in Dumfries, from whence I hope you may get it safe. I heard from my dear Mr. Wood a few days ago by Mr. Kinkead. He writes me he has been ill but has recovered. It is with inexpressible joy I inform you he will, if God spares him live, be with me in about a fortnight. I promise myself more happiness if Heaven permits this impatiently expected meeting, than ever I enjoyed before, tho much has fallen to my lot ever since I was united to this amiable man. Excuse my calling him so. I cannot but think myself excusable in giving him his dues, more especially to one whose good and honest heart I know will rejoice in my felicity. He certainly deserves my utmost praise. He has ever been to me one of the most kind and indulgent of husbands and has and still does, love me with the most extreme affection and unabated ardour. Him I have to thank for all my happiness. Had he not been one of the best of men, I shou'd have been the most wretched of women, but his kind, soothing and gentle goodness has made me the most happy, and while it pleases Heaven to spare him to me I make no doubt shall be ever so.

It is generally thought the fighting is over for this campaign. I am quite in spirits, I tread in air. He has left camp and gone in the country to a friend's home ever since he was ill. From there he is to return home as soon as he settles his business so that he can return. My health is much better than it has ever been since the birth of my little Maria and she thank Heaven, seems mendg. and I hope will get quite hearty. She chatters like a little magpye, and is in my eyes a great beauty. She is the exact resemblance of her Father, his every feature, "Most delicately touch'd." Allow for a fond parent's partiality, but I hope to show her to you yet this winter or early in the spring. My dear Mr. Wood tells me in every letter to hold myself in readiness to take a trip to see you all as soon as he returns. I am vex'd I have it not in my power to send down for the fruit you were so kind as to promise me. If you have dried it, please keep it, if you can spare it, and if I don't go down, I will try to get it up. Mrs. Kinkead and her good man go to housekeeping in about ten days. She desired her compts. to you, Mr. Daniel and all friends. Please remember me also to all inquiring friends. I need not particularise Mr. Daniel to whom I am bound by so many and so great obligations, beside the most sincere esteem and affection. Tell the children I long to see them. Tell Kravy I have still the same wife in view for him that I had when down. She is a fortune in herself and deserves, what I realy think he will be, a clever fellow. She is a miracle of industry. Tell Sally I have one to find for her. Lads are scarce hereabout, but I will find out one to rival George Waugh and Hincher. I shall insist upon Sally returning with us when we go down. I shall be so lonesome when Mr. Kinkead leaves. I must have her, and she will have a playmate just her own age in the second daughter of Mrs. Harrison. Mrs. Wood fails ver fast. This reflection makes me grave and melancholy, as I shou'd lose a kind, a worthy parent, and one whom I most sincerely love and honour. I am, my dear sister, most affectly., and sincerely your obliged,

J. Wood.
(Mrs. James Wood.)

My Dearest Jenny:

I never received your Letter of the 10th instant which came by Post 'till yesterday. I have now an Opportunity of sending this as far as Frederick Town by Colo. Blackburn with Directions to put it in the Post Office there. I am amazed at the Insolence of that scoundrel Aldridge. I shou'd have engaged workmen to repair the house before I left Home but he came to me a few Days before I set off, and told me that he had got nails from Wm. Lupton's Son and that he wou'd take the Opportunity of making the repairs while you were at the Springs. I wou'd not wish to gratify him so far as to give up the house as I have an undoubted right to it 'till the 20th of August; however if you think half of Heth's House is as convenient, I have no

kind of Objection; whatever is agreeable to you will be perfectly so to me. I shall not be Particular in this, as the conveyance is uncertain. Suffice it to assure you that I am in perfect Health, that I wrote yesterday to the General for leave to go Home and that I hope to see My Soul's Treasure nearly as soon as this reaches you. Try my Beloved Jenny, to be well against I am to be the most Happy man alive, in pressing a beloved wife to the fond Bosom of
              Her Truly Affectionate and Tender Husband,
                                            J. WOOD.
Bethlehem, 9th Nov., 1777.

My dearest and only love:

It is now almost two months since the date of the last Letter which I received from your Dear hands. It is Impossible for me to paint my anxiety and Impatience on the Occasion. I am really so unhappy that I am convinced that I don't sleep a single Hour in the night nor do I enjoy a moment's peace of mind, or shall till I hear from my Beloved Jenny. You will receive this by Captain John Mountjoy who sets off tomorrow, but I am happy to tell you my love that I shall set off in three days after him, and if I am not detained longer in Philadelphia than I expect I shall arrive before the letter; I now only wait for His Excellency's Instructions as I am sent by Officers of the Virginia line to represent them in the Assembly of Virginia, and to do some business on my way with the Congress.

Oh, my Jenny how happy I shall think myself if I find you and my Dear little One well and able to go with me to Williamsburg. I am now determined never to be a week from you while I exist. If you can possibly be at Mr. Threlhald's the 10th day of October I shall without Doubt be there; if not the Precise Day in a day or two of it, tho' I shall strive to be there the time affixed; but don't be uneasy as my Business with Congress may detain me two or three days longer. If possible don't fail. My heart will be set on meeting you there, but if any thing prevents you try to be at Colo. Blackburn's.

At the time when the Greatest Expectations prèvailed, that the Enemy were about to leave the Country, I waited upon His Excellency and offered my Commission, but he positively refused to accept it. My reason for taking that time to do it was, that every one thought the war at an End, and that I cou'd not be subject to the least Reflection for quitting the service at such a Period. However I am determined never to return without my Dearest Jenny with whom I can be happy in any place or situation; you will endeavor to have every thing in as much readiness to set out to Wmsburg. as possible.
                            I am,
                    My dear and only love,
                          Yours ever,
                                          J. WOOD.

P. S. We are removed upward of seventy miles from the enemy. Camp West Point, Hudson's River.

28th Septem., 1778.

Note: There is no further mention of the little girl, who must have died at a very early age.

Dr. Sir:

I received a letter from you just before I left Camp but the Hurry of Business there and my being constantly engaged in Business of some Consequence to the army with Congress while in Philadelphia have prevented me from answering it sooner. I am much obliged to you for the Information respecting the Clerkship. If Mr. Keith purposes selling it, I will give him as much as anyone will. I think he ought to give me the refusal, which I shall be obliged to you to mention to him.

I am likely to be detained here for some time. I am charged with a variety of Business to the Assembly from His Excellency—the most material is to urge the necessity of their adopting some vigorous mode to fill up their Regiments, which are greatly reduced. This and many other matters will, I fear, detain me till the end of the Session, which is exceedingly Distressing to me, as my wife is in a very Low state of Health, and I am obliged to return immediately to Camp which will prevent my coming to Frederick, if I am detained here as long as I expect. My wife will be up, if she is able to go with me, which I expect will be the Case.

I wrote to Bobby sometime ago to purchase me some Grain and Fodder Before winter sets in. I have not time by this Opportunity to write to him. Pray remind him of it; the prices will take a great rise as Genl. Burgoyne's army are on their march to Virginia. I want him to increase the Quantity to as much as will fatten what Hogs I have, and serve my wife until spring.

Major Hunter is waiting so that I must conclude with my best wishes to all my Friends.

      I am, Dr. Sir,
       Yr. Aff. friend,
         J. Wood.

Wmsburg., 6th November, 1778.
(No address)

Dr. Sir:

I have inclosed you Lieut. White's Commission with all the Pay due to him which has been recd. by the Paymaster. We are always kept in arrears two or three months—the 6 months pay from Virginia is not yet arrived. The army are moving from this place towards White Plains where the Enemy's whole force have taken the Field.

His Excellency seems to think we shall have a very warm Campaign. I shall be exceedingly glad to hear from you when you have an Opportunity. The Confusion occasioned by our march obliges me to be very short. My best wishes attend my sister, and I am,
         Dr. Sir,
          Yr. aff.,
            JAMES WOOD.
Middlebrook, 2d June, 1779.

           Paramus, N. Jersey
           Oct. 4th, '79.
Dear Bobby:
 I expect to be at home the last of this month and as my Horses are in fine Order, and I shall be exceedingly desirous of keeping them so, I shall be much obliged to you to procure and get it hauled home two Loads of the Best Timothy Hay, and to get my stable chunked and daubed before the weather gets too cold; and that you will get new Felloes put to our Chair and otherwise well repaired as soon as you possibly can. I hope you won't think much of all the Trouble which I give you, as you may be assured I will always be ready to do any thing in my Power to serve you. I should be very glad to know the Prices of Horses in Virginia before I set off. If they sell very high, I wou'd purchase another and bring it with me. I have parted with my Roan for 1500 Dollars, and have got a very likely Bay, which I gave 1600 dollars for. He is a fine Horse and would sell for 2000 Dollars at any time in camp. The Enemy continue quiet, and we have accounts that a very large embarkation is about taking Place.
 Remember me aff. to Comfort, my mother and all Friends, and believe me, Dr. Bobby,
      Yr. affectionate Bro.,
            J. WOOD.

 I shall be glad to hear how all my affairs are. If possible, pray get me a Kitchen and meat House done before cold weather.

Mr. Robert Wood,
near Winchester.

         Charlottesville, 13th July, 1780.
Dr. Brother:
 My being Disappointed in getting my money, I am afraid will be the means of my losing the Bargain you made for the saddle. I am now in Expectation every day of getting my Pay and as soon as I do, I will send the price of the saddle and the £100. I expect Jackey will go by Winchester as I saw him in Richmond about five days ago.
 It will be out of my power to be at Winchester soon. I shall be much obliged to you to advertise and agree with some one to put in a

fall crop on the shares. I think it will be more to my advantage to Hire my Negroes than to put them on the Place. The Person who takes the Place must build a cabin near the new Field, either at his or my own Expense as you can agree. The House Allison lives in I shall want as I expect the Convention Troops will be exchanged. I wish you would inquire and let me know what a log Kitchen 16 x 12 wou'd cost to take it from the stump, for me to find nails. I want to know how my mare and colts are and if the young one is like to get well—what Prospects of Grain, etc.

Remember me to Comfort, Mamma, etc., I am,
Dr. Bro. Yr. aff.
J. Wood.

Irvins House, Aug. 13th, 1780.

Madam:

I take the Liberty to send you two Bottles of Wine.

For the small Quantity I dare not make any Apology as I should have at the same Time a Complaint to make to you of Colo. Wood.

All the Orders he has given out to the Troops were so just and equitable that I found a Pleasure in earnestly recommending to the Troops the exactest Execution of every one of them, but I must acknowledge to You, Madam, that the last Order he has given me for my own Person I think very hard, and punctual Execution of it is really no agreeable task for me.

Please to present my Compliments to Colo. Wood and be persuaded that I am with the most perfect Esteem,
Madam,
Your most obedient & most humble Servant,

(Genl. Specht.)   C. J. W. Specht.

Dr. Brother:

I find it impossible to procure your Interest warrants before Mr. Marshall leaves Town as the auditors are constantly engaged in other Business, but as Mr. White follows in two or three days, it will make no odds.

I have it much at Heart that my two colts shou'd be fed constantly with as much as they will eat, and kept constantly stabled. If you shou'd think they are neglected, I beg you will hire some careful person to do it. I had rather give any Price than that they shou'd suffer.

I will write you more full by Mr. White.
I am,
Dr. B.,
Yrs. Affy.,
J. Wood.

Richmond, 3d Jan., 1786.

Dr. Brother:

I have been with the Continental Commission respecting Mordecai Yarnall's Pay Roll, and to endeavour to get certificates for him as well as for your Horse but was greatly surprised to find the Commissioner wou'd settle no other way than by calling the whole amount Paper money and reducing it by the Seals of Depreciation which wou'd have been next to nothing; it will be Necessary for him to get a more explicit Certificate from Colo. Steele and send it here before the 17th March, as the Commissioner's office will be finally closed on that day.

I am sorry Mr. Smith has parted with his Horse, as I might have probably got him in a Swap, as I am not able at present to purchase. If I had the Mare here I expect I cou'd swap her to advantage. Presume she will be on the way before this reaches you as I wrote last week by Captain Vandeval to request you to send Tom and the Mare by him --------

I am much obliged for your Attention to my Colts and must again request that you will have a watchful eye over my Timber.

I purchased from Mr. Rutherford when here the Balance of an Order on Mr. Norton of £12.12-0 which I paid in cash on his great complainings; pray apply to Mr. R. for the Order as I forgot to get it from him. Pray endeavour to work N. out of the money and pay it to Dr. Mackey to whom I owe seventeen or eighteen Pounds. Maybe it can be negotiated between N. and the Doctor, so as to pay so much of my Debt. Pray do what you can in this matter, as I have been greatly disappointed in getting money. I have never received the money from Alexandria which I expected to be sent to Mr. White at Winchester.

A poor fellow by the name of Jacob Wine, a pensioner, put a warrant into my hands of £12.0. I was in hopes of getting money for it, but find I can't without giving 15 per c. Discount which I am not willing to do. Pray let him know this and that he can get another warrant for his Pension up to the 5th July last upon sending an order in writing to me. The Pension Law is altered. He must as soon as you give him this information get Dr. Mackey or Dr. Baldwin to examine his wounds and certify the Degree of his Disability. A memorandum must be sent with it of the Regiment to which he belonged; where or in what Battle he received the wounds; his age and Place of Residence. Upon receiving this as soon as Possible, I think I can get his allowance increased to £18 per annum which I think he justly merits.

My wife is not yet returned from Stafford, but I expect her with the Monday's Stage.

Remember me affly. to Comfort and children. I shall write to my Mother.

     I am yr. aff. Brother,

             J. Wood.

Richmond, 11th February, 1786.

P. S. Tell Richardson that I have procured a warrant for £14 due to Dennis McCarty, as there were several Claims for what was due to him. I procured the warrant to be given to the person who has the prior right, so that Richardson must prove at what time he made the Purchase before I can let the warrant out of my hands. On these terms I procured the warrant.

Mr. Robert Wood,
near Winchester.

Dr. Brother:

Since I wrote you by Edmondson, I have been so pushed for the money which I told you of sometime ago which was due to the Carolina man for the Balance of the Purchase of the Cattle, that I am left without a shilling to help myself. I must therefore beg that you will turn my wheat the best manner you can into money as soon as you receive this, at least one hundred Bushells; the odd 18 Bushells I wish my Mother to take and make use of. Pray do what you can in this manner as I am really without money for common marketing. My whole Quarter's Salary went to pay off the Debt mentioned. I have some money of Mrs. McDonald's, which I expect her to send for every day. If you can get money for my wheat, if you wou'd give it to her, and take an Order for what you pay her, it wou'd save the Risque of sending money, as I have it in my Possession.

Let me hear from you by Post, as I am really Distressed more than I ever was in my life. Remember me affly. to my Mother and family, yr. wife and Little Boys.

I am,
Dr. Brother,

J. Wood.

P. S. Mr. Kercheval was kind enough to promise to exchange some warrants for me this spring. Tell him that when he comes down it wou'd oblige me greatly if he can accommodate me with about £30 in exchange for Civil List warrants.

Richmond, 10th April, 1786.

Mr. Robert Wood,
near Winchester.

Dr. Brother:

I received your Letter by Mr. Edmondson, which was the first I heard of the writ you mention. I approve what you did as I can easily pay the money. What swelled that Debt so large was an assignment of the 4 years we had Charles, amounting to £39 and an order from Langdon for £37.50 which was due on the acct. of the Cattle. ———

As we intend to spend the summer at home I can't possibly let my House. I mean to be up in June and stay until October. If an Oppy. I shall be glad to have my young horse brought down.
      I am, Dr. brother in great Haste,
         Yr. affc. Bro.,
Richmond, 14th April, 1786.
              J. WOOD.

Dr. Sir:
 I am just now favor'd with your Letter of the 24th ultimo. We really began to think from your long silence that you had forgot us. Be assured that our Friendship has ever been and still is, sincere and affectionate. Mr. Beckley is at present absent; as soon as I see him I will make the enquiries you desire. I am anxious to visit Frederick, but fear it won't be in my power. I can't move without a Horse; the expence of Purchasing, and the inconvenience of keeping him afterwards, I believe will prevent the Pleasure of seeing my Friends this summer. I am afraid our Federal Government is in a bad way. It is now a long time since there has been a Congress to do Business. At present there is not more than six States represented. The Assemblies of Connecticut and New Jersey have lately adjourned without taking the least notice of the requisitions of Congress. The British Ministry have positively refused surrendering the Posts, alledging that we had violated several articles of the Peace, particularly the non-payment of British Debts in Virginia, and Confiscations and the Passage of what is called the Trespass Law, in the State of New York. I think the advocates for paper money increase daily, as well as the Opposition to the Assize Law. I am of Opinion that a spirited Instruction to our Delegates, on those subjects, wou'd have a good effect. There is a great Change in the House of Delegates, about one-half new. From an acquaintance with the last year's members, as well as most of the present, I am inclinable to think our present representation is much the best. I am surprised that the Inhabitants of Winchester cou'd be so easily misled; the Assize Law to them wou'd be of the greatest Consequence. My wife joins in affc. Compts. to Mrs. White and Family. With real esteem I am,
        Dr. Sir,
         Yr. Assured Friend,
            JAMES WOOD.
Richmond, 2d July, 1786.

 P. S. I have inclosed you several Letters containing Commissions as Escheators, which I beg you will forward.

Alexander White, Esqr.,
near Winchester.

Richmond, 14th Jan. 1787.

Dr. Sir:

Mr. Beckley lately put two Civil List warrants of £10 each in my hands for you which I now inclose. Your Letter dated in November did not reach me till the appointment of Escheator was made. Mr. Smith made an Application immediately after his arrival and obtained the Commission. I am extremely sorry that I am unable at present to give you an account of the proceedings of the late long Assembly, the increased Business of the Executive obliged us to meet almost every day during the sitting of the Assembly so that I am almost as little acquainted with the Business of it as if I had been in Frederick. The different laws which were passed are to be divided among the different Printers, so that we hope to have the Business of Printing them completed in two weeks. As soon as this is done, I will forward you a copy to the printer in Alexandria, from whence you will get it by Post. As there will be a vacancy in our district for a Senator, I wish you would consider whether you cou'd not serve without material injury to your private affairs. I am fully convinced every day that a proper and judicious Choice of Members of that House, may one day or other be the salvation of this Country. If you cannot make it Convenient to serve yourself, pray endeavour to impress the Idea of fixing immediately upon a proper person to be proposed, lest an improper one shou'd step forward. I have had thoughts myself of your Brother, nephew Robert, or General Gates, either of whom wou'd meet my entire approbation.

My wife joins in affc. compliments to Mrs. White and family,
With real esteem,
Yr. affectionate friend,

JAMES WOOD.

(No address. Alex. White?)

Dr. Brother:

I received your Letter with the Certificates which I now return with the Interest warrants. With respect to the Plantation, I wish you to do for me as you wou'd for yourself. If you don't hire Ben with it, pray hire him for the best price you can get. I wou'd not engage the place longer than to take off the Spring Crop, but if he shou'd comply strictly, perhaps I may then let it longer. Make the best Bargain you can for the pastures below the House for one year to De La Mark or any other good Tenant.

I find that the money you paid Mr. Moore for Charlie's Hire was for the time you had him on your own account, after you were married—the four years paid by me was before, and while we had him in Partnership, after which I paid him for the year 1776 when I had him on my own account. As to the debt due to Yates, you need be under no apprehension. I hope to be able to pay it soon, as I have already done £270 to Langdon's Exed.—Moore's debt and the

Judgment of the Carolina man from whom we purchased the Cattle.

You would oblige me much by selling the Horse brought up by Rice, and the Colt. I shou'd be willing to take good Bonds payable in six months. Aaron Mercer was to have paid J. Holliday £9 for me. I wish you would inquire whether he has done it, and let me know that I may send him his Bond.

I am,
Dr. Brother,
Yrs. Affly,
J. Wood.

Richmond, 19th Jan., 1787.

Dr. Brother:

I received your letter by Mr. White last night and as he sets off today, I have not been able to make as full enquiry with respect to waggon hire as I cou'd wish. At present I see but little Prospect of your making an advantage by sending your Waggon here. I find there is no constant employment to be had for a Team. The Hire for a single day is 18/ but I discover that getting employ is Precarious. I intended to have enquired of the principal undertakers, and to have endeavoured to make a Contract, but they are out of town. I shall endeavour to get better information and let you know by the first Opportunity.

The price of corn is 18/ per Barrell, oats 2/4 per Bushell and Fodder 6/ per hundred.

I wish to spare no expense in feeding my Mare so as to make the Colt valuable. If Conrad will attend to this I will make him ample satisfaction as also the care of my Horse, as I shall send for him the 5th of June in order to drive up at that time, as I intend to spend the summer at home. Another thing I wish to Trouble you with, which is, to have a sufficiency of Rails hauled and my spring Pastures so inclosed immediately as to prevent anything getting into it. I mean the pasture which includes the Dairy. Whatever expence attends it, I will pay it with Pleasure. I beg you will have it done without loss of time, as it will be of the utmost Consequence to me.

I am,
affly.,
J. Wood.

Richmond 20th April, 1787.

Hond. by Mr. White.
Mr. Robert Wood.

Dr. Brother:

I received your Letter by Mr. Kercheval, and am much obliged to you for the Trouble you have taken by going to Baylor's. If he disappoints me I shall be put to great inconvenience. I shall have no other alternative, I fear, but selling my Certificates; I beg you will continue upon every opportunity to press him to make a payment, at least a part of the Debt. I shall certainly be up by the 15th. My wife has set out already; I am to be at Alexandria the 6th to superintend the sales of the Public Tobacco. I don't wish to hire Ben 'till Fall, as I mean to employ him and Ned while I am up in improving my place. I mean to run a Strait fence from the Corner of your Still House as far as the cross Pasture fence by putting Posts in the ground and nailing on Rails with 20d. nails. I shall therefore be much obliged to you in setting Ben about this business immediately, at least to get the Posts and to put them in the ground at a rail's length by a line. I shall be further obliged to you to get plank for a threshing floor, and to have it layed in Finley's House, as I shall be obliged for want of Money to thresh out my Grain and sell it as soon as I arrive. We have never recd. a shilling of money from the Treasury since October last.

          I am,
            Dr. Brother,
              Yrs. affy.,
                J. WOOD.

Richmond, 25th July, 1787.

Mr. Robert Wood, Winchester.
Hond. by Mr. Kercheval.

Dr. Brother:

I have lately received your two Letters, but Mr. McGuire being waiting, I can't answer them fully. As to the Mill Creek Land I have no Idea of selling. I mean to lease It for my Mother's life and for her Benefit. As to my own Place, I am totally at a loss what to do with it, but must make a flying visit next month in order to determine on it; I am certain I have been greatly imposed on. As to the negroes belonging to the Girls, if they cou'd be hired, I shall be glad, but if not I am willing to pay hire for them rather than they shou'd lose it. Two Guitars were left at Goodlove Heiskill's for them a considerable time ago, but we have never heard whether they came safe. H. wrote me that he had sent them as I gave an order to Mr. Norton's man for them when he returned with a Carriage. If they are not, it would be proper to write to Heiskill to know by whom he sent them.

I am just returned from the seashore where I went on the Business of a Light House. I wished to have written to my Mother, but Public Business rushing on me prevents me, and Mr. McGuire

being impatiently waiting. My prayers and affectionate regards always attend her.
                  I am,
                  Dr. Brother,
                    Yr. Affc.,
                              J. WOOD.

Richmond, 19th Jany., 1789.

Dr. Brother:

I have received your Letter by Mr. Miller. The Governor being absent, I immediately called a Council and have procured his Pardon. A Petition signed by a number of Gentlemen so reputable cou'd not fail to procure a Compliance with their wishes. As the Bearer is extremely impatient, I have not time to answer Mr. McKewan's Letter at present. Please to inform him that I shall make every Possible enquiry to find an Eligible situation for him. At present I believe there is no vacancy of a Clerkship in any of the Public Offices. You may assure him that I shall feel a very Particular pleasure if an Opportunity shou'd offer wherein I can render him service.
                I am yr. affc. Brother,
                              J. WOOD.

Richmond, 9th May, 1789.
Particular Care of Mr. Miller.
Mr. Robert Wood,
Winchester.

My Dear and Honored Mother:

I have long wished with the utmost impatience to see you, but such is my situation, that it has hitherto been entirely out of my Power. Tied by Public Duty, which my country has a right to expect shou'd be punctually observed and performed by me. Add to this, money is so extremely hard to be got that I seldom have as much as would bear my expences. However, at all events, I will be up by Harvest at the farthest.

I beg that you will at all times and on all Occasions make free use of anything on my Plantation. Be assured my only motive for Placing an Overseer and hands there was for your Convenience.

I am grieved to hear from Bobby that one of your Eyes has failed. I trust in God your sight will return, and that your health may long continue. The Bearer being waiting, I must conclude, with every sentiment of the most Perfect Duty and filial Affection.
                My Dr. Mother,
                    Affectionately,
                        Yr.
                              J. WOOD.

Richmond, 9th May, 1789.
Mrs. Mary Wood,
near Winchester.

Richmond, September 16th, 1789.

My dear Mother:
I am Grieved and Disappointed that I have not been able to see you as I expected and intended. Just as I had got everything in readiness to set out, my wife was seized with such a violent Inflamation in her Eyes that it was expected for a long time that she would be totally deprived of Sight. After many weeks close confinement she is much recovered, but has almost lost the sight of one of her Eyes. I shou'd set out myself but the Governor and most of the Council are absent, and I think it extremely hard that poor men shou'd come on Public Business from the remote parts of the State at great expence and Trouble; and shou'd be disappointed through the neglect of Public Officers; such neglect I cannot reconcile with my own Feelings, which confines me much more than others who receive the same Emoluments. The Governor is expected in a week, and as soon as he does, I shall set out, and shall be able I hope to stay a week. I hope and beg that you make use of anything of mine on the Plantation. I have directed Thorp to furnish anything you wanted, telling him that I was in your Debt.

I am most affectionately your,
J. WOOD.

Mrs. Mary Wood,
near Winchester.

New York, 12th January, 1790.

Dear Madam:
I wrote you from Philadelphia where we were detained two days by bad weather. When we sat out the first day we reached Trenton thirty miles—2d day, Brunswick 30 miles—3d day, Elizabethtown 20 miles—4th day (being that day Fortnight on which we left home) 15 miles to New York. It was then a Fortnight to the day appointed for the meeting of Congress, but the arrangement of Family affairs, and the reception and return of the Civilities which the politeness of the inhabitants induced them to show to strangers afforded full employment for us. We (are) just entering on business, so that the Ladies to a great measure will be left to themselves. They have been to one Assembly and once to Mrs. Washington's. These are the only public Places (except the Churches) which they have yet been at. The crowd at Mrs. Washington's was so great (being New Year's day) that I could have no conversation with her. Mrs. Washington returned our visit, but unfortunately Mrs. White and myself were both out. The President seems to be restored to perfect health. I inclose you his speech at the opening of the Session.

I have anxiously awaited to hear from you. My family have all been blessed with perfect health and have met with no disagreeable accidents since their departure from home. They desire to be affec-

tionately remembered to you and the young Ladies, also to Mr. and
Mrs. Wood and their family.
I am with great regard,
Dear Madam,
Affectionately yours,
ALEX. WHITE.

Mrs. Mary Wood,
near Winchester, Virginia.
Free, A. White.

Richmond, April 16th, 1790.
Dr. Sir:
I did myself the pleasure of writing you a long Letter from Norfolk about the 5th of January, but not hearing from you, concluded the Letter miscarried, as I intrusted it to a private hand. Indeed I am confirmed in the Opinion as I wrote to Mr. Dunscomb at the same time, who in a late letter assures me he never received it.

With respect to the Great National Question under consideration I have never ventured to give an Opinion, as it wou'd be naturally supposed that I was interested in the Event. Mr. Madison's plan has been generally reprobated by the Speculators; while the Disinterested of all Denominations admire the goodness of his Heart, but generally think the plan of Discrimination Impracticable.

I have heard very few Objections made to the Proceedings of Congress, except as to the allowance made to the members, which is pretty generally considered as exorbitant. It is objected to by others that a great deal of time is unnecessarily wasted in long Debates on matters of most Trivial Concern. I understand many of the Present Members will be opposed at the next Election. Mr. Giles is candidate for Bland's District, Mr. Harrison for Griffin's and a Mr. Venables for Cole's.

I have inclosed two Letters from my wife, one of them for Mrs. Dunscomb, the other for yourself; also one of my own to Mr. Dunscomb. It being injurious to the Post office, nothing wou'd induce me to inclose Letters to Members but necessity; not being able to find a private Conveyance.

Pray offer my compliments to Mrs. White and the young Ladies, and believe me to be with real esteem,
Dr. Sir,
Yr. assured friend,
JAMES WOOD.

(No address)

Richmond, 13th February, 1793.
Dr. Sir:
I have been favored at different times with your three Letters on the subject of my Accounts. I consider myself particularly

Obliged for your Attention and Trouble. I delayed answering in hopes of receiving from Frederick a Box of papers which I considered useless here, in which was a list of the names of the German Prisoners liberated, the sums respectively paid by them, and the dates. As this Business was Transacted by me at the earnest request of the Minister of War, and the money applied as fast as it was received, and as directed, I thought nothing was necessary for me to do, more than to state exactly from time to time my receipts and expenditures to the Minister of War, which I regularly did—the lists were added up and the aggregate sum entered as a Credit in my Book.

You may recollect the difficulties I had in getting Armand's Legion supplied with Forage. I was obliged to give my own Notes to the People, which did not all come in till the year 1785. Indeed I have reason to believe that some of them for small sums are still out, and which I shall be obliged to pay when presented. It happened you will remember at a very scarce Season, and when the Credit of the States was remarkably Low. If any affidavit of mine shou'd be thought Necessary I will immediately forward it. I have not received a letter or heard from Frederick this two months past.

The inclosed Notification appeared in last Saturday's Paper. When the observations are published I will immediately forward them.

With real esteem,

    I am,
     Dr. Sir,
      Your assured friend,
       JAMES WOOD.

(Address)
The Honble. Alexander White, Esq., of Virginia.
Free
Philadelphia.

        Richmond, 27th Decem., 1794.
Dr. Brother:

I received a Letter from you in the early part of the Session respecting a proposed Application of the Inhabitants of Winchester for permission to carry the water in pipes to the Town. The application has not been made. When it is I shall answer that if it can be done with the General Consent of the people and without injury to Individuals, I shall not have the least Objection. I shou'd have answered your Letter sooner, but have been disabled in my right hand for some time past by Accident, which rendered writing extremely painful. It is now perfectly well, and I am happy to inform you that my health is much better than it has been for more than twelve months past. During that time I had little hopes of ever recovering. However, I am now so well as to conclude I have got a reprieve for a few years to come.

Inform my dear and affectionate Mother that I am well in health and happy. This I know will afford her affectionate heart the greatest pleasure. Tell her at the same time that nothing shall prevent my making a trip this winter on purpose to see her.
       I am,
       Dr. Brother,
        Yrs. Affly.
          J. WOOD.

Mr. Robert Wood,
Near Winchester.

         Richmond, 19th Dec., 1795.
Dr. Brother:

 I received your Letter by Colonel Woodrow, and meant to have answered by his return, but was so occupied about that time by public Business that it really was out of my power to do it. I wrote Doctor Wistar upon the subject you mentioned immediately and forwarded it by Post. With respect to the alteration in the road which is proposed, it will be both Disagreeable and injurious to me—but to Oppose a thing which might be thought a public Benefit I am unwilling. If it shou'd be adopted I hope you will attend to the existing Law, which enacts that where Changes take place the Proprietors of the Land shall be indemnified by a tax to be levied on the County.

 My health which prevented me from spending sometime in Winchester this past summer, is still precarious. I am never three days successively well. Remember me with that affection which I owe to the best of Mothers and tell her that nothing but the want of health shall prevent me from seeing her in the Course of the winter. My love with that of my wife to your family.
      I am yr. afft. brother,
         JAMES WOOD.

Mr. Robert Wood,
Near Winchester.
Hond. by Mr. Page.

        Richmond, 22nd Decem., 1795.
Dr. Brother:

 I wrote you a few days ago by Mr. Robert Page. If you have not received it, you will immediately after this. I have lately seen Bartlet Bennett who informs me that he has found your entries all made in the name of Gideon Grantland—that Grantland in his lifetime made over his right to a Wm. Johnson of Hanover—and that he had purchased Johnson's right presuming that it was a good one. I give you this information as I suspect Bennett and Johnson are combined in order to chouse you out of the Land. I have in my

Possession a small Certificate signed by Grantland to Jno. Wood promising to convey half of a 1000 Acres of Land; whether this is one of Surveys in which you were interested I know not. A Mr. David Laird of Rockingham is anxious to have my father's Books of Surveys and Field Books carefully examined to find whether the inclosed was surveyed by him. The inclosed courses are sent in order to designate the Land. Probably it might have been surveyed in another name so that great attention will be necessary in making the search. I wish much to serve this man, and beg your immediate and particular attention to this Business and that you will as soon as Possible inform me of the result by Post.

I am,
Yr. Affct. Brother,
J. WOOD.

Mr. Robert Wood,
Of Winchester,
Hond. by Mr. Magill.

Dr. Brother:

I have received a letter from you lately as well as the one you mentioned and which I immediately answered; but I suppose it miscarried. I am much obliged by the kind offer which you made of sending a boy and Horses to meet me at Fredericksburg, but such is the nature of my business that I cou'd not be pointed as to the time of meeting them. Otherwise I would avail myself of your Kindness. Although my health has mended greatly, yet I am determined to spend about six weeks at Winchester and Bath. I can easily send my boy and horses back from Winchester, and will depend on my friends to supply me with a Horse while I remain.

Remember me most affectionately to my Mother whom I long much to see—also to your wife and family.

The survey of 15 acres which I made many years ago, I obtained a Patent for about five years ago.

I am,
Dr. Brother,
Yrs. Affly.,
JAMES WOOD.

17th June, 1796
Mr. Robert Wood,
Of Winchester.

Dr. Brother:

I wrote you yesterday in haste, since which I have heard that Major Connell, one of the members, will be a Candidate. The other, Mr. Charles Wells, who is not in the Commission of the peace, has promised me to use his interest for Bobby. I think it absolutely necessary that he shou'd go out immediately and had better board in Charleston or the neighborhood for the winter. Major McGuire is a friend of mine, who will have influence, also Mr. Henderson. John Beck will be sheriff and will not have a vote.

If he can get the vote of six of the Magistrates before any other Candidates set out, he will be secure. If possible, you ought to go with him, as his establishment in life depends on it. I shall now have an Opportunity of going to Winchester after the rise (?) of the Assembly for the express purpose of seeing my Dear Mother, to whom remember me most affectionately.

Yr. Affc. Brother,
J. Wood.

11th Dec., 1796.
Mr. Robert Wood, Winchester.
Colo. McClury.

Winchester, 20th Decr., 1796.

Gentlemen:

Perceiving that the present Session of Assembly has laid off a New County from that of Randolph by the name of Brooke and being informed by Mr. Robert W. Wood of his intention of offering himself to you as a Candidate for the Clerkship thereof, I cannot resist my inclination of mentioning this Gentleman's character, as he is an entire stranger among you and just entering into life. He was born and raised within half a mile of this place and I can with truth say that his conduct from childhood to the present period has been unexceptionable and, without diminution to any applicant for the appointment, that you cannot bestow it upon a more deserving person.

He wrote sometime in my office and since then has applied himself in the same line of business in the County of Berkeley. From his steady attention he has acquired full knowledge of the duty of a County Court Clerk and I have the highest confidence should you appoint him that he will give general satisfaction.

I am Gentlemen,
Your most obedt. Servt.,
J. Peyton.

To the Worshipful Court
of Brooke County
Mr. Wood.

Berkeley County, 20th Decemr., 1796.

Gentlemen Justices of Brooke County:

Mr. Robert Wood who bears this comes into your County with a determination of offering himself as a Candidate for the Clerkship of Brooke County, late part of Ohio, and as I have a thorough acquaintance with him, I take the liberty of laying before you the following relation. Mr. Wood came to live with me in the Clerk's Office of this County, of which I am the Deputy, in the year 1793, with a view to acquire a knowledge of the business relating to that office, and continued with me until the middle of November last. During his stay with me he paid the most unremitted attention to his business, which aided by my instructions has rendered him complete master of his business. Should Mr. Wood meet with your patronage I can with propriety assert that he will discharge the duties of that important trust with integrity, dispatch and satisfaction equal to any person in the State or elsewhere.

I am Gentlemen with esteem,
Yr. obdt.
EDWARD CHRISTIAN.

We, David Hunter and James Anderson, two of the Justices of the peace of the said County Court of Berkeley, do certify that Edward Christian who hath subscribed the above letter of recommendation has been Deputy Clerk of the said County Court for the last five years; that he has discharged the duties annexed to his office with unusual satisfaction, and that the Gentleman with whom he acquired his knowledge of the business justifies us in declaring his abilities in his professional way are not inferior to any person's in the state. We further give it as our opinion that Mr. Wood mentioned in said recommendation is competent to the undertaking of a Clerk of a County Court, and assert that during his continuance in business he conducted himself with every propriety. Certified under our hand this 20th day of December, 1796.

DAVID HUNTER,
JAMES ANDERSON.

Virginia Berkeley, Sct.

I, Moses Hunter, Clerk of the said County Court, do hereby certify that the above named David Hunter and James Anderson. Gentlemen, by whom the above and within certificate was given and who hath subscribed their names thereto, were at the time of doing the same and still are two of the Commonwealth's Justices of the peace in and for the County aforesaid duely and legally Commissioned and sworn and to all certificates by them subscribed as such due faith and credit is and ought to be given as well in Courts of Justice as thereout.

IN TESTIMONY

whereof I have hereunto set my hand and affixed the seal of the said County, the 20th day of December 1796, and in the 21st year of this Commonwealth.

Mo. Hunter.

I do hereby certify that Mr. Edward Christian who has given Mr. Wood the within introduction wrote in my office from the age of fifteen years until he was employed as deputy Clerk of Berkeley County Court in which capacity he now acts. During his continuance with me he acquired full knowledge of the business, and conducts his office with equal propriety to any Clerk in my acquaintance.

Certified under my hand this 22d. day of December 1796.

J. PEYTON, *Clk. W. D. C.*

Dr. Brother:

I have just now received your Letter of the 14th and am surprized you had not received two Letters which I wrote you on the subject of your son Bobby. I informed you of the Division of Ohio, wrote a letter in his favor to the Magistrates and advised that you shou'd go out with him immediately. I thought it still more necessary as I learned that one of the delegates who was here wou'd be a Candidate and wrote you a second Letter. The first was by Mr. Brown, a Brother-in-law of Mr. Peyton's, the second by Col. McClury who was stopped by receiving accidentally a wound by the discharge of a Pistol. If Bobby cou'd get the appointment it wou'd be a provision for life, and a trial ought not to be neglected. I wrote to Colo. Crawford, Clerk of Amherst, not knowing but he might incline to act as a Deputy for some time and received the inclosed answer from him yesterday.

I have long suspected that my affairs have been neglected—but I am prevented from motives of Delicacy from saying or doing any thing immediately as I am determined to be at Winchester between this and the first of March. In the meantime if you cou'd find out and let me know by Post whether the rent of the last year has been paid, as I have wrote on the subject and have received no answer. Remember me affly. to my Dr. mother—your wife and family. I am yr. affc. Brother,

J. WOOD.

Richmond, 24th Dec., 1796.
Mr. Robert Wood of Winchester.
Hond. by Major Holmes.

Richmond, 25th March, 1797.

Dr. Brother:

I received your letter by Mr. Alexander. About three days before his arrival here I had written to Bobby by Mr. Sydnor inclosing a letter to the Magistrates of Brooke, which he will undoubtedly receive before this reaches you. He ought to lose no time in returning and shou'd make it a point to call upon all the Magistrates. I wrote to Dr. Wistar on the 6th January last and recommended your son to his notice and shall always feel a very Particular Pleasure in rendering him any friendly office in my power.

Mr. Alexander waits. I have only time to request you will mention me to my dear Parent with that sincere Affection I always feel for her, and my best wishes for my sister and all your family.

I am Dr. Brother
Yrs. most affectionately
JAMES WOOD.

Mr. Robert Wood,
Near Winchester.
Hond. by Mr. Alexander.

Richmond, 14th April, 1797.

Dr. Brother:

I have received your Letter of the 6th Instant. As I am determined to return to Frederick as soon as my present Appointment expires, I regret that I have no prospect of being able to make so large a purchase as Mr. Norton's Lotts. I have been sinking money here for several years, and no prospect of ever saving myself in the Office I now hold. The expence of Living at this place is beyond all Calculation. I shall try to dispose of my property here as soon as I can and build on my own Land. I met with a very great loss last night. My meat house was broke open and a large stock of excellent Bacon Beef and Tongue stolen, value between two and three hundred Dollars, and what makes it most inconvenient is that Money will not replace it of the same quality. Since my appointment I have been put to immense expence in furniture—a Carriage &c., &c., and I am distressed by this loss exceedingly.

As I have not time to write to Mr. Peyton, I wish you to mention the Circumstances to him. I know not whether he has been able to get what is due to me. If anything is in his hand it will be obliging me in a very high degree if he can find some mode of remitting it to me. Perhaps on the return of the Judges or some Opportunity from the District Court can be found. I wish to know whether I can count upon anything from that Quarter, as my calls for money are pressing —I hope Bobby has set off before this. I am anxious for his success and shall be glad to hear the result as soon as you are informed of it.

Tender my love and best wishes to my Dear Mother and my afft. regards to your wife and family.

I am Dr. Brother,
Yr. afft.,
J. WOOD.

Mr. Robert Wood
Near Winchester.

Richmond, 25th February, 1799.
Dr. Brother:
I received your letter by Mr. Peacock. I saw Grantland's Certificate in the hands of Mr. Wolfe, and was uneasy lest any accident shou'd happen to it. I took it in order to refresh the Memory of Dabney Miller who is the only witness to it, and who is become very drunken and stupid. I have not seen him since as he lives at a distance. I have written to him to call on me when he comes to town, on particular Business. I am in daily expectation of seeing him. I requested the favor of a Mr. Starke who lives in the Neighborhood of the Heirs of Grantland. To him I stated in writing the nature of your Claim, and that you were willing to receive proposals of Compromise upon liberal terms, without which you wou'd institute suit immediately. I expect every day to hear from Mr. Clarke—When I do you shall have immediate notice.

There were two Counties divided the last Session—but upon consulting the delegates from each, who were my particular friends, I am clear in my Opinion that no one but one of themselves wou'd stand the most distant Chance of getting the Appointment of Clerk.
       I am, dear Brother,
         Your affectionate,
            J. Wood.
Mr. Robert Wood,
Near Winchester.
Honored by Mr. Peacock.

Richmond, 9th April, 1799.
Dr. Brother:
I have received your Letter by Mr. Smith—I shall in due time make the application to Mr. Wickham—Being employed by Williams he will be well acquainted with the Merits of the Cause and cannot appear for the Opposite party. With respect to the representatives of Gideon Grantland. I have made every possible inquiry, but can discover nothing satisfactory; his Brother who is a man of responsibility says he was acquainted with the bargain between his brother and J. W.—that they first agreed for two warrants of 1,000 acres each, without any reservation whatever—that afterwards J. W. agreed to let him have another warrant of 1,000 Acres for which one half was reserved and afterwards assigned to you—that G. G. sold but 2,500 acres to Wm. Johnson, who afterwards sold to Bartlett Bennett. The Obligation of Grantland is so Vague and inexplicit that I greatly fear you will find great difficulty in making his estate liable for damages. Grantland who was with me in the business says that his sister-in-law received a letter from Bennett lately, requesting that she wou'd consent to a friendly suit by which he cou'd obtain a legal Title (I fear that there is some Knavery in the

business). The representatives of Gideon Grantland will not come into the measure, and will insist upon seeing the title under which Johnson assigned to Bennett.

       I am Dr. Brother,
         Yrs. affly.,
           JAMES WOOD.

          Richmond, 29th. January, 1800.
Dr. Brother:

 I received your Letter sometime ago, but not having it with me I shall only answer such parts as I now recollect. There has been one County divided this Session. The new County is taken from Russell and Wythe and lies principally on the Waters of Clinch. Whether it wou'd be worth Bobby's while to go to the County I cannot determine. There is but eight Justices Appointed and but one of them known to me. If he goes I will address a Letter to them on his behalf.

 I wish you wou'd speak to my Tenants to be prepared to pay my rent when due, as I shall be in extreme want of it, as I do not draw any thing on my late appointment until June next. I will either come or send for it when due. I shou'd be glad if you wou'd sound them and let me know whether they wish to rent another year, or two years, as I am desirous of again renting. Let me know also what Improvements you think wou'd be to my advantage, and what are their wishes and Expectations.

       I am Dr. Brother,
         Yrs.,
           J. WOOD.

         Richmond, 22nd May, 1801.
Dr. Brother:

 I have been confined for sometime past by extreme illness. I was attacked with a violent cramp in my stomach, which the Doctor says was the gout—I am led to believe it was as my feet have been since affected so as to prevent me from walking—I am now perfectly recovered. I am sorry to tell you that Green's suit has been determined against them by an unanimous Opinion (as I am told) of the Court.

 I wrote Mr. Peyton the day I was taken down, which may not have reached him—if it did not, pray inform him without loss of time that the day I received his money and papers I settled his

Business satisfactorily with the Auditor and have Quietus's in full of all demands, which I will forward to him by the first Opportunity.

W'th real affection
I am
Dr. Brother
Yrs. affly.,
J. WOOD.

P. S. I shall see you soon, perhaps in a fortnight.

Mr. Robert Wood,
Near Winchester.
Favr of Mr. Cochran.

* * * * * * * * *

The letters which slumbered for generations in the old garret at "Glen Burnie" have spoken. In their ingenuous way they tell the story of one who, as chief spokesman, seems to have been true in every relationship of life.

"Well done good and faithful servant: Enter thou into the joy of thy Lord."

Only the finishing touch of the Richmond press is needed to complete the story:

The *Richmond Enquirer*, June 18 and June 29, 1813.

ANOTHER OF THE REVOLUTIONARY PATRIOTS GONE

Died, on Wednesday night, after a lingering indisposition, General James Wood, a member of the Executive Council of Virginia.

On Thursday Evening, the 17th inst., the remains of Gen. Wood were interred at the Episcopalian Church with military honors. At 4 o'clock the corpse, escorted by Capt. Gamble's troop and followed by the clergy, the relatives of the deceased, the Executive, the order of the Cincinnati, and a concourse of citizens, was borne from the residence of the deceased to the Capitol Square. There the body was received by the several volunteer companies of the city and with firing of artillery. The procession then moved to the Church. There the body was borne by the Governor and Lieutenant-Governor, three Revolutionary officers, and the Colonel of the city militia. The procession closed with the firing of artillery, the usual religious rites, and the firing of small arms at the grave.

The Richmond Enquirer, March 7, 1823.

Died—On the night of Tuesday the 4th inst., at her residence in this city, in the 68th year of her age, Mrs. Jean Wood, relict of the late General James Wood, a soldier of the American Revolution and afterwards Governor of Virginia. Of a widely extended circle of acquaintances, this lady has been many years the delight and ornament. She was indeed qualified for distinction in the most enlightened and polished society; for few were ever more remarkably gifted by nature: still fewer there have been, whose minds, tastes and manners have received equal cultivation. But, these attractive qualities did not constitute her chiefest praise: She was an exemplary wife and parent; she was the benignant supporter of those "who were destitute and ready to perish," and whom her energetic and active interposition has often rescued from crime and misery; she was a christian, humble, anxious and devoted in the duties of her religion, the truth and consolations of which she attested with her expiring breath.

The Richmond Enquirer, March 11, 1823.

On last Tuesday night about 11 o'clock, Mrs. Jean Wood, relict of the late Gen. James Wood, in the 68th year of her age, endured her last sufferings.

This records the death of no common woman. Mrs. Wood was equally distinguished for attainments in knowledge, strength of intellect, and richness of imagination. Her conversation was alike instructive and entertaining. She combined grace and dignity with the most winning politeness. And to powers which enabled her to shine in the most brilliant circles, she added a condescension which made her the very idol of the poor. A warmer heart never throbbed in a human bosom. None ever showed more devoted attachment to friends; none, greater compassion to the afflicted.

But it was religion that completed, and gave the finishing touches to her character. She was no ostentatious professor, but an humble believer. And the faith which she never hesitated to avow, was justified by the works which she was always prompt to perform. On the approach of that hour, in which all are expected to be honest and sincere, she thought it prudent to look well to the foundation on which her ALL for eternity was built, and the result was a good hope, through the infinite merit of a Saviour, in the divine mercy. A numerous circle of relatives and friends are deeply bereaved by her removal; but they "sorrow not as those who have no hope;" for they fully believe that in the morning of the Resurrection, she will be raised incorruptible and immortal, and be transformed into the image of that Redeemer, in whom she trusted.

Let not the reader suppose that in this brief sketch of character there is any exaggeration. The writer who pays this humble tribute of affection, has frequently heard those who were connected with the deceased only by the ties of common friendship, say "We never knew her equal."

May her mantle rest on her survivors, and her example be imitated by all who were honored by her acquaintance or blessed with her friendship.

Inscription of tomb of Mrs. Jean Moncure Wood in the Robinson burying ground in Byrd Park, Richmond, Va.

In Memory of
JEAN MONCURE,
Daughter of Rev. John Moncure
of Clermont, Stafford Co., Va.
Born May 22, 1753.
Died in Richmond March 4, 1823.
Married 1775, Gen'l James Wood,
Governor of Virginia
From Dec. 1796 to Dec. 1, 1799.

The Robinson family burying ground is at "Poplar Vale," now Byrd Park, the home of Jean Moncure Wood's grandparents. The handsome old mansion became the Soldiers' Home during the Civil War. The homestead was purchased later by the city for a reservoir and pleasure ground, upon condition that the burial plot remain untouched. A high brick wall surrounds it. From the fine iron gate the graves may be plainly seen.

PART III

THE WESTGATE

CHAPTER XXIII

Romance of Laurence Augustine Washington — His Family — Various Personal Letters — Founding of the Laurence Augustine Washington Society, Children of the American Revolution

1820, March 21st, Tuesday

The perusal of Mr. Paulding's description of the Caphon Rock, brought to my recollection that on this very Rock I first beheld my Mary, and as the incidents of our first acquaintance and subsequent loves will be interesting, perhaps instructive to our children, and as I delight to recall and dwell on the recollection of those pleasing scenes, I will here give a faithful description of them.

I began this note on the 14th, and as I had but a few hours of each day (and some days none) to devote to it, I did not finish it 'till the 21st which date I have affixed to it; altho I did not copy it into this book 'till the 22d.

In the year 1796, I visited Bath, a celebrated watering place, in Berkeley County, Va. I was young, ardent and sanguine, had just entered upon the busy scenes of life, having lately arrived at age, and taken my patrimonial estate, under my own care and protection. My personal deportment, my prosperity, my happiness, were all to be regulated, and influenced, by the force of circumstances, or by my capacity to direct or profit by them. I had taken possession of a comfortable landed estate, and had commenced farming and housekeeping.

Matrimony was the first great object of my most ardent wishes, and was the only subject that could be said to have a real interest and controlling influence over my heart.

I arrived at Bath in the evening, and found several of my acquaintances there, some of whom lodged in the same house I put up at. By one of them, I was informed that most of the young ladies of the place were, the next morning, about to visit the "Caphon Rock," a rock of great resort, from the summit of which one of the wildest, sublimest, and most interesting views of mountain country, interspersed with cultivated vallies, and rivers, was to be seen, which our country afforded, rich as it is, in such scenery. We concluded to take the same ride, and sat out, as soon as our breakfast was over; being sometime after the company, in our departure from the village.

When we arrived at the rock, we found it crowded with the young, the gay and the thoughtless of both sexes. We approached to enjoy the beautiful prospect, for beautiful it is. Mr. Paulding has given a very happy description of it in his Letters from the South.

My eyes had scarcely passed over this delightful landscape before my attention was arrested and my vision irresistibly directed to a particular object that seized on and enchained my whole admiration. The lofty towering mountains which rose in proud and successive elevation over each other, until their blue and fading summits, which seemed to touch the very heavens, were lost in the azure of the distant, retiring horizon—the lovely valley at an immeasurable distance below our feet—the solitary hamlets, with their circling columns of dense smoke, winding slowly up the mountain's top—the two beautiful rivers coursing their romantic passages thro' this enchanting vale—the passing white fantastic clouds of heaven, whirling over our heads, whilst their fleeting shadows glided nimbly over the delightful scene before us, which but a moment before I had beheld with rapture, were now, one and all, unobserved, unheeded and unadmired. My whole thoughts, my whole attention were turned to this new object of delight.

Amongst the ladies we found on the Rock was a Miss Mary D. Wood, who was approaching her 15th year. She was well grown for her age, and had nothing of the child about her, but its sweet, confiding innocence. She was the picture of good health. Her skin was as white as that of the loveliest of her beauteous sex, and the bloom on her fine cheeks was that of nature, acquired and heightened by a life of active industry in the exercise of the cheerful aid she daily afforded an excellent mother, in the management of the domestic concerns, of a large family of growing children.

She was allowed, even by the ladies, to be handsome. The gentlemen all pronounced her beautiful, and in my eyes she was amongst the loveliest of her lovely sex. But it was not the striking symmetry, the sweet harmony of her beauteous features, nor the enchanting tincture of her charming skin, all powerful and captivating as these charms were, that ultimately, so irresistibly bound me to this beauteous woman. It was these that first drew my attention to her and made an impression, which would not soon have been forgotten had I never seen her after the hour we met on the Caphon Rock.

Whilst on the Rock I was not introduced to her, but we knew each other by name. When the party was satisfied with the fine prospect before it, it prepared to return to the village. A gentleman from Winchester (in the vicinity of which Miss Wood lived) a Mr. Adam

Douglass, was one of the gallants to the party of ladies on their trip to the Rock. He helped Miss Wood on her horse. I waited for an opportunity and took advantage of the first that offered to get along side of her on her return to Bath. This station I took good care to hold, to the end of our ride, or rather 'till our arrival in the village. I entered into conversation with her, and found, to my great joy and delight, that she did not assume the airs of distant and stately reserve, because we had not been formally introduced to each other; but that she met my advance towards an acquaintance with a winning sweetness, a kind and frank politeness and unreserve, which greatly increased my admiration for her. In the separation of the ladies, on their entrance into the village, I attended an acquaintance home, and Miss Wood's Winchester beaux attended her to her father's dwelling, for he had rented a house in the village.

It was the custom at that day for the ladies to assemble at the spring to drink the water and to show themselves, and to give the beaux an opportunity also of showing themselves to advantage.

To this place of resort I was punctual in my attendance this afternoon, arrayed in my very best.

From the moment I first beheld this interesting girl, her image had not for one instant been absent from my thoughts. Since we parted, before dinner 'till the hour of expected meeting, at the spring, a space of time had elapsed without my seeming to be conscious of anything which was passing around me. The ladies began to assemble at the spring. I had been there some time. One party arrives; another succeeds; another follows; but the object of my thought is not among them. My eyes are constantly directed toward the street that leads to her dwelling; anxiety is on tiptoe; impatience begins to be felt: at last, the ladies begin to leave the spring, and the hour is arrived which forbids the longer expectation of seeing my little enchantress at the spring! And am I not to see her again until a long, a tedious and sleepless night has intervened? Disquieting thought! If possible this shall not be.

I had some acquaintances who boarded near her father's house. I will pay one of them a visit and perhaps some lucky chance may procure me a sight, if not an interview with this charming girl. And if chance should fail, I could get some acquaintance to introduce me to her father's family.

I posted off and met Mr. William B. Page at the door of his boarding house, which was in the immediate vicinity of Mr. Wood's. He asked me in, but as it was not my wish to be within doors, I told him I preferred remaining where we were.

I was in a kind of feverish impatience, hoping and expecting I hardly knew what; and expecting it only because I wished it. But I could not divest myself of the expectation, because I was unwilling to divest myself of it, that this interesting girl would soon be in motion in the streets. And as good luck would have it she did appear. She left her father's door and was proceeding towards us.

I suppose many young men have had similar sensations to those which this much wished for meeting produced in my bosom. Never! never shall I forget the palpitations of that moment. I thought her still more lovely than she appeared in the morning. Her color more dazzling and striking; the contrast of the white and red more distinctly marked and defined. Upon her lovely bosom, just below the junction of her neck with her chest, there was a spot of extravasated blood, produced by some casual accident, about the size of a hazlenut. The florid coloring of blood was only softened by the transparent covering of white and beauteous skin, which enveloped it. The edges of this beautiful mark were most distinctly defined, and the contrast between it and the lovely white of the surrounding skin, was sweet and enchanting beyond anything I ever saw. I had not seen this mark before, and now viewed it with exquisite delight.

After an awkward inquiry how she felt after her ride, I asked her why we had not the pleasure of her company that afternoon at the spring. She said, at once, with an unaffected freedom that warmed and filled my heart, that she had felt some fatigue from her ride, had lain down after dinner and fallen asleep. That she slept until her mother waked her and told her it was time to dress to go to see Mrs. Pendleton, with whom she was engaged to drink tea. That she had to exert herself to get ready and was then on her way there. The effort of dressing had given her the additional color just spoken of.

I told her I was sorry I was not invited to Mrs. Pendleton's, nor even acquainted with the family, as I would thus be deprived of the pleasure of spending the evening with her, but that I would do myself the pleasure of seeing her safe to the door. When we got to the door, however, we were met by one of the ladies of the family, who had been of the party to the Rock that morning, and who very politely invited me in, knowing who I was, altho' I had not been particularly introduced to her. This invitation was too congenial to my feelings to be refused.

The party was small and dancing the amusement.

All ceremony and unmeaning punctilio were thrown aside and sociality and the finest feelings of the heart contributed to make everyone present as happy as the hours were long.

We broke up late. A Mr. Walker, from Maryland, an old bachelor, and an old acquaintance of Miss Wood's mother, joined me in escorting her home.

I had now a right to call on Miss Wood at her father's house, to inquire into the state of her health after the dance, and should have used it, had no other chance of being introduced to the parents of this charming girl offered. But I requested Mr. Walker to let me know when he called on Miss Wood, that I might accompany him and be introduced by him to her father and mother. This he readily agreed to do and the desired introduction took place, when I again beheld, with increased delight, the sweet, innocent object of all my solicitude.

My course was now clear and I sat about assiduously to improve my acquaintance with this dear girl, and to endeavor to learn her temper, disposition and character, and to make myself interesting, agreeable, and worthy of her.

The first was easily done, for she wore no disguise. She was nature itself in all its guileless, spotless innocence, its open unsuspicious confidence. Too pure and virtuous to use deception herself, she suspected none in others. What her chaste heart conceived her faithful tongue uttered. Her sweet face was the truthful mirror of her spotless bosom, where peace, good will to all the world, a tranquil happiness, held their blestful and eternal reign, unruffled, uninterrupted and undisturbed. As soon as you examined her fine features, your heart instantly yielded to the implicit belief that truth and innocence, and unbounded goodness reigned—the undisturbed possessors of her virtuous bosom, and that no corner was left for any of the vile and baneful passions which deform and debase mankind.

But the most striking trait of her character was an artless plainness and unaffected ingenuousness, which joined to the frank and open confidence and sincerity with which she treated all who approached her, rendered her, to me, the most interesting and beloved human being with whom I had ever become acquainted.

The party at Pendleton's was small. The gentlemen were chiefly elderly, and each had his particular object of attention, or none at all. I, therefore, happily, had no rivals with regard to Miss Wood, and had an excellent opportunity of studying her character. I found her very intelligent for her age, and was very forcibly struck and indescribably charmed with the leading trait of her disposition. I soon perceived that she took all mankind for what they professed to be, and that she had not yet learned that men and women could stoop to the practice of arts, of hypocricy and deception, and that in their common intercourse with each other they were almost anything but what they professed to be. She felt not the necessity of practising this disguise herself, and could not suspect others, of what she herself would have abhorred. Her own heart could never teach her this disgusting, humiliating lesson, and if it had ever been suggested to her by others, the benignity of her nature would not let her believe it.

This night's experience and observation of this artless, innocent and most excellent girl, produced a strong desire to know something of the parents of so much worth and goodness. As soon as I saw them I saw why it was that this sweet, bewitching girl looked on all mankind as her friends and brothers. Her experience of the world had been derived from her own most excellent parents alone, both of whom were models of the finest virtues of the human race. Her own pure heart, with such examples before it, could be nothing but what it really was—the seat of spotless innocence and brotherly love.

As her father has closed his earthly career, I take singular pleasure in passing the following just tribute to his memory.

He was unambitious of being known beyond his own fireside, and there he was deservedly adored. His character and heart were the types of his angelic daughter's. With the fine understanding of a man, the innocence of a child, and a bosom that embraced the whole human family in its benevolent affections, did this most truly good and excellent man devote his whole time, and direct all his efforts to the promotion of the happiness of the dear circle around him, without a wish to attract the public gaze or a single exertion to arrest popular attention. His heart, his soul, his every faculty belonged to his family, and to them were in the first place faithfully given. "He gave his first and best cares to those who had the first and best claims to his protection and tenderness." And when he had done everything for their happiness that he could do, he dispensed his kindness to his neighbours, and in a way known only to those neighbours themselves. I never knew a man I thought so pure. I never loved a man so well.

After the night of Pendleton's party, I lost no opportunity of being in the presence of this sweet girl who I found had gained such an ascendency over me that I was nowhere so happy as when I was conversing with her and studying how I could make myself most agreeable and interesting to her.

The least direct compliment or marked attention would instantly suffuse her cheeks with blushes. And as she was constantly surrounded, in public, by assiduous admirers, some of whose attentions were too plain to be misunderstood, I had often the opportunity of seeing her blush.

Hers was the blush of innocence and nature. Her feelings had never been disciplined, and her face always exhibited the unaffected sensations of her bosom. But such blushes! I see them at this moment as plain and distinct as when they used to spread over her lovely visage, and at this distant day, after a lapse of more than three and twenty years, I recall with exquisite delight the recollection of the ineffable thrillings which those sweet blushes have so often caused to rush thro' my enraptured, my delighted heart.

After a few weeks of this sweet delirium, this enchanting dream, when I began to aspire to the hope of at least making known to this lovely girl the deep interest she had created in my bosom, a gentleman from Winchester, with some of his friends, appeared at Bath, to whom, those friends most confidently asserted, this incomparable woman was solemnly betrothed, and to whom she was shortly to be married. This news was told in a way that gained the belief of every one in Bath, myself perhaps excepted; who might be said to know not what to think, or how to withold a belief, I was so much interested not to receive.

I thought her conduct towards him was not such as it would have been to the man she had so distinguished as to make the blessed depository of her future happiness. But the period of our separation was approaching and I had little time for observation, or remark, and was forced to yield a reluctant and heart-rending acquiescence to the general belief.

From the sincerity and candor of her character and purity of her heart, I was satisfied she would never promise herself in matrimony to any man who had not engaged the whole of her affections. Under these impressions, a silent resignation to my fate, was the only course that I could, with propriety, adopt; and this course I did adopt, with a poignancy of affliction which my young heart had never before known.

All that I felt on this occasion may probably be conceived, but to attempt to describe it would be folly, and the recollection of it even now is painful.

In a day or two we parted, as I then thought; seldom, perhaps never to meet again. My heart bled profusely at every pore at this unexpected, this afflicting, this hopeless separation. I went home and endeavored to become reconciled to my wretched destiny, and I lamented my unfortunate trip to Bath.

Some months after my return home, I was called to Winchester on business. This near approach to the residence of this charming woman awakened the liveliest feelings of my heart. I saw more of her family, but as my thoughts were wholly occupied by her, and the report of her engagement, I could not rest satisfied until I enquired of a friend of mine, who was an acquaintance, a neighbour and a visitor at Mr. Wood's, whom I met in Winchester, into the truth of this heart-rending report. He told me he had no doubt of its truth; that it was the current belief of the neighbourhood; and he supposed her marriage would soon take place. As this gentleman, Major James Singleton was well acquainted with all the parties, with the admirer,

Miss Wood and her family, I could no longer withold my belief from this distressing news. I returned to Winchester in a state of feeling not to be described.

Shortly after my trip to Winchester, I went to the lower part of Virginia and spent the winter at Fredericksburg, at my sister's, who had lately been married.

On my arrival at home, in the spring, I inquired after this dear girl and found that she was not yet married. I was not much acquainted in the vicinity of Winchester and I was laying plans how I should get to Mr. Wood's and again see the dear object of my heart's sincerest devotion.

I began now to suspect that the report of her engagement was designedly set on foot by her Winchester admirer and friends.

Whilst I was debating this matter with myself, a brother of Miss Wood, Dr. James Wood, became an inhabitant of Charlestown, near which I resided, where he intended to practice medicine. We soon became acquainted and a trip to his father's projected. My heart began again to beat high. I told him frankly that I had seen his sister at Bath, and the interest she had created in my bosom. I asked him if she was engaged. He told me that she was not. This revived my hopes, and infused new life through all my frame.

We set out on the 3d of July, 1797, to be present at the celebration on the Fourth at Winchester. We got to Mr. Wood's to dinner. This was a trying meeting to me. An indifferent person would have perceived my confusion, altho I tried hard to conceal it. It was nearly a year since I last saw this interesting woman. She had grown a good deal and improved much in beauty. Her manners appeared to me more engaging and interesting than ever, and all my former feeling returned upon me with redoubled force and ardor.

I found that there was to be a ball the next night in Winchester. I engaged her for partner. At the ball my attentions were too assiduous and particular to escape notice. I was again warned of the old engagement. But this report had now lost its power to deceive and distress me. Her Winchester suitor hung on my skirts all night. The ball was at length over. I had driven her to the ball in my phaeton, and the Doctor, her brother, rode on horseback. Her old admirer took leave of her as we drove off. We got safely home about half a mile from town, but I know not how, during this delightful ball, this dear, this interesting, this enchanting girl, wound around my already captured fluttering heart, such an additional number of soft, indissoluble bands that I determined to lose no time in laying the state of my affections before her.

The Doctor and myself spent several days at her father's, where her old admirer and several other beaux dined the day after the ball. During our stay I had a good opportunity of enjoying the sweet converse of this enchanting girl, whilst each succeeding minute more firmly bound me to her fascinating spell around me.

On my return home, I told the Doctor that my happiness was now indissolubly connected with the interest I had or should be able to make in his sister's affections. That my whole heart and every tender thought of my bosom were irrevocably hers, and that I should not lose one single unnecessary moment in laying the state of my affections before her.

At my earnest request, he promised to return with me to his father's in a day or two when he would leave me to plead my own cause. We accordingly went up again in a few days.

If ever man yet loved as tenderly as I loved and has

made the trying attempt to obtain the object of all his hopes, of all his wishes, he will know what I felt, what I feared, what I hoped, and yet dared scarcely hope, on this interesting occasion. I made out, but how I do not now (nor did I a moment after the dreadful trial was over) recollect, to declare my passion intelligently to her. Happily her own confusion and embarrassment prevented her noticing or recollecting the very awkward and ridiculous figure I cut, and in some measure assisted to restore me to something like tranquility. After the first painful effort was over, the succeeding attempts were less perplexing and distressing to us both.

It is needless to say more on this part of the history of our loves. Suffice it to add, that it was my rare felicity, my singular good fortune, to hold in the heart of this lovely, this charming, this noble woman, a place as dear as my fondest wish could have aspired to even before I had apprized her of the state of my own feelings. With such tender sentiments towards me and such sincerity and candor of character, she did not long let me suffer the painful misgivings, the dreadful fears of doubting affection. The sweet, the delicious confession on the state of her affections was made; the blessed consent to make me happy was given, and I was entranced in the exquisiteness of my enraptured feelings.

She fixed the happy day for our union on the 6th of the succeeding November, on which day she had completed her sixteenth year.

From the time of our engagement 'till the day of our marriage I spent about half of my time at her father's. Delicious moments! Hours of sweet and pure delight! At length the memorable 6th of November, 1797 arrived.

> Let that auspicious day be ever sacred,
> No mourning, no misfortunes happen on it;
> Let it be marked for triumphs and rejoicings,
> Let happy lovers ever make it holy,
> Choose it to bless their hopes and crown their wishes
> That day, that happy day, that gave to me my Mary.

It would seem to be almost unnecessary after what has been said to tell my children what kind of a wife this incomparable woman has made, nor to dilate on the pure happiness, the exalted felicity which such an union must necessarily have produced. But as my opinion of this girl was formed only from such observations as an ardent, sanguine and enraptured lover could make on an unmarried woman, whose interest it was to appear amiable, to all those whose good opinion she values, and as in a judgment thus formed, the blind lover is sometimes egregiously deceived, and the angelic girl loses much of her divinity on becoming a wife, I will not drop this agreeable subject there.

It is a tribute no less due to the virtues of this most noble, most excellent woman, than congenial to the finest feelings of my own heart to declare my deliberate and unshaken conviction, that I have enjoyed with her the purest happiness, the most exalted felicity, the most refined and chastened joys that it ever has fallen to the happy lot of a man to feel.

When this sweet girl announced to me the impressions that I had made on her guileless heart, and that she was willing to make me the happy, the sacred depository of her future happiness, it will be conceived what hours of conjugal felicity and bliss my active sanguine and youthful heart anticipated from this blissful union, it may easily be imagined what moments of connubial joy and transport my throbbing heart told me I should enjoy. Yes: my warm, my ardent, my youthful bosom, had drawn a highly colored picture of my approaching felicity. And yet as highly colored as that picture surely was, I can with perfect truth say, and do it with feelings of the most profound gratitude, to this noble woman, and a due and reverential sense of the mighty obligations to heaven, that the reality far exceeded it. Yes! as happy as I expected to be, as exquisite as I calculated my enjoyments to prove, I was in reality more happy and my enjoyments were more exquisite than my fondest, my wildest imagination had anticipated. And now, at the very moment that my grateful heart is dictating, and my pen portraying this just tribute to the woman of my best affections, when I have been married to her more than two and twenty years, and the afflicting hands of sickness and of time have rudely torn the roses from her cheeks, and planted a thousand wrinkles on her brow, I can truly say that I love and esteem her more than I ever did in the brightest hours of her health, her youth and her loveliness. And that I, at this day, enjoy with this beloved woman, this esteemed and best of friends, some of the most exquisite moments of pure and tranquil felicity, of refined and substantial happiness, that heaven has ever, in its goodness, permitted a frail mortal to enjoy.

Lau. A. Washington.

The marriage of Mr. Washington and Mary Dorcas Wood which took place, as noted, November 6, 1797, was recorded at Winchester and the returns were made by Rev. Alexander Balmain, D. D.

For several years this devoted couple lived at "Hawthorne," which tradition says her father, Robert Wood, gave to Mary Dorcas as a wedding present.

They seem also to have lived at "Richwoods," which had been left to Laurence Augustine by his father,

Samuel Washington. "Harewood," "Cedar Lawn" and "Richwoods" formed the Samuel Washington estate in Jefferson County.

Of the four children of Laurence Augustine Washington and Mary Dorcas Wood, Robert, the eldest, was probably born at Winchester.

At "Red House Shoals," Buffalo, Mason County, now West Virginia, were born the other three—Emma Tell, named for the wife of the Swiss patriot, William Tell, September 22, 1812; Laurence Augustine, Jr., January 5, 1814; and Mary Dorcas, April 10, 1817.

Mr. Washington seems to have possessed the pioneer spirit of change. In 1811 he and his family removed to Mason County. In 1817 they again changed their place of residence to the vicinity of Wheeling, and "Hills," sometimes called "Highlands," became the family seat.

An adopted son, Reuben Short, was a cherished member of the family. In youth he longed to enter the army or navy, but prevented from doing so in spite of the earnest efforts of his foster parents to gratify his desire, he studied law, and in 1826 was licensed to practice by Judge Smith. He died in 1834.

In addition to Reuben Short, Nancy Hardin, a family connection, shared the Washington home and affections. She accompanied Dr. Laurence Augustine, Jr. and his family to Texas, where she remained until her death. She is buried near the Colorado River, in Colorado County, Texas.

Mr. Washington's will dated October 30, 1823, was probated at Wheeling, W. Va. in March, 1824. He died February 15th of that year, in the fiftieth year of his age. His wife died at "Hills," November 9, 1835, aged fifty-four.

The following extracts from personal letters give glimpses of the manners and customs of a little more than a century ago. Methods of travel and communication were so uncertain that the records of watching for visits and letters until hope deferred made the heart sick, are often too pathetic to transcribe. There can be no doubt that the journey by stage or carriage or covered wagon across the Allegheny Mountains was a far more formidable one to Mrs. Comfort Welsh Wood than it seemed to her son-in-law and daughter. She did make the trip in 1818, and the sisters, Comfort, Harriot, Sally, Kitty and Julia were at the hospitable home of their sister at various times; but Mary Dorcas was always very delicate, and she longed for the companionship of her own family with a poignancy that amounted often to homesickness.

Wheeling, Fort Cumberland, Pittsburgh and other places mentioned, were mere villages then, and they were separated by a sparsely settled wilderness threaded by trails leading across high mountains.

The letters of 1824 throw light upon the story with which this chapter opens, and are given out of chronological order. The human element in them all must appeal to every heart.

"Hills," near Wheeling, April 4, 1824.
My dear Mother,
This letter will be handed to you by Mr. Good, a gentleman who possessed the esteem and friendship of my dear Mr. Washington, and for whom I feel similar sentiments. You may perhaps recollect him; he dined with us once whilst you were here.
Your letter of the 6th of March, I received a few days ago. You entreat me to bear my loss with fortitude. I do try, my dear mother, for I know it is my duty to do so, if it were only that I might be able to do my duty more faithfully to my poor children; but if you will only for moment reflect what a partner I have lost, and with what mutual love and confidence we lived together for such a number of years, and that I have not a friend near me to whom I can communi-

cate my feelings and sentiments without reserve, you will say with me that my fortitude is put to a severe trial.

I feel lonely and desolate since I am bereaved of him, who was, and deservedly so, the object of my most tender affections. Our pleasures and amusements were all of the rural or domestic kind, and it was this season of the year that always delighted Mr. Washington most. He would be continually working with his trees and flowering shrubs when his health would admit of it. And the first violet or any other sweet flower which he discovered in the spring was presented to me, accompanied by some endearing sentiment which he was so capable of feeling and expressing. I am now deprived of all those dear, delightful scenes; but I have a melancholy pleasure in attending to the plants and flowers in the green house, and others that were the favorites of Mr. Washington. Yesterday by dear little children came running to me their faces beaming with pleasure to present me the first violets that bloomed in the garden. It had an indescribable effect on my feelings; I was pleased with the attentions of the dear little ones, altho' they produced regrets too painful for me to bear with firmness. I have all the consolation my dear children are capable of affording me. They are indeed a treasure to me. Robert is quite a man in his deportment. He and the other dear children are all the company I have. They are kind and affectionate and all that I could wish or expect from children of their ages. Sweet little Mary is so much like her dear father, that I am afraid I am weak enough to make a pet of her, altho' I am sensible it is the worst thing that could be done for her. I hope and pray that I may be granted the power of keeping them all in the path of virtue and knowledge they have as yet been kept in, but alas! they have lost their guide and preceptor, and God only knows what is best for me to do with regard to the completion of their educations. At this time I cannot form an opinion of what would be best. In my situation how much I feel the want of the endearing attention and sympathy of a fond mother or sister! Your poor child Mary has not even that satisfaction.

I am sorry you have not perfectly recovered your health. I hope when the weather becomes settled it will be quite restored.

Reuben is with me. He attends to the farm, keeps my accounts and assists in teaching the children grammar and arithmetick. Nancy attends to the housekeeping as I have not been able for some time to attend to it.

If Mr. Good does not set out on his journey as soon as he expects, I intend to copy a piece of writing of Mr. Washington's and send you with this, as I feel assured it will give you pleasure to read it. It is a history of our early love.

God bless you all, my dear mother and sisters. Write to me soon.
Adieu, My dear Mother,
MARY D. WASHINGTON.

"Hills," near Wheeling, April 23, 1824.

Dear Kitty,

My mother's letter was longer on the road than is usual. It came by Marietta, which was out of the common route. I wrote to her by Mr. Good, a very worthy old gentleman of my acquaintance, who I suppose has arrived at mother's before this. My increased cares, I believe, have had rather a tendency to rouse me in some degree than otherwise. The calls that my poor dear children make on me for my care and protection bring forth all the energy I possess, and sustain me under my sorrows. To make a just estimate of the very heavy calamity which has befallen me in the loss of my beloved, my most excellent husband, you should be made acquainted with his real character, which approached nearer to perfection than any man's I ever knew, except our revered father's. I have lost my best beloved, the partner of my heart. Oh! if you had witnessed the conjugal felicity we lived in! He was so kind, so tender, so affectionate, and so endearing, you would say, "Alas! my poor sister, well may you mourn, for you have suffered deeply." The future prospect of my life is but as a winter day, short and gloomy, and if it were not for the duty I owe to my poor children, there would be no incitement to struggle against my misfortune, and to endeavour to bear it with fortitude. * * * *

With my love to my dear mother and sisters,
I remain your ever affectionate sister,
M. D. WASHINGTON

"Hills," near Wheeling, May 5, 1824.

My dear Mother,

Repeatedly in the course of the last year, Mr. Washington expressed a wish that you should have a copy of the history of our early loves (which he wrote in March, 1820), thinking with me, it would give you pleasure to know how ardently and sincerely he loved me; and that we

"Loved through wintry age the same
As first in youth we loved."

He would have copied it himself for you, if his leisure or health had permitted him. I have attempted several times to copy it; but it affected my feelings to such a degree that I was not able to go through with it. I have therefore been obliged to get Reuben to do it for me. I should have preferred copying it myself for you, if I could have commanded my feelings sufficiently, but that was impossible. Every scene, every incident is so faithfully and so naturally portrayed that the image, and the very voice of the dear departed object of my earliest and my latest affections seem present whilst I am reading it;

but it is a fleeting vision—I am left to mourn in solitary wretchedness. * * * *

Remember me to my sisters.

I am your ever truly affectionate daughter,

M. D. WASHINGTON

The following letters or extracts are given in chronological order:

Falls of Schuylkill,
20th July, 1811.

To Mrs. Comfort Welsh Wood:

Dear Madam:

We arrived here about two hours since in good health. Our dear little Robert, on whose account I know you have had many anxious moments, has borne the journey better than any of us. He has never been indisposed a single moment since we left Winchester, and has been ever as merry as a little cricket during the whole ride to this place. * * * *

(L. A. W.)

Pittsburgh, 8th October, 1811.

Dear Madam:

We arrived at this place yesterday about twelve o'clock, after as a good a passage over the Alleghaney Mountains as could be expected from the nature of the road.

We spent yesterday afternoon at General Nevill's, where Robert engrossed almost all the attention of the family. * * * * I expect to leave here this afternoon. At Wheeling I will write again. * * * *

(L. A. W.)

Wheeling, 13th October, 1811.

My dear Mother,

We all, black and white, arrived here the day before yesterday in good health. I have not received the smallest injury by the jolting and thumping about which we had an abundance of. * * * *

Mr. W. wrote to you from Fort Pitt, where we spent two days very agreeably. General Nevill's family were extremely polite and attentive to us. We expect to leave this place tomorrow. Mr. W. has engaged a boat in which we shall move down the river. When I get to the end of my journey you shall hear from me again. * * * *

May you, my dear mother, enjoy all the happiness this world can afford is the prayer of your affectionate daughter,

(M. D. W.)

Point Pleasant, 23rd October, 1811.

Dear Madam:
We arrived at Mr. Parks' on the afternoon before the last. We have all enjoyed perfect health. I left Polly, Nancy, and Robert at Parks' and got to this place last night. In the course of the day I shall set out for my land where I expect to arrive tomorrow. I hope to get to house-keeping in three weeks from this time. * * * *

(L. A. W.)

18th November, 1811.

I have taken advantage of the first opportunity which offered to inform my dear mother of our safe arrival at our habitation on the Kanahwa. We were six weeks on the road, but not traveling the whole of that time. We remained several days in Fort Pitt and were detained nearly a week in Wheeling on account of the boat which had to be repaired. We had a pleasant passage from Wheeling to Mr. Parks'. I spent two weeks there, whilst Mr. W. was busily engaged in fixing up the cabin for my reception and a very snug one it is. By next summer we shall have a spacious log dwelling, when I hope and trust I shall have the inexpressible delight of seeing you here. * * * *

(M. D. W.)

Vale of Plenty, December 2nd, 1811.

My dear Mother,
By Mr. Roysten I have an opportunity of writing to you, and as I am persuaded you feel an interest in whatever concerns me, it gives me real pleasure that I can with sincerity tell you I am very happily situated here. I never was more agreeably surprised than when I arrived to see so fine a country after the many shocking accounts I had of it.

We live on a beautiful little hill from which there is a gentle descent all 'round. The hill back of us is by no means so tremendously high as you have heard it represented to be, and the bottom at this place is seven hundred yards wide. Up the river where we shall ultimately fix, it is much wider. I have every reason for liking the country except that it separates me from you, my beloved mother. I never had better health than since I have been out here, and Mr. Washington has almost recovered his sight. * * * *

(M. D. W.)

Red House Shoals, 13th July, 1812.

Dear Kitty:
* * * * I am really glad to hear my dear mother is getting in better spirits. How happy it ought to make you all to witness the returning health and spirits of so good a parent as she has been to us.

Let it be the care of you who remain with her to solace and try to alleviate by your kind affectionate conduct any real or imaginary affliction she may labor under. You will find, my dear girl, it will be the sweetest reflection to you if you are ever separated from your mother, to know you have ever been dutiful and affectionate to her. * * * *

(M. D. W.)

Red House Shoals, January 8th, 1813.
Dear Mother:
 * * * * We are very much in want of a weaver. I have a great deal spun and yet nothing finer than a six hundred wove. I wish we could prevail on one of your Winchester weavers to move here. Do you think it would be possible? * * * *

(M. D. W.)

Red House Shoals, February 22, 1814.
Dear Kitty:
 * * * * I hope mother will not give up the idea of coming here next summer, as I have set my heart on seeing her, and know not how I could bear the dissappointment. She must not forget her promise to bring Julia with her. * * * *

My sweet little Laurence can sit alone, and is the merriest little fellow in the world. I call him "Laughing Lally." Robert and Emma grow finely and are as healthy as can be. * * * *

(M. D. W.)

Red House Shoals, February 3rd, 1816.
My dear Mother:
 * * * * The last I heard of you was by old Bob, who said he saw you a short time before he left Winchester, and you were well; was much pleased to hear of you, even by old Bob; but I should be infinitely more delighted to receive a letter from you. With what unspeakable pleasure do I look forward to the time when I shall see and embrace my dear, my adored parent. I hope my brother James will come with you as he promised.

I mentioned in my last that we expected Reuben to make us a visit. He is with us, and Mr. Washington intends to finish his education at home. Reuben seems to have a perfect recollection of you and begs me to let him write a few lines to you on the same sheet with me. * * * *

Your ever affectionate daughter,

(M. D. W.)

My dear Grandmother:

I have for some time past been anxious to inform you that I still recollect your kind attentions to me, whilst I lived near you, and that I love and shall continue to love and respect you. As my mother is about to write to you by this mail, I cannot longer refrain from paying my affectionate respects to you. My mother has told you that I am to continue at home in future. Amongst other sources of pleasure that this arrangement has produced is this, that I shall have more frequent opportunities of hearing of you in future than I formerly had. For I can assure you it will always delight me to hear of your welfare and happiness.

Accept, my dear grandmother, my love and most affectionate regards,

RUEBEN WASHINGTON SHORT

Red House Shoals, 6th April, 1816.

My dear Mother:

* * * * In consequence of your great weight, I must advise you not to venture to cross the mountain in your chair, but hire a snug, light carriage with four wheels, in which you will travel with much more ease and safety than you could in one with two.

Sometime in November last, Mr. Washington wrote to Mr. Edward McGuire to learn the character of a weaver (of New Town) who wished to remove to this country. He replied to this letter on the 10th of December. After giving the character of the weaver, he casually observed, "Your sister, Miss Comfort Wood, is to be married to Mr. Dailey on Thursday next." * * * *

(M. D. W.)

(*Mrs. Comfort Welsh Wood crossed the mountains in 1818 in a large arm chair which is now at Glen Burnie.*)

Buffalo, Mason County, Va., 10th July, 1816.

My dear Madam:

* * * * Mary has already informed you that our dear little Reuben is at home, and that I don't mean again to send him to a public school.

Many reasons have combined to induce me to undertake the solemn, the holy office of instructor of my children. I shall never send any of them from home again and have concluded to devote faithfully and unremittingly the whole of my time to their education. This undertaking shall be most strictly and scrupulously preformed with all the capacity I possess.

We are now learning botany. Mary, Reuben, Robert and myself are going on together. We assemble in Tom Thumb (a name we have given a house that contains my library and philosophical apparatus), several times a day and go on in our studies together. It would delight you to get a peep at us when we are assembled around our table that holds our microscope, lens and botanical books. We have it strewed with flowers and are investigating their classes, orders, genera, etc. with little Tell and Laurence playing on the floor and begging our flowers as we finish each particular investigation of them. Nancy also joins us but does not take as much interest in the subject as the rest of us. These are to us all, and especially to my dear Mary and myself, hours of the most exquisite enjoyment. Our boys learn with a facility truly gratifying and take a pleasure in my instructions which reward me in a ten-fold degree for all my exertions to improve them.

As soon as I find them flag in the least, I pretend I want to write, or look into some books, when they both scamper out and go to amusing themselves in their own way. * * * *

We have not many neighbors, and they all know my present avocation and my love of home too well to expect regular visits from me or the family. Whenever a visit is made we all go together and talk over our studies on the road from and to our house again. I'll venture to say we are the most constantly employed students in America. * * * * Nearly all my happiness and wishes center in the beloved objects that surround me and are contained in my own doors. Whilst in their endearing society I have few wishes unaccomplished and little else to ask of indulgent heaven. To know of your welfare and that of your daughters and son James will always add to the abundant store of felicity that is accumulated around me; and to see you here would still increase the ample stock of happiness and delight which a beneficent Providence has kindly and profusely bestowed upon me.

I think I can with the most perfect truth declare my firm belief that there is not a happier family on earth than mine. I have no idea of human felicity being more perfect, and I am well assured there is not one in a million any thing like as happy. Our beloved, our esteemed Mary is the center around which we all revolve. She has attracted to herself all the finest feelings of our hearts and justly merits the full measure of love which we all delight to give her. The children are scarcely ever a yard from her. Laurence claims the lap. As soon as he descends from it either to play when he is awake or is put from it when asleep, Emma jumps into it with looks of delight and heart full of joy. When she retires, Robert as large as he now is, glories in possessing it. Reuben leans on her chair with fond delight and plainly shows that nothing but his size prevents his contesting it with Robert, and the summit of my happiness is to be within her reach. From her presence I always go with a reluctance and return to it with rapture. When she gets up to go to the dairy, the poultry yard, or to walk amongst her flowers, Laurence and Tell bounce up from their most engaging plays and pad it with her, one on each side, holding her hands or gown; Robert follows in the rear; Reuben joins them, and I insensibly approach the happy little flock and always feel my heart expand with encreased transport and joy when I have in one view all these dear objects of my tenderest affections. Would to Heaven you could witness our pure unmixed felicity that you might once before you go hence see an exhibition of human happiness as full and perfect as frail mortals are ever permitted to enjoy. Until you can do this, take the above description. It is the best I can give you, and although rigidly true, it will give you a poor and feeble image of the reality it is intended to represent.

Mary joins me in love to the girls. She offers her most affectionate respects to you whilst I assure you of the love, esteem and regard of your affectionate son-in-law,

LAU. A. WASHINGTON

Red House Shoals, August 26, 1816.

Dear Kitty:

You will no doubt be surprised when I tell you that we are going to leave the Kanahwa. Mr. Washington and myself have determined to liberate all our slaves who are of age as soon as the present crop is secured. The difficulty of getting white hirelings in this place, and the opposition some of our near neighbors make to our retaining any of our freed blacks in our service as hirelings make it necessary for us to move to some place where we can either hire white hands, or take Toney and George, who are desirous of spending their days with us. The state of Ohio or Pennsylvania present themselves to our choice. We both prefer the western part of Pennsylvania, as we should then be nearer my mother than we are at present, and she would have a much better road to travel over to come to see us. The reflection that I shall be near my mother, and that she can get to see us with less trouble and fatigue than she could visit us here, help very much to reconcile me to the idea of encountering the trouble of moving and improving a new place. I had thought we were fixed for life, but it has turned out otherwise, and I am satisfied with the prospect of our change of residence, as well as in our mode of living. I am delighted with the hope of seeing my beloved mother and some of my sisters here next spring. Mr. Washington will write to my mother on this subject next week, also on the liberation of our slaves.

Lucy wishes me to inform you that her mother (old Sucky) is dead. She died after a painful illness of several months.

Mr. Washington and Nancy join me in love to you, mother, brother James and my other sisters.

M. D. WASHINGTON

Buffalo, Mason County, Virginia, 27th August, 1816.

My dear Madam:

I had the pleasure to receive your letter of the 7th (in reply to one of mine) by the mail before the last. Particular engagements prevented my answering it by the last mail.

My Mary and myself have latterly had many consultations on the situation of our slaves. We have both upon all the consultation and reflection we could give that very delicate and perplexing subject come to the conclusion that it is better to free them, with all the real and ideal mischiefs which may follow such a course, than to hold them longer in slavery. We are both decidedly of the opinion that the God of nature made them as free as ourselves, and that they are held in bondage by ruffian force and savage violence. These are uncouth terms, and I am sincerely sorry they are so applicable to the case. We both believe it is radically wrong for one person to deprive another of the whole of the products of his labors, and to impose upon him and his posterity forever a state of endless slavery. We cannot believe that any political considerations, and views of personal interest, any prejudices of education, any plans of policy whatever, can make that act right which by the laws of eternal truth and unvarying justice is wrong. And so far from the length of time that this particular, this cruel wrong has existed adding anything to its extenuation, we think it greatly and justly increases the magnitude of the evil.

In the education of our children, it will be the constant study of my Mary and myself to cultivate with ceaseless assiduity and endless care, the integrity of their hearts and the purity of their morals. By a watchfulness that shall never tire and a vigilance that shall never slumber, we will conduct their young minds to the fullest and most complete conviction of the truths of this God-like maxim, "Do not unto others what you would not they should do unto you."

We will implant indelibly in their tender hearts the conviction that the holy obligation of this Divine rule is never to be violated, never to be compromised, never to be evaded. We will teach them that, whilst they are to guard with vestal vigilance and holy care their own personal liberties and rights, they are under an obligation equally holy, sacred and binding, to respect and observe the personal liberties and rights of others.

Precept alone, however eloquently delivered, can never conduct their minds to this sublime conclusion. Our own practice must accord with our instructions or we shall certainly and justly gain their contempt and scorn instead of their love and veneration. How ridiculous, how odious would it appear to them for us to endeavour to enforce on their minds a respect for the rights and personal liberties of others, whilst we ourselves were wrongfully withholding from fifteen of our fellow beings the only boon for which life is worth acceptance. Would not the pure unsullied hearts of these children ask themselves, if they did not propound the question directly to us:

"If you, my beloved parents, would sooner yield your lives than become the slaves of others, whence have you derived the right, and how can you reconcile the act of keeping your fellow beings in slavery?" How could we answer their question or how could we teach them to feel the force of the above Divine precept while we were violating it daily in so gross, so unpardonable an instance?

Upon reflection we were both convinced that to set our negroes free was not only a duty we owed to them and ourselves, which of itself was so imperious as to require no other inducement to its performance than the self-approbation which would most certainly follow it; but that as it regarded the future characters, welfare and happiness of our beloved children, it was an act that could not be longer postponed. We have accordingly announced to those hitherto much injured individuals, that as soon as the present crop is secured, all of them who are of age shall have deeds of emancipation executed to them.

Asa, Maria and Bet, who are under age, will be required to render some years of service as a compensation for our trouble and expense in rearing them. Their time of service (until twenty-one, when, at all events, they shall be set free), will be shortened in proportion to their conduct. We shall reserve Daniel and Lydia for the balance of their lives, as well as old Davy, Mr. Dandridge's slave, who came out with us when we moved here. Polly has told Kitty that his wife, old Suckey, is dead.

It is a source of great and singular delight to me that our beloved Mary has most cordially joined me in this act of justice. As was to be expected from the purity and integrity of her heart, she says she always looked upon the state of slavery in which these much injured individuals are kept in our country, as a standing and deep reproach to a people who are always boasting of the freedom of their institutions, and proclaiming to the world that it is here alone that man walks forth in the true dignity of his nature, and enjoys without alloy that freedom which a beneficent Creator has bestowed on all his works.

Toney and George being very unwilling to leave us, we have concluded to hire them. Our neighbors, however, express great alarm at the idea of their continuing here. As this is the case, and white labourers cannot be had here, Mary and myself have concluded to move to the western part of Pennsylvania. We prefer it to Ohio or Indiana, principally because it will bring us nearer to you than we are at present. If I can buy a small piece of land near the great turnpike road from Wheeling to Fort Cumberland, you will find no difficulty in visiting us.

I have written to different persons in Pittsburgh and Wheeling to know the prices of land, etc. When I hear from them, I shall be able to say when we shall leave this place. You shall know it in time to regulate your much desired visit next spring. On this subject I shall say more when I next write.

Mary joins me in love and affection to you, James Wood, and the girls. Nancy desires to be remembered to you all, whilst I assure you of my sincere regard, respect and esteem.

LAU A. WASHINGTON.

The letters of 1816 show the position of Mr. Washington and his wife upon the subject of slavery, a position which proves them far in advance of their times. They not only freed their slaves but paid the passage to Liberia, of all who would leave them.

The following letters show that they went not to western Pennsylvania, but to the vicinity of the village of Wheeling, W. Va., and made there their future home, undergoing the hardships of such an undertaking rather than offend their neighbors.

Wheeling, 22nd June, 1817.

Dear Kitty:

We arrived here on the first day of this month in good health after a very agreeable journey through part of the Ohio state. Our little Mary was only six weeks old the day we left the Red House Shoals. She was so young that I felt great anxiety on her account, but she bore the journey better than I expected, and is now one of the sweetest and best little girls I ever saw. She has beautiful blue eyes, the finest skin that ever was seen except Robert's, whom she is thought like, but I think her the exact image of her father, who almost idolizes her, and I have the vanity to think (although she is a most engaging little creature), it is because she is called after her mother. He plays more with her than he ever did with either of the other children at her age. * * * *

(M. D. W.)

Hills, 19th June, 1818.

We were extremely delighted, my dear mother, to learn by Reuben's letter that you had safely arrived at Glenburnie. Reuben's letter was dated the 29th of May. * * * *

(M. D. W.)

Wheeling, 23rd June, 1817.

My dear Mother:

We left our late residence on the Kanahwa on Thursday, the 22nd of May, and after a very pleasant and highly interesting journey through a considerable part of the fine state of Ohio, we arrived here on Sunday, the first day of this month. We passed thro' Gallipolis, Chillicothe, Zanesville, etc. A long period of very dry weather had put the roads into the very finest order, and in the most level and in the wildest parts of the country thro' which we passed we traveled with the greatest ease and comfort.

The manners and habits of the people on the road in the very interesting state of Ohio are calculated to arrest the attention and excite the admiration of the most sluggish and unobservant traveler. To Mary and myself they afforded delightful themes for reflection and gave us a gratification we have seldom experienced. As soon as you enter a home you at once see in the manner in which every member of the family goes about whatever they engage in that they feel that they are toiling and working for themselves. They exhibit an earnestness in everything they do which at once assures you it will be well done. There is no confusion, no bustle, no jostling, no orders given in the haughty insolence of petty authority to crouching inferiors. Each member of the family knows its own department and duties and performs them with ease, regularity and silence. Everything goes on like clockwork and each individual being equally interested in the prosperity of the whole, they all draw together and perform with alacrity and cheerfulness their respective parts in the great work of advancing the common and general welfare of the whole. You look around and see none but the sturdy sons and beauteous daughters of industry, freedom, and happiness. Happy, interesting people! I never looked at them in their busy moments of employment without feeling and justly appreciating the delightful influence which the absence of slavery has upon the manners and happiness of a people. In these feelings my beloved Mary most cordially joined me and was, if possible, more delighted than myself.

I have been too much engaged since our arrival here to look out for a place of retreat. I calculate on spending the most of this week (this is Monday) in examining the surrounding country. I shall not, however, purchase hastily, as we are very comfortably fixed here in a rented house that I can keep as long as I please. In it there is a very comfortable room that would hold you and some of the girls, and it will give Mary and myself and the whole family the greatest pleasure to see you and any of the girls who may choose to accompany you and our brother James. Indeed, few circumstances would give me more delight than your company and theirs for as long a period as you can feel disposed to absent yourself from Winchester.

Adieu, my dear mother,
(L. A. W.)

Hills, Tuesday, 1st December, 1818.

My dear Mother:

On the 13th day of this month, Dr. Morton put our dear Mary under a course of mercury, intending to affect her mouth somewhat short of salivation. He at the same time ordered blisters on her breast. * * * *

(A dose of turpentine, calomel and opium is mentioned, and bleedings were of frequent occurrence.)

Hills, Feb. 21, 1821.
My dear Sally:

* * * * Our dear son Robert was taken very ill on the day after the receipt of your letter with a bilious fever and inflammatory rheumatism, which confined him to his bed a week. He has just recovered enough to be able to walk about his room.

I have spent a melancholy winter. About the middle of November, Mr. Washington was taken very sick, and continued to get worse until he became extremely ill before we were aware of it. We sent for a physician, and it turned out to be a most violent inflammatory fever, which confined him to his bed several weeks, and left him so reduced and weak that he was not able to walk across the room for a week after he left his bed. He is now in his usual good health, but he has not regained his flesh. * * * *

I have had more of the rheumatism this winter than I have had since I left Jefferson County. * * * *

Your affectionate sister,
M. D. WASHINGTON.

Hills, Wednesday, 22nd August, 1821.
My dear Mother:

Robert and myself staid a week longer at the Bedford Springs than I expected we should do when I wrote to you from thence. We arrived at home on the second of last month. We came by Pittsburgh. Both of us derived singular advantage from our trip. The waters, air, etc. of that place are certainly highly medicinal. Robert appears to be as hearty as ever he was in his life, and were I to judge from my feelings, appetite and muscular strength I should say that I am restored to a perfect state of health. I had a barrel of the Bedford water sent to me, which my Mary, the children and myself are drinking. Mary thinks the children have derived considerable benefit from its use.

When I got home I found Mr. Henry Berry of Charlestown, Jefferson County, in Wheeling. He had a letter of introduction to me and called to see us the day after my arrival.

He then talked of leaving this part of the country in a short time and promised to convey to you a landscape which Robert has since found here on my return home, and which I should have much sooner answered had not Mr. Berry's movements proved so uncertain. For when I first came home I was fearful that Robert could not finish his landscape in time to go by him. But day after day and week after week have elapsed, and he is not now able to tell when he will set off. He once took a formal leave of his friends in Wheeling, came out here as being so far on his journey home, and instead of proceeding on next morning, he went back to Wheeling.

The fact is that he came out here to court the beautiful Mrs. Swearingen, of Shepherdstown, formerly Miss Sarah Breeding of Harper's Ferry (who has been in Wheeling for some months on a visit to her sister Frazier, at present a resident of this village), and here he has been ever since my arrival almost constantly by her side, gazing on her beauteous face in silent, speechless rapture. Such has been his timidity, that altho' everybody here acquainted with the parties, sees the ardor with which he adores this lovely woman, he has not 'till within a day or two been able to make a formal declaration of his passion to her. From her deportment towards him, it has been for sometime the opinion of my Mary and myself that his suit will be crowned with success. They have been several times here together and we have been with them in Wheeling. * * * *

(L. A. W.)

Hills, Thursday, 29th November, 1821.

My dear Mother:

* * * * Mr. H. Berry left our house for Charlestown on Tuesday, the 28th of August. He took charge of some drawings of Robert, Emma, and Laurence for you, which he promised to deliver himself shortly after his return home. We wish to know if they got safe to hand.

As this has been an unusually sickly fall and we have seen in the public prints and learned from private sources that the citizens of Harper's Ferry, Shepherdstown, and the inhabitants on the watercourses generally in your part of the country have been afflicted with the most fatal epidemic, my Mary and myself have felt some uneasiness at your long silence, and are very anxious to know if your family has had the good luck to escape disease. This anxiety has kept us in a state of unpleasant solicitude for some time past. This solicitude has hitherto been in some measure suppressed by our not seeing any mention of the prevalence of disease in your immediate neighborhood in the Winchester paper, which I subscribe for. But by the "Republican" of the 10th inst., which was received yesterday, we find the death of pastor J. Glass is announced as proceeding from the "prevailing fever". This has given us some fears that the silence of this paper heretofore on the subject of a want of usual health around you has proceeded from a narrow and contracted idea of policy. We hope therefore that you will let us hear the real state of the case as soon as possible.

We are all well here. In this immediate vicinity the people are as well as they ever were. From about forty miles below Wheeling on the Ohio River, as far down as Louisville, at least, a most malignant fever has prevailed which has made most desolating havoc. Amongst others, Mr. John Rutherford has fallen a victim to it.

He wrote to Nancy that he would be here on the first of October. He was taken sick on Saturday, the sixth, and died on Wednesday, the 10th of that month. * * * *

(L. A. W.)

Hills, Sunday, 17th November, 1822.

My dear Sally:

* * * * Kitty kindly offers to send me flowering shrubs and mentions your collection of roses. I wish she had thought of giving the list of their kinds. The rose is a great favorite with both my Mary and myself. This you will readily believe when I tell you that we have growing in my yard and garden nearly a hundred rose bushes. But our variety is not great. I have sent to Philadelphia to purchase the moss and yellow roses and white and yellow jasmine. But I should value any shrubs obtained from you and Kitty vastly more than those procured from any other quarter. The roots that our mother sent out by Nancy and Reuben occupy a distinguished place in our garden and a still more distinguished place in my regard. * * * *

(L. A. W.)

Hills, Monday, 21st April, 1823.

My dear Sally:

When I received your letter of the 17th of last month (which came to hand on the 28th), I was very busily engaged in planting trees and flowering shrubs in our yard. In this occupation I continued in consequence of the great backwardness of the season, until last Monday. I planted 184 trees and shrubs and more than 40 cuttings.

You say that Julia is raising a multiflora rose to send me. Tell her it will be received with pleasure and cultivated with care on her account. * * * *

It is to me a source of singular pleasure to have under my care and protection any plant, especially a flowering one, which has passed thro' the hands and been presented to me by those I love. And when the objects of my affections are at a distance from me and there seems no probability of my ever having the felicity of a personal interview with them, this melancholy consideration binds to my heart with a stronger cord than usual, any plant or other article which has been the offering of their friendship. I look upon it as a kind of mute and humble representation of its donor and never view it without a feeling of affection.

For yourself, Kitty, and the rest of your sisters, I feel the love of a brother, the pure and hallowed affection of a father. To see any of you would give me a pleasure which words can't express. But this exalted happiness I am well assured I shall never enjoy. The great decline in my health for the last twelve months admonishes me that I am not to look forward to events which are to happen even a year or two hence, and of course reminds me that an interview with any of you is out of the question. I am entirely unable to travel, and shall consequently never cross the mountains again; nor do I believe I shall ever be able to go ten miles from my own door. And as none of you would visit my beloved Mary when I with all the powers of persuasion I possessed appealed to every feeling of a sister's heart and solemnly assured you that I considered the presence of one of you as essential to the recovery of her health ultimately, and as absolutely necessary to her peace of mind in the meantime, it would be weakness and folly to expect you here whilst I live and your sister is in health. * * * *

My Mary is very busily engaged in fixing Emma and Laurence for the dancing school. This is the first chance that I have had of having them taught dancing since they were large enough to learn. Emma is in tiptop spirits, and asks a thousand questions respecting it. Laurence does not anticipate quite as much pleasure from it as she does, tho' he is much pleased with the thought of his visits to town to attend the school. Emma is almost grown up. Her mother is only a head taller than she is.

We have taken a room in the tavern, and my Mary will always accompany them to the school, and when they are sufficiently advanced to derive benefit as well as pleasure from cotillion parties at night, she will remain all night with them. Robert and myself will do so occasionally.

My Mary joins me in love to our mother, yourself, and sisters, whilst I assure you of my brotherly esteem and affection.

LAU. A. WASHINGTON

"Hills," Saturday, 2nd August, 1823.

My dear Sally:

* * * * It was not a rose bush that I solicited from you. I have already more than a hundred in my yard, and of almost all the varieties I have ever heard of that will thrive in our climate. I wanted some flowering shrub—a rose, althea, jasmine, flowering almond, snowball, mock orange or any other that you chose to select, if you felt disposed to present it. I told you I wanted some visible memorial of each of you who felt a sufficient regard for me to select a particular one that I might have the pleasure to rear and cultivate it with my own hands; which I would do with delight, because every time I approached it the sight of it would produce the most agreeable sensations by reminding me that it was a gift of affection, and had once passed through the hands of one I loved.

I repeat that each of you who has sufficient regard for me to send me a plant as a gift of friendship may make her own choice. And that I may know them apart, if more than one be sent, I wish each donor to attach a small label to the plant she sends with her name written on it by her own hand. * * * *

(This is the latest letter in the Glen Burnie Collection from Mr. Washington, and probably the latest one extant).

Philadelphia, November 18, 1833.

My dear Grandmother:
* * * * I thought certainly I should have known before this time how I was to get to Virginia; but as yet I have not heard of any opportunity, and unless one offers shortly I shall be obliged to take Laurence from his studies to accompany me, or write for Robert to come on and go to Virginia with me. That, however, I should not like to do, as I do not think it would be altogether safe for him to cross the mountains at this season of the year. I shall, however, be with you certainly before Christmas. * * * *

I have had a very bad cough for two months and was just out of the doctor's hands when I left home. The night we left Wheeling, just one mile this side of Washington (Pa.) about eleven o'clock at night the stage was overset, thrown off the road down a bank, and we were obliged to get out and stand in the road until we could send back to Washington for help to raise the stage. The rain fell in torrents and Laurence thought I had better get into the stage again, turned over as it was, than to stand in the rain; so he put me in and he and the other gentlemen that were in the stage held the horses; but when the men came and brought a light they found that the stage was too much broken to go on so they took the horses out of the overturned coach and went back to Washington for another. There we had to stay another hour in the rain, which you know was not very good for me. We traveled all the way from Wheeling to Frederick Town in the rain, but from there to Philadelphia we had a very pleasant trip. * * * * Laurence joins me in love to yourself and family and to Aunt Kitty.

Believe me your affectionate granddaughter,
EMMA TELL WASHINGTON

Highland, (Hills) August 23rd, 1834.

Dear Uncle:
When my mother received your letter of the 12th inst., she was just recovering from an illness which left her too weak to write, and since that the news of Reuben's death has entirely unfitted her for writing. She has therefore requested me to answer your letter. * * *

We are pleased to hear of the improvement of my grandmother's health and hope to see her in the fall. I think that you may not expect my mother until the middle of next month, for I think that Reuben's death will be the means of postponing her trip for a few weeks. Indeed, her distress is so great that I fear it will have a very unfavorable effect upon her health. * * * *.

With love to you, I remain as ever, your affectionate niece,

EMMA TELL WASHINGTON

(*Emma Tell went as far as Bermuda in search of health. Shells, which she brought as souvenirs, are still at Glen Burnie.*)

Highland, November 5th, 1835.

My dear Uncle:

It is with feelings of the most poignant sorrow I undertake the melancholy duty of apprizing you of my much beloved mother's health. * * * * She is now so ill that hope is scarcely left us. I tremble to think what may possibly be the tenor of my next letter to Glen Burnie.

If it is possible, some of you come and stay with us this winter.

Your nephew,

R. W. WASHINGTON

Highlands, December 4th, 1835.

My dear Grandmother:

Our Aunts Julia and Comfort reached Wheeling this morning and are now with us; they are well, but a good deal fatigued with traveling day and night. * * * *

R. W. WASHINGTON

(*Several weeks, as we know, after the death of the mother.*)

The Laurence Augustine Washington Society of the Children of the American Revolution was founded at Winchester, November 8, 1922, under the auspices of Mrs. J. F. F. Cassell of Staunton, the state director. The members enrolled upon that day at Fort Loudoun were Elizabeth Gold Crawford, John Vernon Eddy, Richard Kurtz Eddy, Louise Baker Glass, Mollie Baker Glass, William Wood Glass, 3rd, Helen Massey, William Protzman Massey, Samuel Jackson O'Neal, John Edward O'Neal, Elizabeth Shannon Rice and John Warren Rice.

The organizing president was Mrs. Katherine Glass Greene. Other senior officers were Mrs. Stuart H. Edmonds, Mrs. Charles W. Trenary and Miss Mary Miller. The junior officers were the members themselves.

Nothing can give a better insight into the character of the man for whom the society is justly named than extracts from his letters. Devoted parent, pioneer, patriot, Christian gentleman, realist as well as idealist, he was far in advance of his times.

The fact that he freed his slaves and sent all who were willing to leave him to Liberia at his own expense, proves him to have been humane to the point of self-sacrifice, almost to that of persecution in leaving his home and undergoing the hardships of making a new one rather than offend his neighbors.

He was a chemist and a devoted botanist. He has left long lists of plants giving both the common and the botanical names, from the gilly flower or "July flower," and "Johnny-jump-up-and-kiss-me," to those that are rare even today.

Cultured and intellectual, he collected a library of more than a thousand volumes and had each bound in calf.

And this before the use of envelopes, and when postal and freight service were most precarious; when railroads and telegraph wires were ore in the mountains, and the idea of them still slumbering in the brains of their inventors.

This, too, when he was suffering acutely from rheumatism and a severe form of malaria of which the early settlers in river valleys were victims, due partly to the primitive development of the science of medicine.

His wife was a fitting helpmeet and worthy of the almost idolatrous devotion of her husband and children.

The Children of the American Revolution could have no more worthy objects of emulation—no finer examples of the beautiful graces.

CHAPTER XXIV

The Founders of the Washington Family in America — Item from General Washington's Will — The Washington and Fontaine Families in Texas

Unusual interest attaches to the family of Washington here at Winchester because of the identification of George Washington with this vicinity as the youthful surveyor of Lord Fairfax, his connection with the Braddock and other expeditions, and his election to the House of Burgesses from Frederick County.

The fact that his nephew, Laurence Augustine Washington, married and lived here and that a patriotic society is named for the latter is an additional reason for recording here fundamentals of universal interest.

We find, then, that John Washington, kown as "The Immigrant," a Royalist and Cavalier, left South Cave in the East Riding of Yorkshire, near the city of Beverley, England, in 1657, with his wife, two children, and his brother, Laurence, and came to Virginia, where he patented a large tract of land in Westmoreland County, about seventy-five miles below the present city of Washington. His wife died soon afterwards, and he married Anne Pope, daughter of a neighboring planter. They had four children: Laurence, John, Elizabeth and Anne.

Colonel John Washington, the immigrant, was very wealthy, very prominent and very pious. He was a member of the House of Burgesses. He fought the Indians and drove them over the "great wall" into the

Shenandoah Valley. He died in 1677, and was buried at his home, Wakefield. He owned part of Mount Vernon, which from this time grew in importance as the seat of the Washington family, until it is now the most famous shrine in America. George Washington and Martha, his wife, are buried there.

Colonel John Washington's eldest son, Laurence, was born at Wakefield, his father's home, about 1661, and died there in 1698, at the age of thirty-seven. He married Mildred, daughter of Colonel Augustine Warner, of Gloucester County, and left three children, John, born in 1692; Augustine (father of George Washington) in 1694; and Mildred, in 1696. All were born at Wakefield.

After the death of her husband, Laurence, Mrs. Mildred Warner Washington and her children moved to England, where she married George Gall, of Whitehaven, Cumberland County. She died there in 1701. In 1712, Gall emigrated to the colony of Maryland, and brought his three step-children with him.

Augustine Washington, father of the "Father of His Country," born in 1694, the second child of Laurence Washington and Mildred Warner Washington, spent most of his early life at Appleby School, in England, returning, as has already been mentioned, to the Colony about 1712. At the age of twenty-one, on April 12, 1715, he married Jane Butler, daughter of Caleb Butler, an emigrant lawyer of Westmoreland County, Va. He bought Wakefield from his older brother John.

Captain Augustine Washington was fond of the sea. He made frequent trips to England, and transported much iron ore. His wife, Jane Butler, died in 1728. She left two sons, Laurence and Augustine. On March 17, 1731, Captain Augustine Washington married Mary

Ball, probably in England. She wrote frequently to her brother, Joseph Ball, in London. She became the mother of George, Betty, John Augustine, Samuel and Charles.

Samuel, for whose son Laurence Augustine the Society of the Children of the American Revolution is named, was born at Wakefield, November 16, 1734. He married, first, Jane Champe; second, Mildred Thornton; third, Lucy Chapman; fourth, Anne Steptoe; fifth, Susanna Perrin. He died at "Harewood," Berkeley County (now Jefferson County, W. Va.), in 1781, and is buried at "Harewood," his home.

These facts are compiled from "Washington, the Man and the Mason," by Charles H. Callahan.

The historian, Norris, says of Colonel Samuel Washington: "He was a conspicuous member of the Court of Justices, lieutenant of the county, and lieutenant-colonel of the militia; also one of the first Justices of the Peace at the organization of the County of Berkeley."

Laurence Augustine, born in 1774, was therefore seven years of age at the time of his father's death.

His mother was Anne Steptoe, the widow of Willoughby Allerton, and the fourth wife of Samuel Washington. Her children were Frederick or Ferdinand, born at "Harewood," who married Lucy Paine, whose sister Dolly, was married at "Harewood" to President Madison; Laurence Augustine, who married in 1797, Mary Dorcas, daughter of Robert and Comfort Welsh Wood, and whose history is being given; and Harriet, who married July 4, 1796, Andrew Parks of Baltimore, son of John and Margaret Parks of Ireland and Baltimore.

The following clause taken from General Washington's will refers to his brother Samuel and his family:

Item

I release, exonerate and discharge the estate of my deceased brother Samuel Washington from the payment of money which is due to me for the land I sold Philip Pendleton (lying in the County of Berkeley), who assigned the same to him the said Samuel; who, by agreement was to pay me therefor, and whereas by some contract (the purport of which was never communicated to me) between the said Samuel and his son, Thornton Washington, the latter became possessed of the aforesaid land, without any conveyance having passed from me, either to the said Thornton, and without any consideration having been made, by which neglect neither the legal nor equitable title has been alienated; it rests therefore with me to declare my intentions concerning the premises and these are to give and bequeath the said land to whomsoever the said Thornton Washington (who is dead) devised the same; or to his heirs forever if he died intestate; exonerating the estate of the said Thornton, equally with that of the said Samuel, from payment of the purchase money which, with interest, agreeable with the original contract with the said Pendleton, would amount to more than a thousand pounds—and whereas two other sons of my said deceased brother Samuel, namely, George Steptoe Washington and Laurence Augustine Washington, were, by the decease of those to whose care they were committed, brought under my protection, and in consequence have occasioned advances on my part for their education at college and other schools, for their board, clothing, and other incidental expenses, to the amount of near five thousand dollars over and above the sums furnished by their estate, which sum may be inconvenient for them or their father's estate to refund, I do for these reasons acquit them and the said estate from the payment thereof—my intention being that all accounts between them and me, and their father's estate and me, shall stand balanced. * * * *

Item. &c. * * * *

G. WASHINGTON

Of the four children of Laurence Augustine Washington and Mary Dorcas Wood, only one, Dr. Laurence Augustine, married. His wife was Martha Dickinson Shrewsbury, and their five children were named James, Walter, Shrewsbury, Emma Tell, Julia and Cecil Wood.

Dr. Washington and his family removed from Red House Shoals to Texas in 1850, before the day of railroads, and experienced all the vicissitudes of life in a new country.

All their children married except Shrewsbury; all have been gathered to their fathers except Julia, Mrs. Sydney Thurston Fontaine.

No data is at hand concerning the families of James and Walter. Emma Tell, named for her father's sister, and born at Red House Shoals, W. Va., married Captain George Lewis Patrick, born at Springville, Alabama. They had nine children: George, Laurence, Margaret, Martha, Isabelle, Charles, Maude, Julia and Emma Louise. Of these, Laurence and Margaret died in infancy; George was killed when twenty-one in a railroad accident in San Luis Potosi, Mexico; Emma Louise died when fifteen years of age.

Of the others, Martha married Thomas Laurence Lewis and lives in Pueblo, Colorado; Isabelle, Stacy Earl Elam, and lives in San Antonio, Texas; Charles, Elsie June Price, and lives in Huntington Park, California; and Julia, Horace E. Collins and lives in San Diego, California. The youngest daughter of Dr. Laurence Augustine and Martha Dickinson Shrewsbury, Cecil Wood, married Mr. Richard Saunders. Their son, Mr. Walter A. Saunders, lives in Pueblo, Colorado. Mrs. Cecil Wood Saunders died in San Diego, California, in 1917. Miss Maude lives in Washington, D. C.

The only surviving child of Dr. Laurence Augustine Washington, Mrs. Julia Washington Fontaine, is now living with her daughter, Mrs. Shirley von Meyer, in New York City. Her husband, Colonel Sydney Thurston Fontaine died while he slept, during the night of Thursday, September 5, 1912. The Galveston Daily news of September 6, after speaking of the shock of his death, says:

"Surviving are his wife, four sons, Dr. Bryce W. Fontaine of Memphis, Tenn.; Laurence W. Fontaine of Denison, Bushrod W.

Fontaine of Galveston and Jules W. Fontaine of San Antonio, and a daughter, Shirley von Meyer of New York.

"The funeral is to be held this afternoon at 5 o'clock from the late residence, 2200 Avenue M. Services will be under the auspices of Humboldt Lodge No. 9, Knights of Pythias, and Camp Magruder No. 105, United Confederate Veterans. Interment will follow in the Episcopal Cemetery. The body of Colonel Fontaine will rest beside that of General Magruder in the plot given by Colonel Fontaine some years ago.

"Judge Fontaine has occupied a prominent place in the public eye for many years. He was judge of the county court at law at the time of his death, receiving the appointment to the newly created bench on April 13, 1911. He went before the democratic primaries July 27 last, and was defeated for the nomination by J. C. Canty, justice of the peace, court "A," a position to which Judge Canty succeeded when Judge Fontaine was appointed judge of the county court at law. Prior to his appointment by the board of county commissioners to the bench of the county court at law Judge Fontaine had been justice of the peace, Precinct 1, court "A," for ten years. He was for about eight years judge of the corporation court. He served several terms as county attorney, and was the first clerk of the former Galveston-Harris County criminal district court. He was for one term city attorney of Denison, Grayson County, Texas.

"As a public official of Galveston County and as a private citizen, Colonel Fontaine was perhaps as extensively known as any man in the city. His erect and commanding figure was a familiar one to all in Galveston, and his friends as numerous as his acquaintance. He was a stanch worker for Galveston and her good name for many years and had been associated with much of her progressiveness.

"Sydney T. Fontaine was born at Houston, Tex., on November 28, 1838. He was the youngest son of Judge Henry Whiting Fontaine and Susan Elizabeth Bryson Fontaine, who came to Texas from Louisville, Ky. His father was judge of the district court of Harris County at the date of the son's birth, and died five days afterward. His father's half brother, Algernon Sydney Thurston, after whom Colonel Fontaine was named, was attorney general of the republic of Texas. His mother, Mrs. Fontaine, returned to Louisville shortly after the death of her husband. Colonel Fontaine was graduated from the Kentucky Military Institute at eighteen years of age. He came to Texas and read law under H. N. and M. M. Potter.

"Colonel Fontaine commanded the first company raised in Texas for the Confederacy. This was Company A, Heavy Artillery. After the battle of Galveston this company was made into a light battery, and, with other batteries, was commanded by him as the Seventh Battalion of Light Artillery.

"Colonel Fontaine received his commission direct from Secretary

Seddon, from Montgomery, Alabama, he being promoted by an act of the Confederate Congress on account of distinguished service. He served on the staff of General Magruder and afterward with General Walker as chief of artillery and ordnance, District of Texas, New Mexico and Arizona.

"He participated in the capture of Union troops at Brazos, Santiago and in the battle of Galveston. He also took part in the engagements in West Texas. He served upon the staff of General Taylor during General Banks' invasion of Louisiana, as inspector of artillery for the Western District of Louisiana. He was in the front with General Taylor and General Wharton, General Majors and Colonel Baylor.

"Following the battle of Yellow Bayou, he reported once more to General Magruder in Texas, and assumed command of his battalion in the field.

"Colonel Fontaine, in 1873, married Miss Julia Washington, daughter of Dr. Laurence Augustine Washington, grandson of Colonel Samuel Washington of Virginia and grand-nephew of General George Washington, the first president of the United States."

In 1915, Mrs. Fontaine visited the home of her father and of her grandfather and grandmother at Wheeling, W. Va.

The following, written at the time, is her description of that visit:

"We have at last made the long talked of trip to the Washington graves on Short Creek, about three miles from Wheeling. We tried but could not get there in a machine on account of a long, steep, narrow, winding road, so Howard got a surry with two horses, and a driver who knew the way. The greater part of the way was thru the beautiful suburban residential section of Wheeling called Woodlawn.

"The home and graves of the Washingtons are on top of a small mountain about 800 feet above the old pike road that leads to Washington. After crossing several bridges and driving thru a beautiful mountain stream we reached the road that winds around the mountain, and which is perilous without gentle good horses and a skillful driver. After going about a mile, stopping several times to let the horses rest a few moments, we reached the top and found beautiful rolling country. Another half mile ride brought us to the gate of the old Washington home.

"We were met by an old man named Meredith Horton, who rents the place from Mr. Nichols, the present owner. Old Mr. Horton, who is about 75 years old, and his wife and three sons cultivate the once fine estate of my grandfather, Laurence Augustine Washington. Old

Mr. Horton told us his father was the manager for my grandfather, and he has lived on the place for fifty years.

"The graves were in a corner of the old orchard that had been planted over a hundred years ago. Over each grave was a large white marble box-like tomb, flat on top and discolored with age, and strange to say in a splendid state of preservation. My grandfather's stone had deep and beautiful carving on the top, with this inscription:

> LAURENCE AUGUSTINE WASHINGTON
> Died February 15, 1824
> In the 50th year of his age

"My grandmother's tomb had a perfectly flat smooth top, with this inscription:

> MRS. MARY DORCAS WASHINGTON
> Died November 9, 1835
> Aged 54 years

"My aunt Emma's tomb had a flat top with this inscription:

> MISS EMMA TELL WASHINGTON
> Died November 20, 1838
> Aged 26 years

"The tombs are absolutely intact. My grandfather's tomb is sunken at one corner. I was amazed to find how young they had died. After lingering quite a while at the graves, planting flowers on them and copying the inscriptions, we asked to be shown over the house. The old man told us that the front of the house, the library, parlor, gallery and the great stone pillars had been moved away. The material was used to build another house about a mile away, but after the house was built the whole structure crumbled to the ground—in protest of the sacrifice, I doubt not.

"There are eight rooms left of the original house, two stories and with an attic, old colonial staircase, rooms with closets and low ceilings. The old stone spring house that old aunt Flora (aunt Emma's negro maid) used to tell me so much about, with the lovely cold spring water flowing thru it, is just as it was one hundred years ago. The yards and grounds are badly kept, or rather not kept at all.

"I had always thought of my grandfather and grandmother as persons in the dim and misty past—quite unreal to me, but his old house and their graves have made them very real, and I now feel in close touch with them."

The available details of the descendants of Laurence Augustine Washington and Mary Dorcas Wood are given, because although Laurence Augustine was born about twenty miles from Winchester, and Mary Dorcas, at "Glen Burnie," and they lived at "Hawthorne," yet the fact that they left the vicinity in 1811, and that no member of their family has lived here permanently since, might lead one to believe that the family was extinct. It is pleasant, therefore, to find that there are so many prominent representatives of this noble pair throughout the length and breadth of the land.

CHAPTER XXV

Miscellaneous Letters — Wills — Indentures — Commissions

1734—At a Court held for the County of Orange on the twenty-first day of January, 1734:

Present—Augustine Smith, John Taliaferro, Thomas Chew, Robert Slaughter, Abraham Field, Robert Green, James Barbour, John Finlason, Samuel Ball, Francis Slaughter, John Lightfoot, James Pollard and Benjamin Cave, Gent. Justices.

James Wood, Gent., produced a Commission from the President and Masters of the College of William and Mary bearing date the 12th day of November 1734 to be Surveyor of this County which being read the said James Wood having taken the Oaths appointed by Act of Parliament to be taken instead of the Oaths of Allegiance and Supremacy and the Oaths of Abjuration and Subscribed the Test was Sworn Surveyor of this County.

A Copy-Teste:
    J. W. BROWNING, *Clerk of Orange Circuit Court, Virginia.*
February 4th, 1920.

1735—At a Court held for Orange County the 17th Day of February 1735. John Read, John Bourke, William Nichols, Oliver Small, Richard Warfin, George Humphrys, William Johnson, John McKenny, William Kelley, Thomas Byrne, Dennis Bryan, James Dyer, David Reach, Arthur Dunn, Francis Billingsby, Martin Bourke, John Stockall and Matthew Stanton, severally made oath in open Court that they were immediately imported from Great Britain or Ireland into this Colony and that this is the first time of proving their importation in order to obtain their rights to Land; all which said persons do assigne their rights to Robert Slaughter, Gent.
                        Copie Test:
                           HEN. WILLIS, *Cl. Cur.*

1737—Ben Burden enters four hundred acres including the Great Plain on the North River of Shenandoah with James Wood surveyor, and by a writing under the said entry assigns the same to the said James Wood.

1744—The sd. James Wood surveyed the sd. 400 acres and

returned a Plat thereof in his own name, with a certificate indorsed that the Land was not claimed by Lord Fairfax.

1746—A Patent issued agreeable to the above mentioned Plat.

1759—James Wood died, having made a will whereby he devised all his land to Mary Wood his widow.

1767—The said Mary Wood gave several Bonds to Mat. Harrison who had married her daughter Mary, and to Elizabeth with whom I am since married; with Condition to convey to the sd. Harrison and to the said Eliz. each one half of the sd. 400 acres and sundry other Tracts of Land when sd. Harrison and Eliz. should agree on a division.

1768—The sd. 400 acres were surveyed in order to a division when it was discovered that about 95 acres thereof lay within his Lordship's Line.

It is to be observed that Col. Wood never claimed the sd. 95 acres since the Line between the King and his Lordship was run, and it can be proved that he declared after running the said Line that he was very glad so small a part fell within it, and that he would have given up the whole if it had done so.

In the sd. year 1768 an Ejectment was brought by Phil. Martin, Esq. to whom his Lordship had granted 430 acres including 80 of the 95 above mentioned, ag. Henry Goare, who was in possession of the said 430 acres. Upon the first calling of the said Ejectment the sd. Mary Wood in whom the Freehold still remained, entered defs. for 100 acres, and upon a survey by order of Court we proved our Boundaries, by which it appeared that 80 acres of the sd. 430 were contained in our Patent, for which we shall undoubtedly be entitled to a verdict at Law. But Mr. Waller's opinion is principally desired. Whether the said Patent is good against my Lord Fairfax, being obtained by means of a certificate, which so far as respects the Land in dispute appears to be false. And whether his Lordship's subsequent consent before the King in Council, and the Act of Assembly in 1748 in consequence of the Decree of the Council have not precluded him from taking advantage of the said Certificate.

ALEX. WHITE.

By the act in 1748 I think Mr. Wood's title to the 95 acres is made good and confirmed, and tho' the Patent as to that part may be said to be obtained by a false Suggestion, yet from the small Quantity included in my Lord's Bounds, and the uncertainty of those Bounds not then run or settled, it appears to be rather a mistake than a willful or designed falsehood, and I think that by the agreement made by his late Majesty and his Lordship, which on the part of the King was no doubt intended for the quiet and Peace of his Subjects as well as for the Benefit of his Majesty, his Lordship's equitable title is also taken away.

BEN WALLER.

THIS INDENTURE made the 25th day of April in the year of our Lord God One Thousand seven hundred and thirty-eight, BETWEEN Just Hite, Gent. of the County of Orange of the one part AND James Wood, Gent. of the County of Orange aforesaid of the other part. Witnesseth, that the said Just Hite for and in Consideration of the sum of five Shillings Sterling to him in hand paid by the said James Wood The Receipt whereof is hereby acknowledged HATH granted Bargained, sold * * * * unto the said James Wood ALL that Tract or parcell of Land situate, lying and being in Orange County Containing by Estimation One hundred Acres of Land be the same more or less and bounded as followeth viz: Beginning at a stake on the west side of Opeckon Run &c. * * * *. TO HAVE AND TO HOLD every part & Parcell Thereof with the Appurtenances unto the said James Wood, &c. * * * * from the day of the date hereof for and during and unto the full end & term of one whole year from thence next Ensuing & fully to be Compleated & Ended YIELDING & PAYING therefor one pepper Corn in & upon the feast of St. Michael the Archangel &c. * * * *

IN WITNESS whereof the said Just Hite hath hereunto set his hand & seal, the day month & Year first above written.

JUST HITE (Seal)

SEALED & DELIVERED in the presence of us
the above mentioned five shillings Sterling being first paid

Thos. Rutherford
    his
Francis X Michael
    mark

A Copy Teste:

C. W. WOOLFOLK, *Clerk.*

At a Court held for Orange County on Thursday ye 27th day of April 1738. Just Hite Gent. Acknowledged this his Lease of Land indented to James Wood Gent. which on the Motion of the said Wood is admitted to record.

Teste:
HEN. WILLIS, *Cl. Cur.*

THIS INDENTURE made the XXVIth day of April in the Year of our Lord God one thousand seven hundred & thirty-eight BETWEEN Just Hite Gent. of the County of Orange of the one part And James Wood Gent. of the County of Orange aforesaid of the other part WITNESSETH that the said Just Hite for & in Consideration of the sum of Ten Pounds Curr. Money to him in hand paid by the said James Wood The Receipt whereof the said Just Hite doth hereby acknowledge, Hath granted, &c. unto the said James Wood: in his Actual Possession now being by virtue of a Bargain & sale to him therof made for one year by Indenture bearing date the Day next before the date of these Presents and force of the Statute for Transferring Uses into Possessions: & to his heirs and assigns forever All that Tract or Parcell of Land Situate lying & being in Orange County Containing by estimation one hundred Acres of Land be the same more or less and Bounded as followeth viz. &c. It being part of a Tract of Land containing five Thousand & Eighteen Acres granted to the said Just Hite by Patent bearing date the third day of October one thousand Seven hundred Thirty and Four AND all houses Gardens Orchards Meadows Comons Woods trees Ways Waters Profits Comodities Hereditaments & Appurtenances whatsoever to the same Belonging or in any wise Appertaining, &c. TO HAVE AND TO HOLD the said Lands Premises & all & Singular & every Part & Parcell thereof with the appurtenances unto the said James Wood his heirs & assigns to the only proper Use and behoof of the said James Wood &c. * * * *. And the said Just Hite, &c. doth Covenant & grant to & with the said James Wood &c. * * * *. That he the said Just Hite now is the true lawfull owner of the said Premises above Mentioned & is Lawfully Seized &c. The Quit rents to become due for the Premises from the time of this sale only Excepted AND Lastly that he the said Just Hite & his heirs the said Premises with the Appurtenances to the said James Wood his heirs & Assigns against himself the said Just Hite his heirs & Assigns & all & every person or persons Whatsoever claiming any thing in the above mentioned Premises shall & will Warrant & forever defend IN WITNESS whereof the said Just Hite hath hereunto Set his hand & Seal the Day month & Year first above Written.

JUST HITE (Seal)

SEALED AND DELIVERED in the presence of us

Thos. Rutherford.
    his
Francis X Michael
    mark

RECEIVED of ye within named James Wood the within mentioned sum of Ten pounds Curr. Money being the Consideration in ye within Deed Mentioned to be paid by him to me on Perfection thereof. WITNESS my hand this 26th day of April 1738.

JUST HITE.

At a Court held for Orange County on Thursday ye 27th day of April 1738 Just Hite Gent. Acknowledged this his Release of Land

Indented with ye receipt endorsed to James Wood Gent. which on the Motion of the said Wood is Admitted to record.
Teste:
HEN. WILLIS, *Cl. Cur.*
A Copy Teste: C. W. GOOLFOLK, *Clerk.*

1742—At a Court held for Orange County on Thursday the 24th day of February 1742.

Present—Robert Slaughter, Robert Green, John Finlasson, Wm. Russell & Good Lightfoot, Gent. Justices. James Wood, Esqr. & John Lewis Gent. having taken the oaths prescribed by Act of Parliament to be taken instead of the oaths of Allegiance & Supremacy & the adjuration oath & prescribed the Test were severally sworn to their Military Commissions the first to that of Colo. of Horse and foot the Latter to that of Colo. of foot.

A Copy-Teste:
J. W. BROWNING, *Clerk of Orange Circuit Court, Va.*
January 9th, 1920.

JAMES WOOD TO THE HONBLE. WM. GOOCH, ESQR. DR.

Decr.	To Ordinary License	to Patrick Ryley	1.15
	To ditto	to Thomas Hart	1.15
	To ditto	to Andrew Campbell	1.15
Jany.	To ditto	to William Hoge, Jr.	1.15
	To Pedlar's License	to John Doones	.10
Mar.	To ditto	to Samuel Devany	.10
	To Marriage License	to Leonard Helms	1.
April	To ditto	to William Mitchell	1.
	To Pedlar's License	to Richard Crunk	.10
	To Ordinary License	to John Hopes	1.15
June	To ditto	to John Neilans	1.15
	To ditto	to John White	1.15
	To ditto	to Duncan Ogullion	1.15
July	To ditto	to Ralph Humfrey	1.15
	To Pedlar's License	to James Welsh	.10
Augt.	To Ordinary License	to Thomas Rutherford	1.15
	To ditto	to Andrew Caldwell	1.15
	To ditto	to Thomas Doster	1.15

£25.00

Received of James Wood, Clk. of Frederick County, the sum of Twenty-Five pounds in full of the above account this 15th day of Mar. 1744.

WILL GOOCH.

Recd. 25th of October, 1744, of Colo. James Wood by the Hands of Mr. Thos. Rutherford Five guineas.

THOS. NELSON, JUNIOR.

GEORGE THE SECOND BY THE GRACE OF GOD OF GREAT BRITIAN FRANCE .& IRELAND KING DEFENDER OF THE FAITH &c. TO ALL to whom these presents shall come GREETING. KNOW YE that for divers good causes & considerations, but more especially for & in consideration of the sum of FORTY SHILLINGS of good and lawful money for our use paid to our RECEIVER GENERAL of our REVENUES in this our Colony & Dominion of Virginia, WE HAVE GIVEN granted and confirmed & by these presents for us our Heirs & Successors do give grant & confirm unto JAMES WOOD one certain tract or parcel of Land containing four hundred acres lying & being in the COUNTY OF AUGUSTA on a branch of the South River of Shenando called CUB RUN & bounded & followeth, to-wit, BEGINNING at a black oak on a hill thence North seventy-seven Degrees East to a hiccory saplin & black oak saplin, thence South seven Degrees, East to two White Oak saplins on a Spur of the Peaked Mountain thence South * * * * to a hiccory saplin; thence North two degrees to the beginning. WITH ALL woods, underwoods, swamps, marshes, low grounds, meadows, feedings, & his due share of all veins, Mines & Quaries as well discovered as not discovered within the bounds of aforesaid & being part of the said quantity of four hundred acres of Land & the Rivers, Waters & Water Courses therein contained, together with the privileges of Hunting, Hawking, Fishing, Fowling, and all other profits, Commodities & Hereditaments whatsoever to the same or any part thereof, belonging or in anywise appertaining, TO HAVE, HOLD, possess & enjoy the said Tract or parcel of Land & all other the before granted premises & every part thereof with their & every of their appurtenance unto the sd. James Wood & to his Heirs & Assigns forever TO BE HELD of us, our Heirs and Successors as of our Mannor of East Greenwich in the County of Kent in free & common soccage and not in capite or by Knights' service; Yielding AND Paying unto us our Heirs & Successors for every fifty Acres of Land & so proportionably for lesser or greater quantity than fifty acres, the fee Rent of one shilling yearly to be paid on the Feast of Saint Michael the Arch Angel & also Cultivating and Improving three acres part of every fifty of the Tract above mentioned, within three years after the date of these presents, PROVIDED always that if three years of the sd. Fee Rent shall at any time be in Arrears & unpaid, or if the said JAMES WOOD, his Heirs or Assigns do not within the space of three years next coming after the date of these presents cultivate & improve three acres out of every fifty of the Tract above mentioned: Then the Estates hereby granted shall cease & be utterly determined & thereafter it shall & may be

Lawful to & for us our Heirs and Successors to grant the same Lands & premises with all appurtenances unto such other person or persons as we our Heirs & Successors shall think fit. IN WITNESS whereof we have caused these our Letters patent to be made. WITNESS our Trusty & Well beloved William Gooch, Esquir., Lieut. Governor & Commander in Chief of our sd. Colony & Dominion at Williamsburg under the Seal of our sd. Colony the XIth. day of January One Thousand Seven Hundred & Forty-six in the XXth year of our Reign.

WILLIAM GOOCH.

James Wood
Patent for 400 acres in Augusta
Examd.
Recorded.

IN THE NAME OF GOD AMEN. I, James Wood being sick and weak of body, yet praised be God of a perfect sense and memory, do make this my Last Will and Testament in manner and form following, that is to say—I give devise and bequeath all my real and personal Estate to my beloved wife Mary on condition that she pay to each of my childrn to-wit: James Wood, John Wood, Elizabeth Wood and Mary Wood, twenty pounds current money of Virginia when they come to age and do hereby appoint her, my said wife, Guardian of my said children, not doubting that she will do a Christian Mother's part to them. And whereas, there are several tracts of land taken up in the name of Robert Groove in which I am a partner, as also several tracts of land taken up in my name by me of which the said Robert Groove is to have a part; I therefore hope and am persuaded that he the said Robert Groove will with Justice and Equity divide the said lands and make deed for said farms according to law to my said wife.

I do hereby appoint and ordain my said beloved wife Mary my whole and sole Executirx of this my last will and testament and it is my desire that no part or parcel of my Estate be appraised. In witness whereof I have hereunto set my hand and seal this eighth day of September, 1746.

J. WOOD.

Signed, sealed, published and declared in presence of James Porten and Thos. Wood.

Fourth Augt. 1746. Agreed with John O'Neal to clear eighteen acres on the Land at the North Mountain where he lives at his own cost for which I am to pay the sd. O'Neal as the same shall be valued by two persons, who are to value the same as if I had found him Diet. Also that the sd. O'Neal is to live on the sd. Land five years from this time clear of paying Rent, and to take care of such stock as shall be put under his care & receive half the Increase & Return the Principal; unless they are lost by accident and not for want of care.

JAMES WOOD.

My good friend Wm. Fairfax, Esq., acquainted me you are Executor of Doctr. Hart. He was indebted to Mr. Wm. Bowden of London in the sum of 42 pounds 10 shillings sterling by bond, which bond with a power of Attorney I have. I beg the favour of your speedy discharge of the said debt and I shall not insist on the Interest though it has run ever since the year 1742. Your answer recommended to the care of Mr. Charles Dick in Fredericksburg will very much oblige, Sir,

Yr. very huml. Servt.,
RICHD. AMBLER.

York Town, April 28th, 1750.
To Colonel Wm. Wood in Frederick County
recommended to the care of Mr. Chas. Dick.

Note by Colo. James Wood: "Advice of an English Bond for 42:10:0 Sterls. Came to hand 9th May, 1750"

29th Sept. 1758.

Dr. Sir:

Jenkins only stays for this and that with Impatience and therefore can't be so pticular as I would otherwise be. I was some days later getg. done than I thought I should be wn. I left you, so that Colo. Green presented yr. petn. before I arrived wch. was opposed by L. Carter and Geo. Johnston and only 'em so that no division was on it. The Bill has been read once and to day is to be read a second time. I make no doubt but it will pass without opposition. This moment an express has arrived from New York with th. agreeable account of Lt. Chs. Hardy taking 6 French ships up the River St. Lawrence. As also by the Grampus sloop of War the pticulars of Marshal Daun's defeat by the King of Prussia, but as yet are not known the Packet being now at the Governor's. The Assembly has done little or nothing, but what is, you may expect by another opportunity. Till then Dr. Sir, Believe me to be

Yr. most Affect. Hble. Servt.,
G. JONES (Gabriel.)

This Indenture made the twentieth day of September in the year of our Lord one thousand seven hundred and sixty between Mary Wood of the Parish and County of Frederick in the Colony of

Virginia, Widow, of the one part and Laughlan McLean of the city of Philadelphia in the Province of Pennsylvania Physician and Surgeon, of the other part, WITNESSETH that the sd. Mary Wood in Consideration of the Covenants hereafter mentioned, Doth by these Presents, put place and bind out as an Apprentice her son John Wood to the sd. Laughlan McLean to be taught the Art of Physick and Surgery; and with him as an Apprentice to dwell, continue and serve from the day of the date hereof until the sd. John Wood shall arrive to the age of twenty-one years, he being sixteen the eleventh of January last, during all which sd. term the said Apprentice his said master well and faithfully shall serve, his secrets keep, his lawful commands everywhere gladly obey, hurt to his sd. master he shall not do, nor wilfully suffer to be done by others, but of the same to his power shall forthwith (illegible) the goods of his said master he shall not embezel or waste nor them lend without his consent to any. At Cards, Dice or any other unlawful games he shall not play; Taverns or Ale houses he shall not frequent, Matrimony he shall not contract; from the Service of his sd. Master he shall not depart or absent himself without his said Master's leave, but in all things as a good and faithful Apprentice shall and will demean himself towards his said Master during the sd. term.

And the sd. Laughlan McClean doth for himself Covenant and promise that he will do his utmost endeavor during the aforesaid term to teach, learn and instruct the sd. John Wood in the Art and profession of Physick and Surgery aforesaid with all things thereunto belonging.

And the said Mary Wood for herself her executors and administrators doth Covenant promise and agree to and with the sd. Laughlan McLean that she will find and provide for the sd. John Wood her son, Meat, Drink, Washing, Lodging and Apparel, both Linnen and Woollen and all necessarys fit and convenient for such Apprentice during the term aforesaid.

IN WITNESS whereof each Party to one of these Indentures hath set his hand and seal the Date above.

LAU. MACLEAN.

Signed, Sealed and Delivered
in the presence of Benjn. Loxley.

A fragment of a letter written by Mary Rutherford to her son John and the only example of hers in the collection, belongs to this period.

* * * * very kind Letters of the 13th and 20th instant * * * * to hear of your Health, and that you go on so well at the Academy, and that Dr. McLean has promised that you shall come Home at Christmass, which I believe will be very agreeable to you as well as to me and all the Family. I have wrote you two Letters before this, but I believe the last never went for want of an opportunity. There will be a safe Hand going from Hence soon, by whom I shall send you some more Linnin, with some Money to purchase yourself Necessarys, such as summer stockings, jacketts, breeches, shoes, etc. The next time you write let me know exactly how your Eye is, and what Washing and Mending is by the year, also by all means write to Doctor Craik, who is much surprised at your * * * * writing to him. Your Sisters and Brothers are well * * * *. Give my Compliments * * * * I remain,

Jacky Dear yr. Loving Mother,
MARY WOOD.

FRANCIS FAUQUIER, ESQ., his Majesty's Lieutenant-Governour, and Commander in Chief of the Colony and Dominion of VIRGINIA:

To George Weedon, Esq.

By Virtue of his Majesty's royal Commission and Instructions, appointing me Lieutenant-Governour and Commander in Chief, in and over this Colony and Dominion of Virginia, with full Power and Authority to appoint all Officers both civil and military, within the same:

I reposing especial Trust in your Loyalty, Courage, and good Conduct, do, by these Presents, appoint you the said George Weedon, Capt. Lieutenant in the Virginia Regiment commanded by Adam Stephen. You are therefore carefully and diligently to do the duty of Capt. Lieutenant by exercising and well disciplining both the inferiour Officers and Soldiers under your Command; and I do hereby command them to obey you as such.

And you are to observe and follow such Directions from Time to Time, as you shall receive from me, or any other your superior Officers, according to the Rules and Discipline of War, in Pursuance of the Trust hereby reposed in you.

GIVEN at Williamsburg, under my Hand, and the Seal of the Colony, this twenty-second Day of May in the Year of his Majesty's Reign, Annoque Domini, 1762.

FRAN. FAUQUIER.

Virginia, Frederick County, Js.

I do hereby certify that James Wood before whom the above deposition was taken, at the time of taking the same, was and still is, one of his Majesty's Justices of the Peace for the said County and that to all depositions by him so taken and subscribed, all due faith and credit ought to be given as well in Justice Court as thereout. In Testimony whereof I have hereunto set my hand and affixed the Publick Seal of the said County this 5th day of January 1764.

JAMES KEITH, C. C.

This Indenture made the Fourth day of March in the year of Our Lord one thousand seven hundred and sixty-five BETWEEN Mary Wood of the County of Frederick in the Colony of Virginia of the one part and James Wood of the County and Colony aforesaid of the other part WITNESSETH that the said Mary Wood for and in consideration of the sum of five hundred pounds current money of Virginia to the said Mary Wood in hand paid by the said James Wood at or before the sealing and delivery of these presents the receipt whereof she doth hereby acknowledge and thereof doth release, acquit and discharge the said James Wood his heirs executors or administrators. By these presents she the said Mary Wood HATH granted bargained sold aliened released and confirmed and by these presents DOTH grant bargain sell alien release and confirm unto the said James Wood (in his actual possession now being by virtue of a bargain and sale to him thereof made by the said Mary Wood for one whole year by indenture bearing date the day next before the day of the date of these presents and by force of the statute for transferring uses into possession) and his heirs and assigns forever one certain tract or parcel of Land containing five hundred and seventy acres be the same more or less situate lying and being on the Branches of Opeckon Creek in the County of Frederick aforesaid; the same being part of a tract of one thousand two hundred and forty one acres of Land formerly granted by the Right Honourable Thomas Lord Fairfax proprietor of the Northern Neck to James Wood Gent. deceased, by deed bearing date the twenty-first day of May in the year of our Lord one thousand seven hundred and fifty-three, and by him devised in his last will and testament to the said Mary Wood as by the said will may fully appear. The courses including the said five hundred and seventy acres of Land are as followeth BEGINNING at a stake and Hickory on a Ridge corner to the entire Tract and running thence along the lines of the same North seventy four degrees West one hundred sixty two poles to two Hickorys and a red oak on the side of a hill thence North three degrees * * * * to two red oaks on a ridge thence North fifty three degrees East * * * * thence So. forty two degrees East seventy nine poles to a locust at the foot of a hill thence South twenty-eight degrees * * * * to a White Oak and Red oak Saplins on a Knowl thence South * * * * forthy five degrees and sixty seven poles to the beginning: and all houses, buildings orchards, ways, waters, watercourses, profits, commodities, hereditaments and appurtenances whatsoever to the said premises hereby granted or any part thereof belonging or in any wise appertaining and the reversion and reversions, remainder and remainders, rents, issues and profits thereof, and also all the estate right, title, interest, use, trust, property claim and demand whatsoever of her the said Mary Wood of in and to the said premises and all deeds evidences and writings touching or in any wise concerning the same TO HAVE AND TO HOLD the said five hundred and seventy acres of Land and all, &c. with their appurtenances unto the said James Wood his heirs and assigns forever * * * *; and the said Mary Wood for herself, &c. doth covenant promise and grant to and with the said James Wood &c. by these presents that the said Mary Wood now at the time of sealing and delivering of these presents is seized of a good perfect and indefeasible estate of inheritance &c. and that she hath good power &c. to convey the same to the said James Wood in manner and form aforesaid and that the said premises now are and so forever hereafter shall remain and be free and clear of &c. charges and incumbrances whatsoever made done committed or suffered by the said Mary Wood or any other person or persons whatsoever (the Quitrents hereafter to grow due and payable to the Right Honourable Thomas Lord Fairfax proprietor of the Northern Neck his heirs and successors for and in respect of the said premises only excepted and foreprized) AND LASTLY that the said Mary Wood &c. hereby granted and released with their appurtenances unto the said James Wood his heirs and assigns against her the said Mary Wood and her heirs and all and every other person and persons whatsoever shall and will warrant and forever defend by these presents. IN WITNESS whereof the said Mary Wood hath hereunto set her hand and seal the day month and year first above written.

MARY WOOD (Seal)

Signed sealed and delivered in the presence of
John Wood
Robert Wood
Elizabeth Wood

Received the fourth day of March 1765 of James Wood the sum of five hundred pounds current money of Virginia the consideration mentioned in the within deed.

MARY WOOD.

Teste,
John Wood
Robert Wood
Elizabeth Wood

At a Court held for Frederick County the 2nd day of July 1765. This Indenture together with the receipt thereon indorsed was acknowledged by Mary Wood party thereto and ordered to be recorded.
By the Court:
JAMES KEITH, C. C.

Articles of agreement indented concluded and agreed upon the twenty-first day of April in the year of our Lord One Thousand Seven Hundred and Sixty Nine, between Martin Pickett of the County of Fauquier of the one part and Burr Harrison of the County of Frederick of the other part; Whereas the said Martin Pickett having this day sold the fee simple Estate of a certain Tract or Parcell of Land containing upwards of Three Hunded Acres, situate lying and being in the County of Frederick on Stony Creek and the said Tract of Land lately the property of John Campbell who gave the same in security of a debt due from him to the late William Pickett deceased, the Dues of which, being obtained from the Proprietor's Office in the name of the said Martin Pickett, and exposed to Publick Auction, and purchased by him at the said sale; Now, the said Burr Harrison doth convenant promise and grant to and with the said Martin Pickett, his Heirs, Executors or Administrators, that he will well and truly pay or cause to be paid to the said Martin Pickett, or to his Assigns the just and full sum of Forty Pounds, Current money of Virginia, on or before the Twentieth Day of October next Ensuing, and the further sum of Forty Pounds like money, on or before the Twentieth Day of April next Ensuing. And the said Martin Pickett doth convenant, promise and grant to and with the said Burr Harrison his Heirs, Executors, or Administrators, that on or before the said 20th day of October next, or at the time of the first payment, make and acknowledge sufficient deeds of lease and Release for the said tract of land unto the said Burr Harrison, his Heirs or Assigns.

And to the true Performance of all and every of the above Articles and Conditions the said Parties do bind themselves to each other in the penalty of One Hundred and Sixty Pounds. In Witness whereof, the said Parties have hereunto set their Hands and seals the day and year above written.

MARTIN PICKET (Seal)
BURR HARRISON (Seal)

Sealed and delivered
in the presence of James Wood

ARTICLES OF AGREEMENT indented etc. this twenty-second day of August in the year of our Lord one thousand seven hundred and seventy-one, between Mary Wood, widow and executrix of Col. James Wood, late of Frederick County in the Colony of Virginia, deceased, of the one part, and Patrick Crawford, of Augusta County, in the Colony aforesaid, of the other part,

WITNESSETH: that the said Mary Wood, in consideration of five hundred pounds current money of Virginia, agreed to be paid to her by the said Patrick Crawford, in manner hereafter mentioned, doth covenant, promise and oblige herself and her heirs to grant and convey to the said Patrick Crawford, his heirs and assigns, eight hundred acres of land (the same less or more) at the foot of the North mountain, on the branches of Muddy creek in the said county of Augusta; being that part of seventeen hundred acres which was assigned to the said Mary Wood in the division between her and Nicholas Green; and that on or before the fifteenth day of November next ensuing.

And the said Patrick Crawford doth hereby bind and oblige himself etc. to pay to the said Mary Wood etc. the sum of three hundred pounds current money aforesaid on or before the said fifteenth day of November next ensuing; or at any time sooner, if a sufficient title can sooner be made to the eight hundred acres of land above mentioned. And also to pay the further sum of two hundred pounds like current money at or before the expiration of one year from this date.

To the true and faithful performance of the said agreement, the said parties do bind themselves, etc. each to the other in the sum of one thousand pounds like current money, firmly by these presents.

In witness whereof the said parties have hereunto set their hands and seal the day and year first above mentioned.

PATRICK CRAWFORD.

The words (the same less or more) being inserted between the 16th and 17th lines from the top of the first page before signing.

Sealed and delivered in the presence of
Rob. Wood.
Alex. White

Recd. 10th May, 1773, from Mr. James Wood five pounds, five shillings and seven d. for interest on his bond to the 25th March, 1773, by the hands of Mr. Rutherford.

ROBT. MILLER, Bursar
Wm. & Mary College.

Mr. Robt. Miller's rect. for £5;5;7, acct. of interest due from Mr. Wood.

Articles of Agreement made and concluded this 24th day of March, 1775, Between John Wood & Richd. Graham. Witnesseth: That the said Wood doth oblige himself to convey all his right and title to three surveys of Land made by Wm. Bennet in the year 1773 lying near Sandy Creek on the Banks of the Ohio River abt. forty miles below the Great Canaway containing about one thousand acres each in all three thousand acres—to say—One full half of the said Lands to Richd. Graham to be divided by a line run from the River through the middle of each tract, the Lands being laid off in two tracts * * * in consideration of which the said Graham obliges himself to furnish five good hands with all necessary tools for building cabbins and clearing and tending said Land in October next; which hands are to be put under an overseer in partnership between the said John Wood and Richd. Graham and continue so, till both the said parties shall agree to divide the said Lands, Servants and Stock * * * and each party to draw his half of the annual produce or profits arising therefrom; the said Graham to pay the said Wood the full amount of the cost of two good Mares which said Wood is to purchase and send down to said Graham about the first of October next to go out with the people, so that said Wood is to be at no kind of expense until the people are settled on the premises.

Witness our hands and seals the day and year above written.

JNO. WOOD.
RICHD. GRAHAM.

Witness:
James Wood
Cochran Gamble

The following is copied from "A Journal of the Convention of Delegates For the Counties and Corporations in the Colony of Virginia," at the Town of Richmond, Friday, January 5, 1776. Found among the documents of the late Daniel Gold, Esq., grandfather of Mrs. Frank Baldwin Crawford, and for many years president of The Bank of the Valley.

Ordered:

"Mr. Bland from the Committee appointed to inquire into the services of Mr. James Wood, who was sent by the House of Burgesses to invite the several tribes of Indians on the western frontiers of this colony to a treaty, according to a resolution of the Council and House of Burgesses in June last, reported, that the committee had, according to order, had the same under their consideration, and that it appeared to them that the said James Wood set out on the 25th of June last, in the execution of his commission; that in his progress through the several tribes of Indians, he was informed that Governor Carleton's emissaries had exerted their endeavors to persuade them to take up the hatchet against this colony; that, in consequence thereof, many of the said Indians entertained very hostile intentions; that the said Wood was frequently in danger of his life, particularly from one of those hostile tribes who had formed a scheme for killing him, but that he discovered their design, and made his escape; that at last, by exerting all his abilities, he happily removed their prejudices, and engaged them, with other tribes, to attend the said treaty, which engagement they accordingly performed, whereby peace and safety was restored to this colony; that the said Wood was near two months employed in the progress of this business, and underwent the greatest fatigues, difficulties, and dangers; and that they had come to the following resolution thereupon, which he read in his place, and afterwards delivered in at the clerk's table, when the same was again twice read, and agreed to.

"Resolved, That the said James Wood ought to be paid by the public the sum of £250 for the great service he hath done to this colony, by his diligent and faithful execution of the commission with which he was intrusted."

IN CONGRESS

The DELEGATES of the UNITED STATES of New-Hampshire, Massachusetts-Bay, Rhode-Island, Connecticut, New-York, New-Jersey, Pennsylvania, Delaware, Maryland, Virginia, North-Carolina, South-Carolina, and Georgia.

To James Wood, Esquire:

We reposing especial Trust and Confidence in your Patriotism, Valour, Conduct and Fidelity, DO, by these Presents, constitute and appoint you to be Colonel of the Twelfth Virginia Battalion in the Army of the United States, raised for the Defence of American Liberty, and for repelling every hostile Invasion thereof. You are therefore carefully and diligently to discharge the Duty of Colonel by doing and performing all manner of Things thereunto belonging. And we do strictly charge and require all Officers and Soldiers under your Command, to be obedient to your Orders as Colonel. And you are to observe and follow such Orders and Directions from Time to Time, as you shall receive from this or a future Congress of the United States, or Committee of Congress, for that Purpose appointed, or Commander in Chief for the Time being of the Army of the United States, or any other of your superior Officers according to the Rules and Discipline of War, in Pursuance of the Trust reposed in you. This Commission to continue in Force until revoked by this or a future Congress.

DATED at Philadelphia 12th. Nov., 1776.

By Order of the Congress,
JOHN HANCOCK, *President.*

Attest: Chas. Thomson, Secy.

HISTORIC EXTRACTS FROM ADDITIONAL LETTERS OF COLONEL JAMES WOOD

To his wife:

I have been nominated by the General Assembly for the command of a Regiment, unsolicited, but as this is only a nomination or recommendation to Congress, I am at full liberty to accept or decline the appointment * * * * *.

Wmsburg, 14th November, 1776.

To his wife:

* * * * I have just returned from Genl. Washington's Marquee where I dined, so that Mr. Kinkead and everyone from Winchester has had the advantage of me in writing. Letters arrived just now which give His Excellency certain intelligence that Col. Barton of the Rhode Island State Troops had taken Major General Prescot and his Aid de camp, and carried them safe to Providence. We have no account of the destination of the Enemy. They have Decamped from Staten Island, and the Fleet are now lying at New York. Whether we shall march to the Northward or return to Jersey no one except the General knows * * * *.

Camp Head Quarters at Clove, 16th July, 1777.

---

* * * * The General has given up all thoughts of saving Philadelphia. The enemy has passed us and are, I dare say, before this time in possession of it. We have had several skirmishes since the battle of the 11th in all of which we have been worsted. We are now thirty-four miles from Philadelphia, and about twenty from Reading, and the general opinion is that there will be little more fighting this campaign * * * *. Colo. Blackburn is in Camp. He arrived yesterday and has entered as a volunteer. Large numbers of the militia were called upon, so that you will have a number of acquaintances in your own situation, or what will be infinitely worse, their husbands dishonored by not stepping forth in the service of their country * * * *.

Camp Head Quarters, 26th Sept., 1777.

In the very entertaining journal of Miss Sallie Wistar, kept during the possession of Philadelphia by the British in 1777, are found some interesting notes concerning Col. James Wood: "October 20, Col. Wood, from what we hear of him and what we see, is one of the most amiable of men. Tall and genteel, of agreeable countenance and deportment, the following lines will more fully characterize him:

> "How skilled is he in each obliging art,
> The mildest manner and the bravest heart."

"Amiable Wood! He is esteemed by all who know him."

THE UNITED STATES OF AMERICA IN CONGRESS ASSEMBLED

To James Wood, Esquire, GREETING.' We, Reposing especial trust and confidence in your Patriotism, Valour, Conduct and Fidelity,

DO by these presents constitute and appoint you to be Colonel of the eighth Virginia Regiment in the Army of the United States, to take rank as such from the 12th day of November A. D. 1776; You are therefore carefully and diligently to discharge the duty of a Colonel by doing and performing all manner of things thereunto belonging. AND we do Strictly charge and require all Officers and Soldiers under your command, to be obedient to your orders, as Colonel. And you are to observe and follow such orders and directions from time to time, as you shall receive from this, or a future Congress of the United States, or Committee of Congress for that purpose appointed, a Committee of the States, or Commander in Chief for the time being of the Army of the United States, or any other your superior Officer; according to the rules and discipline of War, in pursuance of the trust reposed in you. This Commission to continue in force until revoked by this, or a future Congress, the Committee of Congress before mentioned, or a Committee of the States.

WITNESS His Excellency John Jay, Esqr., President of the Congress of the United States of America, at Philadelphia the 20th day of March, 1779, and in the third year of our Independence.

JOHN JAY.

Entered in the War Office
and examined by the Board.

Attest: P. ———, Secretary of the Board of War.

OFFICE OF CLERK OF COUNTY COURT
of Frederick County, Va.,
Winchester, Virginia

Dr. Sir:
The quarter master sergeant of the Light Dragoons will be with you early tomorrow morning, for three days rations. Their number is 93. Capt. Morris will be with you in a few days and will sign the proper returns, which I shall countersign. I have halted them for a few days four miles beyond Winchester. Capt. Johnston will order a waggon to take in the provision.

I am, Dr. Sir, Yours,

J. WOOD.

12th June, 1783
(Address) W. V. Jackson.

Dr. Brother:
I have just procured a certificate for your depreciation while you acted as Paymaster for £46.5.4, on which I have received three years' interest being £8.6.6, which I have sent by Paddy Kirk. The certifi-

cate I will keep in order to get a warrant for the fourth year's interest which will come due the 1st day of next month * * * *.
I am, dr. Brother, affy.,

J. WOOD.

Richmond, 10th December, 1785.
Mr. Robert Wood, Winchester.
By Mr. Kirk with 6 Guineas.

KNOW ALL MEN by these presents, that I, MARY WOOD of the County of Frederick, am held and firmly bound to Elizabeth Rutherford of the same County, in three hundred pounds of the current specie of Virginia, to be paid to the said Elizabeth Rutherford, or her certain Attorney, Executors, Administrator, or Assigns; for which payment well and truly to be made I bind myself, my heirs, executors, and administrator, firmly by these presents, sealed with my seal. DATED THE SEVENTH day of MARCH in the year of our Lord one thousand, Seven hundred and eighty-nine.

The condition of the above obligation is such that whereas the above bound Mary Wood did, on or about the month of March, 1787 for and in consideration of the sum of ten pounds to her in hand paid, bargain and sell unto the said Elizabeth Rutherford in fee simple, a certain lott of ground containing a quarter of an acre, Situate in the town of Winchester adjoining the lotts now in the tenure and occupation of Geor. F. Norton, Robert Long and Robert Carter; and did promise and agree with her, the said Rutherford, when thereunto required, to convey unto her the said Rutherford or her assigns or to such person or persons as she shall by her last will and testament direct, a good clear and indefeasible title in fee simple. NOW if the said Mary Wood shall well and truly perform and execute the above condition then this obligation to be void otherwise to remain in full force and virtue.

Witness my hand the day and year first above written.

MARY WOOD (Seal)

Sealed and delivered in
the presence of
Robert Wood,
Van Rutherford,
R. Rutherford.

A fragment of a letter from Hon. Alexander White:

New York, 20th ———.

Dear Madam:

It gave me great pleasure to learn by a letter from Polly Hite, that your health is in so great a degree restored. I would have wrote you long ago but was ashamed to say I had not heard from you. On this subject I would observe, that taking the states of Virginia, Maryland and Pennsylvania, you cannot find a district * * * * as the one I represent, from which I have * * * * so few letters or so little attention. This however will not prevent my endeavours to promote the public good so long as my Commission lasts. When that ends, I shall depend as heretofore, on a good Providence and my own industry.

I have been so long silent that I know not what to say; the business of congress I have * * * * transmitted to the Printers, by whom you * * * * it retailed. With regard to myself * * * * enjoyed a good state of health, and * * * spirits, as consist with an absence * * * * that is dear, valuable or pleasing to * * * * is no compensation for the loss of Domestic Felicity. To associate with the great men of the Earth, and to share in the Government of an Empire, to me has no charms. I do not flatter you, Madam, when I assure you I have had more pleasure in spending two hours with you when in a low state, than I had last Thursday evening at an Entertainment given by Count de Monstier, the French Ambassador, in honour of the President, when everything splendid, everything which the human mind could devise, or wealth procure to render the Entertainment grand and noble was displayed.

Having mentioned the President, whom I know you love (Mrs. Washington is alive) and honour, I must tell you I never saw him look better, and that I shed Tears of Joy on his arrival. In this I was not singular—the Joy is universal and sincere.

Now for my return of which I can say little, I hope it will not be longer than July. I am constantly engaged, tho' not so talkative as some others, as the News Papers announce. I enclose you one which when perused, I will thank you to send to Woodville. Give my love to the girls and Comfort * * * *. I am with great regard,
Dear Madam,
Affectionately Yours,
ALEX. WHITE.

In the name of God, Amen. I, Mary Wood, of the County of Frederick and Commonwealth of Virginia considering the certainty of death and the uncertainty of the time when it may happen, do make my last will and testament in manner following. In the first place I desire that I may be buried in a decent Christian-like manner and that all my debts may be paid. As to the worldly goods wherewith it hath pleased God to bless me, I dispose thereof as follows: My dwelling house with the yard and garden thereto belonging and all that part of the orchard the remainder in which is not already conveyed to my son Robert Wood, I devise to my said son Robert Wood his heirs and assigns; a lot or parcel of ground lately purchased of Charles Magill situate in the Town of Winchester and one square of lots in the addition to the said town made by my late husband,

Colonel James Wood, I give and devise to my grandsons, sons of Robert, James Wood and Robert Welsh Wood and their heirs, in such manner that my said grandson James Wood shall have his choice either to take the lot purchased of Charles Magill or the square of lots and that either of my grandsons to whose share the square of lots shall fall may take his choice of any square which shall remain undisposed of, and in case my death should happen during the infancy of my said grandsons, the choice may be made by their father or guardian. To my grand-daughter Mary Dorcas Wood I give a new feather bed and furniture and six silver table spoons. To my granddaughters Mary Ann, Elizabeth and Mary Harrison and their heirs, I give and devise to each of them two lots in the said addition to the town of Winchester, such as they shall choose after the choice shall be made of the square of lots above mentioned, my said granddaughters taking their choice agreeably to their ages, beginning with the eldest. To my said grand-daughter Mary Anne Harrison, I give the following slaves, Sarah, Robin, Anne and Charlotte, and an infant son of the said Sarah unnamed and all the issue of the said slave, whether born before my death or after. To my said grand-daughter Elizabeth Harrison I give my slaves Jude and Solomon with all the issue of the said Jude whether born before or after my death. To my said grand-daughter Mary Harrison I give my slaves Charles and Rachell and all the issue of the said Rachell whether born before or after my decease. To my son James Wood I give my slaves Butt, Ned, and Thom, and to my son, Robert, my slaves George, Jack, Lewis, Frank, and John. But my said sons and grand-daughters are not to hold any of my slaves aforesaid longer than until they attain the age of thirty-six years respectively, each of which slaves on his or her attaining the age of thirty-six years is hereby emancipated and liberated from all bondage or claim of service whatever. And my negro man Sy, I do emancipate and set free immediately after my decease. My kitchen furniture, chairs and tables, I desire may be equally divided between my sons James and Robert. My wearing apparel and all my other furniture not herein otherwise disposed I desire may be equally divided among my said three grand-daughters Mary Anne, Elizabeth and Mary Harrison and I do hereby revoke all former and other wills by me heretofore made and do constitute and appoint my said sons James Wood and Robert Wood executors of this my last will and testament. In Witness whereof I have signed, sealed, published and declared this as my last will and testament this 20th day of September, 1790.

                 MARY WOOD (Seal)

Signed, sealed, published and
declared as the last will and
testament of the above named
Mary Wood in the presence of
  Alex. White
  Thos. White

At a Court held for Frederick County the 2nd day of July, 1798 this last will and Testament of Mary Wood decd. was proved by the oath of Alexander White, a witness thereto. And at a Court continued and held for the County aforesaid the 5th day of February, 1811, the negro Sarah who claimed her freedom under the will of Mary Wood decd. produced the same in Court and offered it for probate, which the court refused, the same being opposed by Peter Lauck, who claimed said Sarah as a slave, to which opinion the said Sarah by her counsel filed her exceptions. And at a Court continued and held for the said County the 3rd day of June, 1812, a mandamus was produced from the Judge of the Superior Court of Law for this County directing the Court to receive testimony as to the handwriting of Thomas White one of the witnesses to said will and who does not reside within this Commonwealth. Whereupon Obed Waite appeared as one of the heirs of said Mary Wood and on his motion the further consideration of the same is continued until tomorrow.

And at a Court continued and held for the County aforesaid the 4th day of June, 1812, this will of Mary Wood decd. being proved at a former Court by the oath of Alexander White one of the subscribing witnesses thereto, and it appeared to the Court that Thomas White the other subscribing witness thereto does not reside within this Commonwealth, the signature of said Thomas White was proved to be in the hand writing of said Thomas White by the oath of John White, and the will aforesaid ordered to be recorded.

By the Court: JAMES KEITH, C. F. C.
A copy teste: T. A. TIDBALL, C. F. C.

On the back of one of Col. James Wood's papers the autographs in lead pencil of Archibald Woods, William Griffith, Absalom Ridgely, Zaccheus Biggs, and the note "with many others amounting to 4000. My district Ohio." On the same page, in red ink "Land warrant No. 2419 for 500 acres was issued February 14th, 1792 to James Wood, who was a Colo. of the Virginia line."

MARRIAGE CERTIFICATE

I, Tho. K. Cartmell, Clerk of the County Court for the County of Frederick, State of Virginia, the same being a Court of Record, do certify that there is recorded in this office the marriage of Laurence Aug. Washington and Mary Dorcas Wood, and the rites of said Marriage were solemnized by Rev. Alexander Balmain, Minister, on the 6th day November, 1797. Who made returns of same to the Clerk's Office aforesaid as required by the Statute of Virginia.

Given under my hand on this 9th day of November, 1896.

(Signed) T. K. CARTMELL,
Clerk of Frederick County Court.

A LITTLE GIRL'S LETTER TO HER GRANDMOTHER

Mr. Rutherford's.

My Deare Mama:

I got hear Before Dinner am quite well and was so all the way Turner Behaves very well, and I hop I shall have a most Agreable Jurnay, thay are all a Lafing at me for Writing but I Cannot forbare notwithstanding I saw you this Morning, we forgot Mr. White's surtute and My Cloke which obliges us to send a man to town for them I hope I shall hear you are well I shall pray for youre health and happyness tell I have the Pleasure of seeing you

I am My Deare
Mama Your Loving
Daughtow

ELIZABETH WHITE.

To Mrs. Wood

Richwoods, 2n. Novr., 1801.

Dr. Sir:

From recent information I am well assured that the contest for the Clerkship of Jefferson County will issue between Van Rutherford and Geo. Hite. Morgan is given up now by his own friends. From the calculations, which are made on both sides and on which both parties implicitly rely, Mr. Alexr. White's vote will determine the Election. There are 13 magistrates. The vote will stand six and six exclusively of Mr. White. Therefore you see everything rests with him and Rutherford's friends speak of getting his vote to an absolute certainty.

If you think old Mr. Alex. White would write to his nephew in Hite's behalf you would confer a great obligation on me and a lasting one on him by applying to him. The long intimacy and friendship which have subsisted between you and Mr. White may induce him to interfere, provided he would wish to favour Hite's pretentions. If Mr. R. White would also write 'twould probably have a good effect, but on Mr. A. White's recommendation, Hite places great relyance.

Should Mr. White write, in doing of which he would in a very singular manner oblige Hite, and indeed, myself also, you may carry the letter to Mr. Peyton, who will upon a knowledge of its contents send Robt. Hite down with it.

Lau. Washington has sent for Saml. He will come down with the boy.

With love to Mrs. Wood &c in which Polly joines me,

I am with affection

LAU. A. WASHINGTON.

Mr. Robert Wood, Snr.,
Winchester.

Mr. George Hite was elected first clerk of the court of Jefferson County and served from the organization of the county in 1801 until his death in 1817, when his son, Robert G. Hite was appointed and served until his death in 1823.

Mr. George Hite married Deborah, a daughter of Hon. Robert Rutherford.

I, James Wood of Chelsea in the County of Henrico and Commonwealth of Virginia being at this time in perfect health and memory do make and ordain this to be my last will and testament; that is to say I give and bequeath unto my wife Jean Wood and to her assigns forever all my estate of whatsoever kind, real or personal debts due to me by mortgage or otherwise, subject only to the payment of my just debts if I should leave any unpaid which I trust and hope I shall not—I also appoint my said wife Jean Wood my only and sole executive of this my last will and testament and direct that she shall not be required to give any kind of security for the performance of it, nor that there should be any appraisement made of my personal estate. Having sold a certain tract of land to Valentine Cooper lying and being on Mill Creek in the County of Hardy and continuing upwards of five hundred acres, and on which he now lives, I do give and bequeath the same to the said Valentine Cooper his heirs and assigns forever upon this express condition that he strictly complies with our written agreement by paying the several installments at the periods therein mentioned. In testimony whereof I have written the whole of the above with my own hand (which is well known) and set my hand and affixed my seal to the same this fourteenth day of February One Thousand Eight Hundred and Four (1804).

JAMES WOOD (Seal)

At a monthly court held for Henrico County at the Courthouse on Monday the twenty-fifth of July 1813 this last will and Testament of James Wood deceased was produced in Court by Jean Wood the executive therein named and there being no witness to the said will, Samuel McCraw and William Marshall were sworn and severally deposed that they are well acquainted with the handwriting of the testator and verily believe that the said will and the name there to subscribed are all of the decedents proper handwriting—Whereupon the said will is ordered to be recorded. And on the motion of the said executive who made oath thereto and entered into and acknowledged bond in the penalty of forty thousand dollars, conditioned as the law requires, without security, none being required of her by the testator, certificate is granted her for obtaining a probate of said will in due form.

Teste: J. B. WHITLOCK, *Clk.*

At a monthly court held for Henrico County at the Courthouse on the 4th day of April, 1825 on the motion of John Moncure of "Stafford," who took the oath of an executor and with William A. Moncure, his security, entered into and acknowledged a bond in the penalty of two thousand dollars, conditioned according to law, a certificate was granted him for obtaining letters of administration * * * * on that part of the estate of James Wood deceased, unadministered by Jean Wood the executive, with the will of the said James Wood decd. annexed in due form.

Teste: J. B. WHITLOCK, *Clk. C.*

A Copy teste, Loftin N. Ellett C. L. K. C., March 11th, 1834.

Benjamin Rutherford and Elizabeth his wife were married on November 13, 1744.

Mary, daughter of the said Benjamin and Elizabeth was born November 16, 1747, and departed this life August 17, 1748.

Elizabeth, daughter etc., was born July 25, 1750, m. Samuel Glass.

Robert, son etc., May 22, 1752.

Hannah, November 26, 1754; James, April 26, 1757; Benjamin, October 9, 1759; Ann, October 7, 1761; John Wood, March 12, 1764; Thomas, July 12, 1766; Susannah, April 10, 1768; William, October 4, 1771.

BENJAMIN RUTHERFORD'S WILL

I, Benjamin Rutherford of the Corporation of Winchester, do make this my last will and testament in manner following, that is to say, it is my desire and I do direct that all my just debts be fully discharged and satisfied so soon after my death as the situation of my estate will admit of.

As my daughter, Elizabeth Glass, wife of Samuel Glass, hath always conducted herself towards me as a dutiful and affectionate child, I do in consequence thereof under these impressions hereby devise and bequeath unto her, the said Elizabeth Glass, all my estate both real and personal of what nature or kind so ever to hold to her and her heirs forever, and lastly I do hereby nominate constitute and appoint my friend, John Peyton of Winchester, my whole and sole executor to this my last will and testament hereby ordaining this and no other to be my last will and testament. In testimony whereof I have hereunto set my hand and seal this 14th day of February, 1803.

BENJAMIN RUTHERFORD (Seal)

Signed, sealed, published, pronounced
by the testator as his last will and
testament in the presence of
Thomas McKewan
Thomas Tidball
Robert Hennan

At a Court held for Frederick County the 6th day of May, 1805 this last will and testament of Benjamin Rutherford, deceased, was proved by the oaths of Thomas McKewan and Thomas A. Tidball and ordered to be recorded. The executor therein named being dead, administration with the will annexed was granted to Samuel Glass, he having entered into and acknowledged bond with security in the penalty of One Thousand Dollars, conditioned for his due and faithful administration of the said decedent's estate.

By the Court:
J. A. KEITH, C. F. C.

A Copy Teste: C. C. Brannon, Clerk.

DIED

On Monday last (Nov. 9, 1835), at her residence in the vicinity of Wheeling, Mrs. Mary Washington, relict of Laurence Augustine Washington, aged 54.

Her funeral will take place this day, at 12 o'clock from her late residence. The friends of the deceased are respectfully invited to attend.

Tallahassee, Florida, August 17, 1849.

Dr. Sir:

Your letter of the 4th inst. has been recd. I am in possession of many valuable authentic Revolutionary documents. I have an account of the Services of Genl. Wood through the whole war. He first commd. a compy. from Frederick Co. against the Shawnee towns Dec. 23, 1775, and made a treaty with the Indians at Fort Pitt, at the imminent hazard of his life. For his services Va. ordered his expenses to be paid and £250. I know not whether it was ever recd. He was Col. of the 12th Va. Regt. April 1, 1777. March 24, 1781 he had the command over the prisoners taken at Saratoga. The reduction of the Va. line by the Winchester arrangement, 27th Dec. 1782, which was to take effect 1st. Jany. 1783, is in the handwriting of Gen. Wood. I am very anxious to obtain possession of this paper, as I am convinced it will develop much in relation to the claims of Genl. Wood. If you can find it amongst his papers, send it to me or any other Revolutionary papers. You can get a copy of it if you have not the original from the office of Auditor Heath of Richd. Although it may not appear to you when you see it to be of importance to the claim of Genl. Wood, yet in connection with other documents in my possession it will, I consider be very important. I have lately obtained a very important document through a friend at Washington, one which is kept with great care from the inspection of claimants. It is an account of commutation certificates issued in favor of 1585 officers at the close of the war. On this roll I find a certificate for $5729.04 issued in favor of James Wood, which appears to be for his commutation, as Col. $4500 and the balance for arrearages of monthly pay or money advanced by him for the use of the troops. If you inquire of Mr. Hagner, the 3d. Auditor, if Col. Wood has received his commutation, he will reply he has, as soon as he finds a certificate has been issued in his name, taking for granted that the certificate has been settled by the govt. I consider the issuing of the certificate is as about as good evidence of payment as the giving a note by an insolvent was evidence of payment when seven years after he became so far solvent as to pay interest only, but pleaded the statute of limitations in bar of the debt, which was exactly the case of the United States Govt. until 1828, when Cong. became ashamed of the fraud of the Statute, and disregarded it; since which period they have paid by special acts the commutation some 89 officers. Mr. Gallatin when Sect. of the Treas. in 1810 reported certificates outstanding and unpaid $292,491.25 which at 6 per cent called for by the certificate would now amount to $1,500,000, not $100,000 of which has since been paid by Cong. The accountant of the War Dept., Simmons, stated officially in 1796 that the commutation certificates were delivered to agents for each regt. to be by them delivered to the officers; that several of the agents returned the certificates unissued to the officers, and that others never settled accounts, or accounted for the certificates delivered to them. As these certificates were payable to bearer they were no doubt fraudulently passed off by the departing agents for their own benefit. It also appears officially that John Phelan, a Clerk in the office of John Pierce, Commissioner of army accounts, filled up fraudulently many certificates signed in blank by the Commr. and passed them off for his own benefit. From these facts it is evident that the issuing nor even the funding of the certificates under the act of 4th of Augt. 1790 is any evidence that the certificates have been paid, unless in fraud of the officers, their heirs or assigns. The only chance of justice is to bring the claim before Cong. where I can call the Auditor and Regr. before the Committee to answer questions; and when the Committee will require them not to presume payment, but to prove payment to the officers or their reps. who are entitled. I have many such cases now before Cong. Amongst others the claims of Cols. Jas. Livingston and Philip VanCortlandt, N. York Line. I wish you also to obtain from the Auditor's office at Richd. (Heath) a list of the officers who received certificates for the balance of their full pay under the Act of November session, 1781, including the day of the month and year from which the pay commenced down to the day of the month and year to which the pay was received, and the amount recd. I require the whole list, because many officers who served under Col. Wood at different periods, by having their services, I have his, and it will connect other evidence which I have.

The certificates issued in the name of Col. Wood if not paid with interest, would now amount to $28,418.46, and also to 500 acres county land from U. S. if not recd. Col. Wood recd. from Va. 6666 2/3 acres bountyland, warrant dated 15th Augt. 1782, and 1111 in addn. June 11, 1785. He is returned as having served as Col. to the end of the war, but I have a document signed by him 6th Jany. 1783, as Col. Va. Line, and a certificate signed by him 25th Novr. 1784, as late Brigd. Genl. It seems then he was promoted Brigd. Genl. between 6th Jany. 1783 and the close of the war Novr. 3, 1783; and even if his certificate for com. as Col. and bounty land as Col. has been recd. he must be entitled to difference between the commutation and bounty land of the Col. and Brigd. Genl. which is $34,680, and 350 acres from U. S. and 4000 acres from Va.

I have the name of Robt. Wood as Pay Master to Col. James Wood's regt. Pay Master is not entitled to com. as Pay Master, but as he was taken from a subaltern of the line, as such he may be entitled to com. As Pay Master he may be entitled to bounty land. He has received nothing. When I get the papers written for, I will inform you of my terms for prosecution; they will be moderate.

I formerly lived near Middleburg, Loudoun County.

JOHN P. DuVAL.

N. B. I am known at the War Dept. as an officer U. S. War 1812; at postoffice Dept. as Postmaster, Tallahassee, 1842; at State Dept. as Sect. and Act. Govr. of Florida, 1837-8-9.

One has only to read the letters of Col. James Wood to see that he was often almost in distress for money, and to be convinced that he never received any of the commutation money indicated in the letter of Mr. DuVal.

CHAPTER XXVI

Genealogical Notes — Sketches of the Welsh and Rutherford Families

This is not a genealogical work, nor is it meant to go into detail concerning the present generation, but much confusion has arisen on account of the repetition of family names from generation to generation. For the sake of accuracy therefore, dates are given from original sources, such as the notebook of Colonel James Wood, the prayer-book of Robert Wood, letters, tombstones, family Bibles and family records.

The dates of the births of Colonel Wood's five children are taken from his journal.

The eldest, Elizabeth, born September 20, 1739 (married Hon. Alexander White, member of the vestry of 1764; King's attorney in 1772; member of the House of Burgesses; member of the convention which ratified the National Constitution; member of the first Congress.)

James, General and Governor of Virginia, born January 28, 1741. (Died July 16, 1813. Married Jean Moncure, who died in 1825. One daughter, Maria, who died young.)

Mary, born September 23, 1742. (Married Colonel Matthew Harrison, an officer in the Revolutionary army. Children, Mary Ann married Obed Waite, attorney, banker, and mayor of Winchester. Their daughter Maria Antoinette, married Washington G. Singleton, attorney. Mrs. Maria Offutt Barton is a descendant of this branch.)

John, M. D., born January 1, 1743-4. (Died in 1791; married Susanna Baker; children, Stanhope, James S. Mrs. Lewis Nixon is descended from this branch.)

Robert, born July 27, 1747. (Died in 1801; married on April 2, 1774, Comfort Welsh, born 1751, died 1840, thus attaining the great age of eighty-nine.) Their children were:

James, born January 4, 1775; Robert W., August 17, 1776; Thomas, June 19, 1778; John, November 17, 1779; Richard, October 7, 1780; Mary Dorcas, November 6, 1781; Elizabeth, February 26, 1783; Nancy, November 12, 1784; William, January 5, 1786; Comfort, May 24, 1787; Harriot, June 25, 1788; John 2nd, September 5, 1789; Dolphin, October 4, 1790; Juliet S., September 3, 1793; Catherine, January 27, 1795; Sarah Ann, November 20, 1796; Henry, March 7, 1800; Julia V., August 10, 1801.

Of these, only James, Robert, Mary Dorcas, William, Comfort, Harriot, Catherine, Sarah Ann, and Julia reached years of maturity. Both James and Robert became physicians—only Mary Dorcas, Comfort and Catherine married.

Comfort and James Dailey were married December 14, 1815; four children, Dr. Robert Wood, Jean Welsh, Harriot, Dr. Thomas.

Dr. Robert Wood Dailey (May 11, 1821—April 12, 1902) married Rebecca Harriet Taylor, October 3, 1843. Nine children: Benjamin, attorney, July 15, 1844—October 7, 1912; James, November 6, 1846—December 12, 1909; Judge Robert Wood, April 1849—March 11, 1926; Hon. Comfort Wood, November 7, 1850—April 15, 1908; Griffin Taylor, M. D., September 26, 1852—November 8, 1912; Howland, D. D. S., January 5, 1855, living; Sarah Cornelia, March 19, 1857—October 1, 1899 (married William Nelson Baird, who with five children survived her); Jean Welsh, January 20, 1860, living; Thomas, August 7, 1862, living.

Catherine, or "Kitty," fourteen years younger than her sister, Mary Dorcas, married on December 18, 1832, Thomas Glass, great grandson of Samuel Glass and Mary Gamble, and son of Samuel Glass and Elizabeth Rutherford, through whom the Glass and Wood families were related. This Samuel was a sergeant in Dunmore's War, was in the battle of Point Pleasant in 1774, in the company of Captain John Lewis, and rose to the rank of Captain. His son Thomas, was born in 1792 and died in 1862. He was a lieutenant in the War of 1812. The two children of Thomas Glass and "Kitty" Wood were Ella (1834-1860); and William Wood, who was born on March 14, 1835, and died October 28, 1911. On January 18, 1865, he married Nannie R. Campbell, now living. The seven children of this union, Katherine Rebecca, Harriot Wood, Susan Louisa, Thomas Rutherford, William Wood, attorney, Robert McCheyne, M. D., and Julian Wood, attorney, are all living.

It is a singular fact that of the four male members of the Wood family entering chiefly into this narrative, not one lived to great age. Colonel James Wood was little over fifty; his son, General and Governor James Wood, the oldest of all, but seventy-two; Robert, fifty-four; and Laurence A. Washington, fifty, when called to their reward.

A remarkable coincidence, too, that the wives of the four, the objects of the most tender devotion, long outlived their husbands—Mary Rutherford, by nearly thirty-nine, Jean Moncure, nearly twelve, Comfort Welsh, nearly thirty-nine and Mary Dorcas, by nearly twelve years.

All four were women of remarkable strength and

beauty of character. A tone of the deepest affection and respect pervades the letters of children and grandchildren; and what is more noteworthy, of Hon. Alexander White, son-in-law of Mary Rutherford, and Laurence A. Washington, son-in-law of Comfort Welsh, who seem to have held each in peculiar esteem and veneration.

Of the Glen Burnie estate, received by Colonel James Wood, the founder, from King and Council and confirmed years later by a deed from Lord Fairfax, a substantial part is owned (1926) by the heirs of the late William Wood Glass.

The same is true of "Rose Hill," one of the estates secured by Samuel Glass, "the emigrant," who settled at the headwaters of the Opequon in 1736 with his large family, coming from Bainbridge, County Down, Ireland.

Of the three Glass estates, "Greenwood," "Long Meadows" and "Rose Hill," the last two remain in the original families. Mrs. William D. Simmons (Mary Louise Glass, daughter of the late Robert Presley and Belle Taylor Glass) owns the "Long Meadows" homestead. She is descended from the first Samuel and Mary Gamble, through Robert David and Elizabeth Rust, and Robert Jeremiah and Louisa Bryarly, her father's father and mother.

The only daughter of Colonel Robert Jeremiah and Louisa Bryarly Glass, Sarah Louisa, is the widow of the late Dudley L. Miller. Mrs. Miller spends part of the year at her residence, "Sunnyside," at Stephens City, and the rest with her only living daughter, Cecelia (Mrs. Antrim McKay) in Baltimore, Md.

In the "Glen Burnie" family burying ground, in the rear of the beautiful old garden, are found the graves of Robert Wood, 1749-1801; Comfort Welsh Wood,

1751-1840; Dr. James Wood 1775-18—; Harriot Dailey, 1816-1830; Catherine Glass, 1795-1847; Sarah A. Wood, 1796-18—; Dr. Thomas Dailey, 1822-1862; Comfort Dailey, 1787-1864; Harriot Wood 1788-1866; Dr. Robert Wood, 1776-1855; William Wood, 1786-1872; Julia Wood, 1801-1885; Ella Glass, 1834-1860; Thomas Glass, March 12, 1792-November 13, 1862.

The following sketch of the Welsh family, which became allied with the Wood family through the marriage of Robert Wood and Comfort Welsh, April 22, 1774, is by the well known genealogist, Luther W. Welsh, M. D., of Kansas City, Mo., who upon a request for data, was generous enough to compile this in long hand:

Maj. Jn. Welsh, immigrant ancestor, is named in his will of Jan. 6, 1683-4 (Annap. Wills, 4, 35), as "John Welsh of ye County of Ann Arundell in ye Province of Maryland, Gent." Traditionally, he was of Welsh descent, probably through Eng.

Md. Arch., 5, 30, gives his commission as Justice of the Peace for A. A. Co. on May 4, 1668. The Archives show various renewals of the Commission up to the year of his death 1683-4. From Sept. 13, 1676 (Md. Arch., 15, 130) he was one of the gentlemen Justices of the "provincial organizers of the Court of Ann Arundel."

In 1678 and 1679 (15 Md. Arch.) he was High Sheriff of the County by the appointment of the Governor, and as such the most important official of the county, representative of the Proprietor's power in the county and responsible to the Proprietor alone. (See "The Md. Revolution of 1689," Johns Hopkins Press).

During his incumbency of this position occurred the "Nanticoke War" of 1678, following which on June 6, 1679, he was reappointed to the Quorum as "Capt. John Welsh" (Md. Arch. 15, 253), and 4 mos. later, October 6, 1679, "The Three Sisters," a Balto. Co. tract of 1000 acres, was surveyed for him as "Major John Welsh"—"having been granted unto him by the Rt. Hon., the Lord Proprietor of the Province."

These facts indicate that his titles were of military origin, growing out of the Indian Warfare of 1678. Two years later, Sep. 12, 1681, during a recurrent Indian raid, one man was killed and two Englishmen wounded "on Major Welch's plantation on South river"—a further fact that leaves little room for doubt that Maj. Welsh was in Indian fighter. This incident is given in "Founders of A. A. and Howard Cos.," p. 51, and in Md. Arch., vol. 7.

On Nov. 6, 1683, an "Act for the Advancement of Trade" was enacted. This was a state-wide selection of Commissioners by the Lord Proprietary and the General Assembly, from the several counties of "men of the highest importance, the civil and military officers of the counties," ("Side Lights," vol. 2) for the purchasing and laying out of Town Lands, Ports, etc. In the list of 24 for A. A. Co., six are designated by title, the others as "Mr."—showing the meticulous care of the Gov. and Assembly in the bestowal or recognition of titles in that day. The name of "Major John Welsh" is among the first six of the list (Md. Arch., 7, 610, 611).

His death occurred the following year between Jan. 6, 1683-4, the date of his will, and Mch. 3, 1683-4, when it was probated.

His 1st wife was Anne, widow of Hon. Roger Grosse, by whom he had 2 sons; Capt. Silvester, a Capt. of the Colonial Militia ("The Ancient City," p. 83) and Col. John Welsh, 2d.

To these 2 sons the will of Maj. Jn. Welsh left his plantation on South river, "Arnold-Gray," etc.

Col. Jn. Welsh, of "Arnold-Gray," was b. about 1671-2, and d. 1734. He was one of the Board of Justices and County Commissioners of A. A. Co., 1726-1734, and High Sheriff from 11 Nov. 1732 to 27 June 1733 (Col. Fams., Vol. 7, Bowie). He was a merchant and, like his father, a large landholder. Md. records refer to him as Col. Jn. Welsh. His will is on record at Annap. Liber 21, p. 102. He m. 3. 13. 1700 Thomasin Hopkins (all Hallows Par. reg. 57), da. of Gerrard Thomasin Hopkins, by whom he had das.: Eliz. (presumably m. Wm. Davis), Sarah (m. Samuel Warfield) and Sophia (m. Benj. Hall, of P. G. Co.).

Col. Jn. Welsh m. 2. 1715, Rachel—(last name unknown), and had: Ann, Rachel, John, Thos., Mary, Benj., Elizabeth (2d of the name), Henry O'Neale.

The Da. Ann (b. 1716) m. Capt. Nathaniel Hammond; the son Jn. (known as Capt. Jn. m. Hannah Hammond (da. of Capt. Jn. Hammond and Ann Dorsey, da. of Col. Edw. Dorsey and his 2d wf. Margt. Larkin); the son Hy. O'Neale m. Mary, niece of Jas. Carroll; the son Benj. m. Hamutal Hammond, sis. of Hannah above (so believed, because she m. ——— Welsh, and all the sons of Col. Jn. are accounted for exc. Benj.); and the 2d son Thomas m. Dorcas ——.

Th. Welsh (2d son of Col. Jn. & Rach.) was b. 1.24 1721-2 (A. H.) and d. after 1784. The Prince George Co. census of 1776 gives Th., ae 54, and his wife Dorcas, aged 54, with 4 sons and 5 das. at home; and the will of Henry O'Neale Welsh, dated 16 Dec. 1784, proved 19 Mch. 1794 (Annap. wills, Lib. J. G. No. 1, fol. 399), shows that his bro. Th. was living 1784. The will leaves a bequest to Henry, "son of John Welsh, deceased," and his Dwg. pln. to 2 nephews, Th. King, and "Rd. Welsh, son of Th. Welsh." Evidently Th. was then living.

This will also certainly identifies Comfort Welsh as the daughter of this Th. and his wife Dorcas. Dr. Thos. Welsh, in giving the history of his family (1897) stated that his grandfather Rd. Welsh had inherited the plantation on which he (Dr. Th.) lived, "more than a 100 yrs. ago" from a "distant relative." The relative, as the will above shows, was Hy. O'Neale, son of Col. Jn. (above) and bro. of Capt. Jn., Th. and Benj.

The family record of Dr. Th. Welsh begins with his gdfa. Rd. and names a sister Deborah (m. Nathan Edmonson) and a sister "Comfort, we think" who m. ——— Wood of Winchester, Va., whose "gdchn. were Dr. Thos. Daily & sister." The above data, and the census of 1776, and Brumbaugh's "Md. Records" prove conclusively the following:

Th. Welsh, b. 1721-2, d. aft. 1784 (son of Col. Jn. & Rachel of "Arnold Gray") who (with his bro. Benj.) inherited 2 tracts near the Eastern Branch of the Potomac in P. G. Co., viz., "The Defiance of Williams and Clark" and "Bacon Hall," and possessed other lands, as "Snowden and Welsh," "Richard and John," "Moberly's Rest," "Moberly's Desire," &c. married Dorcas ———; and among their chn. were:

 Rd. M. 1781 Mapsey (Mercy) Prather.
 Comfort (1751-1840) m. Robt. Wood of Va.
 Deborah m. 1788 Samuel Jones and (presumably),
 Eliz. who m. 1781 Joseph Prather.

Richard Welsh, brother of Comfort Wood d. 1. 1. 1833, m. 1781 Mercy Prather. Their children were 1. Benj.; 2. Dorcas; 3. Deborah Lucinda (m. 1822, Jo. Jones, who d. 1823; m. 2. George Beall, who d. 1834) 4. Th. 1789-1873, m. Eliz. Sellman, da. of Major Jonathan Sellman, of the Revolution.

Their eight children were 1. Ann S. D. 1827; 2. Marie Deborah, 1828-1901, m. 1847 Jas. A. Iglehart; 3. Rd. 1830-1891; 4. Sellman ("Semmie") 1832-1911, ae 79, m. Wm. Sprigg Hall; 5. Cath. Howard ("Kate") 1834-1923, unm. ae. 89; 6. Mrgt. Ella b. 1836, m. 1855 Th. Iglehart. She is living, aged 90; 7. Dr. Th. Welsh, 1839-1900, m. 1874 Cath. Waters; 8. Ann Eliz. 1840-1925 ae. 85, m. 1870 Benj. Watkins, son of Dr. Benj. and Mary Hodges Watkins.

From family letters, at least "Kate" and "Semmie" and Deborah (Mrs. Beall) visited their aunt and cousins at Glen Burnie.

Dr. Luther W. Welsh says further:

"My first intimation of the Virginia connection came to me thirty years or more ago, through Dr. Th. Welsh and his older sister, Mrs. Iglehart, of A. A. Co., Md. They sent a copy from an old Bible of Nathan Edmonson, giving their gdfather Rd. Welsh and his sisters, one of whom, "Comfort, we think," m. ——— Wood of Winchester, Virginia.

"When I learned later that my niece, Mrs. Richardson (wife of Rev. Frank Richardson) was located at Winchester, I quickly got the matter straightened out, through your kindness. You will note that through two names "Comfort" and "Dorcas," I was able to discover this connection."

CLAN SONG OF THE RUTHERFORDS

"March, March Ettrick and Teviotsdale!
Why my lads dur na ye march forward in order?
March, March Eskdale and Liddiesdale,
All the blue bonnets come over the border.

"Mount and make ready there,
Sons of each mountain glen,
Fight for your homes
And the old Scottish border."

The ancient Rutherford family of Scotland has been connected with the history of Winchester from the very beginning. When the first court for Frederick County was held November 11, 1743, Thomas Rutherford was sworn High Sheriff, James Wood, Clerk, George Home, County Surveyor. (Cartmell, 19).

Members of the Scotch family seem to have come into the Shenandoah Valley with the tide which set in about 1730, crossing the Potomac River at the Pack Horse Ford, afterwards called Mecklenburg, about a mile east of Shepherdstown.

As to the origin of the family, Burke's "Landed Gentry of Scotland and Ireland" says: "The traditional account of this ancient family is that a man of distinction on the border, having conducted Ruther, king of Scotland, safely through the River Tweed on an expedition against the Britons at a place which from the event was called Rutherford by the king; after his expedition the king bestowed some lands contiguous thereto on his conductor, from which time his posterity assumed the name of Rutherford as soon as surnames became used in Scotland. Be that as it may, certain it is that the family of Rutherford of that ilk from which several other considerable families have sprung having that surname in use south of Scotland, and descended from that family, have always been classed among the most ancient and powerful families of Teviotsdale, Scotland."

The Rutherfords of Scotland are noted as far back as 1140, when Robertus Dominus de Rutherford is mentioned. Sir Robert Rutherford was a friend of Robert Bruce in 1378.

Brief notes gleaned from various sources in the Library of the British Museum which point to the sources of the American branches of the family, are as follows:

Sir Richard Rutherford was ambassador to the court of England, and was in 1400 Warden of the Marches.

Under "Rutherford of Fairnington," it is found that Thomas, the Black Laird, had nine sons, among them Richard, Robert, and John, who helped to restore Charles II. Robert, son of this John, became Rutherford of Bowland, and through the female line was ancestor of Sir Walter Scott, Bart., whose mother was Anne, eldest daughter of Dr. John Rutherford, professor of medicine in the University of Edinburgh. Thomas, of Edgerston and Wells, acquired lands of Bonjedward and Mounthooly, together with land of Hunthill and Scraisburgh, from Robert, Lord Rutherford, who assigned to Thomas the title which he had received from the Earl of Teviot, by virtue of the patent, the only right they had.

Thomas assigned it to his son and successor who declined it, but Captain John Rutherford, collateral, descended from Richard, claimed it.

In 1687 Susanna Riddell assigned her estate to her husband, "Thomas Rutherford of Teviotdale" who died in 1720. He was succeeded by his son, Sir John Rutherford of Teviotsdale, later of Ireland. He was descended from James Rutherford who had married Lady Margaret Erskine (a lineal descendant of Charlemagne through the Duchess of Lorraine).

Sir John married, first, in 1710 Elizabeth Cairncross. Of their nineteen children, "Thomas was baptized July, 1711, at Hunthill, by Mr. Simmeon Riddell; second, John, baptized June 12, 1712; third, William, baptized April 25, 1714, John Simpson, Provost of Jedburgh, and John Bennet, of Chesters, witnesses; fourth, Thomas baptized May 1, 1715, the first Thomas having died; fifth, a daughter, Susanna; sixth, Robert, born May 30, baptized May 31, 1719; Mary, October 28, 1720; James, December 14, 1722; Walter, December 9, 1723; Elizabeth, January 10, 1726; Andrew, July 14, 1727."

Sir Robert, born May 30, 1719, was created a Baron of Russia by Catherine II, in 1768, which title by charter under her own hand, conferred upon him and his posterity the title and dignity of a Baron of Russia.

To the family motto, "Nec sorte, nec fato," Catherine added the adversative, "sed labore et ardore." She presented Sir Robert with a magnificent gold snuffbox set with diamonds and rubies.

Sir Robert purchased back the family property of Fairington in 1779.

His brother, Thomas, married in 1745, Martha, daughter of Alderman Town, of York, and dying in 1749, left a son, John of Fairington, born at Scarborough. His father died at Barbadoes.

John was taken in charge by his uncle, Sir John of Edgerston, and sent to New York to his uncle Walter, owner of "Rutherford County," where a life of adventure awaited him.

He was sent to Detroit, and from there undertook an exploring expedition to the Great Lakes. He set out on May 2, 1763, under Captain Robson, in command of the 77th Regiment. He was captured by the Indians, but escaped and found his way back to Detroit. Afterwards he joined the 42nd Regiment, with which he was connected for twenty years, taking part in both American wars.

He returned to Scotland and settled at Mossburnford, on the right bank of the Jed, three miles from Jedburgh. In 1787 he was visited by Robert Burns. He died there July 12, 1830, in the eighty-fourth year of his age.

His son, John, remained unmarried. Charles married, but left no children. The estate came to Thomas, who married Caroline, daughter of W. Ball. There were nine sons and four daughters of this union. The eldest son, Henry, inherited the estate in 1863, upon the death of his father.

John, an advocate, second son of Sir John, married in November 1737, Ellenor, daughter of Sir Gilbert Elliott, of Minto. Of the sons of John and Ellenor, John and William Oliver, John accepted an independent company of Foot, Province of New York, and was killed at the battle of Ticonderoga in 1758.

William Edward Oliver Rutherford, of Edgerston County, Roxburgh, is descended from John, second son of Sir John, and Ellenor, daughter of Sir Gilbert Elliott.

Seats, Edgerston, Jedburgh, County Roxburgh.

Address, in care of Messrs. Scott and Glover, Hill Street, Edinburgh.

There are many entries of marriages and births in the Jedburgh Parish Registers, among them a few early in 1700, or earlier.

"June 2, 1696, Samuel Rutherford and Margaret Ker, Yetholm parish, gave up their names in order to marriage and were married June 27. 'A Samuel Rutherford' married in 1748 to Euphan Stevenson, and on April 19, 1766, 'Samuel Rutherford' married Isabel Robson.

"May 9, 1718, Sir John Rutherford of that ilk, a daughter born the 6th instant and baptized this day, Susanna," etc.

Much is written concerning the eminent divine, Samuel Rutherford, the author of "The Due Right of Presbytery"; "The Trial and Triumph of Faith"; "Familiar Letters," and the famous "Rex Lex," which after the Restoration in 1660 was burned under his windows in St. Andrews.

He was born about 1600, at Nisbet, Roxburgshire, and died at St. Andrews, March 20, 1661.

He had two brothers, one an officer in the Dutch army, the other a schoolmaster of Kirkcudbright.

The theological services of Samuel Rutherford were great, and he was an able and impressive preacher. Dean Stanley calls him, "The true saint of the covenant."

He received the degree of M. A. at Edinburgh in 1621; became Professor of Humanity; ceased from this office in 1625; studied theology and was settled at Anworth in 1627.

On the 27th of July, 1636, he was cited before the High Commission Court to answer for his nonconformity to the acts of Episcopacy, and for his work against the Arminians. This cost him his position at Anworth and he was banished to Aberdeen. The Covenanters being successful, he returned to Anworth in 1638, and in 1639 was made professor at St. Andrews.

In 1643 he was Scotch commissioner to the Westminster assembly and served four years.

The Restoration brought him into peril and disgrace. He was deprived of his offices and attainted of high treason before Parliament. But while the citation was pending, a more imperative citation was served. In answer to the demand for his presence, he wrote: "I am summoned before a higher Judge and judicatory; that first summons I behove to answer: and, ere a few days arrive, I shall be where few kings and great folk come." (English Hymns: S. W. Duffield, Page 535.)

Samuel Rutherford married Eupham Hamilton, who died in 1630. In 1640 he married Jean McGrath, who with a daughter, Agnes, survived him. All children by his first, and six by his second marriage, predeceased him. Agnes married W. Chiesly, W. S., and left issue.

His pulpit oratory was characterized by a kind of skreigh. So filled with zeal was he when he spoke of Jesus Christ that one felt that he might fly out of the pulpit. He was a little, fair man, naturally of a hot and fiery temper, consumed by zeal which was not relieved by a sense of humor. There is no direct evidence regarding his parentage.

He died in raptures, his last words being,

"Glory, glory dwelleth in Emmanuel's land."

He is buried in the churchyard of the chapel of St. Regulus at St. Andrews.

His tomb has the following inscription:

"M. S. R. Here lyes the Reverend Mr. Samuel Rutherford, professor of divinity in the University of St. Andrews, who died March the 20th, 1661.

> "What tongue, what pen or skill of men,
> Can famous Rutherford commend:
> His learning justly raised his fame;
> True greatness did adorn his name.
> He did converse with things above,
> Acquainted with Immanuel's love.
> Most orthodox he was and sound,
> And many errors did confound,
> For Zion's King, and Zion's cause,
> And Scotland's covenanted laws.
> Most constantly he did contend,
> Until his time was at an end.
> At last he wan to full fruition,
> Of that which he had seen in vision."

(From Thomas Murray's "Life of Samuel Rutherford," in the British Museum.)

Thus far the family in Scotland.

Mrs. Agatha A. Woodson, of Edgefield, S. C., a Rutherford genealogist, says that several of the sons of Sir John Rutherford, of Teviotsdale, and his wife, Elizabeth Cairncross, emigrated to this country.

One of these sons, Thomas, 2nd, illpleased with New Jersey, started southward "on his own horseback." While on this journey, on the Nottoway River in Virginia, Colonel Robert Rutherford was born, April, 1734.

In after years, Thomas, still of a restless disposition moved further south and settled in North Carolina, where he was intimately concerned with the political movements of the colony, as were other members of his family. His son, John, became Lieutenant-General John Rutherford, of His Majesty's forces.

Colonel Robert Rutherford, born in 1734, married first, Dorothea Brooks; second, Mrs. Harrington. He was a member of the first Provincial Congress at Hillsboro, N. C.

Mrs. Woodson says further that the father of Griffith Rutherford had stopped in Wales on his way over to America and married into the Griffith family. He and his wife were both drowned on the voyage to America, and the young son was taken and reared by a family in Virginia. A history of the military operations of General Rutherford is part of the history of the states of North and South Carolina. He died in Tennessee in 1804.

Miss Camilla C. Rutherford is descended from the Griffith Rutherford branch of the family.

Of the Virginia Rutherfords, Mrs. Woodson says: "Robert Rutherford, Congressman from Virginia, member of the House of Burgesses, was the son of Thomas Hugh Rutherford and Sarah or Susan de Montargis. He was born in Scotland in 1728, and educated at the Royal College of Edinburgh. He and his brother, Thomas, settled in Burke County, Penn., then moved to the Valley of Virginia. It is known that one or two of the brothers went farther south."

To quote from Mrs. Woodson again, John Rutherford, Captain of Pennsylvania militia, 177—, died 1804, was probably a son of Thomas Hugh Rutherford and Sarah de Montargis.

The late Mrs. James S. Phillips (Anna Latima Chapline) says in her biographical notes:

"Hugh Thomas Rutherford came to Winchester in 1740, with his sons Robert and Thomas."

Mrs. Danske Bedinger Dandridge in her "Historic Shepherdstown," says: "The Rutherford plantation adjoined that of Colonel James Wood, on which the town of Winchester was laid out, and Hugh Rutherford's daughter, Mary, became the wife of Colonel James Wood. After Berkeley County was formed from a part of Frederick the Rutherfords always lived on their property in that county, and were one of the most prominent families in the community."

The persistent repetition in America of the family names, Thomas, Robert, John, Susan, Mary, Elizabeth, Eleanor, Sarah, indicates that the Virginia families are descended from the Teviotsdale and Fairington Rutherford families of Scotland.

The descendants of Robert Rutherford, the congressman, and of his brother, Thomas, have established family records which are here given in brief.

All biographers are agreed that they were the sons of Hugh Thomas or Thomas Hugh Rutherford and Sarah or Susan de Montargis, his wife. Norris' "History of the Lower Shenandoah Valley," page 250, says that Robert was the son of Thomas, the first sheriff of Frederick County; Mrs. Dandridge, that Mary Wood was the daughter of Hugh; Cartmell, that she was the daughter of Thomas, the sheriff. Clearly, Thomas, the younger brother of Robert, who was born in 1728, could not have been sheriff in 1743. Indeed, Robert would have been only sixteen years of age when he was appointed deputy sheriff in 1744. Benjamin and Mary must have been older children of Thomas Hugh and Sarah de Montargis, all born in Scotland, and if, as Mrs. Phillips says, they came to Frederick County in 1740, Robert's education at the Royal College of Edinburgh must have ended when he was but a child, and there would have been no time for residence in Burke County, Pa.

The identification of Thomas Hugh and Thomas the sheriff as one at least removes all difficulty as to his holding office in 1743. At present nothing definite can be found as to his history before that date. Double surnames were very rare in those days. He perhaps used officially only the strong patronymic, Thomas. All that diligent research upon the subjects has been able to develop is here given. Perhaps this earnest effort to establish facts may bring out what now seems baffling.

The Rutherfords were among those who shared in the "Minor Grants." (Cartmell, 16). Thomas qualified as High Sheriff of Frederick County November 11, 1743. At the June Court, 1744, he received for extra services 1248 pounds of tobacco.

Benjamin and Robert were appointed deputy sheriffs at the January court, 1744, (C. 21).

Colonel James Wood, Captain John Hite and Robert Rutherford were appointed by the General Assembly to settle the accounts of the troops during the Colonial wars. (C. 89).

James Wood and Robert Rutherford were among the trustees of the towns of Stephensburg and Winchester in 1758. (C. 228).

In October, 1776, Robert Rutherford, Thomas Rutherford and Alexander White were among the trustees for Bath, now Berkeley Springs. (C. 231).

Charles Town, established October, 1786, numbered among its trustees John Augustine Washington, Robert Rutherford, William Darke and Alexander White, and became the county seat of Jefferson, upon its erection from Berkeley, November 10, 1801. (C. 234).

Among the old county roads was one from Captain

Rutherford's to the Potomac, and another from the same place to John McCormick's. (C. 50).

From the best authorities, Robert was born October 20, 1728, married on September 13, 1753, Mary Daubein (Daubigny) Howe, widow of Viscount George Augustus Howe (Irish peerage), brother of Lord Admiral Howe. (History of Nations, P. F. Collier, General Index.) George Augustus Howe was killed at Ticonderoga in 1758, leaving one daughter, Margaret, who married Colonel William Little.

Robert Rutherford died in 1805. His wife was born on February 20, 1732; died on June 24, 1813.

Mary Daubein was the daughter of William, and granddaughter of Joseph Daubein (Daubigny), who was born in Dublin, settled in Winchester, and died here at the age of one hundred and three.

The record of Congressman "Robin" Rutherford is too well known to need repetition. His family, brought up at "Flowing Springs," consisted of eight daughters and one son, Thomas Hugh, the seventh child, who died unmarried, aged nineteen.

Of the daughters, the fourth (Hannah), who married a nephew of Colonel John Morrow, left no children. The ninth child, Margaret, died unmarried in Norfolk, Virginia, aged eighteen.

The remaining six daughters became the ancestresses of large and important families:

1. Susan m. in 1780, Colonel John Peyton (see page 92).

2. Mary m. first, Major Henry Peyton, second, Colonel John Morrow.

3. Elizabeth m. first, David Conrad, second, Dr. Davis.

5. Deborah, m. Colonel George Hite, of the Revo-

lution, son of Jacob, and grandson of Jost Hite. Colonel Hite's parents and their young children were massacred by the Indians in South Carolina in 1776.

The Beckwiths, Ransons and Flaggs are among the descendants of Colonel George Hite and Deborah Rutherford.

6. Sarah, m. Daniel Bedinger, b. 1761. Their home was named "Bedford," from a union of the names Bedinger and Rutherford.

Major Henry, George Michael, Daniel and Jacob Bedinger were sons of Henry Bedinger who married Mary von Schlegle, and who died January 22, 1772, in the forty-second year of his age; and grandsons of Adam Bedinger, born near Strasbourg in Alsace-Lorraine, who came to America in 1736. The marvelous Revolutionary War record of Henry, George Michael and Daniel Bedinger is fully given in "Historic Shepherdstown," by Mrs. Stephen Dandridge (Danske Bedinger).

Of the thirteen children of Daniel Bedinger and Sarah Rutherford, the sixth, Elizabeth, m. John Thornton A. Washington; the seventh, Mary, m. Rev. John Love Bryan; the tenth, Henrietta, m. Edmund J. Lee; the ninth, Virginia Anne, m. Hon. William Lucas. Their son, the late Hon. Daniel Bedinger Lucas, the poet and brilliant lawyer, who married Evelina Tucker Brooke, was the father of Miss Virginia Lucas, who lives at the family seat, "Rion Hall," near Halltown, Jefferson County, W. Va. She inherits her father's literary tastes and possesses a legal turn of mind.

Hon. Henry Bedinger, fifth child of Daniel Bedinger and Sarah Rutherford, member of Congress, and in 1853, minister to Denmark, married, first, Margaret Rust; second, Caroline Lawrence. Their daughter Danske, "Little Dane," was born in Denmark.

The daughter of the late Mr. Stephen and Mrs. Danske Bedinger Dandridge, Miss "Violet" (Serena Katherine), lives at "The Grove" ("Rose Brake"), the family residence, at Shepherdstown, and embodies the spirit of her ancestors.

Hon. Henry Bedinger died in 1858, soon after his return from Denmark, of pneumonia contracted at a dinner given in his honor.

8. Eleanor, daughter of Robert Rutherford and Sarah de Montargis, m. James Brown.

Their first child, Robert Templeman, m. Margaretta Brown; their fifth, John Peyton, m. Elizabeth Fulton; their sixth, Sarah Elizabeth m. William Nathaniel Craighill. Of the remaining five the record is not complete.

Thomas, brother of Robert, and son of Thomas Hugh and Sarah de Montargis, married Drusilla Van Swearingen. He died in 1796, leaving a son, Thomas, who m. Mary Darke, daughter of General William Darke. Their daughter, Sarah de Montargis, m. Dr. John Briscoe. Their descendants still live at "Piedmont," the Briscoe homestead near Charles Town.

Van, son of Thomas and Drusilla Rutherford, born 1771, died 1824, married Sarah Marke, d. of John Marke, of Jefferson County.

Their son Thomas, m. Maria Duffield.

Of the children of Thomas and Maria, Ellen m. C. Moore; Virginia, m. McMechan; Mary m. Aisquith; Drusilla m. Packett; Richard m. Forrest. The name of a son, Thomas, is given, the fifth in descent from Thomas Hugh.

The women of the Rutherford family were noted for their beauty, a contributing factor, no doubt, to their great popularity. They certainly possessed solid power and wisdom, as witnessed in many of their descendants.

Wherever found, the original Rutherford families furnished strong leaders in civil and religious affairs.

CHAPTER XXVII

Lists of Frederick County Clerk's Fees for the Years 1744, 1757, 1761 and 1762 — Lists of Officers of the Virginia Line at Winchester and Fort Pitt in 1783 — List of Men Draughted from Hampshire County — Catalogue of the Wood Papers

The following lists are given because the names point to early inhabitants whose descendants may find lost clues to family connections.

LIST OF FREDERICK CLK. FEES BELONGING TO JAMES WOOD, ANNO DOM. 1744

A	Tobacco		Tobacco
Anderson, Colvert	163	Burnett, Daniel	412
Ashley, Thomas Jun	46	Blackburn, Wm.	296
Anderson, John	125	Barrat, John	165
Armstrong, Thomas	55	Breemigem, James	108
Alford, John	23	Beesley, James	131
Anderson, Thomas	51	Blackburn, Easther	131
Armstrong, Robert	78	Beeson, John	150
Alford, Thomas	310	Baker, Isaac	294
Alexander, Zacheus	90	Buttler, Thomas	33
Ashley, Robert	55	Bordens, Exrs.	30
Anderson, Enoch	81	Beeson, William	150
Atkinson, Michael	23	Burkham, Roger	204
B		Black, Patrick	5
Babb, Phillip	70	Berwick, Thomas	361
Brown, Thomas	135	Bryan, Joseph	35
Bowman, George	135	C	
Black, Robert	10	Constant, John	35
Brittan, Samuel	94	Carsey, Christopher	173
Beller, Peter	50	Colson, Tho.	306
Buchanan, Arthur	771	Campbell, Hugh	170
Bryan, Joseph	25		
Byrne, James	20	Carried Over	5764
Borden, Deborah	130	Brot Over	5764
Bumgardner, Peter	35	Crafts, Robert	23

Carrell, Joseph	250
Calmees, Marques	221
Caines, John	55
Chambers, Edmund	30
Counts, John	10
Connell, John	166
Clark, Mary	91
Carrington, Mary	106
Crafts, Robert & Saml. Morris	5
Cunningham, Adam	91
Champ, John	65
Chester, Thomas	288
Collins John & McGuire	33
Cassity, Peter	55
Campbell, Andrew	1053
Cherry, Thomas	65
Colvin, Joseph	150
Collins, John	620
Colvin, William	78
Craigs, David & Archibald	63
Cantrell, Zebulon	120
Curtis, Jonathan	166
Cartlidges, Exr.	46
Crowson, John	33
Carson, John	192

D

Decredow, William	35
Demos, Peter	78
Davis, Wm.	308
Donahue, Daniel	160
Demoss, John & Catherine	150
Dunkham, Mary	101
Denny, Walter	216
Dalton, John	35
Denny, George	101
Daenning, Walter	55
Dennis, Samuel	202
Denton, John	25
Donahue, Henry	25
Davis, Robert	150
Doomes, John	365
Devinne, Hugh	65
Demoss, John	155
Dowland, Henry	322

E

Egarter, Christian	78
Evans, John	290
Ewing, Alexander	120
Edwards, Joseph	85
Earle, Saml.	383
Edzels, Exrs.	80
Carried Over	13423
Brot Over	13423

F

Finler, James	230
Friend, Israel	268
Falconer, Alex.	136
Fearnley, Wm.	273
Fitzsimons, John	401
Fanner, Thomas	131
French, John	55
Fowler, Francis	146
Frost, John	25
Fulton, Mary	78

G

Galbarth, Frederick	50
Gregory, Benja.	15
Gregory, John	73
Griffith, William	1795
Glenn, James	197
Gillespis, Patrick	651
Gibson, Jacob	15
Gilliland, Hugh	55
Gayter, Michael	70
Green, Wm.	120

H

Hood, Rachel	50
Haines, William	5
Holliday, Samuel	76
Harris, Tho.	119
Hatfield, Joseph	33
Hyte, Jacob	279
Hoge, James	256
Harger, Leonard	366
Hanagin, Charles	25
Hedge, Jonas	25
Helms, Leonard	65
Hutchins, Robert	80
Hazor, Jonathan	156
Huston, John	70
Helms, Joseph	155

Haws, Frederick	134
Hart, Thomas	381
Hume, William	113
Hedges, Solomon	170
Hoge, Lewis	241
Hobson, George, Junr.	200
Harrol, John	150
Hollingsworth, Abra	85
Hunt, Roger	80
Hardin, Henry	135
Hardin, Eliza.	91
Carried Over	21747
Brot Over	21747
Hindman, John	110
Harris, John	416
Halling, Wm.	180

I

Ice, Frederick	55
Iohnston, Jacobus	45
Iames, Richard	60
Iay, William	15
Iones, John	160
Isaacs, Samuel	51
Iones, Gabriel	44
Iohnson, Mary	89
Iulian, Rene	35
Iack, Jeremiah	443
Isaas, Elisha	126
Isaacs, Saml. Junr.	120
Iohnstone, George	1058
Iarvis, Thomas	101

K

Keith, John	230
Kelly, John	25
Kelly, David	110
Knott, Peter	85
Keller, Charles	41

L

Lilburn, Ann	51
Lum, Jonas	88
Law, Tho. Capt.	135
Lum, Mary	150
Lyon, Humberton	161
Lawder, Richard	70
Largant, John	116
Linsey, John	60
Lintner, Samuel	40
Loe, Thomas	276
Linwell, John	18

M

Mounts, Joseph	96
McKever, Darby	5
McCormack, John	172
Milbourne, Eliza.	110
Moore, Benja.	213
Martin, Tho.	103
Mitchell, Wm.	1179
McKee, James	630
Morgan, Morgan	25
McHugh, Nichols	46
McDowell, John	135
Carried Up	29230
Brot Over	29230
Miller, Wm.	317
Morgan, Charles	155
Marr, Christopher	15
Morphey, Darby	30
Mitchell, John	515
McCay, Wm.	80
McCracken, James	353
Matthews, Patrick	611
Morgan, Richard	105
Madden, John	145
Mahone, Thomas	106
Mercer, Nicholas	88
Martin, George	144
Miller, John	221
McGuire, Thomas	153
Marlin, Jacob	91
McHugh, Peter	175

N

Nation, Christopher	55
Nichols, John	196
Neal, Hugh	277

O

Osbourn, John	70
Oneal, Garrob	170
Ogullion, Neal	130
Osbourne, Nicholas	135
Oneal, John	5

P

Parrell, Hugh	70

Poore, Jeremiah	111	Rutherford, Benja.	86
Pearson, Eliza.	150	Roark, Bryan	255
Penington, Jacob	133	Rion, John	409
Priest, Thomas	55	Ross, Alexander	80
Purteat, Ann	61	Rutlidge, James	85
Pearson, Abel	194	Richardson, John—Red	23
Peck, Jacob	137	Rogers & Woolf	43
Pooh, Charles	85	**S**	
Pendergrass, Garrob	505	Sheppard, John	122
Peake, Nathaniel	101	Stone, Wm.	25
Pusey, Robert	10	Smith, John	766
Parker, Hugh	55	Shaw, Michael	195
Pugh, Jesse	110	Shurley, Walter	65
Posey, Benja.	567	Smith, John—Blacksmith	55
Penington, Abra	55	Seabin, James	55
Parish, George	137	Smith, Robert	148
		Smith, Jeremiah	205
Carried Over	36036	Shearer, Davis	53
Brot Over	36036	Summerford, Jeffery	75
Perkins, John	190	Swearingham, Van	190
Potts, Thomas	70	Sutton, Joseph	64
Postgate, Thomas	773	Simons, Jonah	289
Poulson, Richd.	5		
Penington, Isaac	141	Carried Up	44448
Poultney, Richard	1027	Brot Up	44448
Price, Aaron	416	Smith, George Audley	61
Quigley, Patrick	60	Simons, Jona.—Ye Infant	560
Quin, John	45	Shippin, Edward	151
R		Seamon, Eliza	5
Rennick, Tho.	360	Stiltwell, Daniel	55
Ross, Wm.	28	Shippin, Joseph Junr.	119
Ross, George	10	Seamon, John	150
Ross, Mary	135	**T**	
Rouss, Wm.	33	Taylor, Samuel	56
Ross, James	120	Teague, Wm.	121
Robinson, Charles	33	Tredan, John	1497
Richardson, John—Black	136	Thornbaugh, Walter	196
Rogers, Edward	424	Turner, Roger	190
Richey, Wm.	130	Thompson, Neil	55
Ryley, Patrick	135	Thompson, Exrs.	150
Rankins, Barbara	60	Turner, Anthony	228
Reid, Wm.	264	Tidwell, Wm.	150
Richardson, Daniel	195	Teator, George	103
Rogers, Wm.	55	Thomas, Nathaniel	183
Robins, Joseph	61	Thomas, Lewis	80
Rankins, Hugh	65	**V**	
Rogers, Catherine	23	Vance, David	155

Vickers, Elisha	45	Brot Over	51827
Vanmetre, Isaac & Henry &c.	100	White, John Junr.	90
Vanmetre, Isaac	43	Wilson, Thomas	96
Vance, Joseph	150	Worthington & Others	93
Vanderpoole, Abra.	342	Welch, James	145
Vanmetre, Isaac & Jacob	15	Waters, Thomas	76
Vickory, Luke	5	Wilcox, John	184
W		Worthington & Others	43
Welton, John	130	Woodfin, John	80
Watkins, Evan	40	Wright, James	150
Worthington & Thomas	20	Williams, John	65
Worthington, Jacob & Others	43	Williams, Joseph	260
Walker, John	156	Warth, Robert	65
Wilson, John	250	Williams, Wm. Revd.	496
Westfoll, Jacob	80	Waring & Son	745
Williams, Edmund	70	**Y**	
Walker, Saml.	170	Yates, Abraham	177
Worthington & Matthews	10	**Z**	
Williams, Vincent	65	Zeigler, George	75
Wanton, John	200		
Winslow, Richd.	60		54767
Worthington, Robt.	881	Buchanan, Robt.	55
Wood, John	5	Griffith, Wm.	96
White, George	211	Shippin, Edward	100
Welton, John Junr.	23		
Carried Over	51827		55018

16th January, 1744-5.

I have Received of James Wood the above Clk's Notes Amounting to fifty-five Thousand & Eighteen pounds of Tobacco wch. I promise to Collect & * * * * account for to the said James Wood * * * * According to Law.

THOS. RUTHERFORD, *Sher. F. C.*

FREDERICK FEES FOR ANNO 1757

Andersons, Exrs.	410	Buckley, Jno.	100	
Alford, Jno.	50	Blackburn, Sam. & Andw.	335	
Abbot, Richd.	100	Burns, Wm.	330	
Allen, Jackson	65	Bryan, Jno.	71	1652
Abut, Jno.	101			
Blackmore, Eus.	90			

Buckley, Abm.	200			Cade, Charles	60	
Burden, Jno.	205			Circle, Andw.	150	
Babb, Pet.	217			Cartmill, Nathaniel	144	
Buck, Tho.	110			Clapham, Joseph	25	938
Burney, Robt.	23					
Boshier, Jno. Adm.	100			Castleman, Wm.	73	
do.	11			Culbertson, Andw.	150	
Bowman, Geo.	225			Cutbeard, Benj.	23	
Bruce, James	106			Chapman, Richard	46	
Blackburn, Wm.	30			Carrot, W.	150	
Bradford, Pet.	23			Chester, D.	40	
Bullock, Tho.	93	1355		do. for his wife	23	
				Coyl, Wm.	50	
Bethell, Jane	140			Clark, Wm.	25	
Brown, James	55			Crisman, Jacob	165	
Bentley, Jno.	65			Conway, Tho.	55	
Bacchus, Pet.	40			Chinowith, Jno.	25	
Boyl, James	264			Conway, James	50	875
Bodken, Lewis	25					
Buckles, Robt.	25			Cooper, Jacob	50	
Boyd, Sam.	65			Connalley, Tho.	86	
Burno, Lem.	55			Carrot, Ann	20	
Berrey, Benj.	119	853		Calvert, Richd.	100	
				Crist, Nicho.	15	
Broughton, Edwd.	50			Duckworth, Wm.	85	
Broughton, Wm.	50			Dawson, Isaac	125	
Brubaker, Abraham	155			Dosker, Tho.	96	
Blair, James	78			Duckworth, Sarah	290	
Buck & McKay, Exrs.	60			Dondal, Mich.	55	
Caton, Tho.	1075			Davis, Wm.	15	937
do. for Meek	25					
Calmes, Margt.	65			s d		
Cockran, Wm.	139			Ewing, Wm.—10:9	340	
Campbell, Andw.	299			Earle, Baylis	88	
Carter, James Jun.	169			Eanney, Geo.	55	
Cromley, James	300	2395		Ellmer, Jno.	50	
				Ellis, Jno.	20	
		6255		Emery, Geo.	25	
Calmes, Wm.	91			Enochs, Hen.	180	
Castleman, Lodo	25			Earle, James	130	
Combes, Jos.	140			Evans, Robt.	75	
do. for Bowen	95			Fitzpatrick, Chas.	25	
Collaghan, Jane	110			Funk, Jno. Capt.	53	1041
Counts, Jno.	75					
Carrot, Jos.	23				10046	

Fife, Jno.	10		Hand, Ph.	15	
Friend, Jonah	85		Hyland, Henry	101	
Funk, Jacob	45		Hougham, Jarvis	220	2399
Forbes, David	155				
Funk, Martin	30			15196	
Fowler, James	196		s d		
do. for Howell	65		Hoge, George—2. 6	40	
Farthingale, Geo.	85		Hames, Mercey	300	
Funkhouser, Jacob	65		Handley, Murtey	201	
do. for his wife	40	776	Harden, Exs.	135	
			Helm, W.	419	
Fox, Hugh	50		Hite, Isaac	30	
French, Ams.	55		Hardin, Jno. Jun.	35	
Fry, Abm. for Ino. Price	90		Hoge, James	10	
Gibson, Jacob	25		Harper, Mich.	180	
Gess, Moses	20		Hagard, W.	110	
Grigsbey, Jno.	23		Harrison, Tho.	53	
Gilleland, Hugh	50		Helm, Tho.	78	1591
Gordon, Exs.	94				
Glenn, Jno.	150		Hobbs, Jos.	25	
Green, W.	70		Hylicks, Geo.	55	
Gess, W.	80		Harrey, W.	73	
Goldsberry, T.	25		Hartley, Jno.	15	
Grub, B.	165	897	Hagan, Jams.	15	
			Harper, Robt. & B. Pearson	130	
do. and wife	15		Hoge, James Jun.	196	
Getgood, Dav.	40		Johnson, D.	93	
Gillam, W.	50		Jones, John	15	
Glass, Jos.	25		Jolliffe, Wm.	30	
Graafe & Panse	40		Jones, James	50	697
Helm, Loo	396				
do. for Waller	103		Jackson, Hugh	78	
do. for Lina Helm, etc.	65		Jones & Pearson	25	
Hayes, Jno.	35		Kelley, W.	55	
Higgons, Tho.	213		Kelley, Mich.	75	
Handshaw, Nicho.	76	1068	Keltner, Exs	180	
			Kennady, Dan.	135	
Helms, Adm.	1202		King, Jno.	45	
Hankins, W.	40		Kemp, Exs.	70	
Hedge, Jonas	190		Keys, Hump	125	
Hardin, Jno.	221		Knight, James	50	838
Heavenrich, Jno.	86				
Helmsworth, Zeb.	218		Lemmon, Jam.	1689	
Hue, Abm.	83		for Tostee	313	
Hart, Tho.	23		Lemon, Tho. Exrs.	75	
			Lemon, Robt. Adm.	40	

do.	75			Marr, Chris.	40	
Lindsey & Exrs.	298			Myre, Ulrick	40	
Lindsey, Jno. Etc.	35			Nicewanger, Mary	115	
Lindsey, Jno.	530			Netherton, Hen.	15	
Londermilch, Jacob	40			Noble, W.	200	
Low, Tho.	445			Opp, Fred	100	
Lewis, Jno.	35			Ott, Jasp.	50	
Long, Henry	45	3620		Odell, Jerem.	58	
				Oyler, Adolph	230	
		21942		Pemberton, Isaiah	40	
Littleton, Charles	35			do. for Geo.	35	973
Lindsay, Ch.	50					
Langdon &c.	150				26950	
Lupton, Jos. &c.	50			Pattison, W.	25	
Leadsom, Tho.	101			Province, Jno.	45	
McDowell, Cap. &c.	90			Paul, Robt. for		
McDaniel, Pat	248			Andw.	85	
Madden, Jno.	277			Pike, Mick. Gt.	70	
McGee, W.	110	1111		do. Adm.	40	
				Pritchard Reese	150	
Morgan, Morg.	276			Pritchard, Samuel	30	
McGuire, Tho.	140			for Jno. Jones	235	
McMachen, W.	68			do. and Barger	50	
McMachen, R.	25			Princebar, Nicho.	100	
McCormack, Jno.	23			Potts, Israel	205	
Mayer, Ulrick &c.	40			Poor, Ann	140	1175
Morgan, R.	120					
McKay, R.	84			Purcell, Dan.	80	
Murphey, Hugh	76			Prince, Jno.	113	
Milbourn, Robt.	50			Pearson, Benj.	116	
Moore, Lewis	426			Paxton, Reu.	15	
do. for Caldwell	130			Pritchard, Pet.	25	
do. Exrs.	310	1759		Perkley, Jacob	10	
				Rogers & Sutton	70	
McGill, Jams.	685			Rutherford, Benj.	111	
McNeal, Jams.	15			Roberts, Jos.	140	
Mealey, And.	25			Redd, Geo.	115	
Mercer, Richd.	65			Roark, Tim.	75	
Miller, W.	190			Ruffner, Pet.	115	985
Miller, H.	35					
Madden, Bridg.	55			Reynolds, W.	190	
Morgan, W.	45			Rout, Pet.	55	
McCracken, Jams.	25			Read, Edw.	45	
Murfey, Darb.	70			Roberts & Helm	111	
Moore, Hen.	55	1265		Ridgway, Josiah	35	
				Richey, W.	30	
Marr, Jno.	50			Rout, Jno.	23	

Robinson, Edw.	93		Shandler, Step.	60	
Roberts, W. Jnr.	78		Stephenson, Rich.	10	
Robinson, W.	90		Stephens, Pet.	25	
Russell & Jardain	40		Shepard, W.	135	
Ruddle, Jno.	75		Spears, Hen.	45	
Reyley, Mary	40		Southard, Step.	15	
Ramey, Dan.	45	599	Shults, God	25	
			Thrasher, R.	65	
Rice, Simeon	135		Thomas, Ellis	45	
Ramey, Ph.	123		Trespaugh, Mart.	66	516
Ruddle, Arch.	45				
Reagan, Rach.	140		Teague, Eliz.	10	
Roberts, W. Sen.	140		Thompson, W.	186	
Smith, Jerem.	221		Thompson, Jos.	100	
Stephens, Law	240		Tipton, Jno.	190	
do. for Jno. Cole	91	1397	Thomas, Nath.	15	
			Vance & Stevens	35	
		31106	Vanmeter, Ab.	300	
Savier, Wm.	60		Vanmeter, Hen.	300	
Swearingen, Van	170		Vance, Etc.	55	
do.	25		Wadlinton, Tho.	85	1276
Smith, Jno.	473				
Scholl & Newman	50				36034
Stewart, W.	150		Wood, Jno.	479	
Scholl, W.	70		Willis, Tho.	40	
Selser, Mathias &c.	10		Worthington, Rob.	768	
Shearer, Jno.	90		Withers, Ralph &c.	35	
Snigers, Ed.	359		do.	175	
Steal, James	189		Wilson, Mary	23	
Sturman, R.	570	2216	Williams, W.	335	
			Wilson, W.	150	
do. for Nealons	48		Wilson, Jams.	35	
Smith, W.	15		Wright, Jno.	175	
Simms, Jno.	30		Williams, Hen.	96	
Speake, Jno.	170		Wade, Geo.	25	
Smith, Geo.	81		Whites, Adm.	25	
Snap, Jno.	50		White, Dav.	25	
Snodgrass, J. & D.	150		Wale, Tho.	15	
Snap, Law.	150		Watson, W.	94	
Shoop, W.	21		Wagoner, Fred	65	
Swearingen, Tho. Jun.	35		Wood, Wm.	23	
Swearingen, Tho. for Shepd.	70		Younge, Goodm.	130	
do.	100	920	Youner, Jacob	55	
			Miller, Wm. on Shenando.	23	
Stewart, Jno.	25		McGuire, Thomas	71	
			Crist, Nicholas	15	

do.	15		39256 & 13/3
Strain, Wm.	54	Cr. by a mistake	12
McGill, James	190		
Townsend, Jacob	86		39244 & 13/3

Received from James Wood, Clerk of Frederick County the within Clerks' notes amounting to Thirty-nine Thousand Two Hundred and Forty-four and 13/3 Pounds of Tobacco to collect and account for according to Law this 16th day of January, 1758.

Teste:
    Jacob Hite   JOHN HARDIN, *Sheriff*.
    T. Rutherford

Frederick

The County	50	James Fowler	60
Thomas Bullock	120	Philips Fitzpatrick	60X
Thomas Caton	490	Joshua Baker	100
John and Jacob Hite	230	Mr. Williams Cocks	150
Murty Hanley	80	Robert Stewart	230
James Hoge	340	William Calmees	70
Thomas Singleton	40X	Mr. John Hardin	430
Mr. Lewis Stephens	670	Mr. Jacob Hite	280
Thomas Caton &c.	20	George Right	185
Mr. William Williams	40	Patrick McDonald	180
Samuel Stanesby	120X	William Richey	70X
Nathaniel Curry	60	Charles Busch	190
John Greenfield	410	Henry Brinker	530
Henry Heath	400	George Michael Lawtinger	40
Francis Silburn	40		
William Porterfield	110		
John Funk	70	Carried Over	6860
Andrew Vance, &c.	70		
Jost Hite	80	Brought Over	6860
Jost Hite & Robert McCoy	215	Thomas Wood	165
		William Cocks & Benj. Grubb	30
John Harding jun.	50	John Leith	10
Henry Moore MacAtree	20	Joseph Walcomott	40
Mr. Gersham Keyes	290	Stephen Rawlings	220
Richard Sturman	40	Mr. James Wood	360
Joseph Parrell	20	John McCormack	40
James Wood & Others	40	Thomas Wood &c.	120
Mr. James Keith	80	Henry Enoch	380
The Right Honble. Lord Fairfax	70	Robert Green	120
Alexander Woodrow	20	Charles Smith	60

Jacob Funk	20	Noah Hampton	30
William Duckworth	110	Taliaferro Stribling & others	70
Jacob Taylor	100	William Ewing	15
Joseph Combs	160	Isaac Dawson & Wm. Cherry	40
Samuel Baldwin	150	William Jolliffe and Benjamin Thornbury	40
Edward Sniggars	150	Mary Wright	40
John Reynolds	80	Godfrey Humbert	40
George House	170	Elizah Isaacs	40
Ann Helm & others	40	John Cary & James Keith	40
Ladowick Castleman	220	Hugh Lyle and Francis Silburn	40
Samuel Pritchard	60	Mary Engle & Henry Loyd	40
Nicholas Schrack	125	Jonathan Langdon	40
John Hardin for Dyre	20	Mary Wood	40
John Smith	20	William McKee	40
Mr. Alexander Woodrow	220	Joseph Thompson	40
John Stewart	120	Thomas Swearingen	40
William Hughes	80	Ann Margaret Mesmore	40
William Hornsby	10	John Daugharty	40
John Hardin for Campbell & wife	50	Eleanor Dwinney	40
Thomas York	60	Samuel Boyd	40
Woolrick Folk	20	Joseph & John Cohill	40
Taliaferro Stribling	40	Simon Carson	40
Mr. Thomas Bryan Martin	40	John Wagener	40
Peter Woolf	40	Margaret Purnell	40
Jacob Chandler	80	Mary & James Loudoun	40
John Greenfield, Thomas Lemon and others	340	Joseph Beeler	40
John O'Neal	60	Simon Taylor	40
Robert O'Neal	40	John Neavil	40
John Lindsey	60	Elizabeth Waters	40
Van Swearingen	50	Jane Baker	40
Thomas Gardner	20	Thomas Sharpe	40
Bastine Frederick	130	George Hollingsworth	40
		Rose Gest	40
Carried Over	11090		
		Carried Over	12865
Brought Over	11090		
Robert Harper & Samuel Stillwell	70	Brought Over	12865
Henry Rinker	90	Katherine Duncan	40
Peter Ruth Smith	70	Elizabeth Matthews	40
Henry Vanmelon	40	Sarah Milbourn	40
Peter Casey	60	Sarah Daugherty	40
Robert Warth	60		
Thomas Lemon	30		

Elizabeth Ramey	40	Samuel Boyd	20
George Sandman	40	John Bowman	100
Elizabeth Johnston	40	Isaac Perkins	770
Henry Loyd	40	Robert Allen	40
Mary Moore	40	David and William Rankin	40
Anne Ulrich	40	Mr. Lewis Neill	20
Sarah Moore	40	William Neill	80
Anne Springer	40	Benjamin Thornburg	240
Elizabeth Morris	40		
Elizabeth White	40		14775
Eve and Henry Wetzell	40		

17th January 1761 Received of the Honble. Mr. Secretary Nelson, by the hand of James Wood, the ticketts according to the above list, amounting to Fourteen Thousand Seven Hundred and Seventy Five Pounds of Tobacco, to collect and account for according to Law. Witness my hand,

VAN SWEARINGEN.

Frederick

The County	100	The Right Honble. Thos. Lord Fairfax	80
Lewis Neill	385	Thomas Swearingen	55
Mary Nisewanger	70	James Lemon	290
Samuel Earle	20	Lewis Neill, &c.	100
Samuel Earle and others	20	Henry Brinker	80
Leonard Helm	210	Elizabeth Paris	90
Susanna Oneil	210	John Cox	50
William Potter	190	John Ashby for Howard	120
Robert Paris	270	Moses Teague	100
Samuel Earle and others	20	John Hardin	420
Joseph Beeler	60	Gersham Keyes	920
William Williams	450	Charles Buck, &c.	20
Melcor Engle	280	John Hardin for Dyre	40
Daniel Murfey	130	Thomas Caton	120
John Madden	110	Thomas Caton, &c.	40
Richard Sturman and Others	150	Carried Over	7340
Nicholas Shrach	150	Brot Over	7340
Andrew Campbell	745	Robert Worthington	140
Peter Lehan	60	Jacob Hite	30
Thomas Millsaps	130	John Murray	80
Henry Heath	450	John Ashby	40
Lewis Stephens	255	Thos. Bryan Martin	40
Colo. James Wood	90	Benjamin Grubbs &c.	70
Robert Paris & others	80	Robert Lemon	90
James Briscoe	130	Aron Jenkins	50
James Cromlie	50		

Hezekiah Clarke	100	Thomas Lemon	160
William Calmees	90	Adam Stephen	110
Thomas Gold, &c.	50	John Greenfield	120
Thomas Wood & others	50	John Hardin	795
Rees Pritchard	60	Robert Harper &c.	110
Thomas Singleton	70	John Lindsey	70
Edward Thomas	40	Noah Hampton	20
Ruth Patton	40	Lewis Stephens	270
William Cocks	40	Bryan Bruin	140
Elizabeth Blackmore	40	Robert Crawford &c.	70
James Gilliland	40	Robert Crawford	70
Christian Nealey	40	Joseph Combs	200
John Boshier	40	William Duckworth	130
John Shearer	40	Robert Steward	30
Van Swearingen	40	William Fowler	70
Elizabeth & Henry Kelhenner	40	Godfrey Hubbard	170
Sarah Duckworth	40	Murty Handley, &c.	50
Elizabeth Peters	40	William Jolliffe	170
Ann Divinney, &c.	40	James Keith &c.	110
Richard Hasebrigg, &c.	40	Robert Parish &c.	140
Richd. Sturman	40	Benjamin Setton	220
Christian Grass, &c.	40	William McMahon	120
Mary Reyley	40	Lewis Stephens & ad.	70
Thomas Lemon	40	Thomas Helm &c.	20
Lewis Moore	40	Taliaferro Stribling & ad.	60
Joseph Lupton, &c.	40	George Wright	190
Isaiah Pemberton	40	William Ramsey &c.	360
Elizabeth Gordon	40	Michael Pyke	60
Frances Ewick	40	Joseph Dark	70
Peter Bacchus	40	John Funk	240
John Price	40	Alexander Woodrow	150
Wm. Robinson	40	Henry Rinker	150
Michael Pyke	40	John Gladin	70
John Crump	20		
			6465
	9400		
Frederick		Brought Over	6465
The County	400	Henry Brinker	50
Thomas Caton	560	James McKay	320
Gersham Keyes	170	John Hurst	50
George Michael Lawbinger	60	William Hurst	50
Patrick McDonnell	40	John McCormick	140
Thomas Bullock	150	Thomas Wood &c.	40
The Adm. of John Maddin Decd.	20	Edward Sniggars & ad.	50
		Samuel Pritchard	70
		John Barnaby Reedy	130
		Thomas Smith	170

Andrew Campbell	100	William Jenkins	40	
Adam Stephen & ad.	65	Edward McGuire	90	
Thomas Cresap &c.	30	Alexander McDonald	90	
Andrew Nance, &c.	150	Isaac Pearce	100	
John Hardin for O'Neal	20	John Stuart	110	
Jost Hite	20	John Ashby	30	
Jost Hite &c.	135	Edward Snickers	90	
Samuel Stainsby Welder	40	Thomas Speake	50	
William Hughes	100	James Craik for Wharton	260	
Thomas Wood	130	William Whitson &c.	90	
Henry Heath	350	Hezekiah Clarke	20	
Charles Buck	355	George Hollingsworth	20	
George Bounds	100	George Hollingsworth & ad.	20	
Lewis Neill	230	Daniel Bush	50	
Thomas Wood & ad.	40	Murty Handley	240	
Woolrick Folk	20	Thomas Hillard, &c.	40	
John Daugherty	100	John Hite & ad.	40	
William Cocks	130	Jane Ruble	40	
Thomas York	10	Catherine Lemen	40	
Thomas Bryan Martin	100	Mary Buff	40	
Thomas Caton &c.	60	Eleanor Archer	40	
John Hardin, Jun.	30	Eleanor & Evan Rogers	40	
James Hoge	200	Robert Worthington	150	
Jacob Hite	280	Jacob Chandler	60	
Isaac Perkins	70	Peter Woolf	20	
Thomas Lord Fairfax	160		13,520	
James Fowler	60	Brought Over	13,350	
John O'Neal	150	Henry Moore, &c.	80	
William Neill	120	Stephens Rawlins	60	
	10,790	Ebreheart Dearing	40	
Brought Over	10,790	Alexander Woodrow & ad.	160	
Bastine Frederick	20	Robert Allen	60	
Philip Fitzpatrick	20	Robert O'Neal	20	
Archibald Wager	200	James Wood & Vestrymen of Frederick	60	
John Funk, &c.	40	George Hollingsworth & ad.	40	
William Meldrum	40	Godfrey Humbert	40	
Richard Morgan	40	Richard Paris	40	
Charles Buck &c.	40	Van Swearingen	40	
William Bailey	30	Robert Tassey	30	
Joseph Beeler	350	Robert Harper	40	
Benjamin Blackburn & ad.	70	Evan Shelburne	10	
Matthias Bush	70		14,240	
Nathanial Curry	70			
Lawrence Harrison	70			
Joseph Jones	70			

2d. January, 1762, Received of Mr. Secretary Nelson by the hand of James Wood the ticketts according to the above list amounting to Fourteen Thousand two Hundred and Forty Pounds of Tobacco to collect and account for according to Law.

THOS. CATON.

Teste:
John Flayton (?)

List of Arranged Officers belonging to the Virginia Line, who are at Winchester and Fort Pitt, whose subsistence for the months of January, February, and March, 1783, is proposed to be drawn by Colonel Wood; exclusive of those with the Southern Army.

(The names of officers are in the handwriting of Colonel Wood, the list of figures, in a different handwriting.)

		1st. REGIMENT	PAY	P. M.	SUB.
Colonel		James Wood	75	32	96
Lt. Colo.		Samuel Hawes	60	24	72
Captains		Wm. Johnston	40	12	36
		John Stith	40	12	36
		Tho. Edmunds	40	12	36
		Abm. Kirkpartick	40	12	36
		John Anderson	40	12	36
		James Williams	40	12	36
		Robert Woodson	40	12	36
Lieutenants		Thomas Martin	26 2/3	8	24
56 2/3		Charles Stockley P. M.	26 2/3	8	24
		Tho. Coverley	26 2/3	8	24
		Samuel Baskerville	26 2/3	8	24
		John Hackley	26 2/3	8	24
		John Harrison	26 2/3	8	24
		Albert Russell	26 2/3	8	24
		Tho. Miller	26 2/3	8	24
39 2/3		Wm. Eskridge, Adj.	26 2/3	8	24
		Jacob Brown	26 2/3	8	24
		James Delaplane, Supposed to have Recd. his Subsistence.			
		Geo. A. Washington	26 2/3	8	24

	John Heth	26 2/3	8	24
	Edmd. Clark	26 2/3	8	24
Surgeon	Cornelius Baldwin	59	16	48
	2d. REGIMENT			
Captain	Samuel Booker	40	12	46
Lieutenants	Richard Claiborne	26 2/3	8	24
	John Drew	26 2/3	8	24
	Elias Langham	26 2/3	8	24
	Wm. Whitaker	26 2/3	8	24
		967 1/3		912

A LIST OF MEN DRAUGHTED FROM HAMPSHIRE COUNTY
(Handwriting Unknown)

The Men Draughted   *The Substitutes*

David Mitchel ——— Thos. Morgan ——— entered with Col. Wood
Abraham Westfall .⎫
Charles Myers ——⎪
William Clark ———⎪   Sick.
Abraham Gum ——⎬ ———————————— On Furlow and to be
Jas. Blackburn ——⎪   in Winchester by the
Philip Switser ——⎪   20th day of March.
Wm. Largent ———⎪
David Allen ————⎭

Thomas Gaff ——— David Gamble
John Rennalds ——— Adam Lancester

John Vanbuskirk ——— Isaac Vanbuskirk
Wm. Fitzgerald ——— Wm. Price   ⎫ Marched with Capt.
Wm. Barber Lewis ——— Jacob Creamer ⎬ Vance.
Peter Timmons
Patrick Lynch ——— Jas. McDow ——— Deserted.
Peter Ashby ——— John Brown   ⎫ Deserters taken.
Edward Williams ——— John Stagg ⎭
Joel Chesser ————————————— On Furlow and to be
George Hersman ——— Danl. Kent ——— at Winchester 24th of
                                                   March.
John Hour
John Homan
Michael Follar
Cornelius Westfall ———⎫
Wm. Engle —————⎪
Thos. Hartly —————⎪
James Conrad ————⎪
James Baker —————⎬ ———————————— Never appeared.
John Rogers —————⎪
Evan Jenkins ————⎪
Richd. Brown ————⎪
Wm. Jane ——————⎪
Saml. Harrison ————⎭

The following list of the papers of Colonel James Wood is taken from Catalogue No. 727, compiled by Stan. V. Henkels at the Book Auction Rooms of Thos. Birch's Sons, 1110 Chestnut Street, Philadelphia, Pa., 1894. Not included in the catalogue are twenty-seven letters of Thomas Jefferson, twenty-four of James Hamilton, twenty of General Burgoyne, exchanges of prisoners, lists of soldiers, etc., one hundred and eighty-three in all.

These were taken from the collection not long after the death of Miss Julia Wood with the consent of the late Colonel William Wood Glass by the late Judge Robert Wood Dailey. They were sold by his daughter during the summer of 1926 to a financier of international fame.

(A. L. S. Autograph letter signed.)

THE PAPERS OF COLONEL JAMES WOOD, OF VIRGINIA, DURING THE REVOLUTIONARY WAR, RELATING MOSTLY TO THE ENGLISH AND HESSIAN PRISONERS CAPTURED AT SARATOGA, YORK AND GLOUCESTER

416 Anderson, Richard C. Distinguished Colonel in the Revolutionary War. A. L. S. Goldmine, December 31, 1799.

417 Armand, Charles, Marquis de la Rouarie. Celebrated French Brigadier-General in the Revolutionary War. A. L. S. (in English). Folio. Staunton, September 21, 1782. To Colonel Wood. With address.
Fine specimen. Rare.

418 Armand, Charles, Marquis de la Rouarie. A. L. S. (in English). Folio. No place, no date. To Colonel Wood. With address.
Fine specimen. Letters of General Armand, in English, are very scarce.

419 Bland, Theodoric. Member of the Congress and Colonel in the Revolution. Gained the confidence of Washington. A. L. S. 4to. 4 pages. November 2, 1779.
   Instructions to Colonel Francis Taylor in regard to the Convention Troops.

420 Bradford, Samuel K. Officer in the Revolutionary War, Aide to General Weedon. A. L. S. 4to. Fredericksburg, December 8, 1782.
   Mentions his appointment as aide-de-camp to General Weedon.

421 Bullitt, Thomas. Officer in the French and Indian War; served under Washington; founder of Louisville, Kentucky. A. L. S. Folio. Dumfries, March 21, 1775. Very rare.

422 Bullitt, Thomas. A. L. S. Small 4to. September 3, 1775.

423 Burnet, J. Major in the Revolutionary War, distinguished in the Southern campaign, Aide to General Greene. A. L. S. Folio. October 10, 1782. To General Muhlenberg. With address.

424 Cary, Archibald. Distinguished Revolutionary patriot and statesman of Virginia. A. L. S. 4to. 2 pages. March 19, 1780. To Colonel James Wood. With address.

425 Crockett, Joseph. Distinguished Colonel in the Revolutionary War. A. L. S. Folio. Fredericktown, New Year, 1781.

426 Crockett, Joseph. A. D. S. (Court-martial). Folio. 2 pages. Albemarle Barracks, November 3, 1780.

427 Crockett, Joseph. A. D. S. Folio. August 9, (1780) and July 28, 1780. 2 pieces.

428 Crockett, Joseph. D. S. Folio. Various dates. Court-martial held at Albemarle Barracks. 6 pieces.

429 Davies, William. Distinguished Colonel in the Revolutionary War. A. L. S. 4to. War Office, January 11, 1782, and D. S., small 4to. 2 pieces.

430 Davies, William. A. L. S. Folio. War Office, December 3, 1782. To General Muhlenberg.

431 Dinwiddie, Robert. Colonial Governor of Virginia. A. D. S. Small 4to. Frederick County, October 17, 1753.

432 Fauquier, Francis. Colonial Governor of Virginia. Parchment D. S. Folio. May 22, 1762.
   Commission of George Weedon as lieutenant in the Virginia Regiment.

433 Fauquier, Francis. D. S. Folio. Williamsburg, October 1, 1758.

Commission of William Woodford as lieutenant in the First Virginia Regiment under command of George Washington.

434 Gates, Horatio. Major-General in the Revolutionary War. A. L. S. 4to. 2 pages. April 3, 1783. To Colonel James Wood. With address.

"America is surely too honorable to be unjust to a brave Body of men, who after Eight Years Toil and Hazard have Established her freedom and independence."

435 Gist, Christopher. Colonel. Accompanied Washington on Braddock's Expedition. A. D. S. Small 4to. November 11, 1752. *Rare.*

436 Gibson, John. Distinguished general in the Revolutionary War. A. L. S. Folio. 2 pages. Fort Pitt, January 6, 1783.

437 Gooch, William. Colonial Governor of Virginia. Parchment D. S. Folio. January 12, 1746.

438 Gooch, William. D. S. Folio. March 15, 1744.

439 Greene, Nathaniel. Major-General in the Revolutionary War. A. L. S. Folio. "Camp before 96, June 15, 1781." To Colonel James Wood. With address.

440 Hamilton, James. Brigadier-General in the British army during the Revolutionary War, and captured at Saratoga. A. L. S. 4to. 2 pages. March 23, 1780. To Colonel Taylor.

441 Hamilton, James. A. L. S. 4to. 2 pages. April 6, 1780. To Colonel Wood.

442. Hamilton, James. A. L. S. Folio. 2 pages. May 13, 1780.

443 Hamilton, James. A. L. S. 4to. 2 pages. Charlotteville, May 13, 1780. To Colonel Taylor.

444 Hamilton, James. A. L. S. 4to. 2 pages. Barracks, June 3, 1780. To Colonel Wood.

445 Hamilton, James. A. L. S. 4to. 3 pages. June 13 (1780).

446 Hamilton, James. A. L. S. 4to. 3 pages. June 25, 1780. To Colonel James Wood.

447 Hamilton, James. A. L. S. Folio. Charlotteville, September 28, 1780. To Colonel John Harris.

448 Hamilton, James. A. L. S. Folio. Leonard's Farm, January 18, 1781. To Colonel Wood.

449 Hamilton, James. A. L. S. Folio. Frederickstown, February 24, 1781. To Colonel Wood.

450 Hamilton, James. A. L. S. Folio. Frederickstown, March 31, 1781. To Colonel Wood.
451 Hamilton, James. A. L. S. Folio. Leonard's Farm. April 13, 1781. To Colonel Wood.
452 Hamilton, James. A. L. S. Folio. May 26 (1780). To Colonel Wood.
453 Hamilton, James. A. D. S. 4to. October 10, 1780.
General orders, October 10, 1780.
454 Hamilton, James. D. S. Folio. Being muster-rolls denoting the state of the Convention Troops in Virginia, signed by General Hamilton and dated May 21, October 29, and November 19, 1780; February 1 and 24, 1781. 5 pieces.
455 Harman, Josiah. Lieutenant-Colonel in the Revolutionary War. D. S. Folio. Headquarters, Ashby Hall, September 13, 1782.
General Greene's orders to the Pennsylvania, Maryland, Delaware, Virginia, North and South Carolina, and Georgia lines, in reference to who shall remain in service to command the troops of each State.
456 Harrison, Benjamin. Signer of the Declaration of Independence. D. S. 4to. November 12, 1782.
457 Harvie, John. Member of the Old Congress and Colonel in the Revolutionary War. A. L. S. 4to. 3 pages. March 9, 1780. To Colonel James Wood.
458 Heister, Daniel. Member of the first House of Representatives. A. L. S. Frederickstown, June 11, 1781. To Colonel James Wood.
459 Heth, William. Officer in the Revolutionary War. A. L. S. 4to. 3 pages. Philadelphia, June 8, 1784. To "Brigadier-General James Wood."
459½ Innis, James. Colonel in the Revolutionary War. A. L. S. Folio. Williamsburg, March 15, 1780.
460 Irvine, William. Brigadier-General in the Revolutionary War. A. L. S. Folio. Yorktown, August 15, 1781. To Colonel James Wood. With franked address.
461 Jackson, William. Officer in the Revolutionary War. D. S. Folio. 1782.
Arrangement of the First Virginia Regiment.
462 Jefferson, Thomas. Signer of the Declaration of Independence and author of that instrument, and Governor of Virginia. A. L. S. Folio. Richmond, May 13, 1780.
Mentions General Washington in reference to the exchange of some of the Convention Troops.
463 Jefferson, Thomas. A. L. S. Folio. 2 pages. Richmond, May 17, 1780. *Fine specimen.*

464 Jefferson, Thomas. A. L. S. 4to. Richmond, January 12, 1781.
465 Jefferson, Thomas. A. L. S. 4to. Richmond, February 15, 1781.
"I have just received information from General Greene that Lord Cornwallis, maddened by his losses at the Cowpens and Georgetown, has burnt his own waggons to enable himself to move with facility, and has pressed forward as far as the Moravian towns, General Greene being obliged to retire before him with an inferior force. We are endeavoring to gather a force around him, from which I hope he will not escape."
Fine specimen.
466 Jefferson, Thomas. A. L. S. 4to. Richmond, February 13, 1781.
467 Jefferson, Thomas. L. S. 4to. Richmond, February 18, 1781.
In reference to the rapid approach of Lord Cornwallis and his army, and ordering the removal of the Convention Troops to a place of safety.
468 Jefferson, Thomas. L. S., folio. Richmond, July 28, 1780; December 15, 1780 and February 3, 1781, and D. S., folio, May 19, 1780. 4 pieces.
469 Lafayette, Gilbert Motier, Marquis de. Celebrated French General in the Revolutionary War. L. S. Folio. Wilderness, June 4, 1781. To Colonel Wood.
Ordering the removal of the Convention Troops to the Eastern States.
470 Lee, Thomas Sim. Member of the Old Congress. A. L. S. Folio. Annapolis, April 10, 1781.
471 Lee, Thomas Sim. A. L. S. Folio. Annapolis, December 21, 1780. To Colonel James Wood.
472 Lincoln, Benjamin. General in the Revolutionary War, and received the submission of the captured troops at Yorktown. A. D. S. Folio. 4 pages. April 26, 1782.
A system on which provisions are to be issued.
473 Lincoln, Benjamin. L. S. Folio. May 6, 1783. To General Muhlenberg. With address.
474 Lyne, G. Officer in the Revolution. A. L. S. Folio. Philadelphia, May 14, 1777. To Colonel James Wood.
"£25 have I given for one suit of clothes made out of indifferent stuff, my coat is blue turned up with white."
475 Mulligan, James. Comptroller of the Treasury during the Revolutionary War. A. L. S., 4to, Philadelphia, June 19, 1781 *(mentions General Washington)*, and A. L. S., 4to, Philadelphia, June 19, 1781. 2 pieces.

476 Monro, George. Distinguished surgeon during the Revolutionary War. A. L. S. 4to. 2 pages. Camp Ashly Hill, South Carolina, November 7, 1782. To General Muhlenberg.
477 Morgan, Daniel. Brigadier-General in the Revolutionary War. A. D. S. Small 4to. March 3, 1780.
Military passport.
478 Morris, Robert. Signer of the Declaration of Independence. L. S. 4to. January 10, 1783.
479 Muhlenberg, Peter. Brigadier-General in the Revolutionary War. D. S. 4to. May, 1783.
480 Nelson, Thomas. Signer of the Declaration of Independence. A. D. S. 4to. October 25, 1744.
481 Nevill, Presly. Officer in the Revolutionary War. A. L. S. Folio. Winchester, January 6, 1783.
482 Nicholas, Robert Carter. 'Revolutionary patriot. D. S. Small 4to. March 2, 1752.
483 Parker, William. Colonel of a Virginia regiment in the Revolutionary War. A. L. S. 4to. North Castle, October 1, 1778.
484 Peters, Richard. Member of the Old Congress. A. L. S. 4to. October 19, 1781. To Colonel James Wood.
485 Peters, Richard. A. L. S. Folio. September 20, 1781. To Colonel James Wood.
486 Reed, Joseph. Member of the Old Congress and Brigadier-General in the Revolutionary War. L. S. Folio. Philadelphia, July 16, 1781.
487 Rawlings, Moses. Distinguished Colonel in the Revolutionary War. A. L. S. Folio. Fredericktown, March 15, 1782.
488 Rawlings, J. W. Colonel in the Revolutionary War. A. L. S. Folio. 2 pages. Fort Frederick, May 24, 1781.
489 Stoddard, Benjamin. Secretary of the Navy and Secretary of War during the Revolution. A. L. S. 4to. September 19, 1780.
490 Stoddard, Benjamin. A. L. S. 4to. 2 pages. June 20, 1780. To Colonel James Wood. With address.
491 Walker, John. Member of the Old Congress and Aide to Washington. A. L. S. Folio. Belvoir, March 6, 1780.
492 Walker, John. A. L. S. 4to. Philadelphia, June 18, 1780.
"*The enemy are still inactive at Elizabeth Town, but the extreme weakness of General Washington leads us to fear they will not long remain so. The People of this country are roused to more than Roman Exertions. They are recruiting and feeding the army at their private expense; should this glorious example extend itself and become general, America will be invincible, but these are trying times.*"

493 Washington, George. First President of the United States and Commander-in-Chief of the American Army during the Revolution. L. S. and autograph postscript of six lines, signed with initials. Folio. West Point, September 19, 1778. To Colonel Wood. With address.

494 Washington, George A. Distinguished officer in the Revolutionary War. A. L. S. Folio. Fredericksburg, December 24. (N. Y.)

495 Washington, Lawrence A. A. L. S., 4to, Rich. Wood November 2, 1801; October 7, 1822, and folio, September 14, 1805. 3 pieces.

496 Weedon, George. Brigadier-General in the Revolutionary War. A. L. S. 4to. Fredericksburg, February 16, 1784. To Colonel James Wood. With address.

497 Weir, John. Distinguished British Surgeon in the Revolutionary War, captured at Saratoga. A. L. S., 4to, June 4, 1778, and D. S., folio. 2 pieces.

498 White, Alexander. Member of the Old Congress. A. L. S. Folio. Winchester, July 17, 1775.

499 White, Alexander. A. L. S. 4to. 2 pages. Richmond, November 14, 1783.

500 White, Alexander. A. L. S. 4to. 2 pages. Richmond, November 22, 1783.

501 White, Alexander. A. L. S. Folio. Woodville, January 3, 1784.

502 White, Alexander. A. L. S. 4to. 2 pages. Richmond, June 20, 1788.

503 White, Alexander. A. L. S. Folio. Richmond, November 5, 1788.

504 White, Alexander. A. L. S. 4to. 3 pages. Philadelphia, December 15, 1788.

505 White, Alexander. A. L. S. 4to. 2 pages. New York, March 8, 1789.

506 White, Alexander. A. L. S. 4to. New York, May 15, 1790.

507 White, Alexander. A. L. S. 4to. March 26, 1791.

508 White, Alexander. A. L. S. Folio (part of signature gone.). Philadelphia, January 19, 1791.

509 British Officers Captured at Saratoga. The Parole of the officers of the British army exchanged, regarding the route to be taken from Virginia to New York, in the handwriting of Colonel James Wood, and signed by thirty British officers. Folio. March 8, 1781.

HESSIAN OFFICERS CAPTURED AT SARATOGA

510 Cleve, H. U. Lieutenant and Aide-de-camp to Riedesel. L. S. 4to. 2 pages. Barracks, March 31, 1780.

511 Cleve, H. U. L. S. 4to. 3 pages. Barracks, April 4, 1780.

512 Gall, Ludwig Frederick von. Brigadier-General. L. S. Folio. "Stantown," March 24, 1789.
   Asking permission to send for the clothes belonging to his regiment, "on board the flag of truce lately arrived at Richmond."

513 Hoijer, William. Lieutenant and Quartermaster of General Riedesel's Regiment. A. L. S. 4to. 2 pages. Barracks, March 25, 1780.

514 Meibom, Charles de. Lieutenant. D. S. 4to. October 9, 1780.
   Signed also by Lieutenant Charles de Lindau.

515 Mengen, ——— de. Lieutenant-Colonel. A. L. S. 4to. Barracks, February 21, 1781.

516 Mengen, ——— de. A. L. S. 4to. 3 pages. Winchester, May 1, 1781.

517 Rhenius, P. W. L. Lieutenant of a Brunswick Regiment of Light Infantry. A. D. S. 4to. Lancaster, June 26, 1781.
   Names of the officers and servants of the regiment of Light Infantry of the Brunswick Troops, which included Lieutenant Cruse, Lieutenant Glade, Lieutenant Rohr, Lieutenant Rhenius and Surgeon Kunze.

518 Riedesel, Friedrich Adolph. Major-General. L. S. Folio. Brooklyn, March 19, 1781.
   Returning thanks to Colonel James Wood for his generous conduct towards the Brunswick Troops of the Convention.

519 Specht, J. W. Brigadier-General. D. S. Folio. Irvin's House, November 17, 1780.
   Return of the officers and persons belonging to Brigadier-General Specht's family, which included Brigade Captain Cleve, Aide-de-camp Lieutenant de Burgsdorff, Judge Advocate General Zincken, Surgeon Bause and Clerk Dehn.

520 Specht, J. W. L. S. 4to. November 27, 1780.

521 Specht, J. W. L. S. 4to. 2 pages. Irvin's House, August 13, 1780.
   Presenting Mrs. Colonel Wood with two bottles of wine.

522 Specht, J. W. L. S. 4to. 2 pages. Staunton, March 8, 1780. To Colonel James Wood.
   Expressing his pleasure at receiving the information that Colonel James Wood was to take command of the Convention Troops.

523 Stain, Carl von. Captain A. D. S. Folio. Winchester, August 20, 1780.
524 Unger, John de. Adjutant and Lieutenant of the Regiment de Rheiz D. S. 4to. Charlottesville, April 6, 1780. *Parole.*
525 Bose, Lieutenant-General Carl von. "Muster-roll of the Present Prisoners of War from the Hessian Regiment de Bose, now at Post of Fredericks Town, March 16, 1782." Folio. 3 pages. Signed by Major Friedrich Henry Scheer.

This highly important muster-roll contains the names of one hundred and ninety-seven officers and privates belonging to the Hessian regiment, commanded by Lieutenant General Carl von Bose, captured at Saratoga.

526 Riedesel, Major-General Friedrich Adolph. Return of the servants belonging to the officers of Major-General Riedesel's Regiment, Brunswick Troops. Folio. 3 pages. Lancaster, June 25, 1781. Signed by Captain Harbord.
527 Muster-roll of the Present Prisoners of the Hereditary German Prince's Regiment, at the Post of Frederickstown, March 16, 1782. Signed by Captain J. H. C. Gebhard.

This important document contains the names of two hundred and seventy-eight officers, privates, etc., in this celebrated regiment, which included Major-General Hachenberg's Company, Colonel de Cochenhausen's Company, Colonel de Tuck's Company, Major Waldenberg's Company, Artillery Detachment and the Company du Corps.

528 Return of the officers and servants from the regiment and artillery of Hesse Hanau. Lancaster, February 26, 1781. Written and signed by Lieutenant-Colonel Lentz. Folio. 2 pages.

Contains the names of sixty-two officers and servants.

529 List of servants belonging to various Hessian officers captured at Saratoga. Folio. 2 pages.
530 Return of clothing lost by the Fourth Virginia Regiment, in the action of the 28th of June, 1778. Signed by Lieutenant-Colonel John Nevill and Paymaster William Baylis. 4to.
531 Savage, Joseph. Surgeon in the American Army during the Revolutionary War. A. L. S. Folio. 2 pages. Frederick County, December 22, 1782. To Colonel James Wood. With address.
532 List of British officers and their servants. (Captured at Saratoga). Frederick Town, April 6, 1781. Signed and written by Major M. P. Kidkman. Folio. 4 pages.

Contains the names of forty-eight British officers and one hundred and fourteen servants.

533 General list of the Detachment of the Royal Artillery, 6th of April, 1781. Folio.

534 Hamilton, James. Brigadier-General British Army, captured at Saratoga. D. S. Folio. November 18, 1780.
   The parole signed by Brigadier-General Hamilton and staff, and other officers of the Convention on their removal from the state of Virginia to Maryland. Contains one hundred and twenty-four signatures of British officers.

535 "List of arranged officers belonging to the Virginia line (First Virginia Regiment), who are at Winchester and Fort Pitt, whose subsistence for the month of January, February, March, 1783, is proposed to be drawn by Colonel Wood." 4to. 2 pages. In the handwriting of Colonel James Wood.

536 Autograph remarks on the nature of the evidence which may be necessary on the behalf of the Commonwealth of Virginia against Henderson and Company's claim to that tract of land and territory, which they pretend to have purchased from the Cherokee Indians and call Transilvania. Folio. 4 pages; and remarks on the nature of the evidence which may be necessary on behalf of the Commonwealth of Virginia against the Indiana Company and George Croghan, Esq., who claim large tracts of land in the neighborhood of Fort Pitt, by a purchase and deed from the Six Nations, made at Fort Stanwix in the year 1768. Folio. 2 pages.
   Two very interesting contemporary documents.

537 Certificates for the exchange of prisoners of the Virginia line for those of the British. Signed by Robert Cooke, Deputy Commissioneer of Prisoners, dated October 23, 1782. 4 pieces

538 Albemarle Barracks, Virginia. Returns of Colonel Taylor's and Lieutenant-Colonel Joseph Crockett's Regiments of the Guards, dated from April to November, 1780.
   These were the regiments appointed to guard the British and Hessian prisoners taken at Saratoga.

539 Paroles given and signed by various British officers, prisoners of war, taken at Saratoga, mostly occasioned by their transfer from Virginia to Maryland. In the handwriting of Colonel James Wood. Dated from March 24, 1780, to February 24, 1781. Folios and 4tos. 12 pieces.

540 Lists of British prisoners of war, captured at Saratoga, York and Gloucester, confined in the barracks at Albemarle, Winchester and Lancaster, 1780-1782; provision returns, regimental returns, muster-rolls, etc. 50 pieces.
   A very important lot of papers.

541 British officers, prisoners of war of the Convention Troops. Autograph letters of various British officers, mostly addressed to Colonel James Wood, etc. 19 pieces.
   Good lot.

542 Courts-martial held at Albemarle Barracks, Winchester and Charlottesville, Virginia; mostly for the trial of Continental soldiers for offences against the Convention prisoners of war, 1780-1782. 7 pieces.
Highly interesting lot.

543 Letters of officers and other participants in the Revolutionary War, mostly to Colonel James Wood; contemporary copies of the Revolutions of Congress, etc. 40 pieces.
All these letters and documents are dated during the Revolution.

544 Letters of Virginia officers written during the Revolutionary War, mostly to Colonel James Wood and General Muhlenberg; relating to military promotions and affairs of importance. 33 pieces.
Highly important and interesting lot.

545 Provisions and clothing returns of the Continental Army at Albemarle, Winchester, etc., 1780-1783. 65 pieces.

546 Broadside. Proposals for publishing by subscription a map of the interior parts of North America. By Thomas Hutchins, Lieutenant in his Majesty's Royal American Regiments and engineer. Folio. No date.

547 Wood, James. Celebrated Colonel in the Revolutionary War; commanded the British and Hessian prisoners, captured at Saratoga, etc. A. L. S. 4to. 2 pages. Richmond, July 2, 1786. To Alexander White. With address.

548 Wood, James. A. L. S. 4to. Richmond, July 25, 1787. To Robert Wood. With address.

549 Wood, James. Thirty-five autograph letters, signed. Folios and 4tos. From September 29, 1777, to May 22, 1801; mostly addressed to his brother, Robert Wood. 35 pieces.

550 Wood, James. Autograph drafts of letters and documents. Folios and 4tos. 41 pieces.

551 Confederate paper money, broken bank bills and Confederate stamp. 13 pieces.

551½ Wood, J. Father of Colonel James Wood. Manuscript dairy kept during the years 1749 to 1754. 12mo.
Contains a short, but very interesting account of Colonel George Washington's expedition from Fort Necessity, for the purpose of attacking the French fort; his retreat back to Fort Necessity, etc.

CHAPTER XXVIII

Winchester, England — The Cathedral City and Ancient Capital of England — Situated Amidst the Beautiful Scenery of the Itchen Valley in the Heart of the Sporting County of Hampshire

"There is no spot in all England better worth study, or more compact with historic associations."—E. A. Freeman.

Winchester, England, is a city of noble mien, and worthy of her distinguished ancestry.

The old area comprised 138 acres within the city walls.

The population taken at the census in 1921 was 23,791.

The city is set on a hill sloping to the east, on the main line of the Southern Railway, between Southampton and London, and sixty-three miles from the great metropolis.

As in the case of Winchester, Virginia, an old map hanging in the Library on High Street gives much data in a condensed form, and a copy of these facts is given here:

THE EAST PROSPECT OF THE CITY OF WINCHESTER

This city stands pleasantly on ye beautiful banks of ye river Itchin and contains about a mile and a half within ye walls, besides ye suburbs; 'twas ye famous city of British Belgae, by Ptolomy and Antoninus call'd Ventae Belgarum, ye Britains to this day Caer-Gwent, ye Saxons Wintancester. The Roman Emperors seem to have had at this place their Imperial weaving shops, where ye Cloaths for ye Emperors; & ye Army as well as Sails for their Ships, Linnen and other necessary furniture, for their houses were wove. Here liv'd that Constans ye Monk, who was first made Caesar & afterwards

Emperor by his father Constantine, & who usurp'd ye Government in opposition to Honorius. In ye Heptarchy 'twas ye seat of ye West Saxon Kings, & their burial place. K. Cenowalch (after ye Convent of ye Roman age was destroy'd) built here A. D. 643 a church very splendid for those times, on ye site whereof Walkelin made Bishop A. D. 1073 erected a Cathedral after ye same model (tho much more stately as Malmesbury observes) & arch'd it with stone. His Successors, contributed to its beauty & magnificence; particularly William de Edington & William de Wickham, who built ye West part of ye Church from ye Choir, as Bishop Fox did ye East end from ye Tower to ye High Altar. 'Twas commended to ye patronage of several, viz. St. Peter, St. Swithin and lastly of ye Holy Trinity; There were also in former days other religious Houses here viz. ye Benedictine Nunnery built A. D. 900 by Alswitha consort to K. Alfred, dedicated to St. Edburg An. Val. 179:7:2 Edwd. ye elder pursuant to his father K. Alfred's will founded a College of secular Canons here which was call'd ye New Minster, but they were removed to Hide. Adam Martin erected a Monastery to ye honour of St. James. John de Pontissar Bishop of the See, founded A. D. 1301 a College for a Provest, 6 Priests and 6 Clerks which was dedicated to St. Eliz an. Val. 112:17:4 ob. William of Wickham before mention'd established A. D. 1387 a College to ye Honour of ye V. Mary consisting of a Warden, 10 Fellows, 1 School master 1 Usher and 70 Scholars 3 Chaplains 3 Clerks 1 Orgenist 16 Choiristers & ye Statutable Servants. Hon. Beaufort Bishop here, half brother to Hen. IV, founded an Alms House within ye precincts of St. Crosses; but he dying before it was established; K. Henry VI incorporated the Members therein under a Rector of their own: By the name of the New Alms House of Noble Poverty; establish'd near Winchester by Hen. Cardinal of England & Bishop of Winchester, son of John late Duke of Lancaster An. Val. £84:4:2. This City sends two Burgesses to Parliament who are Paulet St. John & George Bridges, Esqrs.

(Saml. & Nath. Buck delin. et Sculpt. according to Act of Parliament 1736.)

(Names of the physical features of the map).

1. St. Cross Hospital
2. Navigable River from Southampton
3. Black Bridge
4. Rumsey Road
5. The College
6. The Bishop's Palace
7. Remains of Wolsey Palace
8. St. Michael's Church
9. St. Peter's Church in ye Soke
10. South Gate
11. The Cathedral
12. Bowling Green
13. St. James's burying Ground
14. The King's Palace
15. St. Thomas's Church
16. East Gate
17. St. John's House
18. The Hospital for Clergymen's widows
19. St. Alaunen's Church
20. St. Laurence's Church
21. The County Hall

22. West Gate
23. Lainston
24. Stockbridge Road
25. The North Gate
26. Bowling Green
27. Hide House
28. St. Bartholomew's Church
29. St. John's Church in ye Soke."

(Soke, sac (the legal term), A,-S., and Early Eng. law. Lit., a seeking; hence, either a right of inquiry of hearing and determining, or a duty of seeking or suing in a certain court or the right of exacting such suit. Webster's Unabridged.)

Winchester, as it exists today, in its general plan of the older streets situate within the line of the ancient walls, is almost identical with what it was when the Roman cohorts were here stationed. The High Street was the "Principia."

Winchester was the British, Celtic, Roman, Saxon, Danish, and Norman Capital and the Empire owes much to its influence.

The Saxons at their coming to Winchester forsook their nomadic life, and welcomed the security afforded by the Roman walls.

The Danes, rather than suffer delay, hurried past the strong wall of Winchester; but later on, after a long siege, the city was sacked by the Danes, though not entirely destroyed.

King Ethelred was here married to Emma Elgiva, "the Fair Maid of Normandy" in 1002, and gave her the city of Winchester for her dowry.

King Canute, who married Emma, the widow of King Ethelred, made Winchester his capital, and he and his queen were buried in the Cathedral. Queen Emma was thus the wife of two kings and the mother of two kings, Hardicanute, also buried in the Cathedral, and Edward the Confessor.

In 1340 the Black Death visited the city. In 1363 Winchester lost its wool trade, in 1580 its wine trade, and soon after the manufacture of kerseys and broad-cloths languished, being crippled by the restrictions of the Merchant Guilds. The taking of Winchester Castle by Waller also greatly reduced the importance and prosperity of the city.

The two oldest houses in Winchester are: Old Chesil Rectory, bearing date 1450, and situate in the Soke, outside the East Gate of the city; and "Goodbiete" or "Godbegot" House in High street, of about the same date. The ground on which stands "Godbegot" was given to the Cathedral monastery by Queen Emma, wife of Ethelred and mother of Edward the Confessor, who afterwards married King Canute.

"Ye Olde Hostel" takes its name from Aelfric surnamed Godebegeata or Goodsgetter, its owner in the 10th century. His little manor of half-an-acre or so in Winchester High Street was acquired by Queen Emma and confirmed to her free of all burdens by her husband Ethelred in 1012. Emma bequeathed it to S. Swithun's Monastery in 1052, and her son, Edward the Confessor and his successors on the throne of England secured the prior and monks by many royal charters in its possession. Like the liberty of White Friars in London, the Manor became a sanctuary for criminals and fugitives. It held its own courts, presided over by the steward of the Monastery, until the dissolution under Henry VIII. Then it lost its privileges, but the Dean and Chapter remained owners of several properties in the estate, including Ye Olde Hostel, until 1866. The present building dates from 1558, and was restored by Miss Pamplin in 1908.

The Cathedral of Winchester has witnessed the passage into eternity of many centuries. Already the present church has stood "twice as long as the great Jewish temple of old," and "it is a very moving thing to be able to look back eight hundred years and think of those who have trodden these self-same floors and looked on these massive walls."

A. D. 169. There stood on a portion of the site of the present Minister an early British Church, and the position of its baptistry may be indicated by the ancient well in the Norman crypt.

226. This British Church was transformed into a pagan temple during the Roman occupation.

293. A second Christian Church was erected during the reign of the Emperor Constantine, whose son was for a time a monk in the adjoining monastery.

In 639, Kenwale's Church was built on the site of the early Roman Church, hallowed by Bp. Birinus.

825-60. This Church was enlarged by St. Swithun; and was restored by King Alfred the Great and St. Ethelwold after raids by the Danes.

In 980, King Ethelred was present at the dedication of St. Ethelwold's Cathedral on October 20, by St. Dunstan, besides Bishop Ethelwold, seven other bishops, and nearly every duke, abbot, and noble of England.

Twenty kings of the royal line are buried here, and thirty-five made Winchester their capital.

The present structure (consecrated July 15th, 1093) was at that time the largest, as it is now the longest, Cathedral in Europe with the exception of St. Peter's at Rome.

No church in England is so rich in monuments, with the single exception of Westminster Abbey. The elaborate and magnificent chantry chapels are unrivalled in their way.

The dimensions of the Cathedral at present are: Extreme length, W. to E. 556 feet, 6 inches; extreme breadth at Transepts, 217 feet; of Nave, 250 feet; width of each Transept, 86 feet; height to roof ridge, 109 feet; Tower, height of, 138 feet; Tower, width of, 50 feet.

The Chantries within the Cathedral are some of the finest in the kingdom. Among them, built in 1404 is that of Bishop William of Wykeham. It is situated in the Nave, and was built by Wykeham himself on that part of the Cathedral where, when a boy at school, he loved to pray.

Inscription on Wykeham's Tomb

William surnamed Wykeham lies here overthrown by death;
He was the Bishop of this church and the repairer of it.
He was unbounded in his hospitality, as the poor
and the rich can equally prove.
And was likewise a sage politician and counsellor of the state.
His piety is manifest by the colleges which he founded:
The first of which is at Oxford, the second at Winchester.
You who look upon this monument, cease not to pray.
That for such great deserts, he may enjoy eternal life.

William of Wykeham, Bishop of Winchester for thirty-seven years (1367-1404), took his name from Wickham, near Fareham, Hants, was born in 1324, and died in 1404. He was educated at Southwick and at the Grammar School, Winchester, and though his education was not entirely scholastic or narrowly ecclesiastical, there was no doubt that he could read Latin and French as well as Wycliffe himself. By his energy, graces of person, and good manners, he gained the favour of Bishop Edyndon, who gave him the oversight of the rebuilding of the west end of Winchester Cathedral. At the age of twenty-two his capabilities brought him to the notice of Edward III, when he visited this city, who at once made Wykeham surveyor of the royal works at

Queenborough, Windsor, etc. His pay was one shilling per day. He was ordained priest in 1362, and consecrated Bishop of Winchester in 1367. For six years (1364-1370) he was chief minister to Edward III, and was an executor to the will of Edward the Black Prince. His opposition to the King's mistress, Alice Perrers, caused his banishment from court, and the sequestration of his revenues was ordered upon charges of malversation brought against him by the anti-clerical party. By Richard II he was exonerated from all these charges, and was appointed a member of the Commission of Regency and reinstated as Chancellor in 1389; but he resigned office at the age of seventy. As one of the early founders of colleges he prepared the way for the New Learning which was to give such predominance to the English language. In his buildings he adopted the Perpendicular style.

At this time, when seventy years of age, he undertook the wonderful task of transforming the Norman nave into Perpendicular Gothic. In early life he had conceived the design of his colleges at Oxford and Winchester, and its execution occupied him more than twenty years. He also restored at his own cost a large number of churches and parsonages, and repaired the main road between London and Southampton, rebuilding many bridges.

His income as Bishop and Chancellor must have been equal to 60,000 ℔s. a year.

A prominent trait in Bishop William of Wykeham's character was the equable moderation shown by him under every change of fortune.

If Winchester Cathedral bears the mark of William of Wykeham's genius, and contains his tomb, Winchester College is his own peculiar monument.

The Charter of William of Wykeham, incorporating the College by the name of "Seinte Marie College of Wynchestre," is still kept in the College Muniment Room. It is dated at Southwark, 20 October, 6 Ric. II (A. D. 1382).

In Winchester, long before the Norman Conquest, there had been a grammar school, afterwards known as "The High School." Rudborne, in his history, states that King Ethelwolf and King Alfred were educated at this school.

Bishop William of Wykeham himself had been educated at the High School in Winchester. To promote the study of the Holy Scriptures and to send out into the world an educated clergy that so the "praise of God might be spread" was the object, which he placed in the forefront of his statutes; and the observance of the *curialis modus* was enjoined by his motto, "Manners Makyth Man."

Universal testimony leaves no doubt that "Wykehamists retain in after life a closer sense of brotherhood than do men from other public schools."

Three of the seven bishops sent to the Tower of James II were Wykehamists: Thomas Ken; Turner, Bishop of Ely; and Lloyd, Bishop of St. Asaph.

There is a magnificent War Memorial Cloister to the five hundred Wykehamists who fell in the Great War.

The following is the Thanksgiving for the Founder as at present used on commemoration days:

O ETERNAL GOD, the Life and the Resurrection of all that believe in Thee, always to be praised as well for the Dead as for those that be Alive, we give Thee most hearty thanks for our

FOUNDER, WILLIAM OF WYKEHAM, and all other our Benefactors, by whose Benefits we are here brought up to Godliness and the studies of good Learning * * * *.

Few of Wykeham's relics are kept in Winchester, the great bulk of them being in the custody of the Warden of New College at Oxford.

West's Picture of the "Raising of Lazarus," which stood above the holy table, was purchased in 1899 by Mr. Pierpont Morgan, who presented it to the Wadsworth Athenaeum, Hartford, Connecticut.

The Shrine of St. Swithun, tutor of King Alfred, stands in the Eastern aisle. The Shrine itself, a coffer of "plated silver, gilt and garnished with stones," was confiscated, together with the rest of the Cathedral's treasures in 1538, but some portions of the Purbeck marble base whereon it stood were discovered in 1922, and a theoretical reconstruction of the base was made.

The removal of St. Swithun's body to the inside of the church was said to have been delayed for forty days by continual rain; hence the rhyme:

> St. Swithun's day, if thou dost rain,
> For forty days it will remain;
> St. Swithun's day, if thou be faire,
> For forty days 'twill raine nae maire.

On 25th July, 1554, Philip of Spain was married in this Cathedral to Queen Mary. The queen wore a black dress flashing with gems, with a mantle of cloth of gold. The queen's ladies looked like "celestial angels." The king was presented with the keys of the city by the mayor; the 4,000 gentlemen who attended him must have been an imposing sight.

In 1070, William the Conqueror was re-crowned in the Cathedral by three Papal Legates.

In 1101, Henry I was married here to Queen Matilda.

In 1522, King Henry VIII and the Emperor Charles V came to this Cathedral and viewed St. Swithun's costly shrine. The king, who stayed a week in Winchester, re-dedicated this Cathedral to the Holy Trinity.

In 1570, Queen Elizabeth came in state from the Castle to the Cathedral, and also visited the College.

One of the injunctions of Edward VI was; "All maner of coristars of this said chirche shall from hensforthe suffer their crownes to growe and be no more shaven butt onely ther heare to be roundede and clypped short."

"The simple piety of the early brasses, the odd conceits of the Elizabethan elegiacs, the ponderous and fulsome prose of the eighteenth century, the strange medley of our own day, all are represented here."

(H. J. Hardy, M. A.)

West of the Cathedral is the Thomas Thetcher Tombstone:

In Memory of

THOMAS THETCHER

A Grenadier in the North Regt.
Of Hants Militia, who died of a
Violent Fever contracted by drinking
Small Beer when hot the 12th of May,
1764. Aged 26 Years.

In grateful remembrance of whose universal goodwill towards his Comrades, this Stone is placed here at their expence, as a small testimony of their regard, and concern.

> Here sleeps in peace a Hampshire Grenadier
> Who caught his death by drinking cold small Beer.
> Soldiers be wise from his untimely fall
> And when yere hot drink strong or none at all.

> This memorial being decay'd was restored by the Officers of the Garrison A. D. 1781.
>
>> An honest Soldier never is forgot
>> Whether he die by Musket or by Pot.
>
> This Stone was placed by the North Hants Militia when disembodied at Winchester on 26th April 1802 in consequence of the original Stone been destroyed.

Among interesting women buried in the Cathedral are Jane Austen and Mrs. Montagu.

Jane Austen has not only a Memorial Window beneath which she is buried, but a Monumental Brass in the North aisle, as well as a floor slab.

The window inscription is as follows:

> JANE AUSTEN
>
> known to many by her writings, endeared to her family by the varied charms of her Character, and enobled by Christian Faith and Piety, was born at Steventon in the county of Hants Dec. XVI, MDCCLXXV, and buried in this Cathedral July XXIV, MDCCCXVII
>
> "She openeth her mouth with wisdom and in her tongue is the law of kindness."

She was the daughter of Rev. George Austen, formerly Rector of Steventon.

Mrs. Montagu was an admirer of Shakespeare, and founder of the Blue Stocking Club, and the Chimney Sweepers' Friend. A friend of Dr. Johnson and of many literary and artistic celebrities, the "feather-room" at her house in Portman Square, London, is commemorated by William Cowper, the poet.

In the North aisle is found the curious inscription to the Two Brothers of Avington:

"A Union of Two Brothers from Avington. The Clerks' Family were Grandfather, Father, and Son, successively Clerks of the Privy Seal. William, the Grandfather, had but two Sons, both Thomas's, their wives both Amy's and their heirs both Henry's and the heirs of Henry's both Thomas's. Both their wives were inheritrixes, and both had two sons and one daughter, and both their daughters issueless. Both of Oxford, both of the Temple, both officers to Queen Elizabeth and our noble King James. Both Justices of the Peace, both agree in arms, the one a Knight, the other a Captain.

In the South Transept is the Tomb of IZAAK WALTON, "The Prince of Fisherman," author of The Compleat Angler, etc. (floor slab).

INSCRIPTION

Here resteth the body of

MR. IZAAK WALTON

Who died the 15th of December, 1683

Alas! Hee's gone before,
Gone, to return noe more,
 Our panting Breasts aspire
After their aged Sire,
 Whose well-spent life did last
Full ninety Years, and past.

But now he hath begun
That which will nere be done,
 Crown'd with eternal Blisse,
We wish our Souls with his."

Bishop Ken is said to have written this inscription. The Mortuary Chests—"a shelter for the bones of half-forgotten dynasties"—are placed over the side screens of the choir. Bishop Henry of Blois, who erected the former apsidal screens of the choir (1129-71), collected the bones of kings and saints who had been buried in the crypts, and placed them in wooden chests. Bishop Fox (1524) placed these bones in chests, inside two of which are more ancient chests. Two of the present chests date from the Restoration of 1661.

Among ancient epitaphs at Winchester College is the following: Edmund Hodson Clerk and Fellow of this College, died the 8th of August, 1580.

> Whoso thou art, with loving harte,
> Stande, read, and thinke on me,
> For as I was, so now thou art,
> And as I am, so shalt thou be.

On the Western wall of The School-room at Winchester College is an inscription with emblems:

Aut Disce.—A mitre and crosier, as the expected rewards of learning.
Aut Discede.—An inkhorn and sword, the emblems of the civil and military profession.
Manet Sors Tertia Caedi.—A rod.
A free translation—Learn, leave, or be licked.

Grocyn, the Grecian, headed College Roll in 1463. While still a schoolboy, a girl threw a snowball at him, which event Grocyn commemorated in Latin verse, of which the English is:

> My Julia smote me with a ball of snow;
> I thought that snow was cold; but 'tis not so,
> The fire you wakened, Julia, in my frame
> Not snow, nor ice can cool; but answering flame.

The judges, the sheriffs, and chief lawyers of the realm lodged in chambers in Winchester College, while they held their Court in the Great Hall of Winchester Castle for the trial of Sir Walter Raleigh, who was

"The Trusty Servant," Winchester:

A Piece of Antiquity, Painted on the Wall adjoining to the Kitchen of Winchester College.

A Trusty servant's portrait would you see, / This emblematic figure well survey;— / The porker's snout—not nice in diet shows; / The padlock shut—no secrets he'll disclose; / Patient the ass—his master's wrath to bear; / Swiftness in errand the stag's feet declare; / Loaded his left hand—apt to labour saith; / The vest—his neatness; open hand—his faith; / Girt with sword—his shield upon his arm / Himself and master he'll protect from harm.

condemned to death for high treason against James I, but subsequently reprieved. After his release from prison he sailed for the coast of Guiana, with fifteen armed ships on an unsuccessful search for gold. On his return, in 1616, the King, partly to please the Spaniards, ordered his execution.

In the Library of Winchester College there are some exceedingly rare manuscripts, the most valuable being the Vulgate (12th century) in three volumes, imperial folio, with splendid illuminations, and Bede's Ecclesiastical History (10th century).

There is also a Translation of the Bible into the Indian language, by John Eliot, 1663, printed in New England—the first Bible printed in America.

In the passage outside the kitchen at Winchester College is the curious picture of The Trusty Servant. The Latin words of its descriptive account are attributed to Dr. Christopher Jonson (Head Master, 1560-71).

Tradition says it was given to William of Wykeham by a German monk, as a portrait of a serving man at foundation of College, A. D. 1393. It must have been covered up with plaster, etc., for some years, as it was rediscovered, and an early scroll, preserved in the College archives, says 15s. was paid in 1560 for the repainting of the picture. The figure was dressed at this date in a buff-coloured jerkin. A picture of the figure in this dress is preserved in the archives of the College. It received its present Brunswick uniform in honour of a visit paid by George III in 1778. The painter was William Cave, of Winchester.

> Colour of Dress at the present time:
> Coat—blue (a greeny tinge of blue).
> Collar, cuffs, breeches—red.

Stockings—white.
Trimmings of coat—gold lace and buttons.
Strap round waist—leather, light coloured.
Shirt sleeves—white.
Broom, etc., for wood ashes not coal.

On June 27th, 1884, T. R. H. the Prince and Princess of Wales (King Edward VII and Queen Alexandra) visited the College. In his reply to a loyal address from the Senior Scholar, the Prince said: "The presence of the Lord Chancellor reminds me not only that William of Wykeham filled the same office, but also that no other School in England can boast of so many recent representatives on the woolsack."

The Great Hall of Winchester Castle, completed A. D. 1235, is a portion of the ancient Castle, which was one of the fortresses built by William the Conqueror, and the records of which show that it has been the scene of great and important events.

Hence Rufus started on that hunting expedition to the New Forest from which he never returned. He was hurriedly buried, without the services of the Church, under the Tower of Winchester Cathedral, "many looking on and few grieving." The fall of Walkelin's Tower at Winchester, A. D. 1107, was at the time regarded as a judgment for burying in a sacred precinct so profane a person as William Rufus.

The Hall was originally Norman, and was transformed into the Early English style of architecture by Henry III, and again (1380) altered by Richard II. In it the Parliaments of England sat for nearly 400 years. The King's commission has been executed there for upwards of six centuries: some of the most important laws have been passed, and some of the greatest trials heard in it, notably those of Sir Walter Raleigh and Lady Alice Lisle.

The especial treasure of the Great Hall at the present day is King Arthur's Round Table, which hangs on the wall.

The tradition of a round table was common to all Celtic nations. The earliest account we have of it is an order by the builder of the palace (about the time of Henry III—1253) to construct a wheel of fortune. A Round Table was usually established for the feasting of the knights and for encouragements of tournaments and military pastimes, and is said to have been the precursor of the Order of the Garter.

The earliest written authority for a Round Table is the Roman de Brut of Wace, the Norman (1155).

Caxton's Morte d'Arthur (1485) mentions this table as proof of the existence of King Arthur. History shows that it was considered as a curiosity in the time of Henry VII.

This table was repainted in the time of Henry VIII, and since then the same style has been repeated.

It has seats for King and 24 knights. Its diameter is 17 feet.

> And so great Arthur's seat old Winchester prefers,
> Whose Round Table yet she vaunteth to be hers.—*Drayton.*

The City Cross, 43 feet high, was erected during the reign of Henry VI, probably by Cardinal Beaufort. An earlier market cross originally occupied this site. The present Cross was repaired in 1835, and restored by Gilbert Scott in 1865. The principal figures are:

William of Wykeham, with the book of statutes of his College and Pastoral Staff;

Laurence de Anne, Mayor of Winchester.

King Alfred the Great.

St. John the Evangelist (the only old figure remaining).

In the top niches are eight figures, namely: SS. Thomas, Maurice, John, Peter, Laurence, Bartholomew, Swithun, and the Blessed Virgin.

The King Alfred Statue, near the Guildhall, stands about eighteen feet high, and the pose is easy and graceful. The right hand held aloft grasps the cross-hilted sword, the symbol of the Christianity which was to combat the power of heathenism. On the front of the bronze base is the inscription recording the name of the sculptor,

HAMO THORNYSCROFT, R. A.
Sc. 1900

whilst carved on the pedestal is the one word, eloquent in its simplicity—

AELFRED

The far-famed, and at one time wealthy, Hyde Abbey is reached from Hyde Street. It was built by King Henry I and Bishop William Giffard, in Hyde Mead, outside the north gate of the city, to replace the New Minster, which had been founded by King Alfred the Great inconveniently near to the Cathedral. The Abbot and monks took possession of their new buildings in Hyde Meads in 1110, and removed with them not only the relics of the saints, but the remains of King Alfred himself, and other illustrious dead. The Abbots of Hyde were afterwards honoured with a mitre, and a seat in Parliament as peers of the realm.

Outside the city gates northward was the Hospital of St. Mary Magdalene, originally founded for nine lepers by Bishop Toclyve in the twelfth century, now totally destroyed; and on the southern highway, beneath the British earthwork on St. Catherine's Hill, lay the charming Hospital of St. Cross, also founded in the twelfth century to provide doles of bread and beer for all wayfarers and pittances for one hundred dinners daily, besides a hospital for thirteen aged brothers.

The wayfarers' dole is still presented to every visitor.

The form of the Cross worn by the black-gowned Brothers (of Bishop Henry of Blois' Foundation, 1136 A. D.) is a cross potent, because its arms terminate in potents, the name anciently given to a crutch. It is also called a cross baton or Jerusalem cross, since it appears in the insignia of the Kingdom of Jerusalem established by the Crusaders.

The present West Gate on its western side is fourteenth century work, though probably during the Roman occupation a round archway, similar to the one existing at Lincoln, occupied the site. The footways on each side are modern. The openings above the outer Gate through which molten lead was poured on the besiegers, the arrow slits, and the grooves in which the portcullis worked should be noticed. The grotesque heads with large holes for mouths are said to be the openings through which the drawbridge chains were worked. The great ditch which ran along the western front of the Castle Walls was some yards away. The "cage" was at the foot of the steps leading to the chamber over the Gate, and here for centuries vagrants and night walkers were locked up by the city beadle. The South and West Gates were formerly kept in repair by the prior of St. Swithun's.

In 1591 the gate was shut at seven in the evening and opened at seven in the morning. In the chamber above the archway is the ancient city coffer of the sixteenth century with four locks; the standard bushel and weights of the time of Henry III, Edward III, Henry VII, Elizabeth, William III, and George I; and a warder's horn of Henry the Second's time.

A building on the north, where now stands "The Plume of Feathers," was the Porter's Lodge. In Queen Elizabeth's time it was a prison for freemen who offended the Mayor, and also for debtors. Often prisoners made their escape, and others died there from infectious diseases. In 1753 the room over the gate was let as a smoking room, but the "cage" or "little ease" was used until recent years for disorderly persons. The cheesemen up to 1794 held their fair near this gate.

Outside the gate there stood formerly the King's hawk house, a seagulls' house, and a spital for lepers. Queen Emma's palace was near by on the north side of High (Cyp or Cheap) Street, and not far from the outer gate were five bordelli or shantes, there put for the love of God wherein belated travellers might find night shelter.

* * * * * * * * * * *

Except for the ancient map of Winchester which was copied from the original, the outstanding features here recorded are quoted, compiled and adapted from the "Illustrated Guide to Winchester," by the late William Thorn Warren, Warren and Son, Ltd., as being the most reliable source available.

The attention of visitors especially is directed to that scholarly production.

Today interest seem to center in the Cathedral, the College and the visitors from all over the world. These represent religion, education and travel, the three chief elements of civilization, and constitute an ideal atmosphere.

* * * * * * * * * *

CONCLUSION

It augurs well that a scion of so noble a city as Winchester, England, should have founded her Virginia namesake. True it is that Winchester in the smiling Shenandoah Valley can boast no such stately monuments as those which have withstood the flight of centuries in the English city, but she has bared her sword in every American war since her foundation, and her contribution to the World War was of her choicest sons.

Inasmuch as she has worked in the spirit of William of Wykeham, whose life was devoted to the glory of God and to the uplift of his fellowmen, she has succeeded, and only in that spirit can she really progress, whatever may be her outward signs of prosperity.

Due to the inaccessibility or non-existence of accurate information, much is left incomplete as touching the lives of Colonel James Wood, father and son, and so as touching the beginnings of Winchester.

The subject is closed with regret, but with the hope that

> "In the hereafter angels may
> Roll the stone from its grave away."

INDEX

Acadians, The	78
Act Establishing Winchester	33
Adair, William	12
Adams, John	149, 248
Adams, Samuel	147
Addison, Joseph	98
Addresses	
Gov. Harry F. Byrd	151
Capt. Robt. Y. Conrad	60
Calvin Coolidge, The President	145
Miss Kate Innes Harris	133
Albemarle Barracks	165, 210
Albemarle, Earl of	85
Alexandra, Queen	424
Alexandria, Va.	63, 107
Alfred the Great	414, 417, 426
Allegheny Mountains	304
Allen, Ethan	137
Allerton, Willoughby	327
Ambler, Richard	341
Amherst, Sir Jeffrey	85, 107
Annapolis	189
Anderson, Robert	126
"Angerona"	91
Appleby School, England	326
Aquia Church	155, 159
Arbuckle, Mrs. Robert	56
Armstrong, James	248
"Arnold-Gray"	367
Arrangement, Va. Line 1780	241
Arr. First Va. Regt.	241
Atkinson, Mrs. Wm. M.	125
Atkinson, Rev. Wm. M., D.D.	124, 128
Austen, Rev. George	420
Austen, Jane	420
Avirett, Rev. James B.	91
"Bacon and Hale"	368
Baker, Rev. Joseph	91, 125
Baker, Mr. W. H.	56
Baker, Mrs. Wm. Hartman	126
Bainbridge, Ireland	365
Barnum, Mrs. Frances C. B.	56
Beckers, George	127, 128
Baird, Benjamin	114
Baird, Robert Wood	114
Baird, William	114
Baird, William N.	363
Baldwin, Dr. Robert	93
Baldwin, Dr. Stewart	93
Ball, Joseph	327
Ball, Mary	327
Ball, Samuel	334
Balmain, Rev. Alexander, D.D.	127, 128, 302, 355
Barbadoes	371
Barrett, Dr. Kate Waller	17, 93, 159
Barrett, Rev. Robert South	159
Barbour, James	16, 334
Barton, Col.	350
Barton, David Walker	103
Barton, Mrs. Eleanor Offutt	133
Barton, Lieut. Robert T.	55
Barton, Hon. Robert T.	103
Barton, Mrs. Robert T.	94
Baylis, Billy	251
Bath	287, 288, 290, 378
"Bedford"	380
Bedinger, Daniel	380
Bedinger, Hon. Henry	381
Bedinger, family	380
"Belvoir"	30
Bennet, William	347
Berkeley, Lord	31
Bethlehem, Camp near	255, 259
Beverley, England	325
Bible, John Eliot's	423
Bible, Vulgate	423
Billingsby, Francis	324
Bill of Rights	152
Bishop, Thomas	99
Blackburn, Col.	350
Blair, James	154
Bland, Theo.	248
"Bleak House"	39
Blue Coat School	102
Blue Ridge, The	18, 31, 41, 46, 129, 154
Board of Arrangement, Va. Line	140
Bonjedward	370
Boscawen, Admiral	62, 107
Boscawen Street	43
Bourke, John	334
Bourke, Martin	334
Boyd, Alexander	88
Boyd, Rev. A. H. H., D.D.	113, 124
Boy Scouts	55
Braddock, General Edward	61, 65, 70, 74
Braddock, Expedition	35, 47
Braddock Memorial	47
Braddock Monument	53
Brandywine, Battle of	139
Brannon, C. C.	359
Brown, Dr. Gustavus	155
Browning, J. W.	334
Browning, Robert	114
Bryan, Dennis	334

Buchanan, Miss Mary Spottiswoode ---------- 54, 55, 73, 75
Buena Vista, Battle of ------------ 74
Bullitt, Theo. ---------------------- 198
Buffalo, Mason Co. ---------------- 313
Bull, William --------------------- 126
Bumstead, Albert ------------------ 143
Bunker Hill, Battle of ------------ 137
Burden, Ben ---------------------- 334
Burgoyne, General ------ 139, 229, 399
Burke's, "Landed Gentry" --------- 369
Burns, Robert --------------------- 372
Bush, Philip ---------------------- 127
Butler, Caleb --------------------- 326
Butler, Jane ---------------------- 326
Byrd, Col. ------------------------- 16
Byrd, Gov. Harry Flood ------ 145, 151
Byrd Park ------------------------ 283
Byrd, Com. Richard Evelyn -------- 143
Byrd, Col. Wm. II ---------------- 159
Byrne, Thomas -------------------- 334

Caldwell, Andrew ------------------ 24
Callahan, Charles H. -------------- 327
Calmes, Marquis -------- 22, 24, 198, 32
Cameron Street ---------------- 43, 124
Camp before '96 ------------------ 192
Campbell, Andrew ------------------ 22
Campbell, John -------------------- 85
Campbell, Mrs. Mary B. ----------- 56
Campbell, Nannie R. -------------- 364
Canute, King --------------------- 412
"Caphon Rock" ---------- 287, 288, 289
C. A. R. ---------------------- 324, 327
Carkins, Jasse -------------------- 24
Carleton, Governor ---------------- 348
Carroll, Joseph ------------------- 39
Carson, Mrs. Adam C. ------------- 58
Carter, L. ------------------------ 341
Carter, Shirley ---------------- 52, 56
Cartmell, Thomas K. --------------
------------------- 12, 14, 40, 42, 166, 355
Catherine II ---------------------- 371
Cary, Archibald --------------- 134, 137
Casey, Miss. ---------------------- 91
Cassell, Mrs. J. F. F. ------------ 322
Cave, Benj. ------------------- 16, 324
Cave, William --------------------- 423
"Cedar Lawn" --------------------- 303
Century Club --------------------- 58
Chandlee, C. ---------------------- 26
Charlemagne ----------------------- 371
Charles I ------------------------- 138
Charles V, Emperor ---------------- 419
Charles Town, W. Va. ---- 298, 378, 281
Charlottesville, Va. ------- 139, 211, 261
Charter Members, Fort Loudoun Chapter, D. A. R. ------------- 95
Charter Members, L. A. W. Society C. A. R. ---------------------- 322

Chastellux ------------------------ 86
Chelsea --------------------------- 357
Chesterton, Gilbert K. ------------ 129
Chester, Thomas ------------------- 22
Chiesly, Agnes (Mrs. W.) --------- 374
Chew, Thomas ------------------ 16, 34
Christ Church --------------- 113, 127
"Churches of Old Va." ------------ 155
City Cross ----------------------- 425
Civic League ---------------------- 58
Clan Song of the Rutherfords ----- 369
Clark, Susan Peyton ---------- 92, 103
Clark, Judge William L. ------ 92, 124
Clement, Maj. W. T. -------------- 55
Clinton, George ------------------ 248
Clove ---------------------------- 350
Coat of Arms
  Queen Anne,
  I and II George ---------------- 115
Cohongoroota --------------------- 20
Cohongueroota -------------------- 46
Coldstream Guards ---------------- 62
Colepepper Grant ----------------- 30
Colepepper, Lady Catharine ------- 30
Coleridge, Samuel Taylor --------- 103
Coles, Isaac --------------------- 165
Colonial Convention -------------- 165
Colonial Dames at Braddock Celebration ------------------------ 56
Colonial and Revolutionary Winchester ------------------------ 119
Colorado River ------------------- 303
Conrad, Miss Bessie -------------- 55
Conrad, Dr. Daniel B. ------------ 74
Conrad, Mrs. Daniel B. ----------- 57
Conrad, David ------------------- 379
Conrad, David Holmes ------------ 42
Conrad, Capt. Robert Y. --- 49, 57, 58
Conrad, Mrs. Robert Y. ----------- 56
Constitutional Convention -------- 135
Convention Troops ---------------- 166
Coolidge, Calvin, The Pres. -- 145, 154
Cooper, Valentine ---------------- 357
Cornstalk ------------------------- 89
Cornwallis, Lord -------------- 51, 190
Counties
  Augusta ------------------------ 18
  Berkeley --------------- 50, 116, 287
  Clarke ------------------------- 50
  Cumberland --------------------- 147
  Down, Ireland ------------------ 365
  Frederick (See Frederick)
  Hardy -------------------------- 357
  Henrico ------------------------ 357
  Jefferson ---------------------- 50
  Morgan ------------------------- 50
  New Kent ----------------------- 99
  Orange 16, 18, 20, 115, 334, 336, 377
  Page --------------------------- 50
  Rutherford --------------------- 372

WINCHESTER, VIRGINIA, AND ITS BEGINNINGS 433

Shenandoah -- 50
Spotsylvania -- 17
Stafford -- 155
Warren -- 50
Westmoreland -- 326
Wood -- 136
Court of Enquiry -- 208, 209
Courts Martial -- 210, 213, 215
Cover, Mr. Thomas -- 56, 91
Cover, Mr. Loring A. -- 56
Cowper, William -- 421
Cox, Mrs. William Ruffin -- 76
Craighill, William N. -- 381
Craik, Dr. -- 70, 82, 343
Crawford, Mrs. C. Grattan -- 92
Crawford, Capt. -- 164
Crawford, Mrs. Frank B. -- 348
Crawford, Patrick -- 347
Crown Point -- 84
Crum, Mrs. Charles L. -- 93
Cumberland Valley Depot -- 87
Custis, Mrs. Martha Dandridge -- 51, 99, 107
Dailey, Benjamin -- 113
Dailey, Hon. Comfort Wood -- 113
Dailey Family -- 363
Dailey, Griffin -- 114
Dailey, James -- 113
Dailey, Jean Welsh -- 364
Dailey, Dr. Robert Wood -- 13
Dailey, Judge Robert Wood -- 399
Dailey, Dr. Thomas -- 368
Dailey, Thomas -- 114
Dandridge, Adam Stephen -- 54
Dandridge, Mrs. Danske B. -- 377
Dandridge, Serena K. (Violet) -- 381
Dandridge, Col. Wm. -- 54
D. A. R. -- 129
Dark, Maj. -- 252
Darke, Mary -- 381
Darke, Sarah de Montargis -- 381
Darke, Gen. William -- 378, 281
Darlington, John W. -- 93
Darley, Felix O. C. -- 82
Daubein (Daubigny) Joseph -- 397
David, the psalmist -- 144
Davidson, John -- 48
Davis, Dr. -- 379
Davis, Mrs. W. B. (Harriot Wood Glass) -- 364
Davis, William -- 367
Declaration of Independence -- 32, 153
Declaration of Rights -- 138
Deeds and Indentures, 336, 339, 341, 344, 345, 346, 347, 352.
Deed from Lord Fairfax -- 36
De Jumonville -- 48, 108
Detroit -- 372
Dickens, Charles -- 39
Dinwiddie, Governor -- 47, 48, 49, 50, 80, 82, 84
Dorsey, Col. Edward -- 367
Douglass, Adam -- 290
Duff, William -- 38
Dumfries -- 249
Dunbar, Joe -- 24
Dunbar, Col. Thomas -- 49, 50, 61
Dunmore, Lord -- 90, 133, 136, 137, 147, 162
Dunmore's War -- 89, 364
Dunn, Arthur -- 354
Du Quesne, Marquis -- 61
Dutch, Mess, The -- 126
DuVal, John P. -- 361
Dyer, James -- 334

East Riding -- 325
Ecclesiastical History, Bede's -- 423
Edict of Nantes -- 155
Edmonds, Mrs. Stuart H. -- 323
Edmonson, Nathan -- 368
Edward VII, King -- 424
Edward VI -- 419
Edward III -- 416
Edwards, Rev. William B. -- 43, 112
Edwards, Gov. William -- 162
Edynton, Bishop -- 415
Election of the First President -- 247
Elliott, Sir Gilbert -- 372
Elliott, Ellenor -- 372
Emerson, Ralph Waldo -- 51
Empire Theatre -- 94
Episcopal Church -- 43, 112, 140
Episcopal Female Institute -- 142
Erskine, Lady Margaret -- 371
Ethelred, King -- 414
Ethelwolf, King -- 417
Executive Council of Va. -- 136, 140

Fairfax's Addition -- 14
Fairfax, Thomas, Lord, 14, 17, 23, 24, 30, 32, 33, 37, 40, 42, 44, 45, 83, 127, 129, 325, 335.
Fairfax, Denny Martin -- 41
Fairfax, William -- 341
Fairnington -- 370, 371, 377
Farmer, Thomas -- 20
Fauquier, Gov. Francis -- 343
Field, Abraham -- 334
Finlason, John -- 334
First Newspaper -- 112
"Flowers and Weeds of the Old Dominion" -- 159
"Flowing Springs" -- 397
Fontaine, Col. Sydney Thurston -- 329
Fontaine, Mrs. Julia Washington -- 329
Ford's Writings -- 100, 161
Fort Cumberland -- 99, 304
Fort Du Quesne -- 50, 65, 78, 107

Fort Frederick _____ 218
Fort Loudoun _____
_____ 36, 54, 79, 81, 84, 91, 92, 97
Fort Loudoun Chapter, D. A. R. __ 93
Fort Loudoun Seminary _____ 55, 94
Fort Necessity _____ 35, 48, 89
Fort Pitt _____ 135, 137, 359
Fort Venango _____ 48
Fox, Bishop _____ 422
Franklin, Benjamin _____ 65, 85, 101
Fredericksburg _____ 16, 243, 298
Frederick County _____
13, 14, 18, 24, 26, 50, 79, 97, 107, 116
145, 324, 359, 377.
Frederick County, First Officers __ 116
Frederick Parish ___103, 112, 136, 140
Frederick Town _____ 24, 43
Frederick Town, Md. _____ 48, 49

Gage, Col. _____ 67
Gall, George _____ 326
Gallatin, Secretary _____ 360
Gamble, Cochran _____ 348
Gamble, Mary _____ 364
Garrison Orders _____ 198-207
  Brig. Smallwood, Maj. Adams,
  Maj. Kirkpatrick, Brig. Wayne,
  Maj. Stephenson, Major Minnis,
  Brig. Muhlenberg, Col. Williams,
  Maj. McCormack, Gen. Wayne,
  Col. Williams, Maj. Kirkpatrick,
  Gen. Wayne, Col. Humpton, Maj.
  Hitchcock, Brig. Muhlenberg, Col.
  Gaskins, Maj. McCormack, Brig.
  Wayne, Col. Gist, Maj. Minnis,
  Brig. Muhlenberg, Col. Nichols,
  Maj. Kirkpatrick, Brig. Muhlenberg, Col. Hawes, Maj. Porterfield,
  Brig. Smallwood, Maj. Massey,
  Maj. McCormack; Brig. Muhlenberg, Maj. Clark, Maj. Minnis;
  Brig. Smallwood, Maj. Grier,
  Major Minnis, Brig. Muhlenberg,
  Col. Hawes, Maj. McCormack,
  Brig. Smallwood, Col. Brant, Maj.
  Porterfield.
Gates, Horatio _____ 193
General Assembly ___ 105, 165, 275, 349
General List, Royal Artillery _____ 217
George I, King _____ 428
George II, King _____ 12, 14, 18, 74
George III, King _____ 136, 153
Gifford, Bishop William _____ 426
Gist, Christopher _____ 48
Glass, Belle Taylor _____ 365
Glass, Catherine or "Kitty" _____ 364
Glass, Elizabeth Rutherford _____ 358
Glass, Ella _____ 364
Glass Family _____ 364
Glass, Katherine R. _____ 52, 57

Glass, Louisa Bryarly _____ 365
Glass, Mary Louise _____ 365
Glass, Robert David _____ 365
Glass, Robert Jeremiah _____ 365
Glass, Dr. Robert McC. _____ 56
Glass, Robert Presley _____ 365
Glass, Samuel _____ 358, 365
Glass, Thomas _____ 364
Glass, William Wood, Jr. _____ 94
Glass, William Wood, Sr. _____
_____ 113, 364, 365, 399
Glen Burnie _____
__21, 26, 53, 112, 113, 315, 333, 365
Glen Burnie, Graves at _____ 365
Goare, Henry _____ 335
"Godbegot House" _____ 413
Goethe, J. W. Von _____ 128
Gold, Daniel _____ 348
Gooch, Gov. William _____ 19, 338
Graham, Rev. J. R., D. D., ____ 93, 128
Graham, Richard _____ 347
Grampus, Sloop of War _____ 341
Grant, Major _____ 89
Grantland, Gideon _____ 279
Graves of Revolutionary Heroes ___ 125
Gray, Robert L. _____ 52
Great Canaway _____ 347
Great Hall, Winchester Castle ____
_____ 422, 424, 425
Great Meadows _____ 35, 48, 71, 73
Greene, Col. _____ 341
Green, James, John, Moses, Robert
_____ 38, 324
Green, William _____ 24, 32
"Greenway Court" _____ 26, 30, 54, 83
Griffin, Sam _____ 248
Greene, Katherine Glass _____ 323
Griffith, Mrs. Richard E. _____ 56
Grim, Charles _____ 126
Grocyn, the Grecian _____ 422
Grosse, Hon. Roger _____ 367

Hack, Mrs. Annie R. _____ 56
Hagner, Mr. _____ 360
Haines, George W. _____ 52
Haines, G. Reginald _____ 53
Halket, Sir Peter _____ 49, 65
Halifax _____ 84
Hall, Benj. _____ 367
Hall, William Sprigg. _____ 368
Hamilton, David _____ 92
Hamilton, Eupham. _____ 374
Hamilton, Gov. _____ 49
Hamilton, James _____ 399
Hammond, Capt. John _____ 367
Hampton Roads _____ 49
Hancock, John _____ 247, 349
Hardicanute, King _____ 412
Hardin, John _____ 392
Hardin, Nancy _____ 803

Hardy, Lt. Charles	341
"Harewood"	303, 327
Harper, Robert	46
Harris, Kate Innes	133, 142, 145
Harrison, Carter Henry	147
Harrison, R. H.	248
Harrison, Burr	345, 346
Harrison, Mathew	27, 335, 337
Harrison, Mrs. Thos. W.	56
Hart, Dr.	341
Hatcher, Lt. Richard Felix	92
"Hawthorne"	21, 302, 333
Hays, Mark	126
Heiskell, Adam	127
Heiskell, George	126
Helm, Meredith	22
Helphenstine, Maj. Peter	126
Hening's Statutes	42
Henkels, Stan. V.	399
Henry VIII	419, 425
Henry I	419, 426
Henry VII	425
Henry VI	425
Henry III	424
Henry of Blois, Bishop	421, 427
Henry, Patrick	79, 138, 141, 147, 148, 153
"Highlands"	303
Hill, Rev. William, D. D.	128
"Hills"	303
Hilsborough, Lord	164
Hite, George	356, 380
Hite, J.	24
Hite, Jacob	392
Hite, John	106, 112, 378
Hite, Jost	31, 35, 37, 336, 380, 352
Hite, Polly	352
Hite, Robert G.	327
Hoge, George	22
Holborne, Admiral	84
Holmes, David	127
Holmes, Judge	102
Home, George	369
Homes, Walter	121
Hopes, John	24
Hopkins, Rev. Abner C., D. D.	128
Hopkins, Gerrard Thomasin	367
Hospital of St. Cross	427
Hospital of St. Mary Magdelene	426
House of Burgesses	48, 97, 101, 104, 115, 135, 137, 147, 325, 348, 327
Howe, Viscount George Augustus	379
Howe, Mary Daubein	379
Huck, Miss Hallie	56
Hunthill	370
Huntington, Samuel	248
Humphrey, Hannah	24, 32
Humphreys, George	334
"Hunting Creek"	30
Hyde Abbey	426
Hyde, Rev. John P., D. D.	91
Iglehart, Jas. A.	368
Iglehart, Thomas	368
Indian Warriors	89
Innes, Col.	82
Irving, Washington	30, 71, 85, 107, 108
Irvins House	262
Itchen River	410
Items, James Wood's Note Books	109
James I	154
James Wood Chapter, D. A. R.	133, 141
Jamestown, Va.	143, 153
Jay, John	247, 351
Jedburgh	371
Jedburgh, Parish Registers	373
Jed River	372
Jefferson, Thomas	101, 138, 147, 153 399
Jefferson, Thomas, letters	188, 189, 190, 193
John Kerr High School	55
Johnson, Dr. Samuel	420
Johnson, William	334
Johnston, Capt.	341
Johnston, George	341
Johnston, Mrs. Robert D.	75
Jolliffe, Mrs. George	56
Jolliffe, William	23
Jones, Alex. T.	52
Jones, Maj. Francis B.	92, 103
Jones, Gabriel	25, 32, 88, 100, 102, 104, 106, 116
Jones, Gabriel, Letter from	341
Jones, Joe	368
Jones, Louisa Peyton	93
Jones, Samuel	368
Jonson, Dr. Christopher	423
Jost Hite's Fort	53
Kanahwa River	315
Keith, James	343, 345, 355, 359
Keller, George W.	93
Kelley, William	334
Ken, Thomas	417, 421
Kenwale's Church	414
Keppel, Commodore	63
Kercheval, Andrew W.	195
Kercheval, Mr.	264, 268
Kercheval, Samuel	12, 14, 135
Kerr, John	92
King Alfred Statue	426
King Arthur	425
Kinkead, Mr.	350
Kinzol, Henry	92
Knights of the Golden Horseshoe	129
Kurtz, Adam	126
Kurtz, Frederick	126
Lacy, Rev. Horace, D. D.	57
Lamb, Charles	103
Lauck, Peter	126, 355

Lauck, Simon _____ 126
Laurence Augustine Washington
  Society C. A. R. _____ 322
Lee, Charles _____ 139
Lee, "Light Horse Harry" _____ 97
Lee, Richard B. _____ 248
Lee, Richard Henry __ 128, 147, 148, 152
Lee, Gen. Robert E. _____ 128
Lemen, Robert _____ 24
Leonard's Farm _____ 191
Letters, 1780 _____ 166-186
  From James Wood to Maj. Forsyth,
  Gen. Specht, John Harvie, Gen.
  Washington, Board of War, Col.
  Grayson, Col. Archibald Cary, Gov.
  Jefferson, Edward McGuire, Col.
  Southall. Maj. Cleve, Gov. Jefferson, Gen. Hamilton, Gen. Wilkinson, John Walker, Lt. Taylor,
  County Lieuts., Capt. Read.
  To his wife _____ 250-259
  Personal, to his Brother Robert
    and Others _____ 260-281
Letters _____ 187-193
  To James Wood from Gen. Adam
  Stephen, Gen. Washington, Gen. J.
  W. Von Specht, Gov. Thomas Jefferson, Baron Von Riedesel, Gen.
  James Hamilton, Marquis de Lafayett, Gen. Nath. Greene, William
  Irvine, Robert Morris, Gen.
  Horatio Gates.
Letters. Miscellaneous _____ 195-247
  Andrew W. Kercheval, Philemon
  Waters, Adam Stephen, Gen.
  Washington, Henry Peyton,
  Charles Ridgely, Thos. Bullitt,
  Jas. Hamilton, Lt. Col. Crockett,
  Richard Peter, Lt. Col. DuMengen,
  James Wood, Moses Rawlings, Col.
  Val. Eckert, J. Barnett, W. Jackson, Jos. Savage, Gres. G. Nevill,
  Dennis Ramey, Wm. McGuire, Annie McDonald.
Lewis, Gen. Andrew __ 88, 90, 127, 135
Lewis, Col. Charles _____ 89
Lewis, Fielding _____ 73
Lewis, Thomas _____ 103, 104
Lexington, Battle of _____ 137
Liberia _____ 315, 323
Licenses _____ 338
Lightfoot, Col. _____ 338
Lightfoot, John _____ 334
Lisle, Lady Alice _____ 425
List of men draughted from Hampshire Co. _____ 398
List of Officers, Va. Line, 1783 ____ 397
Little Meadows _____ 66
Little, Thomas _____ 22
Livingston, James _____ 361

London _____ 410
"Long Meadows" _____ 365
Long, Robert _____ 352
Loudoun, Lord _____ 83, 84, 107
Loudoun Street _____ 90
Louisburg _____ 85
Lucas, Hon. Daniel B. _____ 380
Lucas, Miss Virginia _____ 380
Lupton, Daniel W. _____ 56
Lupton, Edmund _____ 55
Lupton, Hon. S. L. _____ 56
Lutheran Church _____ 54
Lyman, General Phineas _____ 160
Lyons, Mrs. James _____ 57

Madison, Dolly Paine _____ 327
Madison, James _____ 128, 248
Magill, Fanny Bland _____ 93
Magill, Mr. _____ 274
"Manners Makyth Man" _____ 417
Map in Rouss City Hall _____ 118
Marke, John _____ 381
Marke, Sarah _____ 381
Marriage Certificate, L. A. Washington and M. D. Wood _____ 355
Marshall, Ann Maria _____ 103
Marshall, John _____ 140, 147
Marshall, William _____ 357
Martin, Col. _____ 83
Martin, Phil. _____ 335
Martin, Col. Thomas Bryan _____
  _____ 14, 83, 100, 106
Mason, George _____ 138, 152, 155
Mayer, Hon. Brantz _____ 135
Mayhew, Rev. Jonathan _____ 147
Maynard, Mrs. Virginia Faulkner __ 126
McCormac, H. B. _____ 56
McCraw, Samuel _____ 357
MacDonald, Judge Rose _____ 52, 57
McGrath, Jean _____ 374
McGuire, John _____ 246
McGuire, William _____ 247
McGuire, Dr. Wm. P. _____ 56
McKay, Mrs. Antrim _____ 365
McKenny, John _____ 334
McKewan, Thomas _____ 359
McMachen, William _____ 22
Meade, Bishop William _____ 128, 155
Mecklenburg _____ 369
Memphis, Tenn. _____ 161
Middlebrook _____ 200, 202, 207
Middleburg, Loudoun Co. _____ 361

Military Commissions,
  McGuire, John _____ 245
  Weedon, Capt. George _____ 343
  Wood, James, Col. of Horse and
    Foot _____ 338
  Wood, James, Col. 12th Va. Battalion _____ 349

Wood, James, Col. 8th Va. Regiment 351
Military Company of Adventure .. 160
Military Correspondence 195, 248
Miller, Mrs. Dudley L. 56, 355
Miller, Mrs. John 56
Miller, Mary 323
Miller, Robert, Bursar 347
Miller, William 116
Milton, John 144
Milton, John 248
Minor Grants 40, 41
Minor, Stephen 24, 32
"Miss Josephine Ford" 143
"Moberly's Desire" 368
"Moberly's Rest" 368
Moncure, Anne Brown 133
Moncure, Jean .. 133, 140, 159, 358, 364
Moncure, Jean, Letter from 155
Moncure, Rev. John 128, 155
Monmouth, Battle of 139
Monroe, James 140
Monstier, Count de 353
Montagu, Mrs. 420
Montargis, Sarah or Susan de 377, 381
Montcalm, Marquis de 84
Moore, Andrew 248
Morgan, Gen. Daniel ....
  .... 52, 66, 90, 125, 126, 127, 128, 245
Morgan, Morgan 22
Morgan, J. Pierpont 418
Morris, Capt. 351
Morris, Robert 193
"Morte d' Arthur," Caxton's 425
Morrow, Col. John 379
Morton, Mrs. Margaret Strother .. 103
Mortuary Chests 421
Mossburnford 372
Mount Hebron Cemetery 54, 113, 124
Mount Hebron Dedicatory Services.. 124
Mount Hebron, Oldest Graves 125
Mount Vernon ....
  .... 30, 63, 73, 99, 107, 162, 326
Mountholly 370
Muhlenberg, Gen. Peter 126, 245

Nail, John 92
Neill, John 24, 32
Neill, Lewis 22
Nelson, Thomas, Jr. 12, 83, 339
"Nemo" (Miss Kate McVicar) 56
Nevill, Gres. G. 244
New College, Oxford 418
New Forest, The 424
Newport, John 23
New York 270, 352
Nicholas, William 324
Nisbet 373
Note Book, James Wood, Jr. 165
Note Book, James Wood, Sr. 108

Norfolk, Va. 137, 147
Norris, J. E. 12, 377
Norton, Geo. F. 352
Nova Scotia 44, 78

Oaths of Allegiance, etc. 334
Obituaries
  Col. Sydney T. Fontaine 329
  Gov. James Wood 281
  Mrs. Jean Wood 282
Officers
  Gen. Daniel Morgan's Co. 127
  James Wood's Chapter, D. A. R. _ 141
Ohio River 347
Old Aquia Church 155, 156
Old Chesil Rectory 413
Old Lutheran Church 127
Old Map, Rouss City Hall 118
Old Streets, Winchester, Va. 121
Old Map, Winchester, England ... 410
O'Neal, John 340
O'Neale, Henry 367
Opekenough 20
Opequon Church 53
Order of the Garter 425
Orkney, Earl of 85
Otis, James 147
Otto, John Tobias 127
Overwharton Parish 155, 156
Oxford 112

Pack Horse Ford 369
Page, Jno. 248
Page, Wm. B. 291
Paine, Lucy 327
Pamplin, Miss 413
Paramus, N. J. 261
Parker, Josiah 248
Parkersburg Chapter, D. A. R. ... 121
Parks, Andrew 327
Patrick Family 329
Patrick, Capt. Geo. L. 329
Paulding, Mr. 287, 288
Peacock, Mr. 279
Peacock, Admiral 143
Pendleton, Edmund 138, 148, 152
Pendleton, Mrs. 292
Pendleton, Sarah 54, 57
Pere Marquette 60
Peyton, Col. Henry 92, 197
Peyton, Col. John ....
  .... 92, 275, 277, 356, 359, 379
Peyton, Louisa Morrow 92
Phelan, John 360
Philip of Spain 418
Philips, Col. 74
Phillips, Mrs. James S. 376
Philadelphia ... 165, 254, 272, 349, 350
Pickett, Martin 345, 346
"Piedmont" 38

Pierce, John	360
Pitt, William	84
Pittsburgh	304
Pocahontas	154
Point Comfort	44
Point Pleasant, Battle of	89, 133, 364
Point Pleasant Chapter, D. A. R.	141
Pollard, James	334
Pope, Anne	325
"Poplar Vale"	283
Port Tobacco	155
Posey, Capt.	163
Postage, Thomas	23
Pot-O-Make	46
Potowmack	45
Prather, Joseph	368
Prather, Mapsey (Mercy)	369
Presbyterian Church, The	93
Prescot, Maj.-Gen.	350
Pritchard, Housan K.	121
Purcell, Mrs. Benj. Ladd	52, 154
Putnam, Israel	78
Queen Elizabeth	419, 428
Quiriough	46
"Raising of Lazarus," West	418
Raleigh, Sir Walter	422, 425
Raleigh Tavern	147
Rappahannock River	45
Rawlings, Moses	219, 233
Reach, David	324
Read, Harikenson	39
Read, John	334
"Red House Shoals"	303, 329
"Rex Lex"	373
Rice, L. E.	92
Rice, Mrs. Warren	56
"Richard and John"	368
Ri__chardson, Mrs. Frank	369
"Richwoods"	302, 356
Richmond	262 and ff. 352
Riddell, Simeon	371
Riddell, Susanna	371
Ridgely, Absalom	355
Ridgely, Charles	197
Riedesel, Major,-Gen.	191
Rio Grande	74
"Rion Hall"	380
River Tweed	369
Roberdeau, Gen. Daniel	125
Robinson, Speaker	101
Robert Y. Conrad Post	129
Romney, W. Va.	13
Rooker, Rev. Wm., D. D.	124
"Rose Brake"	381
"Rose Hill"	365
Ross, Alex.	17, 21
Roszel, Col. Brantz M.	56
Round Table, Kind Arthur's	425
Rouss City Hall	14
Roxburgshire	373
Russell, Mrs. James B.	56
Russell, William Greenway	119, 126
Rust, Elizabeth	365
Rutherford, Benjamin, family	358, 378
Rutherford, Camilla C.	376
Rutherford, Elizabeth	352
Rutherford, Deborah	357, 380
Rutherford of Fairnington	370
Rutherford, Family in America	375
Rutherford, Family in Scotland	369
Rutherford, Gen. Griffith	376
Rutherford, Hugh Thomas	27, 369, 376, 379
Rutherford, Dr. John	370
Ruth__erford, John	29, 381
Rutherford, Sir John	373
Rutherford, Mary	27, 112, 377
Rutherford, Robertus Dominus de	370
Rutherford, Hon. Robert	92, 112, 347, 357, 376, 377, 378
Rutherford, Samuel	373, 374, 375
Rutherford, Sir Robert	371
Rutherford, Thomas, the Black Laird	370
Rutherford, Thomas	22, 336, 339, 377, 387, 392
Rutherford, Thomas of Teviotdale	371
Rutherford, Van	352, 356, 381
Rutherford, William E. O.	372
Rutledge, John	248
Sandy Creek	347
Santa Anna, Gen.	74
Saratoga, Battle of	139, 359
Savage, Joseph, Surgeon	242
Scarborough	371
Schlack, Grover	56
Schultz, John	126
Schuyler, Mrs.	189
Scott, Rev. Alexander	155
Scott, A.	250
Scott, W. W.	12, 18, 21
Scott, Sir Walter	370
Scraisburgh	370
Seal of Frederick County	107
Seal of Frederick County, quarterings	115
Sellman, Maj. Jonathan	368
"Selma"	21
Sesqui-Centennial, The	145
Shawanese, the	133, 134
Shawnees	90, 359
Shawnee Springs	53
Sharpe, Governor	62
Shenando	18
Shenandoah National Park	154
Shenandoah River	53, 154, 334
Shenandoah Valley Academy Cadets	55
Shenandoah Valley	46, 129, 326

WINCHESTER, VIRGINIA, AND ITS BEGINNINGS 439

Short, Reuben _____ 303
Shrewsbury, Martha D. _____ 328
Six Nations _____ 90
Slaughter, Francis _____ 334
Slaughter, Robert _____ 334, 338
Small, Oliver _____ 334
Smith, Prof. "Archie" Magill _____ 125
Smith, Augustine _____ 16, 334
Smith, Edward _____ 87
Smith, Capt. John _____ 45
Smith, Gen. John _____ 125
Smith, Judge _____ 303
Smith, Miss Kinnie E. _____ 142
Smith, Meriwether _____ 148
Smith, Rev. Wm. D., D. D. _____ 57
"Snowden and Welsh" _____ 368
Society for Abolition of Slavery __ 136
Society of the Cincinnati _____ 136, 140
Society of Colonial Dames _____ 53
Southampton _____ 410
Southwick _____ 415
Sparks' Writings _____ 162
Specht, Gen. C. J. W. _____ 262
Sperry, Jacob _____ 126
Sperry, Peter _____ 127
Spottswood, Col. _____ 87
Spottswood, Gov. _____ 45
"Spring Gardens" _____ 21
St. Andrews _____ 373, 375
St. Clair, Col. St. John _____ 62, 68
St. Dunstan _____ 414
St. Ethelwold _____ 414
St. John's Church _____ 129, 141
St. Lawrence River _____ 341
St. Pierre, Legardeur de la ___ 48, 60
St. Peter's Cathedral _____ 414
St. Regulus Chapel _____ 375
St. Swithun _____ 414
St. Swithun's Shrine _____ 148, 419
Stackhouse, James _____ 87
Stackhouse, Stephen _____ 87
Stanley, Dean _____ 373
Stanton, Matthew _____ 334
Stephen, Gen. Adam _____ 48, 90, 135
Stephen, Susan _____ 54
Stephens, Lewis _____ 106
Stephensburgh, Trustees _____ 14, 106
Steptoe, Anne _____ 326
Stewart, Capt. _____ 70
Stevenson, Robert Louis _____ 59
Stockall, John _____ 334
Story of the Braddock Sash _____ 72
Stratton, Seth _____ 126
Streit, Rev. Christian _____ 127
Student Loan Fund, D. A. R. _____ 95
Sturman, John _____ 24
Suit in Chancery _____ 38
Swartzwelder, Mrs. _____ 91
Swearingen, Thomas _____ 100
Swearingen, Van _____ 394

System for Provision to be Issued _ 236

Taliaferro, John _____ 16, 334
Tallahassee, Fla. _____ 359
Tanacharicon, Half-King _____ 48
Tanquary, W. W. _____ 56
Taylor, Lucy _____ 128
Taylor, Gen. Zachary _____ 73
Telfair, Edward _____ 248
Teviotsdale _____ 369, 375
"The Defiance of Williams and Clark" _____ 368
"The Plume of Feathers" _____ 428
"The Three Sisters" _____ 366
"The Trusty Servant," Win. College _____ 423
Thicketty Run _____ 67
Thomas Thetcher Tombstone _____ 419
Thomson, Charles _____ 349
Thornyscroft, Hamo _____ 426
Thurston, Rev. Charles Mynn ____ 128
Ticonderoga _____ 84, 137, 372, 379
Tidball, Thomas A. _____ 355, 359
Tilford, Mrs. Flora J. _____ 56
Toclyve, Bishop _____ 427
Town, Alderman _____ 371
Treaty of Utrecht _____ 78
Trenary, Mrs. Charles W. _____ 328
Two Brothers of Avington _____ 421

University of Edinburgh _____ 370
Unveiling Braddock Memorial _____ 57

Valley Forge _____ 139
Van Braam, Jacob _____ 47
Vance, Davis _____ 22
Van Cortlandt, Philip _____ 361
Van Fossen, Capt. J. C. _____ 91
Van Metre, John _____ 17, 20, 46
Van Swearingen, Drusilla _____ 381
"Vaucluse" _____ 103
Vergennes, Count de _____ 107, 108
Virginia Company of London _____ 44
Virginia Company of Plymouth __ 44
Virginia Line _____ 28
Visiting Colonial Dames _____ 56
Von Meyer, Mrs. Shirley _____ 329
Von Steuben, Baron _____ 139

Wager, Archibald _____ 133
Waite, Judge Obed _____ 126, 355
"Wakefield" _____ 326
Walkelin's Tower _____ 424
Walker, Rev. Cornelius _____ 128
Walker, Mrs. Gen. John B. _____ 56
Walker, John _____ 135, 137
Walker, Mr. _____ 293
Walker, Dr. Thomas _____ 90, 105, 135
Waller, Ben _____ 335
Walton, Izaak _____ 421

Wappatomaka	42
Ward, Dr. Julian F., Mayor	57
Ward, Hon. Robert M.	129
Warfield, Samuel	367
Warfin, Richard	334
Warner, Col. Augustine	326
Warren, William Thorn	428
Washington, Augustine	326
Washington, Emma Tell	303, 321, 322
Washington, Gen. George	16, 31, 35, 47, 54, 64, 79, 86, 87, 100, 104, 107, 147, 161, 326, 350.
Washington's Dogs and Horses	86
Washington's Election, 1758	97
Washington's Election, 1789	247
Washington's Letters to James Wood	100, 161, 162, 164, 187
Washington's Well	93
Washington's Will, item from	328
Washington, George A.	243
Washington, Col. John	325
Washington, Laurence Augustine	287, 302, 325, 333
Washington, L. A., Letters from	307 and ff.
Washington, Laurence Augustine, Jr.	303, 308
Washington, Mrs. Martha	326
Washington, Mary Dorcas Wood, Letters 304 and ff.	
Washington, Robert Wood	303, 322
Washington, Col. Samuel	327
Washington, Col. Samuel, wives of	327
Waters, Catherine	368
Waters, Philemon	196
Watkins, Benjamin	368
Weedon, George	343
Welsh, Comfort	368
Welsh Family	366
Welsh, Maj. John	366
Welsh, Dr. Luther W.	366, 368
Welsh, Richard	368
Welsh, Dr. Thomas	368
West Gate	427
West, Hugh	100
Westminster Abbey,	129, 414
West Point	187
Wheat, Rev. J. C., D. D.	142
Wheeling, W. Va.	303, 315, 331, 359
Wheeling, Washington Tombs at	332
White, Alexander	27, 249, 265, 271, 272, 335, 347, 353, 355, 356, 362, 365, 378
White, Elizabeth	356
White, Rev. Henry M., D. D.	128
White, John	22
White, Thomas	355
White, William Spottswood	92
Whitlock, J. B.	358
Wilderness	191
William the Conqueror	418, 424, 425
William and Mary College	16, 18, 149, 154, 347
Williams, Hon. R. Gray	129
William Rugus, King	424
Williamsburg Resolutions	138, 152
Williamsburg	13, 50, 99, 134, 153, 155, 162, 260, 349
Willis, Henry	16, 336, 338
Will's Creek	35, 48
Wills	
Benjamin Rutherford	358
Col. James Wood	340
Gov. James Wood	357
Mary Rutherford Wood	353
Wilmington, Camp near	251, 253
Wilson, Woodrow	145
Winchester Castle	413
Winchester Cathedral	413, 414, 415, 419, 422
Winchester Cathedral Tower	424
Winchester College	416, 418, 422
Winchester, England	13, 26, 410, 429
Winchester Evening Star, The	56
Winchester, Va.	11, 13, 14, 30, 35, 41, 43, 47, 50, 64, 99, 101, 144, 249, 237, 299, 325, 378, 429.
Winchester, Va., Inc.	107
Winchester, Va., Trustees	106
Wistar, Miss Sallie	350
Wister, Wm.	239
Wood, Catherine	364
Wood, Comfort	13, 113, 304, 353, 368
Wood, Elizabeth	335
Wood Family	362
Wood, Col. James, Jr.	28, 90, 92, 113, 129, 133, 137, 139, 145, 155, 161, 165, 349, 350, 355, 358, 359, 361, 364, 399.
Wood, Col. James, Sr.	11, 12, 13, 14, 16, 17, 18, 20, 23, 24, 28, 31, 32, 33, 36, 83, 88, 100, 104, 106, 108, 112, 129, 334, 337, 338, 341, 343, 348, 364, 369, 378, 392, 429.
Wood, Gen. James, Life of	133
Wood, James, Jr. Note Book	166
Wood, James, Jr. Pres. Board of Arrangement	244
Wood, James, Jr., Treaty with the Indians	348
Wood, Dr. James	298
Wood, Jean Moncure	282, 283, 357
Wood, Miss Julia	399
Wood, Mary Dorcas	288, 289, 304, 327, 333, 364
Wood, John	28, 345, 347
Wood, Robert	28, 87, 113, 139, 345, 347, 352, 356, 361, 368
Wood, Thomas, Jr.	24
Woodcock, John S.	14
Wood's Addition	14

Woods, Archibald _____ 355
Woods, Rev. Wm. H., D. D. _____ 128
Woodson, Mrs. Agatha A. ____ 375, 376
Woolfolk, C. W. _____ 336, 338, 345
World War _____ 429
Wren, Sir Christopher _____ 154
Wurtring, Daniel _____ 24
Wycliffe _____ 415
Wykeham, Bishop William _____

_____ 415, 417, 423, 424, 429

"Ye Olde Hostel" _____ 413
Yorktown, Fall of _____ 140
Yosemite Valley _____ 45

Zimerman, Andrew _____ 17
Zimerman, Christopher _____ 17
Zane, Isaac _____ 145